Adventures in Writing

An Introduction to the Writing Process with Readings

Adam U. Kempler

Prentice
Hall

Upper Saddle River, New Jersey 07458

Library of Congress Cataloging-in-Publication Data

Kempler, Adam U.
   Adventures in writing : an introduction to the writing process with readings / Adam U. Kempler.
      p. cm.
   Includes index.
   ISBN 0-13-094372-X
   1. English language—Rhetoric. 2. College readers. 3. Report writing. I. Title.
   PE1408 .K478 2003
      808'.0427—dc21

2002151016

VP, Editor-in-Chief: Leah Jewell
Sr. Acquisitions Editor: Craig Campanella
Editorial Assistant: Joan Polk
Exec. Managing Editor: Ann Marie McCarthy
Production Liaison: Fran Russello
Project Manager: Patty Donovan/Pine Tree
   Composition

Prepress and Manufacturing Buyer: Ben Smith
Art Director: Jayne Conte
Cover Designer: Jayne Kelly
Cover Art: David F. Gallagher/Lighteningfield.com
Permission Specialist: Kathleen Karcher
Manager, Prod/Formatting & Art: Guy Ruggiero
Marketing Manager: Rachel Falk

This book was set in 11/13 Times Roman by Pine Tree Composition, Inc.,
and was printed and bound by Hamilton Printing Company.
The cover was printed by Phoenix Color Corp.

© 2003 by Adam U. Kempler
Pearson Education, Inc.
Upper Saddle River, New Jersey 07458

Printed in the United States of America
10 9 8 7 6 5 4 3 2 1

ISBN: 0-13-094372-X

Pearson Education LTD., *London*
Pearson Education Australia PTY, Limited, *Sydney*
Pearson Education Singapore, Pte. Ltd
Pearson Education North Asia Ltd, *Hong Kong*
Pearson Education, Canada, Ltd., *Toronto*
Pearson Educación de Mexico, S.A. de C.V.
Pearson Education—Japan, *Tokyo*
Pearson Education Malaysia, Pte. Ltd
Pearson Education, *Upper Saddle River, New Jersey*

This book is dedicated to Jennifer;
her support made it possible.

"There are three rules for writing well.
Unfortunately, no one knows what they are."
—W. Somerset Maugham

Contents

Preface   **xi**
To the Instructor   **xiii**

INTRODUCTION   WHY AND HOW WE WRITE   **1**

1   Why Learn to Write?   **1**
What Is Literacy   2
Why Did Literacy Spread in Recent History?   2
How Literate Are Adults Now in the United States?   2
What Are Some Benefits of Literacy?   3
How Does a Person Raise His or Her Level of Literacy?   4
What Are the Purposes of Writing?   5

2   What is Involved in the Process of Writing?   **8**
What Is Involved in the Process of Writing?   9
Prewriting   9
Writing   11
Rewriting   13
What Are the Traits of Effective Writing?   20

PART ONE   PREWRITING   **25**

3   What Does a Writer Consider Before Writing?   **25**
What Might a Writer Consider Before Writing?   26
What Might a Writer Consider in Choosing a Writing Subject?   27

4   How Does a Writer Generate Ideas?   **33**
Why Are Prewriting Techniques Useful in the Writing Process?   34
What Are Some Useful Prewriting Techniques?   35

**5   How Does a Writer Narrow a Topic, Generate Topic
      Sentences, and Create a Thesis Statement?**   **44**
What Are Topics, Why Do Writers Need to Narrow Them,
      and How Does a Writer Narrow a Topic?   45
What Are a Topic Sentence and a Thesis Statement,
      and Why Do Writers Use Them?   47
How Do Writers Create Topic Sentences and Thesis Statements?   48
Where Does a Writer Place Topic Sentences and Thesis Statements?   53

**6   How Does a Writer Support and Develop a Topic Sentence
      and a Thesis Statement?**   **59**
What Is Support, and Why Do Writers Need It?   60
What Are the Different Types of Support?   61
What Are the Guidelines for Using Support?   62
How Does a Writer Generate Support?   66

7   How Does a Writer Find Specific Information?   **70**
Why Can Sources of Information Help Your Writing?   71
What Are the Basic Types of Sources of Information?   72
What Are the Basic Methods for Writing About What You Have Read?   74
Why Should You Acknowledge a Source?   82

8   How Does a Writer Organize Ideas?   **85**
What Is an Outline, Why Do We Use It, and How Does It Fit
      into the Writing Process?   86
What Is the Format of an Outline?   86
What Can Be Included in an Outline?   87
How Does a Writer Choose an Order for Presenting Ideas?   91
What Are Some Guidelines for Creating an Outline?   99

PART TWO   WRITING   **107**

9   How Does a Writer Write the First Draft?   **107**
What Is a Rough Draft and Why Write One?   108
What Should Writers Focus on in the First Draft?   108

What Should Writers Not Focus on in the First Draft? 111
How and Why Can a Computer Help at this Stage
    of the Writing Process? 113

**10 How Does a Writer Move Smoothly from One Idea
to the Next in Sentences and Paragraphs? 116**
What Are Transitions, and Why Are They Needed? 117
What Types of Transitions Can a Writer Use Between Sentences? 118
Where Are Transitional Expressions Placed in a Sentence,
    and How are They Punctuated? 121
Repeating Key Words (Synonyms, Antonyms), Ideas,
    and Sentence Patterns 122
Using Pronouns 123
What Types of Transitions Can Be Used Between Paragraphs? 125
How Can You Avoid Making Your Writing Worse by Using
    Transitions Incorrectly? 127

11 How Does a Writer Apply the Writing Process to the Essay Exam? 131
What Are Essay Exams? 132
Why Are Essay Exams Used? 132
What Are the Unique Challenges That Essay Exams Impose? 132
What Are Strategies for Succeeding on Essay Exams? 133
Proofreading Your Essay 138

12 How Does a Writer Use a Computer to Write? 142
Why Are Computers Needed? 143
How Can You Find a Computer for Writing? 143
What Are the Different Ways to Use a Computer in the Writing Process? 144
Prewriting 144
Writing 145
Rewriting 145
What Are Strategies for Coping with Computer Challenges? 147

PART THREE REWRITING 151

13 How Does a Writer Improve a First Draft? 151
What Is Revision? 152
Why Is Revision Needed? 153
Who Revises Writing? 153

How Is a Paper Revised?   154
Revision Checklist   154
Directions for Using the Revision Checklist   156

14   Have Words Been Chosen Well?   **161**
What Does Choosing Words Well Involve?   162
Why Is Choosing Words Well Important?   162
How Does a Writer Eliminate Slang?   163
How Does a Writer Eliminate Clichés?   164
How Does a Writer Eliminate Sexist Language?   165
How Does a Writer Eliminate Wordiness?   167
How Does a Writer Add Omitted Words?   170

15   Are Sentences Free of Fragments?   **172**
What Is a Sentence?   173
What Are Fragment Sentences, and Why Should They Be Eliminated?   176
What Are the Four Types of Fragments, and How Do Writers
      Correct Them?   177
How Do Writers Recognize and Correct Fragments
      in Their Own Writing?   184
Why and When Do Professional Writers Use Fragments?   185

16   Are Sentences Free of Run-Ons?   **187**
What Are Run-On Sentences, and Why Should They Be Corrected?   188
What Are the Two Types of Run-Ons and the Six Ways
      to Correct Them?   189
How Do Writers Recognize and Correct Run-Ons
      in Their Own Writing?   197

17   Do Subjects and Verbs Agree?   **201**
What Is Subject-Verb Agreement, and Why Is It Important?   202
What Must a Writer Know in Order to Address Difficult
      Situations in Subject-Verb Agreement?   204
How Do Writers Recognize Subject-Verb Disagreement
      in Their Own Writing?   216

18   Have ESL Trouble Spots Been Avoided?   **219**
What Are the Advantages of Knowing Two Languages, and Why
      Should ESL Trouble Spots be Addressed?   220
How Does a Writer Make a Point?   221

How Does a Writer Use Articles Correctly?   221
A Closer Look at Noncount Nouns   223
What Are the Twelve Tenses of Verbs?   227
How Does a Writer Avoid Common Trouble Spots with Verbs?   231
How Does a Writer Start Sentences with *it*?   248
How Does a Writer Avoid Using Double Negatives?   253
How Does a Writer Create Questions?   255
How Does a Writer Use Prepositions to Show Time and Place?   256
How Does a Writer Use Pronouns Like *I* and *me*?   257

19   Have Words Been Spelled Correctly?   **261**
Why Is Spelling Words Correctly Both Difficult and Important?   262
What Are Four Common Spelling Rules?   263
How Does a Writer Form Plurals?   266
How Does a Writer Form Possessives?   269
How Does a Writer Form Contractions?   270
What Are the Most Commonly Misspelled Words?   271
What Are the Most Commonly Confused Words?   273
How Does a Writer Avoid Common Incorrect Word Forms?   279
When Does a Writer Spell Out Numbers?   281
Should Writers Be Aware of Differences in American
    and British Spelling?   282
How Does a Writer Improve Spelling?   283

20   Have Capital Letters Been Used as Needed?   **286**
What Are the Four Main Rules of Capitalization?   287
Can Computers help with Capitalization?   293

21   Has Parallel Structure Been Used?   **298**
What Is a Parallel Structure?   299
Why Is Parallel Structure Used?   299
When Is Parallel Structure Used in the Writing Process,
    and How is Faulty Parallelism Revised?   301

22   Has Basic Punctuation Been Used Correctly?   **309**
What Is Punctuation, and What Does It Do for Writing?   310
What Are End Marks, and How Are They Used?   311
When Should a Writer Use Commas?   313
When Should a Writer Not Use Commas?   320
Basic Punctuation Summary   321

23   Has Other Punctuation Been Used Correctly?   **324**
How Does a Writer Use Semicolons?   325
How Does a Writer Use Colons?   326
How Does a Writer Use Parentheses?   328
How Does a Writer Use Dashes?   329
How Does a Writer Use Quotation Marks?   329
How Does a Writer Use Italics?   332
How Does a Writer Use Brackets?   332
How Does a Writer Use Ellipses?   333
How Does a Writer Use Apostrophes?   334
How Does a Writer Use Hyphens?   336
How Does a Writer Use Slashes?   338

Appendix A   Readings for Writing   **345**
Poems   345
Short Readings   369
Recommended Books   404

Appendix B   Additional Writing Topics   **404**

Appendix C   Basic Punctuation   **406**

Appendix D   Other Punctuation Summary   **408**

Appendix E   Parts of Speech   **410**

Appendix F   Block Business Letter Format   **414**

Appendix G   Answer Key to Exercises   **415**

Appendix H   About the Companion Website   **446**

Index   447

Preface

Several years ago, a few instructors and I were frustrated at not being able to find a satisfactory text for an introductory writing class. We would select one text and try it for a semester or two, but then set it aside for one reason or another: too difficult to understand, too grammar oriented, too few practices, etc. We would select and try another text for a little while, but experience the same results. I realized that a better text must exist, so I began to search for it.

I mailed a letter to the English Department Chairs at all community colleges in California (107 at the time) requesting textbook recommendations. Many chairs responded, and my list of recommended texts grew. Then, I requested desk copies of these texts from publishers and evaluated 46 books, creating a table that compared their strengths and weaknesses. Upon completion of this research, I realized that—although several good books existed—the book that we sought had not yet been written. We needed a book that introduced students to the process of writing, a book that was organized according to that process, a book that explained how to incorporate technology into the writing process, and a book that was sensitive to our diverse student population by addressing ESL trouble spots.

This text, the culmination of five years of research and writing, fills that need. First, it introduces students to the complex process of writing through a simple organization: prewriting, writing, and rewriting. While doing so, it builds sentence skills, teaches grammar, and provides practice in sentence combining. This approach benefits students because they need to understand the big picture— the process of writing—early in their writing education. Second, this text offers an entire chapter on computers, computer tips throughout the text, and Internet-based writing assignments in every chapter, making this text ideal for classes with computer components, classes taught in computer labs, web-supported classes, self-paced classes, online classes, etc. Third, this text serves our diverse student population by addressing the writing concerns of students who are learning English as a second language; these concerns are addressed both in a separate chapter and in the form of tips throughout the text.

Finally, I would like to thank the following reviewers: Jessica Carroll, Miami-Dade Community College; Patrick Haas, Glendale Community College; Sarah Kirk, University of Alaska-Anchorage; Richard W. Rawnsley, College of the Desert; Mark Branson, Davidson County Community College; Janet Cutshall, Sussex County Community College; Andrew B. Preslar, Lamar State College—Orange.

Adam U. Kempler

To the Instructor

This text was written for students who want an introduction to writing, and it has the following components:

1. **The Sentence-Level Component:** This text explains in detail elements that often challenge students on the sentence-level: subject-verb agreement, fragments, run-ons, tense shifts, spelling, capital letters, faulty parallelism, periods, question marks, exclamation points, commas, colons, semicolons, quotation marks, parentheses, and sentence combining.

2. **The Process Component:** A few years ago, I discovered the results of some research at a conference of the National Council of Teachers of English: teaching grammar outside of the context of students' own writing does not necessarily improve writing. In other words, to be most effective, students must address their own grammar problems in their own writing. In addition to grammar practices, then, students need writing assignments. To provide writing assignments, instructors must also introduce students to the process of writing. This text introduces that process through a simple organization: prewriting, writing, and rewriting. It also provides more than 100 introductory-level writing assignments, including the following types: academic assignments (requiring critical thinking), journal assignments, creative assignments, Internet-based assignments, and non-Internet-based assignments. Each chapter concludes with group and individual writing assignments, and Appendix *A* provides eight short readings and twenty-two poems with writing assignments following each work. Appendix *B* provides twenty-five additional introductory-level writing prompts. In the rewriting section of this text (the longest of the three sections), students are taught how to recognize and address the most common grammar problems in the context of their own writing.

3. **The Internet Component:** This book contains URL's for more than 80 websites that provide grammar instruction, grammar practice, ESL instruction, writing instruction at Online Writing Labs (OWL's), and writing assignments, such as the examples below:
   - For information on transitions, visit Harvard's Writing Center at http://www.fas.harvard.edu/~wricntr/documents/Transitions.html.
   - For a fun writing assignment, examine the challenges and successes of one musical group in an essay by visiting the Rock and Roll Hall of Fame and Museum at http://www.rockhall.com.
   - For ESL tips, visit Ohio University's ESL Page at http://www.ohiou.edu/esl/english/grammar/index.html
   - For an online writing quiz on fragments, visit Capital Community College at http://webster.commnet.edu/cgishl/quiz.pl/fragments add1.htm?cgi quiz form=1
   - For assistance with basic punctuation, visit the Weber State Writing Center at http://catsis.weber.edu/writingcenter/an introduction to comma u sage.htm.
   - For a creative writing assignment, describe an image on display at the Smithsonian National Museum of American History at http://americanhistory.si.edu/.

This text also provides an entire chapter (12), on how to use a computer in the writing process. Finally, this text provides a web page that supports the text: http://www.prenhall.com/kempler/. This site provides the following: how to use this textbook, sample syllabus, editing exercises, sentence-combining practices, and support for each chapter (objectives, self-grading quizzes, chapter-test answers, group assignments, web destinations, and writing assignments that develop critical thinking skills).

4. The ESL Component: The longest chapter in this text is the ESL Chapter (18). It covers the following:

- Advantages of knowing two languages
- Why ESL trouble spots should be addressed
- How to make a point
- How to use articles correctly
- The 12 tenses of verbs
- How to avoid common trouble spots with verbs
  - Irregular verbs
  - Troublesome irregular verbs
  - Gerunds and infinitives
  - Progressives
  - Modals
  - Subjunctive mood
  - Tense shifts
  - Passive and active voice
- How to avoid repeating subjects
- How to start sentences with *here* and *there*
- How to start sentences with *it*
- How to use adjectives
  - Word order with adjectives
  - Punctuating adjectives
  - Using present and past participles as adjectives
- How to avoid using double negatives
- How to create questions
- How to use prepositions to show time and place
- How to use pronouns like *I* and *me*

Since many native English speakers also have challenges with issues in this chapter, it should be used as a resource for all writers.

5. The *Why* Component: This book attempts to answer the question *why*. The first chapter addresses the question "Why learn to write?" Furthermore, the practices try to teach why specific writing rules exist. For example, in Chapter 19, students are taught about spelling. Practice 2 asks students to correctly spell the plural forms of words and indicate which of eight rules dictates the spelling for each word. Requiring students to identify the rule that dictates the spelling helps them to understand why words are spelled as they are and remember how to spell them correctly.

Finally, I welcome feedback from instructors and students about this text. Please contact me at the following address:

Adam Kempler
c/o Craig Campanella
Senior Editor, English
Prentice Hall
1 Lake Street, Suite 4F
Upper Saddle River, NJ 07458

Why learn to write?

"One writes to make a home for oneself, on paper, in time and in others' minds."

—Alfred Kazin

LEARNING OBJECTIVES

1. Learn what literacy means.
2. Learn why literacy has spread in recent history.
3. Learn about literacy in the United States.
4. Learn about the benefits of literacy.
5. Learn how to increase your literacy.
6. Learn the purposes of writing.

PRE-READING QUESTIONS

1. What do you think the word "literacy" means?
2. What percent of adults in America do you think lack the ability to read a simple children's story?
3. What can someone accomplish with written communication that might be more difficult to accomplish with oral communication?
4. Can you raise your level of literacy without going to school? Why or why not?
5. Take a minute to consider a few of the reasons that you write. When you write something, why do you do it?

WHAT IS LITERACY?

A simple definition would be the ability to read and write, but the Workforce Investment Act of 1998 defines literacy in America as "an individual's ability to read, write, speak in English, compute and solve problems at levels of proficiency necessary to function on the job, in the family of the individual and in society" ("Frequently Asked Questions"). This definition clarifies the connection between a person's ability to apply language skills and his or her ability to succeed in a group.

WHY DID LITERACY SPREAD IN RECENT HISTORY?

During the Middle Ages, writing began to replace functions that had previously been performed by oral language, such as indenturing of servants, deeding of property, displaying evidence at trials, recording the lives of saints, etc. According to the *Britannica Online,* "As literacy began to be required for these vital social purposes, oral language came to be seen as loose and unruly and lacking in social authority" ("Writing"). Those who developed their oral language skills into written language skills gained the ability to fill key social roles, and members of society respected them for their abilities.

HOW LITERATE ARE ADULTS NOW IN THE UNITED STATES?

The National Institute for Literacy addresses this question:
To determine the literacy skills of American adults, the 1992 National Adult Literacy Survey (NALS) used test items that resembled everyday life tasks in-

volving prose, document and quantitative skills. The NALS classified the results into five levels that are now commonly used to describe adults' literacy skills.

Almost all adults in Level 1 can read a little but not well enough to fill out an application, read a food label, or read a simple story to a child. Adults in Level 2 usually can perform more complex tasks such as comparing, contrasting, or integrating pieces of information but usually not higher-level reading and problem-solving skills. Adults in Levels 3 through 5 usually can perform the same types of more complex tasks on increasingly lengthy and dense texts and documents.

Very few adults in the United States are truly illiterate. Rather, there are many adults with low literacy skills who lack the foundation they need to find and keep decent jobs, support their children's education and participate actively in civic life. Between 21 and 23 percent of the adult population or approximately 44 million people, according to the NALS scored in Level 1. Another 25 to 28 percent of the adult population, or between 45 and 50 million people, scored in Level 2. Literacy experts believe that adults with skills at Levels 1 and 2 lack a sufficient foundation of basic skills to function successfully in our society ("Frequently Asked Questions").

If you consider for a moment that half of the adults in the United States are not sufficiently literate to function well on the job, in the family, and in society, then you begin to see the extent of our problem.

The following sentences taken from actual letters received by the Stanislaus County Welfare Department provide a few examples of communication casualties.

1. I cannot get sick pay, I have 6 children, can you tell me why?
2. My husband got his project cut off 2 weeks ago and I haven't had any relief since.
3. I am forwarding my marriage certificate and my 3 children, one of which was a mistake as you will see.
4. In accordance with your instructions. I have given birth to twins in the enclosed envelope.
5. I want money as quick as I can get it. I have been in bed with the doctor for 2 months and he doesn't do me any good. If things don't improve, I will have to send for another doctor.

WHAT ARE SOME BENEFITS OF LITERACY?

Now that we have looked at the extent of the literacy problem in the U.S., we can better appreciate the benefits of literacy.

First, writing preserves ideas more accurately than oral communication. *Britannica Online* notes, "Writing allows exactly repeatable statements to be circulated widely and preserved. It allows readers to scan a text back and forth and to study, compare, and interpret at their leisure" ("Writing"). Consider, for example, the significance of writing in education. How would an education be different without written curriculum, procedures, materials, assignments, and tests?

Second, writing often carries a greater significance than oral communication. Isak Dinesen, in her autobiographical *Out of Africa,* reported on the response of people of the Kikuyu tribe to their first exposures to written texts: "I learned that the effect of a piece of news was many times magnified when it was imparted in writing. The messages that would have been received with doubt and scorn if they had been given by word of mouth . . . were now taken as gospel truth" (Dinesen, 123). People receive communication similarly today. A letter of complaint, for example, will probably solicit thoughtful consideration whereas the same complaint left as a phone message would probably produce a less-favorable result.

Third, democracy depends upon literacy. Democracy in the United States means government by the people, and for the people to fulfill their responsibilities as citizens, they must be able to consider issues, discuss ideas, and express their opinions. In other words, they need to be able to read, write, speak in English, and compute and solve problems.

Fourth, writing often leads to truth, organization, and individualism. As a society adopts the practice of writing, history replaces myth, and science replaces magic. Writing allows organized legal systems to develop through rules and procedures. Although writing has replaced some face-to-face communication with depersonalized administrative procedures, it has also created authors. As authors flourish, society recognizes the importance of the thoughts of individuals ("Writing").

Fifth, literacy enhances opportunities and understanding. For example, many opportunities for advancement in work, education, and society depend upon levels of literacy. In addition, the ability to understand people, problems, science, technology, history, etc., depends upon literacy. Also, enjoying, understanding, and appreciating cultures, perspectives, and forms of art depend upon literacy. Ultimately, the more literate we become the more easily we may understand ourselves and the world in which we live.

HOW DOES A PERSON RAISE HIS OR HER LEVEL OF LITERACY?

Raising one's literacy level involves education. *Britannica Online* notes that "whereas oral language is learned quite independently of whether it is taught or not, literacy is largely dependent upon teaching" ("Writing"). For example, when a person comes to America, he or she may "pick up" the ability to speak English without ever taking a class or studying English. Such a person, however, has not raised his or her literacy level in terms of "the ability to read, write, compute and solve problems at levels of proficiency necessary to function on the job, in the family of the individual and in society." Education provides the opportunity to develop these abilities.

I have noticed the rise in my own literacy through a variety of forms of teaching: first through my parents, then through my K to 12 teachers, then through my university professors, and finally through self-instruction. One of my most influential teachers was Mrs. Butler, my high school photography teacher. On many occasions during my freshman year, she gave me permission to skip her class to read in the library. I read whatever I wanted to read, and she would give me things to read like "A Letter from Birmingham Jail" by Dr. Martin Luther King, Jr. Then she would ask me questions about what I read; we discussed books, ideas, and authors many times. This process continued long after her class ended. I probably read twenty-five books during this period. In retrospect, I see a dramatic rise in my own literacy through the teaching of Mrs. Butler. Reading well-written books showed me good writing. Reading many books enhanced my reading speed so that the process of reading became almost effortless. Discussing books and ideas taught me to appreciate and question other perspectives.

Many other instructors, also, have contributed to the rise of my literacy, particularly my ability to write, through teaching. Each English instructor, and many other instructors who have promoted literacy, has contributed to the life-long process of raising my literacy level to its current position, which allows me to function comfortably in my job, in my family, and in society. The purpose of this book is to be one source of raising your level of literacy by teaching you about the process of writing.

WHAT ARE THE PURPOSES OF WRITING?

Thomas Jefferson wanted the British to know that the colonies would no longer be treated unfairly and ruled by England, so he drew up the Declaration of Independence. Pickard and Johnson needed to hire people to work in the office of their engineering firm, so they created a job description that said, "Must be able to communicate well orally and in writing," and they required all applicants to take a grammar and writing test. My grandmother wanted to share some insights with me, so she wrote the following in my journal three years before she passed away, "I hope that you will always enjoy your life as much as I have mine. It isn't really what happens to you that counts. It's how you take it, how you feel about it, and what you get out of it, that counts." Whether it's Thomas Jefferson or my grandmother, when a person knows how to write, he or she may make a point effectively through the process of writing.

We write for many reasons: to inform, to argue, to complain, to correct, to solve problems, to organize, to praise, to recognize, to make money, to remember, to entertain, to mourn, to articulate emotion, to express imagination, to pass tests, to fulfill assignments, to explore the world and ourselves, and to enjoy life. In short, we write to communicate. What did you write last? Why did you write it?

 ## PRACTICE

Answer the following questions on a separate piece of paper or on a computer.

1. How does the Workforce Investment Act of 1998 define literacy in America?
2. During the Middle Ages, writing began to replace what?
3. With time, oral language came to be seen as what?
4. According to the National Adult Literacy Survey (NALS), how many million Americans today lack a sufficient foundation of basic skills to function successfully in our society?
5. List five benefits of literacy.
6. Literacy largely depends upon what?
7. What are five purposes of writing that are important to you?

GROUP WORK

1. Consider, discuss, and list the five most common situations in which you write.
2. Consider, discuss, and list three benefits of literacy in your future.
3. Consider, discuss, and list five steps that you can take to raise your literacy level.

TEST (TRUE/FALSE)

1. Literacy involves only reading and writing.
2. Writing replaced oral language because oral language lacked social authority.
3. About half of the adults in the United States today lack the level of literacy needed to function successfully in society.
4. Writing allows statements to be repeated exactly.

5. Writing often carries more significance than oral communication.

6. A democracy can function well with citizens who are mostly illiterate.

7. Writing has contributed to the recognition of the importance of the thoughts of individuals.

8. Raising our literacy level can help us to more easily understand ourselves and the world in which we live.

9. Raising one's literacy does not involve education or teaching.

10. Alfred Kazin said, "One writes to make a home for oneself, on paper, in time and in others' minds."

WRITING ASSIGNMENTS

1. Academic Assignment: Visit the International Literacy Explorer at http://www.literacyonline.org/explorer/overview.html and learn the estimate of illiterate people in the word today, examine three social consequences of low levels of literacy, and discover the economic, social, and political rationales for promoting literacy. Also, visit the National Institute for Literacy at http://www.casas.org/lit/litcode/Search.cfm to learn the estimate of literate adults in your city. Use the information at these two websites and in this chapter to write a short paper on literacy in which you examine problems associated with illiteracy and propose methods of raising people's levels of literacy.

2. Journal Assignment: Explain everything that you have learned in this chapter: "Why learn to write?"

3. Creative Assignment: Visit Harvard's Peabody Museum of Archaeology and Ethnology at http://www.peabody.harvard.edu/, and view the Exhibitions On-Line. Select an image that you like, and describe it in a one-page essay. For tips on writing descriptions, visit Purdue University's Online Writing Lab at http://owl.english.purdue.edu/handouts/general/gl_describe.html.

Chapter 2

What is involved in the process of writing?

"One learns to write by writing and revising, not by consciously learning and rhetorically applying the 'rules.'"

—Robert J. Connors

LEARNING OBJECTIVES

1. Learn what is involved in the process of prewriting.
2. Learn what is involved in the process of writing.
3. Learn what is involved in the process of rewriting.
4. Learn what effective writing is.

PRE-READING QUESTIONS

1. Suppose that you were given a writing assignment at the beginning of the semester in which your instructor asked you to describe a significant event in your life. If you had one week to turn in your one-page answer, what would you consider doing *before* writing that paper?
2. How many stages or steps in the writing process would that assignment involve for you? What would you do at each stage? How could a computer help you with your writing?

3. Would you prefer to be given this assignment as an in-class essay? Why? How would that change the steps or stages of the writing process?
4. Suppose that you finished the writing assignment the day before it was due, and you were proofreading it for mistakes. What kinds of mistakes would you look for first? Why?
5. How do you define effective writing?

WHAT IS INVOLVED IN THE PROCESS OF WRITING?

If your instructor asks you to write an essay that is due in one week, then the paper that you hand to your professor is the **product** of your writing. The steps that you go through to create that paper constitute the **process** of your writing. This process and the number of steps in it will vary from writer to writer and from situation to situation. Most authors in most situations, however, engage in one form or another of three stages in the writing process: prewriting, writing, and rewriting.

PREWRITING

Before any writing is done, ask yourself a few questions. First, why are you writing this? The answer to this question will provide you with the need for or purpose of the writing. Second, for whom are you writing this? The answer to this question will tell you who your audience is. Third, what will you write about that will be meaningful to you and your audience? The answer to this question will provide you with your content. Fourth, what attitude will you take towards your writing? The answer to this question will determine the tone of your writing. Having answers to these questions early in the prewriting process will help you to stay focused by guiding you towards effective writing.

Patricia Martinez received a short writing assignment in which she was asked to make a point about something she had learned, illustrate the point with an example, and analyze its significance in her life.

In the prewriting stage of her work, she started to answer the questions above. First, she was writing this paper in order to earn a good grade in the class, and she hoped to improve her ability to write in the process. Second, she was writing this paper knowing that all of her classmates and her professor would read it. That carried ramifications: she had to be comfortable sharing the experience.

With these questions answered, she needed to generate some lessons learned, and a short list provided a way of doing that.

Things I've Learned

1. Be honest.
2. I can accomplish what I set my mind to.
3. Real friends won't stab you in the back.
4. Life is fragile.
5. I love sports.

To support her list of lessons learned, Patricia needed examples or illustrations, a cluster provided a format for generating them.

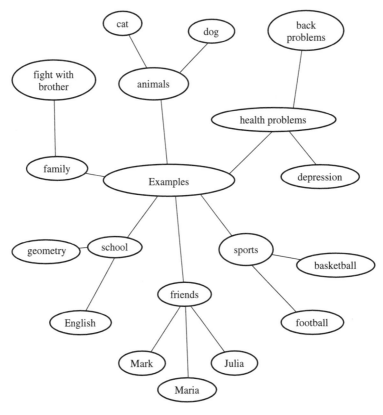

After creating a cluster with a dozen ideas or so, she considered which point and story might best fill her need to do well on the assignment and be significant to her audience. For her point, she chose "I can accomplish what I set my mind to." For her example or illustration, she chose "Football," and she decided to approach this incident with a serious tone.

 While a cluster generates ideas, an outline organizes ideas, and her professor asked her to type an outline with an introduction, a body, and a conclusion and about five ideas under each heading:

I Introduction: Accomplishments
   A. Armstrong's words
   B. People on the moon
   C. The price
   D. The reward
   E. Thesis: I can accomplish what I set my mind to.
II Body: Football
   A. Setting (time, place, people, background)
      1. Patricia
      2. Martin Luther King, Jr. High School
      3. Football field
      4. 70 boys
      5. Ages 14
      6. Summer
   B. Rising Action (conflict begins)
      1. People stare
      2. They walk away
      3. Mean comments
   C. Climax (most intense part of the conflict)
      1. Fighting
      2. Boys picking fights with me
      3. Coach's reaction
      4. Punishment
      5. No water
   D. Falling Action (story concludes)
      1. My reaction
      2. 3 months of summer
      3. The regular season (some problems)
III Conclusion: Significance of Experience
   A. Accomplish goals
   B. Deal with people, situations
   C. Strong person
   D. Believe in myself

WRITING

 With the outline complete, Patricia typed her first draft, simply hoping to record a full account of her story by using her outline as a guide.

Football

    In 1969 Neil Armstrong stepped onto the moon and said that's one small step for a man, one giant leap for mankind. Getting to the moon took alot of work and a lot of money it was difficult. But it was worth the reward. We learned alot from reaching that goal. I have learned that I can accomplish what I set my mind to.

It was the summer morning of June 21, 1995. When I woke up around 5:00a.m. The reason I woke up so early is because I was about to do one of the most scariest things of my life. I had made a choice to do something that people wouldn't understand or like it very much. I had gotten ready and my family had said don't worry be strong everything will be all right. They all gave me a hug and wish me good luck. My family had left to work. I was so nervous that I couldn't eat all I could do is walk around house. I did that for a half an hour or so until my friend Luis came over and asked if he could take me to school for support.

As we got to Martin Luther King, Jr. High School I felt that I wanted to turn back that it was a mistake. I knew in my heart that's not what I wanted to do. So as I continued walking closer to the football field I felt that I was going to die. It got worse as I reach the field all the boys were all ready lined up in rows. There were Parents there. I went up to the coach and had asked him if he need my name? He had my name on the list so then he had checked off my name and told me to go to the end of the line. As I did the exercises with every one else. I could hear all the Parents yelling at me so were the rest of the guys, but not only did they say things the guys were moving away from me, but before they move away they also spit on me. They said things like this Bitch, Mexican trash, you don't belong here, you are a stupid beaner, you want to be a guy, no one wants you here, go back to Mexico, get away you freak, leave, and bad words like that. Things like that as we were doing push-ups it was hard to focus on the push-ups the coaches were coming around and counting, but they never told them to shut up. I felt really bad. I just kept telling my self to be strong and ignore them. It was hard, but I did. It is kind of weird that I grow up with all of them and they know me and they know what kind of a person I am. Yet they treaded me like a dirt. They all knew I want to pay football I don't understand why it was a suprize to them like they didn't believe me before. For the rest of the day I was treaded just as bad or worse. I did every thing just as good as they did. They still said things and tried to pick fights with me and they wouldn't even fight far. If I was walking some where the hit be from behind. they always did things like that. If I were to defend myself I would get extra laps after practice. So now know matter what I did it was not good enough for them. I did every thing just as good as they did and know what I did I could never please them. They just kept trying to make me quite. They kept doing just as bad or worse day in

day out. I had gone throw hell weeks with them and they still did n
stop. When some of them couldn't even handle it I didn't cry like they
did I even tried to help them throw it. They continued to do so many
bad things for like two more months. They had all thought I had done it
for the attention they found out that they were wrong. The next four
months left they came around and we all got along step for the guys
that will never except me just because I'm a girl. I had finish the season
with all of them and then continued on basketball season. Know matter what they did they just made my stronger. I learned so much that
year like how my family supported me throw every thing that happened. I learned how to deal with people. Also never quite no matter
what happens. I learned to believe in my self and that I could do anything I put my mind on. That I made my goals and dreams come true.
That I can deal with any situation now.

Adapted from Patricia Martinez

Patricia's first draft is complete, and an interesting story has started to emerge. Of
course, she has quite a bit of work left in the writing process to prepare it so that
her audience can read, understand, and appreciate it effortlessly.

 ## REWRITING

Improving the first draft requires rewriting, and this can be done easily on a computer. Who may read your work to give you feedback for rewriting it? Your professor may set guidelines for you, but feedback through proofreading may be obtained
from yourself, fellow students, tutors, On-Line Writing Labs (OWLS), teachers, etc.

How does an author begin revising his or her work? Writers will benefit
from making global revisions first, if necessary. In other words, before doing anything else, look at the big picture. Try to answer the questions asked in the
prewriting stage. Has the author accomplished the purpose of the writing? Is the
writing appropriate for the audience? Is the writing significant to the author and
the audience? Is the essay organized appropriately for the subject? Is the tone
suitable for the subject, purpose, and audience?

After global revisions have been made, sentence-level revisions can be
made. These revisions involve looking for one type of error at a time through
proofreading aloud. The most serious errors should be sought out first. Proofreading should be conducted so that the paper sits between proofreadings. Some errors to look for include the following:

1. Fragments
2. Run-ons

3. Subject-verb disagreement
4. ESL and verb errors
5. Misspelled words
6. Incorrect use of plurals and possessives
7. Incorrect use of capital letters
8. Lack of parallel structure

Lamar and Nadine provided Patricia with the following feedback on her paper during peer revision in class.

Football

In 1969 Neil Armstrong stepped onto the moon and said ^*use quotation marks* that's one small step for a man, one giant leap for mankind. Getting to the moon took ~~alot~~ *a lot* of work and ~~alot~~ *a lot* of money it was difficult. But it was worth the reward. We learned alot from reaching that goal. I have learned that I can accomplish what I set my mind to.

It was the summer morning of June 21, 1995. When I woke up around 5:00a.m. The reason I woke up so early ~~is~~ *was* because I was about to do one of the most scariest things of my life. ~~Were~~ I had made a choice to do something that people wouldn't understand or like it very much. I had gotten ready and my family had said don't worry be strong everything will be all right. They all gave me a hug and wish me good luck. My family had left to work. I was so nervous that I couldn't eat all I could do is walk around *the* house. I did that for a half an hour ~~or so~~ until my friend Luis came over and asked if he could take me to school for support.

As we got to Martin Luther King, Jr. High School I felt that I ~~wanted to~~ *might be* ~~turn back that it was a mistake~~ *making a mistake*. I knew in my heart ~~that's not~~ *that it wasn't* ^ what I wanted to do. ~~So as~~ *As* I continued walking closer to the football field I felt that I was going to die. It got worse as I reach the *football* field all the boys

were ~~all ready~~ *already* lined up in rows. There were Parents there *watching the rest of the guys*

to make sure things were okay . I went up to the coach and had asked him if he

∧ explain more about this here

need my name? He had my name on the list so then he

had checked off my name and told me to go to the end of the line. As I

did the exercises with every one else. I could hear all the Parents yelling

at me so were the rest of the guys, but not only did they say things the

guys were moving away from me, but before they move away they also

spit on me. They said things like this Bitch, Mexican trash, you don't be-

long here, you are a stupid beaner, you want to be a guy, no one wants

you here, go back to Mexico, get away you freak, leave, and bad words

like that. Things like that as we were doing push-ups it was hard to

focus on the push-ups *when* the coaches were coming around and count-

ing, but they never told them to shut up. I felt really bad. I just kept

telling my self to be strong and ignore them. It was hard, but I did. It is

kind of weird that I grow up with all of them and they know me and

they know what kind of a person I am. Yet they treaded me like a dirt.

They all knew I want to ~~pay~~ *play* football I don't understand why it was a

~~suprize~~ *surprise* to them like they didn't believe me before. For the rest of the

day I was treaded just as bad or worse. I did every thing just as good as

they did. They still said things and tried to pick fights with me and they

wouldn't even fight far. If I was walking some where ~~the~~ *they* hit *me* be from

behind. ~~they~~ *They* always did things like that. If I were to defend myself

I would get extra laps after practice. ~~So now know~~ *rewrite* matter what I did

it was not good enough for them. I did every thing just as good as

they did and know *matter* what I did I could never please them. They just

kept trying to make me quite. They kept doing just as bad or worse day

in day out. I had gone throw hell weeks with them and they still did
not stop *even when some of them were crying because they couldn't handle it* . ~~When some of them~~
~~couldn't even handle it~~ *get through it* I didn't cry like they did *I still helped them* ~~I even tried to help~~
~~them throw it~~. They continued to do so many bad things for like two
more months. They had all thought I had done it for the attention they
found out that they were wrong. The next four months left they came
around and we all got along ~~step~~ *except* for the guys that will never except me
just because I'm a girl. I had finish the season with all of them and then
continued on basketball season. Know matter what they did they just
made ~~my~~ *me a* stronger *person* . I learned so much that year like how my family
supported me throw every thing that happened. I learned how to deal
with people. Also never ~~quite~~ *give up* no matter what happens. I learned to believe in ~~my self~~ *myself* and that I could do anything I put my mind ~~on~~ *to*. ~~That~~ I
made my goals and dreams come true. ~~That~~ I can deal with any situa-
tion ~~now~~.

Patricia made a global revision first; she decided that instead of starting her example or story at her house at 5:00 a.m., she would start her story on the football field at 7:00 a.m. She also made the majority of corrections that her fellow students recommended, realizing that most of their suggestions would improve the paper. She then made some additional improvements before handing in her second draft, along with the first draft, outline, and cluster, to the instructor for further feedback. The second draft follows with the instructor's corrections and comments.

Football

In 1969 Neil Armstrong stepped onto the moon and said, "That's
one small step for a man, one giant leap for mankind." Getting to the
moon took a lot of work and a lot of money *run-on sentence—insert period It* ~~it~~ was difficult. *insert comma—see option 1 but* ~~But~~ it was worth the reward. We learned a lot from

reaching that goal. I *insert "also" as a transition* ^ have learned that I can accomplish what I set my mind to.

It was 7:00 *insert space* ^ a.m. on June 21, 1995 on the Martin Luther King, Jr. High School football field. The first day of practice was about to begin. There were close to 70 guys on the field. When I walked on to the football field, everybody stood still, *omit comma* ^ and stopped talking. They ~~stopped doing whatever they were doing and~~ stared at me, *omit comma—see option 4* ^ until the coach said, "Line up in rows to start to stretch." We had to line up but *reword this* whatever line I got in they would all walk away *run-on sentence—see option 1* ^ .

The coach had told the guys to stop walking away from the line, but that was the only time he told them to stop. When we started doing push-ups *insert comma—see option 5* ^ all the guys started yelling mean things to me. They said things like, "You don't belong here, you stupid beanner, go back to Mexico *run-on sentence* ^ . No one wants you here, leave, you're a bitch *run-on sentence* ^ . You're a freak, Mexican trash," and other bad words. They didn't just say things, they went as far as to spit on me and hit me from behind *run-on sentence* ^ . They always did things like that, and the coaches never said or did anything about it.

They continued to harass me anyway they could to get me into trouble. The guys would pick fights with me, even though they knew we were not allowed to fight with each other. When the coaches saw the guys bothering me *insert comma—see option 5* ^ they never did or said anything to them about it. If I defended myself and fought back *insert comma—see option 5* ^ I would get extra laps after practice. The guys were so mean that they would not allow me to drink water. We were given a few minutes to drink water and during that time I would hear them saying things like, "Don't let Martinez drink water" *run-on sentence—see option 1* ^ . It was a very hot summer and

run-on sentence—see option 1

we would practice from the morning until the nighttime   .
                                                                          ^

Every day, five days out of the week, they continued to harass me day in

and day out, all the time.

They would get me so mad that I wanted to quit. Why should I

have to quit something I love just because people are mean? They

would never give me a break no matter what I did it wasn't good

run-on sentence

enough   . I went through hell for weeks just like they did, but I
                    ^   *run-on sentence*

omit

still ⫯ did everything they did I could never please them   . They
      ^   ^
                                                          run-on sentence

harassed me for three months then they finally stopped   . The
                                                          ^

next four months they came around and were nice to me, but there

were still a few guys that would believe that I didn't deserve to be on

                                                    omit comma—see option 4

the same field as them. That is ok with me,   because I
                                                      ^

learned that you can't please everyone. I went on to finish the football

                                      boy or girls?

season. I also played on the basketball team.
                                      ^

I learned that I can do anything I put my mind to, no matter what

anybody says. I learned how to deal with people and certain situations.

I learned that I'm a strong person, and that I believe in myself. I learned

that I could challenge myself, and succeed in my goals.

*This essay is very personal and interesting. You have a strong final paragraph
with several good ideas in it, but avoid starting each sentence with "I." Combine
some sentences using the five options. Watch run-ons throughout paper.*

Patricia considered her instructor's feedback carefully and rewrote the paper
again before submitting it as a third draft.

Football

In 1969 Neil Armstrong stepped onto the moon and said, "That's one
small step for a man, one giant leap for mankind." Getting to the moon
took a lot of work and a lot of money. It was difficult, but it was worth

the reward. We learned a lot from reaching that goal. I also have learned that I can accomplish what I set my mind to.

It was 7:00 a.m. on June 19, 1995 on the Martin Luther King, Jr. High School football field. The first day of practice was about to begin. There were close to 70 guys on the field. When I walked on to the football field, everybody stood still and stopped talking. They stared at me until the coach said, "Line up in rows to start to stretch." We had to line up, but they would all walk away from whatever line I got in.

The coach had told the guys to stop walking away from the line, but that was the only time he told them to stop. When we started doing push-ups, all the guys started yelling mean things to me. They said things like, "You don't belong here. You stupid beanner. Go back to Mexico. No one wants you here. Leave. You're a bitch. You're a freak, Mexican trash," and other bad words. They didn't just say things; they went as far as to spit on me and hit me from behind. They always did things like that, and the coaches never said or did anything about it.

They continued to harass me anyway they could to get me into trouble. The guys would pick fights with me, even though they knew we were not allowed to fight with each other. When the coaches saw the guys bothering me, they never did or said anything to them about it. If I defended myself and fought back, I would get extra laps after practice. The guys were so mean that they would not allow me to drink water. We were given a few minutes to drink water, and during that time I would hear them saying things like, "Don't let Martinez drink water." It was a very hot summer. We would practice from the morning until the nighttime. Every day, six days out of the week, they continued to harass me day in and day out, all the time.

They would get me so mad that I wanted to quit. Why should I have to quit something I love just because people are mean? They would never give me a break. No matter what I did. It wasn't good enough. I had to endure hell week just like they did. I could never please them. They harassed me for three months; then, they finally stopped. The next four months they came around and were nice to me, but there were still a few guys that would believe that I didn't deserve to be on the same field as them. That is ok with me because I learned that you can't please everyone. I went on to finish the football season. I also played on the girl's basketball team.

This experience is significant because it taught me a lot. It taught me I can do anything I put my mind to, no matter what anybody says. I learned how to deal with people and certain situations. I learned that I'm a strong person, and that I believe in myself. I learned that I could challenge myself, and succeed in my goals. If I want to, I could be the first person to step foot on Mars.

Take a minute to consider the entire process that Patricia Martinez has gone through. Her instructor gave her a writing assignment, and her first step in the writing process involved creating a list and a cluster of possible ideas. From one idea on her list and one idea on her cluster, she created an outline that organized her thoughts. From that outline, she wrote a first draft. She then made a global revision by eliminating the entire scene at her house before she reached the football field, and she made corrections based on feedback from her classmates in the second draft. Feedback from her instructor permitted her to make several sentence-level revisions in her third draft, which focused mostly on correcting run-ons. Each step in the process allowed her to develop or refine her ideas.

Is she finished? Her paper still has some errors and room for improvement. Then when does the process of rewriting end? To answer this question, an author must return to the first question in the writing process: why am I writing this? If a student's third draft of an essay meets his or her need to earn a good grade in a class, then the author may be finished with that piece of writing. The answer will vary from author to author and from situation to situation. Many levels of quality in writing exist. Certainly, Patricia's essay at this point reflects effective writing.

WHAT ARE THE TRAITS OF EFFECTIVE WRITING?

Effective writing meets the needs of the writer and the reader. Much effective writing, particularly college writing, has the following four traits:

Trait 1: Make a Point

Patricia Martinez has a point, and it appears in her outline ("I can accomplish what I set my mind to"), which she created in the prewriting stage of the writing process. The author tells the reader the point of a paragraph in the topic sentence and the point of an essay in the thesis statement; these ideas are explained in Chapter 5.

Trait 2: Support the Point

Patricia's story about playing football in high school supports her point; she generates the details of this story in the prewriting stage of the writing process also. Imagine her point sitting by itself: "I can accomplish what I set my mind to."

Without her story, which is her example or evidence, her readers probably would not believe her point. Imagine a lawyer in court claiming that someone is guilty of murder without producing specific, clear evidence. The jury probably would not believe the lawyer. Support or evidence is the reason that we believe someone's point. These ideas are discussed in Chapter 7.

Trait 3: Organize the Ideas

Patricia's outline—also part of the prewriting process—helped her to organize her ideas. She used an introduction, a body, and a conclusion, and she decided to organize her story chronologically, i.e., according to time. Without a method of organization, her readers would not be able to understand her point. Imagine a child presenting to you all of the ingredients of a cake mixed together in an incorrect order. Perhaps you would not even recognize it as a cake; it certainly would not appeal to you. A baker, on the other hand, could make and present a cake that would appeal to your sense of sight, smell, and taste. Organization determines the way in which something is presented, and organization is the reason we are able to understand and appreciate someone's point. These ideas are clarified in Chapter 8.

Trait 4: Present the Ideas in Error-Free Sentences

Writers attempt to achieve error-free writing in the final stage of writing—rewriting—and not before then. Errors in sentences call attention to themselves and distract and confuse readers. On the other hand, error-free sentences, like organized ideas, allow readers to understand a point easily; they also lend credibility to the writing because they reflect the author's education and skill in communicating. In other words, error-free sentences enhance the likelihood that the reader will understand and agree with the author's point. These ideas are discussed in Chapters 13–23.

PRACTICE

 Answer the following questions on a separate piece of paper or on a computer.

1. How is the process of writing different from the product of writing?
2. What are the three stages of the writing process?
3. What are four questions that a writer should ask him- or herself in the prewriting stage of the writing process?

4. What is the purpose of creating a cluster?
5. How can an outline help in the writing process?
6. Should a writer be concerned with writing error-free sentences when writing the first draft? Why or why not?
7. Name three people who can read your paper to give you feedback on it.
8. Does a writer make sentence-level revisions or global revisions first? Why?
9. What are the four traits of effective writing?
10. Which of the four traits of effective writing are addressed in the prewriting stage of the writing process?

GROUP WORK

1. Consider, discuss, and list three pros and three cons of peer revision. Do you have experience with peer revision of writing assignments? If so, how beneficial was the experience? How have your peers been helpful in revision? Have your peers ever given you incorrect advice during the rewriting process?
2. Discuss whether more emphasis has been placed on the product or on the process of writing in your education so far. List three examples to support your position.
3. Consider, discuss, and record your group's comments on the three general stages of the writing process: prewriting, writing, and rewriting. Which stage of the writing process do you anticipate being the easiest? Most difficult? Most time-consuming? Most beneficial? Explain your reasons for each of your positions.

TEST (TRUE/FALSE)

1. The product of your writing involves prewriting.
2. The process of your writing involves prewriting, writing, and rewriting.
3. The reason for a work of writing is not an important consideration.
4. A writer's audience refers to those people who will read the writing.
5. One purpose of a cluster is to generate ideas.
6. One purpose of an outline is to organize ideas.
7. A writer should try to write error-free sentences in the first draft.
8. One draft of an essay is usually enough to produce effective writing.

9. Global revisions should be made after sentence-level revisions.

10. Presenting ideas in error-free sentences is a consideration of the rewriting stage of the writing process.

WRITING ASSIGNMENTS

1. Academic Assignment: Write a short essay in which you make a point about something that you have learned, illustrate the point with an example, and analyze the significance of what you have learned. For tips on making a point through a thesis statement, visit The Writing Center at the University of North Carolina at http://www.unc.edu/depts/wcweb/handouts/thesis.html.

2. Journal Assignment: Explain everything that you have learned in this chapter: "What is involved in the process of writing?"

3. Creative Assignment: Visit the Museum of Modern Art at http://www.moma.org/, and view the collections. Select an image that you like, and describe it in a one page essay. For tips on writing descriptions, visit Purdue University's Online Writing Lab at http://owl.english.purdue.edu/handouts/general/gl_describe.html.

Chapter

What does a writer consider before writing?

"Easy writing makes hard reading."

—Ernest Hemingway

LEARNING OBJECTIVES

1. Learn what to consider before writing.
2. Learn what to consider in choosing a subject for writing.

PRE-READING QUESTIONS

1. Can someone learn to write well?
2. How can making a commitment to learning to write well improve your writing?
3. What tools would you want to have before writing something?
4. How do you choose a subject for writing?
5. When you write something, do you think about who the readers will be?

WHAT MIGHT A WRITER CONSIDER BEFORE WRITING?

Attitude

First, consider your own attitude toward writing by answering the following questions.

1. Is writing easy for you?
2. Do you like writing?
3. Do you ever write anything for enjoyment, like a poem?
4. Have you enjoyed your English teachers?
5. Have you earned good grades in your English classes?

If you have more *no* answers than *yes* answers, you may have had many negative writing experiences, which influence your attitude about writing. If this is the case, realize that you can now begin to have a series of positive writing experiences and develop a positive attitude about writing. To accomplish these two things, you need to realize the following:

1. People are intelligent and can learn to write well. Consider one of your talents or skills. How did you become good at it? First, you are intelligent, and second, you probably practiced quite a bit. The same applies to writing. Because you are intelligent, you can also learn to write well through instruction and practice.
2. As Rita Smilkstein has pointed out in *Tools for Writing: Using the Natural Human Learning Process (Instructor's Manual),* people love to learn (p. 15). Learning is a natural process that starts at birth and is very satisfying. Consider a two-year-old girl at a park. If you sit down on a bench and watch her, you will see her learning about other kids, bugs, swings, gravity, language, etc. Kids are naturally curious and love to explore and learn new skills. Although the settings and the skills change, this process remains satisfying throughout our lives.
3. Learning to write well is a lifelong process, not a semester-long process. Compare writing to playing a musical instrument. You would not expect to be playing the vio-

lin well in an orchestra after one class. To learn how to write well, we need to engage in an ongoing process of instruction and practice. Consider taking many English classes and writing in a journal on a weekly basis for the rest of your life.

Since your current attitude toward writing will influence everything that you write in the future, developing a positive attitude toward writing will make the process more enjoyable and productive.

Commitment

Learning to write well also requires commitment. Twenty miles into a marathon, runners often hit "the wall." At this point, the strain and fatigue of the marathon test the stamina of the runners. Continuing is difficult. Committed runners, nevertheless, finish the race. The writing process also requires endurance. Success will come by working hard long after the initial excitement of an idea passes.

Tools

 Your writing tools will depend upon what you are writing. For some assignments in college, you only need a pencil, a sheet of lined paper, and a quiet place. For a journal assignment, you might need a pen and a journal. For an essay assignment, you might want to use a computer. If you don't own one, consider buying a disk and becoming familiar with your campus writing center where you can have access to a computer and a tutor who can give you feedback. To research a subject, you will want to become familiar with your campus library as well.

Finally, don't overlook your instructor; take advantage of him or her by stopping by regularly during office hours. Think about your professor's situation: he or she may have 35 students in each of 5 classes. You may be 1 out of 175 students, and your professor may struggle just to remember your name. You will gain an advantage by making yourself stand out. Initiate frequent contact so that he or she may get to know you well and help you with your writing in a one-on-one setting. The best time for this to occur is during your professor's office hours. Visit and discuss your ideas. Bring chocolates! Review progress on your essay together, and ask lots of questions at each stage of the writing process. Show your completed work to your professor before the due date; this will give you time to refine your paper before your instructor evaluates it for a grade. Your instructor may be the most valuable writing tool at your disposal; initiate contact.

WHAT MIGHT A WRITER CONSIDER IN CHOOSING A WRITING SUBJECT?

Several factors come into play when choosing a subject about which to write.

Directions

The directions that you receive on a writing assignment will significantly influence the subject about which you choose to write. For example, in Chapter 2 Patricia Martinez responded to her instructor's assignment to make a point about something she had learned, to illustrate the point, and to analyze the significance of the point in a one- to two-page, double-spaced, typed essay, due in two weeks. This assignment limited her options: her paper had to include a true story that contained a conflict and brought about a new perspective.

Reread the directions a couple of times before beginning any work. Approach your instructor for clarification if necessary. A professor once distributed a test with 165 questions, asked students to read the directions on the first page, follow them, and leave the test on his desk on their way out. The directions asked students to complete only the first eight questions. Some students turned in the test after a few minutes and walked out. Other students panicked in an attempt to answer all 165 questions in the allotted time, and they agonized over material which they had not yet learned. Following directions carefully will save you a lot of time and fundamentally influence the decision for a writing subject.

Purpose

The reason why you are writing something is the purpose for it. Knowing that you are writing to entertain, to inform, or to persuade will help you in the writing process. Writing a play could be an example of writing to entertain. Explaining the problem of graffiti at a park in a letter to the city council is an example of writing to inform. Attempting to obtain employment by submitting a cover letter and résumé is an example of writing to persuade. When writing in or out of your college setting, you may be writing for more than one of these three reasons. For example, you may write a paper in which you both explain capital punishment laws to your readers and take a position on the issue; such a paper would both inform and persuade readers.

Significance

The most important suggestion in this book about writing is to write about something that is significant to you, something that you enjoy or feel strongly about, and finding that topic is always the most important step in the prewriting stage of the writing process.

Several advantages exist for writing about issues, experiences, or ideas that are significant to you. First, the writing process is longer and more difficult than students of writing often imagine, so feeling strongly about a topic will sustain a writer through this period. Imagine spending eight hours in the process of writing your next essay. Since time is a function of interest, the topic that you choose will determine how much you enjoy that process and how quickly time appears to pass. Although your professor may narrow or limit your options for topics, you will usually have some choices. Within those choices, you will be responsible for selecting a topic that carries significance to you.

Second, issues of significance to you typically interest your audience, the readers of your writing. Conversely, if your topic and your own writing do not interest you, how could they be of interest to your readers? This is a common pitfall to avoid. One of my students once read his research paper on World War II to the class, and I interrupted him, "By the tone of your voice, you don't sound interested in this subject. Are you?"

He thought for a moment and then said, "Not really." He continued, "I thought *you* would be interested in it." We then reviewed the point that topics of significance to *the writer* tend to interest the reader.

Third, you probably already know something about subjects that are significant to you. For example, if you have been surfing for ten years and you know quite a bit about the sport, you will probably have a positive experience writing about it. You will be able, for example, to discuss the equipment needed, the best beaches for surfing, the best techniques for beginners, problems to avoid, etc. Since learning is enjoyable, your readers will naturally be interested in learning about surfing, even if they have no interest in trying the sport. If you have never tried surfing in your life, you know nothing about the sport, and it carries no significance to you, you should pick a different writing topic because, generally, your strongest writing will flow from subjects about which you have some experience and knowledge.

Fourth, issues of significance to writers tend to produce effective writing, i.e., writing that makes a point, that supports a point, that has organized ideas, and that presents those ideas in error-free sentences. In other words, writers tend to produce their highest-quality writing on issues of significance to them. Although some students enter a writing class feeling like they hate writing, all students feel passionately about some things: relationships, hobbies, drug abuse, women's rights, movies, friends, the environment, cars, music, religion, sports, history, art, etc., and selecting these topics to write about is crucial to sustain interest in the author and the audience and to produce high-quality writing.

Audience

Whoever reads a particular piece of writing is considered the audience. In college, your peers or classmates may be part of your audience, and your instructor will be part of your audience.

Some important questions to consider about your audience follow:

1. Is the audience interested in the subject?
2. How much does the audience know about the subject?
3. What does the audience need to know about the subject?
4. Does the audience already have an opinion or attitude about the subject?
5. Do I want to try to change the audience's opinion or attitude about the subject?
6. Will the audience resist hearing a new perspective on the subject?
7. Would humor be appropriate with this audience and this subject?

The answers obtained from these questions will help the writer know how to best approach the audience through writing.

Tone

Tone refers to the attitude that an author has toward his or her writing and audience. I recently felt a desire to express my frustration with a manufacture defect in the turn signal of my Toyota Camry. My frustration inspired me to write a letter to the owner of a local Toyota dealership. After considering my problem, my audience, and my desired solution, I decided to write with a respectful tone, explaining the problem without criticizing the owner, my car, or the company. The owner responded in a letter by crediting my account with enough money to pay for the malfunctioning part. Had I expressed my frustration in a tone of anger or sarcasm, the results would not have been as productive. Using an appropriate tone requires considering the position of the readers and the most effective way to address them.

Writing to fill a need, choosing a subject that carries significance, considering the audience, and using an appropriate tone contribute to effective writing by increasing the likelihood that an audience will consider and agree with a writer's point.

PRACTICE

Answer the following questions on a separate piece of paper or on a computer.

1. What three facts can help us to develop a positive attitude toward writing?
2. How is a positive attitude helpful in the writing process?
3. How is the writing process like running a marathon?

4. Can you list five tools of writing?
5. Why is following writing directions important?
6. What are the three purposes of writing?
7. What are three reasons that choosing a significant subject to write about is important?
8. What are four important issues for writers to consider about audiences?
9. Define *tone*.
10. How can an author's tone contribute to effective writing?

GROUP WORK

1. To promote a positive attitude about writing and literacy in general, discuss a favorite reading (book, play, short story, poem) and a favorite writing assignment of each member of the group. Keep the discussion positive by avoiding war stories and whining. Then, list each book and assignment and explain in writing the reasons that made each of these experiences positive.
2. Describe your writing center on campus in a paragraph. What are the hours of operation? What qualifies a person to use the center? What equipment is available? What on-line resources are provided? What technical assistance is available with writing on computers? In what ways will tutors and writing coaches assist in the writing process?
3. To find potential writing topics of high interest, discuss and list a dozen ideas that are of significance to members of your group, ideas about which you feel passionately and would like to learn more.

TEST (TRUE/FALSE)

1. People are intelligent enough to learn how to write well.
2. People love to learn.
3. People can learn to write well in a semester.
4. Learning to write well requires a commitment.
5. Access to a computer is not necessary in today's English classes.
6. It is possible to entertain, inform, and persuade all at once in writing.
7. An author who knows his or her subject well will have an advantage over an author who does not.
8. In college writing, your audience is always just your teacher.

9. What the audience needs to know about a subject is important to consider.

10. Tone refers to the reader's attitude toward a piece of writing.

WRITING ASSIGNMENTS

 1. Academic Assignment: Visit the National Wildlife Federation at http://www.nwf.org/ and use their *search* to obtain information on one endangered species. Use this information to write a short essay in which you explain the current condition of an endangered plant or animal, the causes of the condition, and propose solutions to improve the situation.

 2. Journal Assignment: Explain everything that you have learned in this chapter: "What does a writer consider before writing?"

 3. Creative Assignment: Visit the National Gallery of Art at http://www.nga.gov/, and take an on-line tour. Select an image that you like, and describe it in a one-page essay. For tips on writing descriptions, visit Purdue University's Online Writing Lab at http://owl.english.purdue.edu/handouts/general/gl_describe.html.

How does a writer generate ideas?

"The idea is to get the pencil moving quickly."

—Bernard Malamud

LEARNING OBJECTIVES

1. Learn why prewriting techniques are useful in the writing process.
2. Learn nine prewriting techniques.

PRE-READING QUESTIONS

1. Why can generating writing topics be difficult?
2. How do you now generate ideas for a writing topic?
3. How can a computer be useful in the prewriting process?
4. How can drawing be useful in the prewriting process?
5. How can questions be useful in the prewriting process?

WHY ARE PREWRITING TECHNIQUES USEFUL IN THE WRITING PROCESS?

Have you ever been given a writing assignment and stared at a blank piece of paper, not knowing what to write about or where to begin? Perhaps you write something down, then scratch it out. This can happen when writers are trying to produce high-quality work at the beginning of the writing process; ironically, seeking perfection early may prevent writers from progressing in the writing process. Imagine playing professional baseball. The best hitters strike out more often than they hit the ball. That's the nature of the game, but they have no fear of stepping up to the plate, and when they swing, they swing hard. They enjoy the challenge, and they know the possibilities. Writing is like that. The process of generating ideas to write about involves generating many ideas. Most of them will not be developed into paragraphs or essays, but after a writer puts enough ideas on a piece of paper, her or she will notice that one or two of them have great potential.

College professors often set parameters on writing subjects and then require students to select their own specific topics. For example, in Chapter 2 Patricia Martinez had to make a point about a lesson she had learned. How did Patricia generate ideas? She created a cluster, a common prewriting technique. The objective in a cluster is to generate as many ideas as possible; think of them all as potential writing topics. Do not evaluate them at this point, thinking, for example, that one idea is too ridiculous to add to other ideas on the page. Just write each one down and move on. Generally speaking, these ideas are to be recorded quickly, with the emphasis on quantity, not so much quality. Allow one idea to lead to another; do not interrupt the flow of ideas to evaluate one of them. Just think and write. Try to generate twenty ideas in ten minutes using any one of the techniques described below. Finally, remember that while many of these prewriting activities may be completed in pen or pencil, some of them can be accomplished easily on a computer. Try all of the techniques in this chapter, and then continue to use just the techniques that work best for you, modifying them as need requires.

Remember these guidelines as you try each technique.

1. Generate as many ideas as possible, or explore one idea as thoroughly as possible.
2. Do not reject or evaluate any ideas.
3. Rules of English such as grammar, spelling, punctuation, logic, etc., do not apply to prewriting. This is not a finished product for sharing with other people, so set aside concerns about correctness.
4. Remember (from Chapter 3) to work with ideas that
   • Fulfill your writing assignment
   • Interest you
   • You know something about (or at least would like to know something about)

WHAT ARE SOME USEFUL PREWRITING TECHNIQUES?

1. **The Internet**

   The Internet can provide writers with many ideas quickly. Begin with one of the main search engines like Excite, Yahoo!, or AltaVista. Type in an idea that you wish to explore. For example, you might want to write about Mount Everest. In the search box, you could type *Mount Everest,* which might lead to 300,000 websites. Because these search engines produce so many related sites, you will want to narrow your search. Ask yourself what about Mount Everest interests you. Typing *Mount Everest* and *hiking* and *dangers* might lead to about 3,000 websites. Through this method of searching, writers can quickly explore many ideas about an area of interest.

2. **Sketching**

   Imagine that you have been given the assignment to describe a favorite place in a short essay. As William Strong explains, one prewriting technique would involve drawing a rough sketch of the place (p. 31). You may simply use a pencil to sketch some stick figures. Good artwork is not important; however, including as much detail as possible is important since your sketch will be converted to words. This technique helps writers when they want to describe how things appear, such as an animal, a person, a painting, a house, a scene, etc. In the sketch below, a student responds to the assignment to describe a place of personal significance, which he will later describe in words.

A FAVORITE CAMPGROUND

3. Idea Mapping

   Idea mapping is similar to sketching, except that an author explores an idea by both drawing several sketches on a page and adding words beneath the pictures. William Kelly and Deborah Lawton explain the nature of this process:

> Idea Mapping is a freewheeling prewriting technique that attempts to stimulate both hemispheres of your brain. When you idea map, you write words and create images such as icons, scribbles, sketches, and symbols. According to the theory underlying this technique, the words you include flow from the left side of your brain, the home of logic and analysis. The sketches and doodles you create arise from the right side of your brain, the home of creativity. (p. 24)

   Below is an idea map drawn to generate ideas in response to a teacher's request for an essay explaining the process of something.

HOW TO SURF ON YOUR HEAD

Catch a wave!

Kneel on board
- stay in center
- maintain balance

Headstand
- place head down
- stabilize with hands
- raise feet

4. Brainstorming or Listing

   Brainstorming also uses free association. It involves writing down all the ideas that come to mind for an assignment or about a subject. Start with a title to provide some focus. Then, simply list as many ideas as you can on a piece of paper or on the computer. Your brainstorming will be like a grocery list in form. The list should include words and phrases, not complete sentences. Brainstorming can be done individually, with a partner, or in a group. When a group brainstorms, one good idea often triggers another in a process that combines thinking about a topic, talking about possible ideas, and recording these ideas in writing. Ideas may be generated with or without a time limit; just write as quickly as you can. Do not try to place ideas in any kind of order, do not reject bad ideas, and do not stop adding new ideas to your list. After you are finished, put a line through unwanted ideas, organize the ideas, and star or circle good ideas. Good ideas may be further developed through additional brainstorming or clustering.

Below is a list of ideas generated in response to an assignment that requested solutions to the problem of loss of natural resources.

Preserving Natural Resources

Laws that protect national parks, air, water, etc.

Water conservation

Recycling

Clean transportation

Using less energy at home

Nuclear energy

Stop deforestation

Stop use of CFC's

Avoid oil spills

Avoid nuclear war, accidents, etc.

Solar energy

Insulate house

5. Clustering (Webbing or Mapping)

Once a subject has been selected, clustering allows writers to generate specific ideas in an organized fashion. Start with a central idea; this could be a subject upon which you have settled, or this could be your assignment. Put it in a circle in the middle of your page.

Then, draw lines like spokes coming from the center of a wheel to smaller circles that represent related ideas. These smaller circles may even be connected to circles that are smaller still with more spokes. Notice that the circles that are the farthest from the middle are the most specific. Eventually, you will find a topic for writing that is specific enough to manage (see figure on p. 38).

6. Branching

Branching provides another way of generating ideas in an organized way, just like clustering. Start by putting your main idea at the top of the page as a title. Then put major supporting ideas down the left side of the page, leaving plenty of space between ideas. Draw branches to the right with minor supporting ideas. Continue branching to the right with specific details. To show the similarity between clustering and branching, the cluster (referred to above) has been recreated using the branching method shown on p. 39.

7. Free Writing

Free writing is an unstructured activity in which one writes without stopping in an attempt to produce many ideas in a short time. The writer disregards fears and inhibitions and warms up in the writing process through free association. If you have no direction yet for a subject or topic of your paper, just start writing. If you al-

CLUSTERING

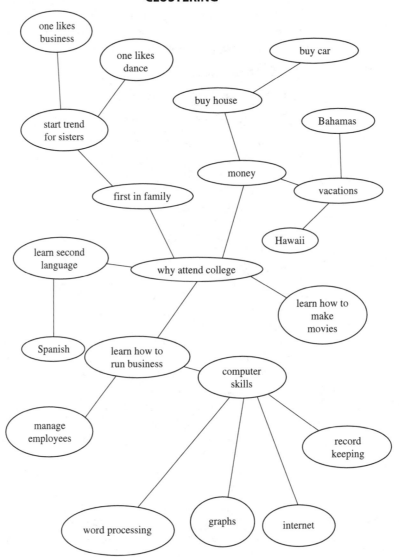

ready have a subject for your paper, focus your free writing by giving it a title at the top of the page. Do not evaluate ideas. Do not worry about grammar, spelling, punctuation, or correctness. Simply record ideas as quickly as they come for ten minutes without stopping. When ideas do not come, continue to record ideas, even if that means writing, "I have nothing to say. I have nothing to say. I have nothing to say." until something comes to mind. When you are done writing, read your free writing. Circle or underline ideas that might be worth developing in a paper.

BRANCHING
MAIN IDEA: WHY ATTEND COLLEGE?

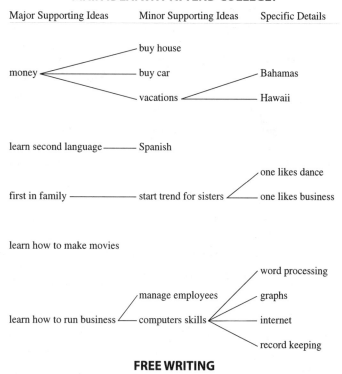

| Major Supporting Ideas | Minor Supporting Ideas | Specific Details |

FREE WRITING

Returning to school at 31

School is hard now that I'm older. Most of the others in class look about 18 just out of high school, those were fun times. I wasn't serious about college then, I started but dropped my classes my second semester. Jerry and me moved to Arizona to get a way, but my job didnt work out. What shall I write, What shall I write. Want a job working at a bank but I need computer skills for it. My class in Word and Excel will let me get a higher paying job this summer. I like my film class alot. A couple other students in class look my age, one guy is for sure older than me. Now I'm here to learn, I want to be here.

8. Journal Writing

   Journal writing is personal and private, so you may, again, write without being evaluated. It is like focused free writing, except it is not timed. As a result, it is relaxed and reflective, which often leads to insight. Take time to think as you write. Journals often include significant experiences and private thoughts, but they may include anything: actions, conversations, thoughts, explorations, observations, perspectives, etc. They may also contain prewriting techniques: sketches, lists, clusters, branches, free-writes, etc. Since practice makes performing any task easier, students of writing often benefit a great deal from writing in a journal for about fifteen minutes five times per week.

In 1942 Anne Frank, her family, and some friends went into hiding in a secret annex above an office building in Amsterdam for a period of two years before the Nazis discovered them. During this period of hiding, Ann recorded her thoughts in her diary; in the following entry she focuses on religion:

> People who have a religion should be glad, for not everyone has the gift of believing in heavenly things. You don't necessarily even have to be afraid of punishment after death; purgatory, hell, and heaven are things that a lot of people can't accept, but still a religion, it doesn't matter which, keeps a person on the right path. It isn't the fear of God but the upholding of one's own honor and conscience. How noble and good everyone could be if, every evening before falling asleep, they were to recall to their minds the events of the whole day and consider exactly what has been good and bad. Then, without realizing it, you try to improve yourself at the start of each new day; of course, you achieve quite a lot in the course of time. Anyone can do this, it costs nothing and is certainly very helpful. Whoever doesn't know it must learn and find by experience that: "A quiet conscience makes one strong!"
>
> Yours, Anne (p. 256)

9. Questioning or Interviewing

Where would we be without questions? When we have a problem, whether we realize it or not, we ask a question like, "Do I have the tools that I need to fix this flat tire?" Socrates taught by asking questions. Information in this book is presented in a question-and-answer format. Modern technology is the result of questions asked by scientists and engineers. Without questions, how could society progress?

Writers often ask the journalistic questions (5 *W*'s and *H*): Who? What? Why? Where? When? and How? You may start by creating questions about a topic using these six words. The journalistic questions will help you to consider a topic from a variety of angles, and the process of asking questions will automatically cause you to narrow your topic. Of course, these questions may cause you to consider other questions worth asking, and you will probably approach each writing assignment or situation with a set of tailored questions. After you have asked a dozen questions about a topic, try to answer some of these questions yourself. Your answers to these questions may be developed into paragraphs in your writing assignment. Below are some questions and answers about the subject of sex education being taught in public schools.

Main Idea: Sex Education in Public Schools

1. Who will decide if sex education should be taught in public schools? Who are the target students who would receive sex education in public schools? Who will be teaching the material? Who will determine what is included in the instruction?

Perhaps teachers, administrators, and parents will make the decision and determine what will be taught. This education will be received in the higher grades of elementary school or middle school. Health teachers will provide the education.

2. What will the curriculum include? What will the curriculum exclude? What are the pros of sex education in public schools? What are the cons of sex education in public schools?

The curriculum could include the changing body, methods of birth control, decisions about sex, sexually transmitted diseases, etc. The pros of sex education include students knowing about their bodies, being able to make informed decisions about sex, and being able to avoid diseases. The cons of sex education might include stimulating kids to become sexually active early and parents not being able to control delivery of sex education.

3. Why are these students being taught this subject? Why are they not being taught this subject at home?

Students need this subject to know about their bodies and the changes that occur as boys and girls grow into young men and women. Some parents teach their kids about sex education. Some parents don't.

4. Where will the students be taught these subjects? Where will the materials and supplies for the class come from?

Students will be taught these subjects in their health classes in school. School districts will supply all of the materials and supplies for the classes.

5. When will these students receive this information? When is the best time to have this education in a student's life?

Students will receive this information in sixth and seventh grade. This is the best time for this education because kids' bodies are changing then.

6. How will teachers know if students have learned the material? How will parents feel about it?

Teachers can test students on the information after the instruction. Parents can be notified before instruction to give permission.

You will probably want to find additional answers to these questions from parents, teachers, administrators, kids, and from written sources. If you interview someone, consider taking notes or recording the conversation with permission. If you consult the Internet, an encyclopedia, a book, or an article for answers to your questions, record the name and publication information of the source, and in your writing, acknowledge these sources.

PRACTICE 1

Using one of the main search engines on the Internet, find five potential writing topics. Enter a word or phrase that you wish to consider as a writing topic, like espionage. After you visit a few websites and see what ideas are discussed, return to your search engine and add additional words to espionage to provide focus to

your search, like espionage and equipment. Repeat this process until you have found five topics. Write on a separate piece of paper or on a computer.

PRACTICE 2

Create an idea map that explains a process with which you are familiar. Include as many stages as the process requires. Include as many details as possible. Write on a separate piece of paper or on a computer.

PRACTICE 3

Select one of your ideas from one of the practices above and generate more ideas through listing, clustering, or branching. Write on a separate piece of paper or on a computer.

PRACTICE 4

Select one of your ideas from one of the practices above and free write or write a journal entry. Do not concern yourself with grammar, spelling, punctuation, or correctness. When you are finished writing, read your paper. Circle or underline ideas that might be worth developing in a paper. Write on a separate piece of paper or on a computer.

PRACTICE 5

Select another one of your ideas from a previous practice, and place it at the top of a page. Generate a dozen journalistic questions (5 W's and H); then, seek answers to your questions through interviews and research. Write on a separate piece of paper or on a computer.

GROUP WORK

1. In your group, pick a general topic to brainstorm. Then, list at least a dozen ideas about it as quickly as you can. Limit yourself to five minutes. Be as specific as you can. When you are finished brainstorming, circle your three favorite ideas.

2. Pick one of the topics that you generated in Practices 1 to 4 (or select a new topic); then, generate fifteen to twenty ideas through clustering.

3. Pick one of the topics that you generated in Practices 1 to 4 (or select a new topic); then, create at least six questions using the *5 W's* and *H*. Finally, generate answers to these questions in your group.

TEST (TRUE/FALSE)

1. Trying to produce high-quality work at the beginning of the writing process may block progress.
2. Use correct grammar when free writing.
3. Try to generate ideas for writing about topics that interest you.
4. Generally, adding additional words to a search on the Internet will produce additional web sites.
5. Idea mapping allows writers to use both sides of their brains in the writing process.
6. Clustering and branching help to narrow a subject down to a manageable topic.
7. Free writing allows writers to generate ideas based on free association.
8. Journal writing should always be timed like free writing.
9. Questioning helps writers to consider topics from new perspectives.
10. Ask the same set of questions about every topic.

WRITING ASSIGNMENTS

1. Academic Assignment: Visit The U.S. Conference of Mayors at http://usmayors.org/uscm/home.asp to find the name and address of the mayor in your city and your city's website with current local issues. Write a letter to your mayor (or a member of your city council) expressing your opinion on a local issue. Provide ample support or reasons for your opinion. Begin the writing process by generating ideas about local issues with one of the prewriting techniques discussed in this chapter. For further explanation on prewriting techniques, visit Purdue University's Online Writing Lab at http://owl.english.purdue.edu/handouts/general/gl_plan1.html.

2. Journal Assignment: Explain everything that you have learned in this chapter:"How does a writer generate ideas?"

3. Creative Assignment: Visit the Smithsonian National Museum of American History at http://americanhistory.si.edu/. Select an image that you like, and describe it in a one-page essay. Begin by using one of the prewriting techniques described in this chapter, like sketching. For tips on writing descriptions, visit Purdue University's Online Writing Lab at http://owl.english.purdue.edu/handouts/general/gl_describe.html.

Chapter 5

How does a writer narrow a topic, generate topic sentences, and create a thesis statement?

"You can get help from teachers, but you are going to have to learn a lot by yourself, sitting alone in a room."

— Theodor Geisel ("Dr. Seuss")

LEARNING OBJECTIVES

1. Learn what topics are and why writers need to narrow them.
2. Learn how to narrow a topic.
3. Learn what a topic sentence and a thesis statement are.
4. Learn why writers use them.
5. Learn how to create them.
6. Learn where to place them.

PRE-READING QUESTIONS

1. Would you rather write about a broad topic like music or a narrow topic like the reasons for the breakup of your favorite band? Why?
2. Do you remember the first goal of effective writing? If you don't, check the beginning of Chapter 2.
3. What does a topic sentence do for a paragraph?

4. Where in a paragraph may the reader expect to find a topic sentence?
5. How is a thesis like a topic sentence?

WHAT ARE TOPICS, WHY DO WRITERS NEED TO NARROW THEM, AND HOW DOES A WRITER NARROW A TOPIC?

A topic is a subject for discussion, and many subjects are too broad to be discussed in a paragraph or an essay. For that reason, writers need to understand how to narrow a topic.

In Chapter 4, a student created a cluster to generate potential ideas for writing a paper about why someone should attend college. Notice that as the circles move away from the center, they become more specific topics, better writing topics. That is because the process of clustering not only generates topics, but it narrows them as well. Generally, narrow topics are better than broad topics. To further narrow one of the topics from the cluster in Chapter 4, a new cluster can be created with any of the words from the original cluster. This process of creating a second cluster narrows the topic to a manageable size, as in the example below:

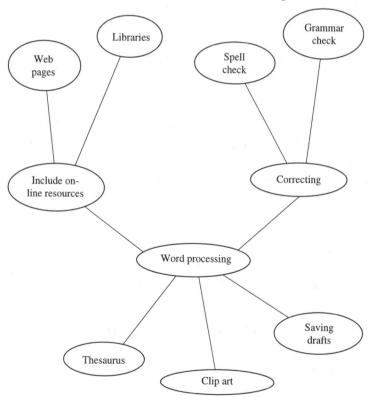

A flowchart is another way of visually arranging ideas in a way that also narrows topics, and a computer may be used to accomplish this, as in the example below:

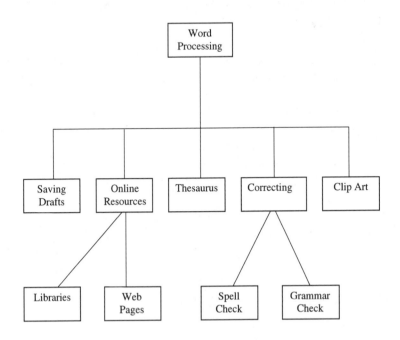

The Circle Diagram provides a third method for narrowing topics. Start with a large circle on the page and topic just inside of it. Smaller circles are added to the inside of this large circle, each one being a narrower and narrower topic. As noted by Audrey Roth in *The Elements of Basic Writing*, "The resulting circle diagram looks like a target with writing in each circle" (p. 41), as in the example on p. 47.

PRACTICE 1

Number the following sets of topics, with number 1 being the narrowest and number 3 being the broadest.

Example: _2_   California   _1_   Los Angeles   _3_   United States

1. ___ people   ___ women   ___ literate women

2. ___ baseball   ___ sports   ___ pitching

CIRCLE DIAGRAM

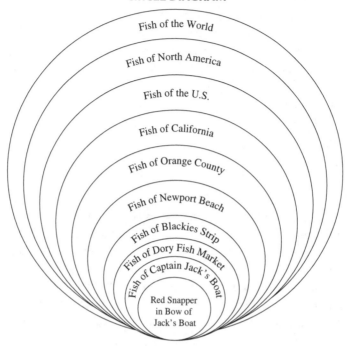

Fish of the World

Fish of North America

Fish of the U.S.

Fish of California

Fish of Orange County

Fish of Newport Beach

Fish of Blackies Strip

Fish of Dory Fish Market

Fish of Captain Jack's Boat

Red Snapper in Bow of Jack's Boat

3. ___ universities ___ education ___ classes

4. ___ key boards ___ computer hardware ___ computers

5. ___ city buses ___ transportation ___ public transportation

PRACTICE 2

Generate a potential writing topic, and narrow the topic by creating a cluster, a flowchart, or a circle diagram. Include a dozen ideas in your work. Write on a separate piece of paper or on a computer.

WHAT ARE A TOPIC SENTENCE AND A THESIS STATEMENT, AND WHY DO WRITERS USE THEM?

Once you have narrowed a topic, you need to make a statement about that narrowed topic in a special sentence. This unique sentence focuses your writing by controlling what you discuss. If your writing task involves writing one paragraph, then you need to begin by writing a controlling sentence that is called a topic sentence. If your writing task involves writing an essay, then you need to begin by writing a controlling sentence that is called a thesis statement.

The topic sentence and the thesis statement are best understood after reviewing the goals of effective writing that were discussed in Chapter 2:

1. Make a point.
2. Support the point.
3. Organize the ideas.
4. Present the ideas in error-free sentences.

Topic sentences and thesis statements help us to accomplish the first step in effective writing: make a point. In other words, they define what will be discussed in a paragraph (a group of sentences that reveals the author's perspective on a subject) or an essay (a group of paragraphs that reveals the author's perspective on a subject), and they provide a forecast to the readers about what is coming up the way that a sign on the freeway notifies drivers that the next exit leads to Dodger Stadium. A topic sentence or thesis statement tells readers what lies ahead; it's a commitment by the author to move in a certain direction.

HOW DO WRITERS CREATE TOPIC SENTENCES AND THESIS STATEMENTS?

Below is a table that shows how writers move from a topic to a narrowed topic to a topic sentence or thesis statement:

Topic	Narrowed Topic	Topic Sentence/Thesis Statement: The writer's perspective about the narrowed topic
Fish	Fish caught by the Dory Fishermen	The red snapper caught and sold by Captain Jack of the Dory Fishermen are fresh and nutritious.
Yosemite National Park	Bears at Yosemite National Park	Backpackers in Yosemite National Park should store food in bear-proof canisters.
Ice Skating	Ice skating in the Olympics	Russian female ice skaters will have another strong presence in the next Olympic Games.
Word Processing	Web pages and word processing	Information and images on web pages can be used to bring word processing documents to life.
Basketball	Michael Jordan and basketball	Michael Jordan is the best basketball player of all time **because** of his shooting percentage (1), his attitude on the court (2), and his playoff victories (3).

Notice the form of the last thesis statement in the table on page 48: it makes a statement, follows with the word *because,* and then gives a few reasons to support the statement. This format works well in some writing situations because it organizes the essay, enabling each reason to be discussed in a separate body paragraph.

Also, keep in mind that two different authors could start with the same narrowed topic but take the topic in different directions, as in the examples below:

> Backpackers in Yosemite National Park should store food in bear-proof canisters. Backpackers in Yosemite National Park should store food in trees using the counterbalance technique.

In other words, the topic sentence/thesis statement controls the direction of the writing and makes all the difference in where the author is going.

Notice that the topic sentences/theses statements in the table on page 48 have some traits in common, and these traits constitute the six guidelines for topic sentences/thesis statements:

1. They fit the writer's assignment or need.
2. They cover a topic of interest to the writer.
3. They make a discussable point.
4. They are written in one complete sentence.
5. They represent the writer's perspective.
6. They can be supported and developed with details in one paragraph or one essay.

Consider each of these guidelines for a moment.

1. The topic sentence or thesis fits the writer's assignment or need. If you have received a writing assignment from a college professor, reread it. Make sure that you understand it; if you do not understand it, ask for an explanation. Teachers usually have very specific ideas in mind when they give a writing assignment, but the assignment is not always communicated clearly by the instructor nor understood well by students. Initiate contact with your instructor if you have any questions about the direction of your writing.

2. The topic sentence or thesis covers a topic of interest to the writer. Remember from Chapter 3 that the most important advice in this book is to write about something that is significant to you, something that you enjoy or about which you feel strongly. When you write about something that is of significance to you, four positive consequences will follow: the topic will sustain your interest through the writing process,

your writing will sustain the reader's interest, the writing process will be easier because you probably already know something about the topic, and you will tend to produce your best writing when discussing a topic that carries special significance to you.

3. The topic sentence or thesis statement makes a discussable point. Writing in college or academic writing attempts to explain truth, the way things really are. Of course, your topic sentence or thesis attempts to describe the truth as you now see it. Intelligent people disagree on the truth, and the truth for one intelligent person may change with time as additional information or experience creates new perspectives. Generally accepted facts, however, do not need to be explained because most people already agree with them. For example, if a student states that the sun is hot, who will disagree with that? Most people already share the same perspective, so that statement makes for a poor topic sentence or thesis statement because it is not discussable. The following sentence could serve as a useful topic sentence: Solar energy should power the majority of automobiles of the future.

4. The topic sentence or thesis is written in one complete sentence. A complete sentence, a sentence that has a subject, a verb, and one idea, will help to ensure that the statement is actually a topic sentence or thesis statement, and not just a title or narrowed topic.

5. The topic sentence or thesis statement represents the writer's perspective. Since good writing makes a point, and since academic writing attempts to reveal truth, a good topic sentence or thesis statement must state the writer's perspective.

6. The topic sentence can be supported and developed with details in one paragraph, and the thesis statement can be supported and developed with details in one essay. Think of the topic sentence or thesis statement as a circle around a set of ideas. Ideas outside of that circle cannot be discussed in that paragraph or essay. For example, imagine that the circle is a fence, and the writer must decide where to place it: around the pool, around the trampoline, around the garden, around the backyard, around the house, around the neighborhood, etc. The challenge in writing involves creating the right size circle, not too large, and not too small. Circles for paragraphs, obviously, must be smaller than circles for essays since they discuss writers' perspectives about narrow topics. Circles for essays, then, must be a little larger since essays discuss writers' perspectives about slightly broader topics, and they discuss them in greater detail.

PRACTICE 3

 To show that you understand how to narrow a topic and create a topic sentence/thesis statement, complete the following table. Write on a separate piece of paper or on a computer. The first one has been completed as an example.

Topic	Narrowed Topic	Topic Sentence/Thesis Statement: The writer's perspective about the narrowed topic
Printers	Low-cost color printers	The Hewlett Packard DeskJet 1600 is the best low-cost color printer for the money.
Education		
Twins		
Skiing		
Websites		
Space Travel		

In creating topic sentences and thesis statements, students should be aware of common challenges.

Problem	Example of Poor Sentence/Thesis Topic Statement	Reason for Poor Sentence/Thesis Topic Statement	Example of Better Topic Sentence/Thesis Statement
Announcement of subject	The giant panda is an endangered animal.	This sentence only announces a subject. It does not take a discussable position on it.	Reproductive programs can restore the giant panda population.
Statement of fact/non-discussable	The people were forcibly evacuated from their villages.	This sentence simply states a generally-accepted fact and is not discussable.	The evacuation of people from their villages led to the current civil war.
Too broad to support	Using animals for testing products is unethical.	This statement applies to many animals and many products.	Spraying hair spray in the eyes of chimpanzees for product testing is unethical.
Too narrow to support	Reading books by Dr. Seuss regularly to children promotes their language development.	This topic sentence would not allow the writer to discuss books by other authors.	Reading books regularly to children promotes their language development.
More than one idea	Hang-gliding is a dangerous sport, and scuba diving is expensive.	Two different aspects of two different ideas should not be discussed in one paragraph or essay.	Hang-gliding is a dangerous sport.
Vague or general	Collecting coins is interesting.	"Interesting" is a vague word that does not provide the reader with much information.	Coin collecting is a hobby that can open new worlds of friendships and cultures to collectors.
Indirect or uncommitted	First aid could help some time, if someone wanted to learn it.	This sentence does not make a point, is not direct, and is not committed.	Everyone should be able to provide first aid in an emergency.

Problem	Example of Poor Sentence/Thesis Topic Statement	Reason for Poor Sentence/Thesis Topic Statement	Example of Better Topic Sentence/Thesis Statement
Unclear or poorly worded	Students and cultures that mix show better for everyone in college.	The writer of this sentence has not taken the time to reread and reword the topic sentence.	Diverse student populations at colleges enhance appreciation of cultural diversity.

PRACTICE 4

Change the following poor topic sentences/thesis statements to better ones. Write on a separate piece of paper or on a computer. The first one has been completed as an example.

Problem	Example of Poor Topic Sentence/Thesis	Your version of a better topic sentence or thesis statement
Announcement of subject	My essay is about stress management.	Applying stress management techniques can lower blood pressure, create positive thinking, and produce effective behavior.
Announcement of subject	My paragraph will discuss adoption.	
Statement of fact/ non-discussable	Exercise helps people stay in shape.	
Too broad to support	Parents should protect their children against diseases.	
Too narrow to support	The Johnson's second daughter should be breast-fed for eight months.	
More than one idea	Extra curricular activities in high school help students to enjoy school, and picking the right major in college helps students find an enjoyable career.	

Problem	Example of Poor Topic Sentence/Thesis	Your version of a better topic sentence or thesis statement
Vague or general	Central Park is great.	
Indirect or uncommitted	Perhaps students with disabilities might be given equal access to public schools.	
Unclear or poorly worded	Because weather patterns have to changed.	

WHERE DOES A WRITER PLACE TOPIC SENTENCES AND THESIS STATEMENTS?

Writers should also become familiar with the location of the topic sentence and the thesis statement in a paragraph or essay. Typically, writers place a topic sentence in the first sentence of a paragraph; however, writers sometimes put them in the middle or at the end of a paragraph. Writers typically place a thesis at the end of the introduction, but it may be placed anywhere in the introduction. Notice the parallels between the paragraph and the essay in the following diagram, particularly the locations of the topic sentences and the thesis statement. Remember that the exact number of supporting sentences in a paragraph and the exact number of paragraphs in an essay will vary, but the basic structure will remain constant, see figure on p. 54.

A paragraph makes a clear point in the topic sentence. All body sentences support that point. The conclusion returns to the clear point in the topic sentence. Notice how the following student paragraph follows the correct format:

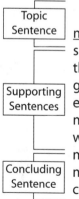

Topic Sentence

Supporting Sentences

Concluding Sentence

   I would have to say my most prized possession is my quilt because my grandmother gave it to me (**Topic Sentence**). When I was twelve, she asked me to pick out colors that I wanted in my quilt. We went to the fabric store, and picked out blue and different floral material. My grandma spent 2 months on this quilt. When she gave it to me, I was so excited. I immediately ran home and put it on my bed. It is funny when my friends stay at my house, they always ask to use the quilt. They always claim thy sleep better with it. Who knows, grandma's quilt may be more soothing than a regular blanket. Since the quilt is so special to me, I will have to retire it one day. When that time comes, I will put it in a cedar box. That way I can pass it down to my children.

Adapted from Jennifer Parker

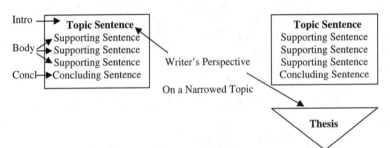

Paragraph

Intro ⟶ **Topic Sentence**
Supporting Sentence
Body ⟶ Supporting Sentence
Supporting Sentence
Concl ⟶ Concluding Sentence

Writer's Perspective

On a Narrowed Topic

Essay

Introductory Paragraph

Topic Sentence
Supporting Sentence
Supporting Sentence
Supporting Sentence
Concluding Sentence

Thesis

First Body Paragraph

Topic Sentence
Supporting Sentence
Supporting Sentence
Supporting Sentence
Concluding Sentence

Second Body Paragraph

Topic Sentence
Supporting Sentence
Supporting Sentence
Supporting Sentence
Concluding Sentence

Third Body Paragraph

Topic Sentence
Supporting Sentence
Supporting Sentence
Supporting Sentence
Concluding Sentence

Concluding Paragraph

Thesis

Topic Sentence
Supporting Sentence
Supporting Sentence
Supporting Sentence
Concluding Sentence

Where a paragraph makes its point in a topic sentence, an essay makes a clear point in the thesis statement. All paragraphs support that point. Notice how the following student essay follows the essay format:

Which College Should One Choose?

Intro

Let learning be an adventure of your choice **(Topic Sentence)**. Mary Traub is a high school graduate interested in going to college. She is very confused and unsure of exactly what she wants to learn in college. She was an underachiever in high school, but she enjoys learning. She is not sure she can comfortably leave home so soon after high school. She also has financial problems. Mary, like many other students in high school or adults returning to school, has a big decision to make. To ease this situation, she and others should first attend their local community college before attending a university **(Thesis Statement)**.

Body

Attending a community college can save a student money **(Topic Sentence)**. The expenses at the community college are insignificant compared to expenses at a university. For example, tuition may only cost a hundred dollars at a community college compared to thousands of dollars at a university. Books, parking fees, health fees, and other fees are very reasonable at the community college level. In addition, the student housing costs are eliminated as they would be living at home. Add it all up and community college is more affordable than a university.

Beside being affordable, the community college is considered an excellent transition from a high school to a university **(Topic Sentence)**. A community college campus is like a blanket that embraces the student whereas a university campus is like going into a foreign land where the natives are restless. In other words, a community college campus is less intimidating than a university campus. Applying and being accepted into a community college is much easier than at a university. At a community college, an undecided student can take additional time to decide what major he or she will take. The student can take classes in different fields to see which field he or she would like best. Going to a community college will help a student adjust to college. Community college prepares a student to take that final step towards a university.

Along with being a transition from high school to a university, most community colleges are more geographically convenient than a university **(Topic Sentence)**. There are more community colleges than universities in a state. In fact, community colleges are usually within a few miles of home whereas universities can be much farther away. Being located close to home makes the community college easier for students to attend, which helps cut the student's driving time and transportation costs. Altogether, community college is more convenient to attend than a university.

Concl.

High school graduates, like Mary Traub, interested in attending college should attend a community college before attending a university (**Thesis Restated**). The advantages include saving money, enjoying a transitional opportunity, and taking advantage of a geographical convenience. Consider all the stress that an eighteen-year-old person faces: leaving home, assuming adult responsibilities, initiating new relationships, etc. In addition, college students will want to maintain a high grade point average. Why make this period in a person's life more difficult than it already is?

Adapted from Jennifer Hendrix

Finally, students should be aware of two things. First, a thesis statement will often evolve as a student gains additional information about a subject because this additional information influences the writer's perspective on the topic. For this reason, consider your thesis statement at this point in the writing process a working thesis. Second, although most forms of academic writing include topic sentences and thesis statements, exceptions do occur. Narrative essays, essays that tell a story, for example, typically do not have topic sentences and thesis statements.

PRACTICE 5

Locate and underline the topic sentence in the following paragraphs.

1. Everyone should have the right not to be exposed to secondhand smoke. The diseases that one can get from secondhand smoke are deadly. My mom smokes around me, and it's very uncomfortable to be around. I can't stand the smell; I get a headache every time I smell smoke. Fortunately, society is putting restrictions on smoking in public areas. We can't stop people from smoking, but I wish they would realize what they are doing to other people. They know what could happen to them, but they don't think about the serious health problems that can hurt non-smokers.

Adapted from Michelle Lugo

2. Did you know that women in some countries may only have one child? In China, couples are limited to one child, two if the first one is a girl because males are favored over females. This policy is viewed as a solution to China's population problem (over one billion people). Women who do not comply with the policy are subject to fines or perhaps forced abortions. Women should be free to have as many babies as they want, boys or girls.

Adapted from Peter Whang

3. Since the creation of sports cars, teenagers have been illegally racing on the street. Whether it is for fun or for money, these kids will race no matter what. As some of these races take place, there is an occasional fatal collision; this is why they are illegal. Los Angeles city should put together a safe drag strip for legalized street racing because this would cut down on collision injuries. There would be an entrance fee. Part of it would go to the winners, and part of it would go to other city funding. Also for precaution, an ambulance and police vehicles would be nearby. This would allow teenagers to do something that they love—legally.

Adapted from Jared Ramero

GROUP WORK

1. As a group, generate a potential writing topic, and place it in the middle of a cluster. From the original thought, narrow the topic by branching off into at least fifteen specific ideas.

2. As a group, generate a potential writing topic, and place it just inside a large circle. From that original thought, narrow the topic by placing each subidea in a smaller circle. Include ten ideas in your circle diagram.

3. As a group, generate your own topics, narrowed topics, and topic sentences/thesis statements on a separate paper or a computer. Follow the example below.

Topic	Narrowed Topic	Topic Sentence/Thesis Statement: The writer's perspective about the narrowed topic
Maps	Topographical maps	Forest rangers should distribute free topographical maps to all hikers in an attempt to reduce the number of "lost hikers" annually.

TEST (TRUE/FALSE)

1. Generally, broad topics are better for writing than narrow topics.
2. A cluster will narrow a topic.
3. Ideas at the bottom of a flow chart are more specific than ideas at the top.
4. Ideas on the outside of a circle diagram are very specific.
5. The first goal of effective writing is to make a point.
6. A topic sentence defines what will be discussed in an essay.
7. A thesis statement reveals the writer's perspective on a narrowed topic.
8. The topic sentence or thesis should fit the writer's assignment or need.
9. A topic sentence is usually the first sentence of a paragraph.
10. A generally-accepted statement of fact will make for a good thesis.

WRITING ASSIGNMENTS

1. Academic Assignment: Visit the International Federation of Red Cross and Crescent Societies at http://www.ifrc.org/ to read their latest news and reports. After reading about a world problem, narrow your one problem into specific causes and effects using clustering or a flowchart. Then, write an essay in which you clearly distinguish between the causes and the effects of the problem. Remember to include a thesis statement in the introduction of your essay. For additional explanations about writing thesis statements, visit The Writing Center at The University of North Carolina at http://www.unc.edu/depts/wcweb/handouts/thesis.html.

2. Journal Assignment: Explain everything that you have learned in this chapter: "How does a writer narrow a topic, generate topic sentences, and create a thesis statement?"

3. Creative Assignment: Visit The National Museum of Wildlife Art at http://www.wildlifeart.org/Frame_HomePage.cfm. Select an image that you like, and describe it in a one-page essay. For tips on writing descriptions, visit Purdue University's Online Writing Lab at http://owl.english.purdue.edu/handouts/general/gl_describe.html.

How does a writer support and develop a topic sentence and a thesis statement?

"Writing is manual labor of the mind: a job, like laying pipe."

— John Gregory Dunne

LEARNING OBJECTIVES

1. Learn what support is and why writers need it.
2. Learn the different types of support.
3. Learn the guidelines for using support.
4. Learn how to generate support.

PRE-READING QUESTIONS

1. If you were a lawyer defending an innocent client charged with murder, how would you convince the jury of the truth?
2. What specific evidence would you use to establish the long-standing good character of your client?
3. What facts would you present to prove logically that the crime could not have been committed by your client?

4. How would you present these facts? Would you show pictures, present records, call witnesses to the stand? Would you consider the gender, ethnicity, personality, education, and general make-up of the jury?
5. How is a lawyer defending a client before a jury like a writer making a point to an audience?

WHAT IS SUPPORT AND WHY DO WRITERS NEED IT?

Remember that the general pattern for a paragraph and an essay contains three parts: (1) tell them what you will tell them, (2) tell them, and (3) tell them what you told them. In Chapter 5, we learned that a topic sentence and a thesis statement accomplish the first step—tell them what you will tell them—by making a point that reveals the author's perspective on a subject. In this chapter, we will learn how the body of the paragraph or essay accomplishes the second step—tell them—by developing and explaining the topic sentence or thesis statement. Of course, the concluding sentence or summary accomplishes the third step—tell them what you told them—by restating the topic sentence or thesis statement.

If the topic sentence or thesis statement is a commitment, then the support is the fulfillment of that commitment. Notice how the underlined sentences in the following paragraph support the topic sentence:

Billy Johnson could not have committed the murder because he has an established record of good character **(Topic Sentence)**. For example, Billy has been involved in feeding the hungry by volunteering one evening each month for two years to distribute food to homeless people at the Food Pantry. Also, Billy has coached baseball for Pacific Coast Little League for three years. He has publicly demonstrated his philosophy that good character on the field is more important than winning by his positive comments to his players, and his record of 18 wins and 27 losses shows that. Finally, Billy has been serving as the District Commissioner for the Boys Scouts of America for the past seven years. This organization builds good character in boys and advocates obedience to laws. A close examination of Billy Johnson reveals that his good character makes him an unlikely suspect in this murder case.

As that paragraph demonstrates, support interests readers, proves a point, and influences reader's perspectives or understanding. In other words, as Susan Anker explains in *Real Writing with Readings,* "Without support, you *state* the main point, but you don't *make* the main point." Since support is imperative to good communication, it remains the second goal of effective writing (discussed in Chapter 2):

1. Make a point.
2. Support the point.
3. Organize the ideas.
4. Present the ideas in error-free sentences.

With an understanding about what support is and why we use it, we are prepared to consider different types of support.

WHAT ARE THE DIFFERENT TYPES OF SUPPORT?

Reasons are just one type of support for a topic sentence or thesis statement. The type of support that you will produce will be determined by the writing question or prompt. Consult the following table for common types of support:

Essay Questions or Writing Prompts	Corresponding Types of Support
Write a detailed account of a personal experience in which you learned a valuable lesson.	Illustrate through narration.
Give a brief overview of the main points of the Indian War of 1622.	Summarize through narration.
Clarify how classical conditioning works.	Explain by giving details.
Explain the process of energy flow through ecosystems.	Describe the steps in the process.
Define *imprinting*.	Provide the meaning or definition.
Are you in favor of the death penalty as punishment for certain crimes?	Provide reasons for your argument.
Explain the reasons for the Spanish presence in the Philippines. What were the consequences of their presence?	Analyze the causes and effects.
What challenges did Americans face in the Great Depression, and what remedied the situation for them?	Explain the problems and the solutions.
What are the similarities and differences of short-term and long-term memory?	Compare and contrast.
What are the functions of the various levels of national courts?	Explain the types or kinds in a classification.

Not only do different types of support exist, but writers sometimes use more than one type of support in a writing situation.

PRACTICE 1

Explain what type of support could be used in response to the following questions or writing prompts. Write on a separate piece of paper or on a computer. Choose from the types of support in the table above.

Essay Questions or Writing Prompts	Corresponding Types of Support
1. Are you in favor of allowing euthanasia to be practiced?	
2. Explain how play therapy works.	
3. Explain *passive compliance*.	
4. What started the Cold War, and how did it effect the world?	
5. What are some challenges in establishing a public relations program, and how can these challenges be addressed?	
6. What are the similarities and differences between Down's Syndrome and Turner's Syndrome?	
7. Describe three kinds of rock.	
8. Give a brief overview of the Gulf War.	
9. Give an account of an experience that created an aversion.	
10. Explain how asexual reproduction works.	

WHAT ARE THE GUIDELINES FOR USING SUPPORT?

1. **Support your point.** Do not simply reword your topic sentence or thesis statement. Also, only support a point that relates to your topic sentence or thesis statement. Notice how the following examples have both weak and strong supporting sentences for the topic sentence below:

    Topic Sentence: Billy Johnson could not have committed the murder because he has an established record of good character.

    Poor Support: Billy has always been a good person.

    This supporting sentence simply rewords the topic sentence in vague terms; it does not support the topic sentence with evidence. In other words, it does not say *how* Billy has been a good person or has good character.

    Poor Support: Billy was at Central Park at the time of the shooting.

    This supporting sentence does not develop the author's point, that Billy could not have committed the murder because "he has an established record of *good character.*"

    Strong Support: For example, Billy has been involved in feeding the hungry by volunteering one evening each month for two years to distribute food to homeless people at the Food Pantry.

This supporting sentence is strong because it supports the author's point about how Billy has good character.

2. Be specific and concrete. When writing a description or a narration, write to the five senses by describing how things appear, smell, feel, taste, and sound. When writing to inform or persuade, use specific names, quantities, and details. Specific details will *show* something to your readers, not *tell* something to your readers. Do not use vague and abstract words.

Vague and Abstract Words to Avoid		
a lot	great	sad
awful	happy	small
bad	nice	stupid
big	old	very
fine	okay	wonderful
good	pretty	young

Consider the following examples:

Topic Sentence: Billy Johnson could not have committed the murder because he has an established record of good character.

Poor Support: Billy has always been friendly and a great guy.

This supporting sentence is vague; it does not support the topic sentence with concrete evidence. In other words, it does not say *how* Billy has been friendly and a great guy.

Strong Support: Also, Billy has coached baseball for Pacific Coast Little League for three years. He has publicly demonstrated his philosophy that good character on the field is more important than winning by his positive comments to his players, and his record of eighteen wins and twenty-seven losses shows that.

This supporting sentence is strong because it specifically identifies the little league, the number of years coached, the coaching philosophy, and the win-loss record.

3. Use support that relates to your audience.

Topic Sentence: Billy Johnson could not have committed the murder because he has an established record of good character.

Poor Support: Billy used to invite neighborhood kids over to play handball after school when he was a kid.

This supporting sentence might be of interest to children, but since a jury is composed of adults from the community, they would be more interested in Billy's actions as an adult.

Strong Support: Finally, Billy has been serving as the District Commissioner for the Boys Scouts of America for the past seven years. This organization builds good character in boys and advocates obedience to laws.

> This supporting sentences might work well because a random sample of members of the community sitting on a jury would probably have heard of and have respect for a well-known national organization like the Boy Scouts of America and those who volunteer in it.

4. Use an adequate quantity of support.

Topic Sentence: Billy Johnson could not have committed the murder because he has an established record of good character.

Poor Support: Billy has coached baseball for Pacific Coast Little League for three years. He has publicly demonstrated his philosophy that good character on the field is more important than winning by his positive comments to his players, and his record of eighteen wins and twenty-seven losses shows that.

> Although these two supporting sentences provide quality support, they provide an insufficient quantity to support the topic sentence.

Strong Support: For example, Billy has been involved in feeding the hungry by volunteering one evening each month for two years to distribute food to homeless people at the Food Pantry. Also, Billy has coached baseball for Pacific Coast Little League for three years. He has publicly demonstrated his philosophy that good character on the field is more important than winning by his positive comments to his players, and his record of eighteen wins and twenty-seven losses shows that. Finally, Billy has been serving as the District Commissioner for the Boys Scouts of America for the past seven years. This organization builds good character in boys and advocates obedience to laws.

Notice that all five of the supporting sentences assembled together form a sufficient quantity to make the author's point and influence the reader's perspective or understanding. Although no exact number of supporting sentences exists, generally, five to eight supporting sentences will provide a sufficient quantity to support a point in a paragraph.

PRACTICE 2

Circle the three specific supporting words in the list of five that follows a topic sentence:

1. Topic Sentence/Thesis Statement: The 1971 Volkswagen bus is deteriorating.
   a. Upholstery
   b. Engine

   c. Bad
   d. Headliner
   e. Ugly

2. Topic Sentence/Thesis Statement: Alligators and crocodiles have some similarities and differences in their features.
   a. Snout
   b. Skin color
   c. Awful
   d. Roar
   e. Big

3. Topic Sentence/Thesis Statement: Soil is composed of several items.
   a. Rocks
   b. Wonderful color
   c. Pebbles
   d. Nice odor
   e. Dead leaves and sticks

4. Topic Sentence/Thesis Statement: Cezar Chavez organized migrant farm
   workers through the establishment of the United Farm Workers Union.
   a. 1966
   b. Mexican Americans
   c. Awful situation
   d. Dolores Huerta
   e. A lot of work

5. Topic Sentence/Thesis Statement: Yosemite preserves a variety of trees.
   a. Coniferous forest
   b. Beautiful
   c. Young trees
   d. Ponderosa pine
   e. Douglas fir

PRACTICE 3

*Find the vague and abstract words in the following sentences. Then, rewrite the
sentences by replacing the vague and abstract language with specific and concrete details that communicate by showing instead of telling. Write on a separate
piece of paper or on a computer.*

1. A lot of doctors do a good job with their patients.
2. College is wonderful because the classes are great.
3. The young psychiatrist said I was okay.
4. The alarm system at the power plant is fine.
5. Old Mrs. Helrick in Human Resources is very nice.

HOW DOES A WRITER GENERATE SUPPORT?

 The prewriting techniques described in Chapter 4 will be very helpful in generating support. Begin by writing your topic sentence or thesis statement at the top of a blank piece of paper or on a computer. Then, choose a prewriting technique like questioning, brainstorming, or clustering to generate additional ideas, as in the examples below.

Topic Sentence/Thesis Statement: Losing weight should be a slow process that involves changing eating habits.

Questioning

Questions	Answers
How slow should the process of losing weight be?	Three-month diet (marathon, not a sprint)
How many weeks should it take to lose ten pounds?	Two months
If weight is lost quickly, will it be regained eventually?	Probably
What is involved in the process of losing weight?	Diet and exercise
How many hours per week should someone exercise?	At least thirty minutes, every other day
How many calories per day should someone eat to lose weight?	1800
What and how much should someone drink to lose weight?	Eight cups of water, plus fruit juices daily
How should eating habits be changed?	More healthy foods, less junk food
What should be eaten more?	Grains like wheat; vegetables like carrots, cucumbers, lettuce; fruit like watermelon, pears, bananas
What should be eaten less?	Fast food like Wendy's and desserts like apple pies, cakes, chocolate candy bars

Brainstorming

1. Set conservative goals
2. Five pounds in one month (not more)
3. Record weekly weight
4. Use accurate scale

CLUSTERING

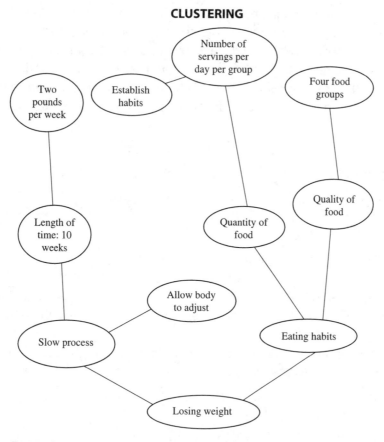

5. Monitor diet for several weeks (at least six)
6. Stop eating some foods: candy (M & M's, Skittles)
7. Eat less of some foods: meat, fat, fast food (McDonald's, Burger King), desserts (ice cream, doughnuts)
8. Eat more of some foods: grain (wheat), vegetables (carrots, broccoli), fruit (apples, bananas), juice
9. Eat consistently (three meals per day)
10. Eat moderate quantities

PRACTICE 4

Select a topic sentence/thesis statement that you created in Chapter 5 or create a new one now, and place it at the top of a blank page. Generate at least ten specific supporting ideas using questioning, brainstorming, or clustering. Write on a separate piece of paper or on a computer.

Questioning, brainstorming, and clustering produced at least ten ideas each with many specific details that could be used to support the topic sentence. The ideas follow the guidelines by supporting a point, being specific and concrete, relating to the audience, and being adequate in quantity. Although not all of the ideas generated need to be used in writing a paper, a sufficient amount of support now exists to make the job easy.

PRACTICE 5

Reread the student essay about going to college in Chapter 5. Write on a piece of paper or on a computer.

1. List three specific details from the first body paragraph about community colleges saving money on a separate piece of paper.
2. List three specific details from the second body paragraph about community colleges being a good transition from high school to a university on a separate piece of paper.
3. List three specific details from the third body paragraph about community colleges being conveniently located on a separate piece of paper.

GROUP WORK

1. As a group, select a topic sentence that you created in Chapter 5 or create a new one now, and place it at the top of a blank page. Write one paragraph together containing at least five supporting sentences. Make sure that each sentence follows the four guidelines for using support in this chapter.
2. As a group, select a topic sentence/thesis statement that you created in Chapter 5 or create a new one now, and place it at the top of a blank page. Generate at least ten questions using the journalistic questions described in Chapter 4 (Who? What? Why? Where? When? and How?). Then answer the questions as a group.
3. As a group, select a topic sentence/thesis statement that you created in Chapter 5 or create a new one now, and place it at the top of a blank page. Generate at least ten specific supporting ideas using brainstorming or clustering.

TEST (TRUE/FALSE)

1. Support develops or explains the topic sentence or thesis statement.
2. Support will interest your reader because people are naturally curious about specific details.
3. Support will not change the reader's perspective.
4. A reworded thesis may be an example of a good supporting sentence.
5. Avoid vague and abstract support.
6. A description of an animal should never include how it smells.
7. Directions for a writing assignment for children should not include the word *circumlocution*.
8. Three supporting sentences will provide enough evidence to back-up any topic sentence.
9. Questioning, brainstorming, and clustering are three techniques that can produce support for a topic sentence or thesis statement.
10. All supporting ideas generated through questioning, brainstorming, or clustering should be used in the first draft of the paragraph or essay.

WRITING ASSIGNMENTS

1. Academic Assignment: Visit BizRate.com at http://www.bizrate.com and choose a product or service that you know well or can easily research. Write an essay in which you try to sell your product or service based on its good points. For an additional explanation on developing a paragraph with specific support, visit The Writing Center at the University of North Carolina at http://www.unc.edu/depts/wcweb/handouts/paragraphs.html.

2. Journal Assignment: Explain everything that you have learned in this chapter: "How does a writer support and develop a topic sentence and a thesis statement?"

3. Creative Assignment: Visit The Reynolda House, Museum of American Art at http://www.reynoldahouse.org/. Select an image that you like, and describe it in a one-page essay. Begin by using one of the prewriting techniques described in this chapter to generate specific details. For tips on writing descriptions, visit Purdue University's Online Writing Lab at http://owl.english.purdue.edu/handouts/general/gl_describe.html.

Chapter 7

How does a writer find specific information?

"Good writing is a kind of skating which carries off the performer where he would not go."

— Ralph Waldo Emerson

LEARNING OBJECTIVES

1. Learn why sources of information can help your writing.
2. Learn the basic types of sources of information.
3. Learn a couple of basic methods for writing about what you have read.
4. Learn why you should acknowledge a source.

PRE-READING QUESTIONS

1. What do you recall the definition of support being from Chapter 6?
2. If you are going to write a paper for a college class, what could be the benefit in reading about your subject before writing your paper?
3. If you wanted to learn more about skydiving before you wrote a paper on it, what would you read, and where would you go to find it?
4. How do you use facts and ideas from other writers in your papers?

5. If you want to use information in your paper that you find while reading about your subject, how could you show your readers that some of the ideas in your paper come from another author?

WHY CAN SOURCES OF INFORMATION HELP YOUR WRITING?

To answer this question, we need to recall the four traits of effective writing from Chapter 2:

1. Make a point.
2. Support that point.
3. Organize the ideas.
4. Present the ideas in error-free writing.

We also need to recall from Chapter 6 that support involves developing and explaining the topic sentence or thesis statement, and the guidelines for support are as follows:

1. Support your point.
2. Be specific and concrete.
3. Use support that relates to your audience.
4. Use an adequate quantity of support.

With these guidelines, we can see why sources of information can help our writing. In order to make a point and support it with enough specific concrete details that relate to our audience, sometimes we need more information than we alone possess. Of course, writers rely on what they already know first, but when their own knowledge or experience is not enough to produce effective writing, then they must search for specific information.

Sources of information can help our writing in another way, too. Reading improves writing. As a result, when we read good writing frequently, we see how writers express their ideas well with specific support and error-free sentences, and we will more easily be able to express our ideas well, too.

As a writer in college, your first task at this point in the writing process is to determine if you have enough specific information to support your topic sentence or thesis statement. Consult your professors for each writing assignment to find out if they want, encourage, or require you to consult sources before writing a paper. Because this book is an introduction to the writing process, this chapter will simply introduce you to the process of consulting and using other sources. Your future writing classes will probably teach you how to write research papers that draw heavily on other sources.

WHAT ARE THE BASIC TYPES OF SOURCES OF INFORMATION?

1. Yourself.

Many writing assignments in introductory writing classes in college simply require you to rely upon the knowledge and experience that you already possess. Do not underestimate yourself as a rich resource of concrete details to support your points in your writing. Consider Patricia Martinez's essay titled "Football" in Chapter 2. She relied entirely upon herself in generating the concrete details to support her point and tell her story, and she generated them through clustering, one of the prewriting techniques described in Chapters 4 and 6. You should realize, however, that many advanced college classes require you to consult and incorporate other sources in the writing process.

2. Other people.

An easy way to obtain additional information is to talk to people with experience or knowledge in the area about which you will write. You may use the journalistic questions explained in Chapter 4 (5 *W*'s and *H*): Who? What? Why? Where? When? and How? Of course, these questions may cause you to consider other questions worth asking, and you will probably approach each writing assignment or situation with different questions. If you interview someone, take notes or tape-record the conversation (with permission) so that you will be able to use this information as you write.

3. The Internet.

One of the fastest ways to obtain additional information is through the Internet, as explained in Chapter 4. Begin with one of the main search engines like Excite, Yahoo!, or AltaVista. Type in key words from your narrowed topic. For example, you might want to write about the dangers of hiking Mount Everest. Type in *Mount Everest* and *hiking* and *dangers*; this will lead to about three thousand websites. Many of these sites will provide you with facts, stories, and concrete details to support your topic sentence or thesis statement.

As you search on the Internet, realize that not everything that you read will be useful, accurate, or true. Because anyone can post almost anything on the Internet, you should understand that the Internet is like a swap meet, where some information that you find will be high-quality; other information will be low-quality. Most of the material that you find on the Internet has not passed through the rigorous process of publication, so the challenge of assessing the validity and credibility of information at any website rests upon the shoulders of the browser.

4. Reference Materials.

Unlike many websites, reference works like dictionaries and encyclopedias consistently provide high-quality information on a wide variety of topics, and some of them are available both in libraries and on the Internet. Reference materials provide a good introduction to a topic that you want to research. If you want to know exactly what a term means, you may easily get a specific definition from an online dictionary like *Webster's Dictionary* at http://www.m-w.com/netdict.htm. Type in a word or term that you may not know well like "affirmative action," and you will be given the definition: "an active effort to improve the employment or educational opportunities of members of minority groups and women." If you want specific information about a narrowed topic like the first man to travel to the moon, you may easily visit an online encyclopedia like the *Concise Columbia Encyclopedia* at http://www.encyclopedia.com. Type in "space exploration," and you will be led to "human space exploration," which will provide you with a summary of space travel to the moon, space stations, and space shuttles. In encyclopedias, one article will also lead you to many other related articles.

5. Journals, Magazines, and Newspapers.

   Campus and public libraries carry subscriptions to many journals, magazines, and newspapers. After going to a library, use one of the computer terminals to access the online catalogue. The catalogue will allow you to search for an article on your narrowed topic in a few different ways: by word, by topic, or by publication. Try searching by word or topic first by entering key words from your narrowed topic. If you type "abortion and health risks," the online catalogue will list many articles by title that relate to your narrowed topic. Click on a title that interests you, and you will be given additional information about the article: the title, the author, the magazine (or journal or newspaper), the date of publication, volume number, page number, number of pages in length, abstract (summary), etc. The full text of the article will also appear on your screen. Read the abstract or skim the article. If you want to use it, print it out for careful reading at home or send it to your home through e-mail. If you want a different article, continue searching.

6. Books.

   At a campus or public library, you may also access books. Use one of the computer terminals to access the online catalogue for books on your narrowed topic. You will be allowed to search by subject, title, author, or key word. Try searching by subject or key word first by entering key words from your narrowed topic. If you type in "electric cars in America," the online catalogue will list books by title that relate to your topic. Click on the title that interests you, and you will be given additional information about the book: the title, author, publisher, holdings (call number, location in the library, and status), number of pages in length, description of contents of the book, etc. Read the description of the book. If you want to use it, write down the call number, title, author, and location of the book in the library. If you want more books, continue searching. When you are finished searching, find your books in the library and check them out for careful reading at home.

PRACTICE 1

Choose a prewriting technique from Chapter 4; then, generate fifteen ideas drawing upon your own knowledge and experience to create specific support for a topic sentence or thesis statement that you created in Chapter 5. Write on a separate piece of paper or on a computer.

PRACTICE 2

Find at least ten specific facts that support a topic sentence or thesis statement that you created in Chapter 5 by using a search engine, an online reference material, or an online catalogue. Write on a separate piece of paper or on a computer.

PRACTICE 3

Visit your campus or public library, and use one of the computer terminals to access the online catalogue. Search for a book that might contain at least ten specific facts supporting a topic sentence or thesis statement that you created in Chapter 5. When you find a book with useful information in it, check it out for careful reading at home.

WHAT ARE A COUPLE OF BASIC METHODS FOR WRITING ABOUT WHAT YOU HAVE READ?

The first basic method for writing about what you have read is summarizing. A summary is a brief retelling of a longer document in your own words. For example, a summary of a three-page article might attempt to recount the main points of the article in a one half-page paragraph. Longer summaries are easier to write than shorter summaries, but the ability to write concise, accurate, summaries serves college writers well. Below are some guidelines for writing summaries.

1. Photocopy and read the entire document to understand the big picture, main point, or author's thesis before writing your summary. As you read the photocopy, pay special attention to the title, subtitle, introduction, and headings because they will indicate the direction of the article. Also, as you read, highlight the main points with a marker, take notes by writing on the article itself, or take notes on separate paper if you are reading an original library document.

2. After you read the entire article, create an outline. Begin your outline with an introductory sentence that states the name of the author, the title of the reading, and the main point of the entire reading. In parentheses, add the name of the publication and the date. This is called citing your source. The first sentence of your outline might look like this: In "The Diminishing Elephant Population" (*National Geographic,* May 14, 1999), Craig Hammer argues that poaching has been the main cause of the decline of the elephant population.

3. Reread the original article adding one line at a time to your outline (see Chapter 8) after rereading each paragraph or section of the original document. Pay special attention to the highlighted sentences and your notes. The outline should cover the au-

thor's main points in the same order and with the same emphasis as they were presented in the original document.

4. Write your summary based on your outline. Although the length and nature of the original document will influence the length of the summary, try to limit your summary to one 100-word paragraph.

5. Use a neutral tone. Be as objective as possible in the summary. Do not insert your own opinion as you are summarizing another person's ideas; omit references to yourself by writing in the third person (see *What should writers not focus on in the first draft?* in Chapter 9).

6. Default to present tense (see *Tense Shifts* in Chapter 18).

7. Use your own words to retell or rephrase the main points. Do not simply copy a few key sentences from an article into a paragraph and call that a summary.

8. Proofread your summary. As William S. Robinson and Stephanie Tucker suggest in *Texts and Contexts: A Contemporary Approach to College Writing,* "In particular, compare the spelling of titles, authors, and other names and key terms with that in the original document." Taking time to do this will help you to produce error-free writing.

9. Finally, after you have written your summary, ask yourself the following question, as Teresa Ferster Glazier recommends in *The Least You Should Know about English: Writing Skills*: "Would someone who had not read the article get a clear idea of it from your summary?" If you have followed these guidelines carefully, the answer will be *yes*.

Below is an example of an article, a simple outline, and a summary of the article. The author had to write many drafts to be able to reduce the summary to one hundred words or less.

Dr. Death, Be Not Proud by Abigail Trafford

In the end, he seemed more buffoon than firebrand, more bizarre than revolutionary. The man called Dr. Death came across during his trial as a little weird—his bumbling words of defense more pathetic than provocative. By the time a Michigan jury convicted Jack Kevorkian of second degree murder last week, his defiant stand on "mercy killing" was a kind of whimper.

Good riddance! That's the view of many of those who care for dying patients—physicians, nurses, social workers, ministers, family caregivers. To them, the retired pathologist with his suicide machines and in-your-face support of euthanasia had given dying a bad name. They oppose him on deep moral and medical grounds.

Yet Dr. Death served a purpose. He illuminated the terrible ways of dying in the United States and highlighted the real gaps in caring for people at the end of their lives. By his own account, he has helped 130 people kill themselves since

1990. Each case dramatized deficiencies in the health care system and in society in dealing with such issues as unremitting pain and loss of control—loss of mind and personhood. With headlines as his sword, Kevorkian forced Americans to confront "hard deaths" in which suffering cannot be relieved, function cannot be restored and dying may be the best outcome. When is death a release? Should people have a right to end their lives? To die the way they want to die? And what about the burden on loved ones—the financial and emotional costs of a long, devastating illness? What is the definition of a meaningful life? Who decides?

From Janet Adkins, the woman with Alzheimer's who went to Kevorkian in 1990, to Thomas Youk, the man with Lou Gehrig's disease, whose death by lethal injection was videotaped and broadcast on "60 Minutes," Americans walked through these questions and asked themselves: "What would I do if . . . ?"

At the same time, by grabbing headlines, Kevorkian dominated the debate on dying, drowning out less inflammatory voices. The movement to improve the care of the dying has accelerated in the last five years. Largely unnoticed by the public, a quieter revolution in medical centers and family rooms has gone a long way to change how people with life-threatening illness are supported and treated.

Leaders in this movement, such as physician Joanne Lynn with Americans for Better Care of the Dying, point to real gains. Control of pain, she says, is much more sophisticated, and the use of such potent drugs as morphine has increased. "We're a lot better in taking care of pain, particularly the pain of cancer," she said. Twenty years ago, people were afraid to give such drugs, even in hospices, because they were narcotics. "We don't see that anymore," she said.

The emphasis, she continues, is on having choices. There is no one "right" way to die. Oregon, for example, has led the nation on the issue of physician assisted suicide. For several years, end-of-life care was the subject of a major political debate in the state, making people think about the issues raised by Kevorkian's headlines. Instead of hiding out in a Michigan motel, Oregonians are able to request physician help in ending their lives. But it is not the only choice. In the first year of the state's "compassion in dying" program, 56 patients requested help, and of the 34 who have since died, only 10 were the result of physician assistance. Meanwhile the use of opioid drugs increased dramatically in the state. Said one advocate: "In the wake of real patient choice, death in Oregon has improved."

In hospitals across the country, people increasingly sign advance directives to let caregivers know how they wish to be treated if they cannot speak for themselves. The National Institutes of Health is sponsoring research into end-of-life medicine. Numerous enterprises with names like "Project on Death in America" and "Death With Dignity National Center" have emerged to promote better care.

Several recent books have galvanized both the public and the medical community on this subject, including the bestselling "How We Die," by Sherwin B. Nuland.

All of this activity in the quiet revolution is providing alternatives to Dr. Death and his suicide machines. The goal is to make death "good" enough that checking in with Kevorkian will no longer be seen as necessary.

That's a worthy goal. But there's still a long way to go. A major obstacle is fear. So many people have had "bad" experiences with watching loved ones die. How many times have people said: "Well, if it gets too bad, I can always call Kevorkian."

In a recent issue of the Journal of the American Medical Association, researchers identified the five end-of-life issues that patients care about most: "receiving adequate pain and symptom management, avoiding inappropriate prolongation of dying, achieving a sense of control, relieving burden and strengthening relationships with loved ones."

Surely this is something a trillion-dollar health care system ought to be able to do. People should not have to rely on Kevorkian as a backup.

The hope is that the quiet revolution in "good dying" can make enough progress so that the country won't need a Kevorkian to kick around any more.

The Washington Post (Mar 30, 1999)

An outline and brief summary follow:

   I Summary of "Dr. Death, Be Not Proud"
      A. In "Dr. Death, Be Not Proud" (The Washington Post, March 30, 1999), Abigail Trifford discusses improving euthanasia in America.
      B. Dr. Death (Jack Kevorkian) raises questions
      C. Joanne Lynn's positive contribution: choice
      D. Books
      E. Hope for improving dying

In "Dr. Death, Be Not Proud" (*The Washington Post,* March 30, 1999), Abigail Trafford discusses improving euthanasia in America. Although Jack Kevorkian was convicted of second-degree murder for his methods of euthanasia, he raises many questions about dying. Physician Joanne Lynn has made positive contributions by reducing the suffering of those dying. Lynn points out that patients today have more choices than they used to about using drugs and requesting help in dying. Some books have been written on how to improve dying, but fear remains an obstacle. Trafford hopes that our health care system can make improvements with end-of-life issues.

PRACTICE 4

Visit your campus or public library, and use one of the computer terminals to access the online catalogue. Search for an article in a journal, magazine, or newspaper (or on the Internet). When you find an article of interest, print it out for careful reading at home or send it to your home through e-mail. Then, create a simple outline for a paragraph, and write a 100-word summary of the article. Write on a separate piece of paper or on a computer.

The second basic method for writing about what you have read is a summary and reaction. Often in college writing, you will be asked to read something and write a paper that includes both a summary of a reading and your reaction to it. Follow the guidelines for writing a summary to complete the first part. To write the second part, state your agreement or disagreement with the author (see *Thesis Statement* in Chapter 5) and why you believe so (see *Support* in Chapter 6). Below is an article, simple outline, and short essay (including a summary and reaction).

Is the Death Penality Cruel and Unusual by John Barry

On May 2, 2000, the State of Arkansas put 28 year-old Christina Riggs to death for killing her two children. The execution method was lethal injection. According to a witness, the executioners planned to administer the shot through veins in her elbows, but when they had trouble finding one, Riggs gave them permission to inject through her hands. A confessed murderer, Riggs had admitted to smothering her two children when potassium chloride failed to kill them. While Riggs at first attributed the murders to depression, the prosecution argued that she had killed her children because they had become an inconvenience to her lifestyle. Witnesses had seen Riggs singing karaoke on several nights prior to her children's deaths.

In 1967, a moratorium was placed on the death penalty as the Supreme Court debated its constitutionality. In 1972, the Supreme Court ruled that the death penalty violated the Eighth Amendment, which protects Americans from "cruel and unusual" punishment—largely because it was determined not to be applied fairly. In 1976 the Court ruled that, in certain cases, the death penalty was a legitimate punishment, and now, it is practiced in all but 13 states and the District of Columbia.

Since 1977, 611 people have been executed in the United States. In the last year, executions in the U.S. have been carried out at an increasing rate, with more than half of the executions since 1976 having occurred in the last five years.

On One Hand . . .

Our criminal justice system has no basis for deciding whether an individual deserves or does not deserve to live. Because the death penalty is the one punishment that can never be reversed, it is always unjust—our courts should be proven incapable of error before using it. Despite one being carried out every 3.5 days—the current rate of executions in the U.S.—a plague of violent crime continues, proving that the death penalty is not working as a deterrent either. The death penalty is just one more way to get revenge in a society that is already consumed with violence. Many countries have already abolished the penalty. The United States, which has always taken a strong stand for fairness in criminal justice systems, should join those nations in denouncing capital punishment.

On the Other Hand . . .

Capital punishment is both constitutional and morally right. Prisons are used to reform criminals, but in certain cases—when guilt is unmistakable and the accused has a history of violent behavior—society has the right to demand the ultimate punishment. It doesn't make sense to give someone who has been convicted of murder the chance to commit another. But this happens all too frequently. This April, in Minneapolis, a 32 year-old man was arrested for the murder of a woman. The same man had been convicted of a third-degree murder in 1987. In Texas, Algernon Doby was captured after shooting a pregnant woman and killing her boyfriend, only seven months after Doby had been paroled for a previous murder. With such continual failures in our justice system, Americans deserve to know that murderers will face the same fate as their victims.

- This April, Congressmen Bill Delahunt (D-Mass.) and Ray LaHood (R-Ill.) introduced the Innocence Protection Act, the House version of Sen. Patrick Leahy's (D-Vt.) bill. It is designed to ensure that death-row defendants are completely represented and have access to DNA evidence. "We must be sure that every legal and technological method is provided to determine guilt in capital cases," said LaHood. LaHood supports capital punishment.
- According to Amnesty International, more than two countries a year on average have abolished the death penalty in law since 1976. Seventy countries, including Australia, Germany, and Spain, refuse to impose the death penalty for any crime.
- On March 22, in Beeville, Texas, a convicted killer already serving a life sentence was indicted Tuesday for murder in the death of the prison guard Daniel Nagle. Robert Lynn Pruit, 30, had been serving a life term for a murder committed when he was 20.
- An ACLU study released this month found that lawyers whose clients ended up on Virginia's death row were six times more likely than other lawyers to be

disciplined in the course of their careers. One of every 10 defendants sentenced in Virginia was represented by a lawyer who at some point had lost his or her license, the study found.

- In 1992, Roger Keith Coleman was strapped into his electric chair while protesting his innocence. Coleman claimed he had an alibi and that a post-trial DNA test indicated that a second person was involved. But the Supreme Court of Virginia refused to hear the case because the lawyer filed a day late.

- There are currently 459 inmates on Death Row in Texas. There are 368 in Florida. There are 29 in Virginia.

http://speakout.com/activism/issue_briefs/1230b-1.html (May 3, 2000)

An outline and brief summary follow:

I Introduction: Capital Punishment
   A. Question
   B. Definition
   C. Thesis statement: In "Is the Death Penalty Cruel and Unusual?" (http://speakout.com/activism/issue_briefs/1230b-1.html), John Barry explores the pros and cons of capital punishment, but ultimately Americans should join together in banning the death penalty.
II Body: Summary of "Is the Death Penalty Cruel and Unusual?" by John Barry
   A. Christina Riggs's story
       1. Executed on 2-2-00
       2. Killed two children
       3. Confessed murders
       4. Lethal injection
   B. History of Supreme Court Rulings
       1. 1967 moratorium on death penalty.
       2. 1972 death penalty violates 8th amendment.
       3. 1977 death penalty permitted in certain cases.
       4. Now it is practiced in most states.
       5. 611 deaths since 1977.
   C. Cons
       1. Society has no right to decide about death.
       2. Not reversible.
       3. Courts make errors.
       4. Not a deterrent.
       5. Many countries oppose death penalty.
   D. Pros
       1. Morally right.
       2. Society has right to decide death in certain cases.
       3. Murderers should not be allowed to kill again.
       4. Murderers should experience what their victims experienced.

III Conclusion: Reaction
    A. Thesis restated: Capital punishment should be banned.
    B. Equal to slavery.
    C. Unconstitutional.
    D. Disrespects life.
    E. Unmerciful.
    F. Wastes recourses.

Notice how the ideas in the outline have been converted to an essay.

What is capital punishment? It is the death penalty for committing a crime. If a person has committed the most serious crime—murder—should the punishment be death? John Barry explores the pros and cons of capital punishment in "Is the Death Penalty Cruel and Unusual?" (http://speakout.com/activism/issue_briefs/1230b-1.html), but ultimately Americans should join together in banning the death penalty.

Barry begins his article by explaining that Christina Riggs was twenty-eight years old and living in Arkansas when she was put to death for murdering her two children. She confessed to killing them, and lawyers argued that they were an inconvenience to her. After potassium chloride failed to kill them, she smothered them to death. For murdering them, she was put to death through lethal injection.

Barry explains that in 1967 the Supreme Court put a moratorium on the death penalty in order to decide what position to take on the issue. In 1972, they decided that the death penalty was "cruel and unusual punishment." Later, in 1976, the Supreme Court decided that the death penalty did not violate the Constitution. Since 1977, 611 people have been executed.

On one hand, society has no right to decide if someone should be killed, and the decision cannot be reversed. Also, lawyers, judges, and courts make mistakes, so innocent people can be put to death. Furthermore, crime has continued to increase, so the death penalty is not working as a deterrent. Finally, many countries oppose the death penalty.

On the other hand, Barry argues, the death penalty is morally right. In certain cases—when no mistake has been made and when the criminal has a history of violence—society has the right to decide if the death penalty is appropriate. Murderers should not be allowed to kill again, which happens now. Also, murderers should experience what their victims experienced.

Although John Barry explains both sides of the issue, Americans should agree to ban capital punishment in the United States. Capital punishment is just like slavery and branding. Executions should not be allowed in any civilized society; furthermore, they are unconstitutional. The death penalty is both "cruel and unusual punishment." Executions show society that human life is no longer respected for those who make mistakes in life. Not only does the death penalty show no mercy, but it also wastes resources through court and lawyer fees. A humane society should not deliberately kill human beings.

Adapted from Buniel Chang

PRACTICE 5

Visit your campus or public library, and use one of the computer terminals to access the online catalogue. Search for an article in a journal, magazine, or newspaper (or on the Internet). When you find an article of interest, print it out for careful reading at home or send it to your home through e-mail. Then, create a simple outline with an introduction, a body, and a conclusion, and write a short essay that includes a summary and reaction. Write on a separate piece of paper or on a computer.

After you become familiar with summarizing and reacting to sources, you will be prepared to take other classes that teach how to write research papers that incorporate quotes and document sources in a Works Cited page according to the Modern Language Association format.

WHY SHOULD YOU ACKNOWLEDGE A SOURCE?

Remember that the first guideline for writing a summary is to begin your summary by referring to the author, the title of the reading, and the main point of the reading. This is acknowledging your source. Citing your source in this way gives credit to the author whose ideas you are using, and it allows readers to know where to find the full original source. Failing to do so leads the readers to believe that you generated all of the ideas in your paper yourself. As Diana Hacker explains in *A Writer's Reference*, to misrepresent yourself in this way, whether it is done intentionally or unintentionally, "is a form of dishonesty known as plagiarism" (p. 260). Plagiarism carries unpleasant consequences that range from receiving an F on the paper to expulsion from the university without the opportunity of returning. Professionally, plagiarism may result in costly lawsuits.

GROUP WORK

1. As a group, select one topic sentence or thesis statement that you created in Chapter 5. Then, create a series of at least six journalistic questions (explained in Chapter 4) to generate specific support. Then answer the questions as a group.

2. As a group, select one topic sentence or thesis statement that you created in Chapter 5. Then, visit *Webster's Dictionary* at http://www.m-w.com/netdict.htm and the *Concise Columbia Encyclopedia* at http://www.encyclopedia.com to find at least ten specific facts to generate specific support.

3. As a group, select one topic sentence or thesis statement that you created in Chapter 5. Visit your campus or public library, and use one of the computer terminals to access the online catalogue. Search for at least ten specific facts in a journal, magazine, or newspaper article. When you find an article with useful information in it, print copies of it for each member of your group or send copies to your homes through e-mail.

TEST (TRUE/FALSE)

1. Making a point is one of the four traits of effective writing.
2. Supporting your point involves using specific, concrete details.
3. Writers always know enough facts and have enough experience to support their points without reading.
4. You should consult your professors for each writing assignment to find out if they want, encourage, or require you to consult sources before writing your papers.
5. Most advanced college classes do not require you to consult other sources in the process of fulfilling your writing assignments.
6. Most of the material that you find on the Internet has not passed through the rigorous process of publication.
7. Short summaries (about 100 words) are easy to write.
8. Summaries should include all specific examples and details from the original source.
9. Summaries should include the opinion of the person writing the summary.
10. Writers should give other authors credit for their ideas by acknowledging sources.

WRITING ASSIGNMENTS

1. Academic Assignment: Visit http://speakout.com/ or a website of your choice and learn both sides of a controversial issue. When you find an article of interest, print it out for careful reading at home or send it to your home through e-mail. Then create a simple outline with an introduction, a body, and a conclusion. Write a short essay in which you summarize the article and formulate your reaction to it, as in the student essay in this chapter. For assistance with searching the World Wide Web, visit the Purdue's Online Writing Lab at http://owl.english.purdue.edu/handouts/_research/r_web-search2.html.

2. Journal Assignment: Explain everything that you have learned in this chapter: "How does a writer find specific information?"

3. Creative Assignment: Visit the Savador Dalí Museum at http://www.savadordalimuseum.org and view the collections. Select an image that you like, and describe it in a one-page essay. For tips on writing descriptions, visit Purdue University's Online Writing Lab at http://owl.english.purdue.edu/handouts/general/gl_describe.html.

How does a writer organize ideas?

"A place for everything and everything in its place."

—Isabella Mary Beeton

LEARNING OBJECTIVES

1. Learn what an outline is, why we use it, and how it fits into the writing process.
2. Learn the format of an outline.
3. Learn what to include in an outline.
4. Learn how to choose an order for presenting ideas in an outline.
5. Learn some guidelines for creating an outline.

PRE-READING QUESTIONS

1. What is a benefit of writing an outline before writing a complete draft of a paragraph or essay?
2. If you were assigned to write an essay that explains how to do something like build a model rocket, in what order would you present the ideas or directions in your paper? In other words, how would you decide what direction to give first, second, third, etc.?

3. If you were writing a paper in which you explained three reasons that support capital punishment, where would you place your strongest argument, at the beginning, in the middle, or at the end of your paper? Why?
4. If you were describing the details of a photograph in a paragraph, how would you decide what to describe first, second, third, etc.?
5. What would you do if in the process of writing an essay by looking at your outline you remembered an important point that should be added to your paper?

WHAT IS AN OUTLINE, WHY DO WE USE IT, AND HOW DOES IT FIT INTO THE WRITING PROCESS?

Imagine that someone on the phone has consented to go out with you this weekend on a first date. You take down directions to the person's house on the back of a napkin. Saturday evening arrives, and you leave your house with napkin in hand to pick up your date. That napkin is a map that will get you were you want to go. An outline is also a map. As you write, you will need a detailed outline to keep you moving in the right direction. It will help you to avoid straying from your destination, your topic, or your point. It also creates unity, provides support, and offers organization. Finally, your outline (along with the rest of your prewriting work), documents your authorship, which becomes important if you are ever charged with plagiarism. Ultimately, if you were not to use an outline in the process of writing, you could waste a lot of time and end up lost and frustrated.

To see how the outline fits into the process of writing, recall the four steps of effective writing from Chapter 2.

1. Make a point.
2. Support the point.
3. Organize the ideas.
4. Present the ideas in error-free sentences.

The outline particularly helps the writer to accomplish step three, *organize the ideas.*

WHAT IS THE FORMAT OF AN OUTLINE?

Outlines use the following format to organize information into categories and subcategories with numbers and letters. Include a minimum of two points in each subcategory.

I

    A.

    B.

      1.

      2.

        a.

        b.

          (1)

          (2)

            (a)

            (b)

II

WHAT CAN BE INCLUDED IN AN OUTLINE?

Most outlines will be divided into three general parts: an introduction, a body, and a conclusion. The introduction states the main point, the body develops it, and the conclusion emphasizes it.

Introduction

An introduction captures the reader's attention and usually concludes with a thesis statement (occasionally, a thesis statement is not needed, such as in a narrative essay). An introduction can often be accomplished in one paragraph, but some writers find it difficult to introduce a paper that they haven't yet written. For this reason, the introduction may be written last. Below are some methods of introducing an essay:

1. Ask a question.
2. Include an interesting quotation.
3. State a surprising fact.
4. Provide a story or example.
5. Give an analogy.
6. Present a thesis statement.

Body

The body supports the thesis statement. This support typically requires several paragraphs. The exact type (or types) of support that will be appropriate for a writing assignment will be determined by the writing question or prompt (see

Types of Support in Chapter 6). Below are general guidelines for support (see *Guidelines for Support* in Chapter 6).

1. Support your point (thesis statement).
2. Be specific and concrete.
3. Use support that relates to your audience.
4. Use an adequate quantity of support.

Conclusion

The conclusion drives your main point home, and writers can usually accomplish this in one paragraph. Because readers will best remember what they read last, make the conclusion memorable. Begin your conclusion by paraphrasing the thesis statement. As you write, consider the following ideas for concluding an essay:

1. Refer back to the thesis statement.
2. Summarize the body.
3. Explain the significance of your point.
4. Offer advice.
5. Propose a perspective or an action.
6. Conclude where the essay began by referring to something in the introduction.

The outline for a paragraph can be as simple as the one created below, which describes a process. The purpose, audience, tone (see Chapter 3), and topic sentence (see Chapter 5) were established before writing the outline.

Purpose: To complete a short writing assignment by describing a process.
Audience: Professor and fellow college students.
Tone: Serious
Topic Sentence: Wolves practice a form of birth control.

I Narrowed Topic: wolves and birth control.
  A. Topic Sentence: Wolves practice a form of birth control.
  B. Supporting Idea: food supply
  C. Supporting Idea: five to nine babies with plenty of food
  D. Supporting Idea: two to three babies when lacking food
  E. Concluding idea: wolf population mirrors food supply

Notice how the short paragraph below follows the outline.

Believe it or not, wolves do practice a form of birth control. The key factor in this process is the food supply. Wolves frequently eat small animals like rodents. Sometimes they hunt large animals like caribou in packs. When either food supply is abundant, female wolves will give birth to five to nine pups. When the food supply is sparse, female wolves will give birth to two or three pups. In this way, the wolf population stays at a level that the food supply can support.

Below is a simple outline for an essay. It contains an introduction, a body, and a conclusion, and it summarizes an article. The purpose, audience, tone (see Chapter 3), and thesis statement (see Chapter 5) were established before writing the outline.

Purpose: To complete a short college essay assignment that summarizes an article.

Audience: Professor and fellow college students.

Tone: Serious.

Thesis Statement: The article "The Crew of the Challenger Shuttle Mission in 1986" by Jason Wood (*Aviation,* December, 1986) explains the backgrounds of the seven astronauts on the mission.

I Introduction: Personal experience
   A. Topic Sentence: My Challenger experience
   B. Supporting Idea: January 28, 2986
   C. Supporting Idea: Elementary school
   D. Supporting Idea: Watching television
   E. Supporting Idea: The explosion
   F. Supporting Idea: My experience at home
   G. Supporting Idea: Mom's explanation
   H. Supporting Idea: Mom's tears
   I. Supporting Idea: No survivors
   J. Thesis Statement: The article "The Crew of the Challenger Shuttle Mission in 1986" explains the backgrounds of the seven astronauts on the mission.
II Body: Summary of article
   A. First Supporting Point
      1. Topic Sentence: Five NASA employees
      2. Supporting Idea: Francis R. Scobee (commander)
      3. Supporting Idea: Michael J. Smith
      4. Supporting Idea: Judith A. Resnik (second woman to orbit)
      5. Supporting Idea: Ronald E. McNair (black American)
      6. Supporting Idea: Ellison S. Onuzuka
   B. Second Supporting Point
      1. Topic Sentence: Two non-NASA employees
      2. Supporting Idea: Gregory B. Jarvis (liquid-fueled rockets)
      3. Supporting Idea: Christa McAuliffe (teacher)

III Conclusion: significance of this event
    A. Restated Thesis: This article reviews the backgrounds of the seven astronauts.
    B. Supporting Idea: bond with Christa McAuliffe
    C. Supporting Idea: reduce common people in space
    D. Supporting Idea: reduce manned missions

Notice how her short essay below adheres to her outline.

The Challenger

The day had finally come; the first teacher was going into space. It was January 28, 1986, at about 8:40 in the morning, and my whole elementary school was waiting to see the takeoff. My eyes were glued to the television, and I heard all the students count down to the blastoff. The Challenger finally lifted off the ground, and the whole school cheered. The shuttle's graceful launch gave my classmates and me a great thrill. After barely one minute in the air, however, a ball of fire immersed the Challenger. The explosion looked like fireworks on the Fourth of July. A silence fell over everyone, and I could not believe what I had just witnessed. My teacher hurried to the television to turn it off; however, the damage was already done. We all sat still, and no one knew what to say. My teacher acted very calm and tried to explain to us what just happened.

I could not wait for school to be over that day and go home. When my mom picked me up, she was quick to ask me if I watched the liftoff. I told my mom that my class, as well as the rest of the school, watched the Challenger explode. My mom told me that the news said that there was a leak in one of the two solid rocket boosters. The leak caused the main liquid fuel tank to explode. Then, with tears in her eyes, my mom explained that none of the astronauts had survived. The article "The Crew of the Challenger Shuttle Mission in 1986" by Jason Wood (*Aviation,* December, 1986) explains the backgrounds of the seven astronauts on that mission.

The crew consisted of five men and two women, and five of the crew members were NASA employees. The commander of the Challenger was Francis R. Scobee. He was the pilot of the fifth orbital flight that took place before the Challenger, so he was an experienced astronaut and the right person to handle a history-making mission. The second member of the crew was pilot Michael J. Smith, and the Challenger was his first space flight. The first mission specialist was Judith A. Resnik, who became the second American woman to orbit space. Ronald E. McNair was the second mission specialist; he was one of the first three black Americans selected for the astronaut cadre. The last of the three mission specialists was Ellison S. Onizuka, and the Challenger flight was his second shuttle mission.

The last two members of the crew were not official NASA employ-ees. Gregory B. Jarvis was a payload specialist for Hughes Aircraft Cor-poration and Communications Group. Hughes, a main NASA contractor, made Gregory available for the Challenger flight. His mission was to gather new information on the design of liquid-fueled rockets. The last member of the crew was Sharon Christa McAuliffe, the first teacher to fly in space. Christa taught at Concord High School in Concord, New Hampshire. Christa was selected through a nationwide contest that was searching for a gifted teacher who could communicate with stu-dents from space.

As the "The Crew of the Challenger Shuttle Mission in 1986" points out, the seventh crew member was a gifted teacher, an average Ameri-can, a person with no space experience, and this explains why the acci-dent had such a significant impact on the nation. Because of all the publicity devoted to the Teacher in Space Program, all Americans were watching what was supposed to be a proud, patriotic moment. People felt a special bond with Christa McAuliffe because of her status as a high school teacher. However, since the explosion, support for sending non-astronauts into space on NASA missions has decreased. Also, Americans think twice about supporting a mission that sends any human into space if a robot can do the job.

Adapted from Stacy DeCandido

Stacy's essay follows her outline closely, but that is not always the case. For example, when writing a rough draft based on an outline, a writer's ideas often evolve, and that's positive. This allows writing to improve at each step of the process. In other words, the outline serves as a guide, not a straitjacket.

Now that you are familiar with the format of outlines, you are prepared to become acquainted with the various methods of presenting ideas.

HOW DOES A WRITER CHOOSE AN ORDER FOR PRESENTING IDEAS?

Presenting your ideas in a logical order allows your readers to easily understand your thoughts. Before you write your outline, consider three methods of develop-ment: time, space, and importance.

The Time Method

Developing your ideas by time allows your readers to understand events according to when they happened. The time method works well when you are writing about events through narration. You may narrate events using one of two types of time order:

- First to last (chronological)
- Last to first

Reconsider Stacy DeCandido's opening paragraph in "The Challenger," which uses the time method. Does she narrate the event from first to last or from last to first?

Obviously, she orders her ideas from first to last, which is most often the case in a narration, and that order allows the reader to easily understand her story.

PRACTICE 1

Arrange the details that support the topic sentence below by numbering them in the order that they occurred. Sometimes more than one order is possible.

Example:

Topic Sentence: To drive a stick shift, do the following.

Type of time order: first to last

Supporting details:

   _3_ put car in first gear
   _5_ increase speed
   _2_ engage clutch
   _4_ disengage clutch while accelerating
   _1_ start the car in neutral

1. Topic Sentence: Follow a few steps to surf a wave.

   Type of time order: first to last

   Supporting details:

      ____ walk into the water
      ____ wax the surfboard

_____ paddle out to the waves

_____ put on the wetsuit

_____ catch the wave and stand up

2. Topic Sentence: Writing an essay involves several steps.

   Type of time order: first to last

   Supporting details:

   _____ narrow a topic

   _____ generate a tentative thesis statement

   _____ create an outline

   _____ brainstorm some topics

   _____ write a rough draft

3. Topic Sentence: Your valentine will love a romantic date.

   Type of time order: first to last

   Supporting details:

   _____ take your valentine to your favorite restaurant

   _____ take a moonlit walk on the beach

   _____ give your valentine a card and a gift

   _____ kiss your valentine

   _____ call your valentine and set up a date

4. Topic Sentence: Bears scavenge for all types of food.

   Type of time order: first to last

   Supporting details:

   _____ heard noise outside tent

   _____ saw bear eating cookies out of icebox

   _____ banged pans together and made noise

   _____ talked about what to do

   _____ unzipped tent door

5. Topic Sentence: Adding an image to your report will bring it to life.

   Type of time order: first to last

   Supporting details:

_____ save the document

_____ locate the image that you want inserted

_____ adjust the size of the image to fit the document

_____ copy the image

_____ paste the image into the document

The Space Method

Developing your ideas by the space method allows your readers to imagine the place or thing that you are describing as you imagine it. The space method works well when you are writing about a physical object or place through description. Ten common types of space order follow:

- Top to bottom
- Bottom to top
- Left to right
- Right to left
- Front to back
- Back to front
- Near to far
- Far to near
- Largest items to smallest items
- Smallest items to largest items

Inspect Melissa Chapel's paragraph below, which uses the space method, to determine what type of space order she uses to describe a photograph.

A picture shows a slight breeze in the trees. A short wall stretches across a field. A little girl and a little boy sit on the wall, and they are both crossing their legs. The girl is wearing a dress that seems to be a size too big. It is purple with pink polka dots, and she is wearing cream tights to keep her legs a little warmer. Her hat is tilted while the floral box which holds the hat rests next to the little boy. The little boy is wearing a little suit which consists of tan pants, a green jacket, and a red bow tie. The girl is looking at the boy while licking her lips, making sure he is following her every move. The boy is looking down at her with his spoon in the air trying to sneak a peek in her cone to see if she has the same amount of ice cream. Even though the picture is silent, their expressions are felt, and the saying, "I scream, you scream, we all scream for ice cream," fills the silence.

Can you visualize the picture? What type of space order did she use? Melissa decided to present the items in the photograph from largest to smallest, starting with the breeze and the wall, and ending with the kids' expressions.

PRACTICE 2

Select a type of space order (near to far, back to front, bottom to top, etc.), and number the details that support the topic sentence below. Answers will depend upon the type of space order selected.

Example:

Topic Sentence: The '67 Mustang looked brand-new.

Type of space order: top to bottom

Supporting details:

    _5_ clean, black tires
    _1_ black convertible top
    _2_ gleaming, red paint
    _4_ tan upholstery
    _3_ an engine that roared like a tiger

1. Topic Sentence: The American flag is composed of symbols.

    Type of space order: _____

    Supporting details:

        ____ red stripes
        ____ white stripes
        ____ white stars
        ____ blue background

2. Topic Sentence: The first bicycle was invented in 1840.

    Type of space order: _____

    Supporting details:

        ____ tires
        ____ seat
        ____ frame
        ____ handlebars
        ____ peddles

3. Topic Sentence: The horse is useful to people because of its build.

   Type of space order: _____

   Supporting details:

   ___ legs
   ___ head
   ___ back
   ___ tail
   ___ neck

4. Topic Sentence: Computer components can be upgraded easily.

   Type of space order: _____

   Supporting details:

   ___ monitor
   ___ mouse
   ___ harddrive
   ___ keyboard
   ___ speakers

5. Topic Sentence: Plastic surgery can alter someone's face.

   Type of space order: _____

   Supporting details:

   ___ nose
   ___ eyes
   ___ ears
   ___ chin
   ___ cheeks

The Importance Method

Developing your thoughts by importance allows your readers to understand your ideas according to their importance, value, or interest. The importance method works well in an argument or explanation through illustration, definition, classification, comparison and contrast, problem and solution, or cause and effect. Four types of importance order follow:

- Most important to least important
- Least important to most important
- General to specific
- Specific to general

Examine the following paragraph, which uses the importance method, to determine what type of importance order the author uses to explain the effects of alcoholism.

> Parents that have alcohol problems usually will begin to have a chain reaction of problems in their families. Alcoholic parents often begin to abuse their children. Once a young person experiences child abuse, she no longer desires to stick around. This dreadful challenge, called child abuse, is the biggest cause of teenage runaways. Young people become afraid of their surroundings, and they think life would be like a playground if they could only get away. When young people run away, they begin to develop negative attitudes; they think nobody cares about them. All young people will face some kind of challenge; they all are looking for love to guide them through each challenge. There are many teenage runaway shelters where young people can go to seek advice on child abuse and other problems; there are plenty of people who are willing to listen and care for young people and help them with their challenges.
>
> Adapted from Michelle Goodwin

What type of importance order did Michelle use? Michelle chose to explain alcoholism from the least important facts (the problems associated with it) to the most important facts (the assistance available to the victims).

PRACTICE 3

Select an importance order (most important to least important, least important to most important, etc.), and number the details that support the topic sentence below. Because readers are most likely to remember the things that they have read last, writers often choose to order their ideas from least important to most important. Answers will depend upon the type of importance order selected.

Example:

Topic Sentence: Americans should protect the environment.

Type of importance order: least important to most important

Supporting details:

    _2_ recycling paper, plastic, aluminum at home
    _5_ laws that protect endangered species
    _3_ recycling paper, plastic, aluminum at work
    _1_ supporting environmental organizations
    _4_ educating children about natural resources.

1. Topic Sentence: Tougher gun laws will reduce crime.

   Type of space order: _____

   Supporting details:

       ____ gun laws needed in the future
       ____ current gun laws and crime rates in America
       ____ victims of gun crimes
       ____ how laws influence criminals
       ____ current gun laws and crime rates in other countries

2. Topic Sentence: Reducing class size improves education.

   Type of space order: _____

   Supporting details:

       ____ national statistics on class size and success rates
       ____ state statistics on class size and success rates
       ____ benefits of small classes to teachers
       ____ school district statistics on class size and success rates
       ____ benefits of small classes to students

3. Topic Sentence: Staff diversity adds breadth of perspective in institutions.

   Type of space order: _____

   Supporting details:

       ____ lack of diversity in universities
       ____ lack of diversity in businesses

___ problems with lack of diversity
___ benefits of staff diversity in institutions
___ history of diversity in American institutions

4. Topic Sentence: Several factors contribute to youth crimes.

Type of space order: _____

Supporting details:

___ lack of positive role models
___ lack of fathers in homes
___ glamorizing of crimes by media
___ lack of quality education
___ poverty

5. Topic Sentence: Solutions to domestic violence exist.

Type of space order: _____

Supporting details:

___ classes
___ individual counseling
___ support groups
___ family counseling
___ self-help books

Again, note that not only one type of order is correct. Now that you understand the three methods of development, you are ready to create your own outlines. As you do, keep the following ideas in mind.

WHAT ARE SOME GUIDELINES FOR CREATING AN OUTLINE?

1. Write in pencil or type on a computer so that you can easily modify your outline.
2. Before writing the outline, put the purpose, audience, tone, order, and topic sentence or thesis statement at the top.
3. As you complete the outline, work in the following order:
   a. First, write the full thesis statement twice, once at the end of the introduction and again at the beginning of the conclusion.
   b. Second, fill in the topics for each body paragraph.
   c. Third, insert all of the supporting ideas for the body paragraphs.
   d. Fourth, complete the introduction and conclusion.

4. Limit the number of major sections in an outline.
5. Use words and phrases for informal outlines, full sentences for formal outlines.
6. Provide ample specific support (see Chapter 6).
7. Use the standard system of numbers and letters for creating new levels of specificity.
8. Use at least two subdivisions per category.
9. Symmetry is not required in your outline; i.e., if you have two points under a heading, you may have five points under a parallel heading.
10. Use the outline as a map or guide, not a straitjacket. When you write your rough draft, you may add to or delete from your outline to improve your work in progress.

PRACTICE 4

Create an outline by responding to one of the writing prompts below and filling in the blanks on the outline, or write an outline based on one of your own topic sentences from Chapter 5. Remember that outlines are flexible, so just use the forms below as a guide. For example, if you need seven lines for supporting detail in your paragraph, then expand your outline to allow for your support. If you need to add additional levels of specificity, expand your outline to accommodate your ideas.

Writing Prompts:

- Narrate a significant experience in your education.
- Narrate a process with which you are very familiar.
- Describe a place or location where you enjoy being.

PARAGRAPH

Purpose:

_____

Audience:

_____

Tone:

_____

METHOD OF DEVELOPMENT: (CHECK ONE)

☐ time   ☐ space   ☐ importance

Type of order: (first to last, top to bottom, general to specific, etc.)

_____

I Narrowed Topic: _____

    A. Topic Sentence: _____

    B. Supporting Idea: _____

    C. Supporting Idea: _____

    D. Supporting Idea: _____

    E. Supporting Idea: _____

    F. Concluding Idea: _____

PRACTICE 5

Create an outline by responding to one of the writing prompts below and filling in the blanks on the outline, or write an outline based on one of your own thesis statements from Chapter 5. Again, remember that outlines are flexible, so just use the form below as a guide. For example, if you need seven lines for supporting detail in a paragraph, then expand your outline to allow for your support. If you need four supporting paragraphs in the body of your essay, then expand the body of your outline. If you need to add levels of specificity, expand your outline to accommodate your ideas.

Writing Prompts:

- Explain why you do or do not support capital punishment.
- Argue for or against honoring same-sex marriages.
- What are some solutions to the problem of unwanted teenage pregnancies?

ESSAY

Purpose:

_____

Audience:

_____

Tone:

_____

METHOD OF DEVELOPMENT: (CHECK ONE)

☐ time   ☐ space   ☐ importance

Type of Order: (first to last, top to bottom, general to specific, etc.)

_____

I Introduction

  A. Topic Sentence: _____

  B. Supporting Idea: _____

  C. Supporting Idea: _____

  D. Supporting Idea: _____

  E. Thesis Statement: _____

II Body

A. First Supporting Point

1. Topic Sentence: _____

2. Supporting Idea: _____

3. Supporting Idea: _____

4. Supporting Idea: _____

5. Concluding Idea: _____

B. Second Supporting Point

1. Topic Sentence: _____

2. Supporting Idea: _____

3. Supporting Idea: _____

4. Supporting Idea: _____

5. Concluding Idea: _____

C. Third Supporting Point

1. Topic Sentence: _____

2. Supporting Idea: _____

3. Supporting Idea: _____

    4. Supporting Idea: _____

    5. Concluding Idea: _____

III Conclusion

    A. Refer to Thesis Statement: _____

    B. Supporting Idea: _____

    C. Supporting Idea: _____

    D. Supporting Idea: _____

    E. Concluding Idea: _____

GROUP WORK

1. As a group, select one topic sentence you created in Chapter 5 or create a new one now. Then, brainstorm specific details and place them in an outline for a paragraph. Follow the format and guidelines provided in this chapter.
2. As a group, select one thesis statement that you created in Chapter 5 or create a new one now. Then, brainstorm specific details and place them in an outline for an essay. Follow the format and guidelines provided in this chapter.
3. As a group, create an outline of this chapter. Follow the format and guidelines provided in this chapter.

TEST (TRUE/FALSE)

1. You should define your point (topic sentence or thesis) before creating an outline.
2. An outline is like a map.
3. Skipping the outlining step in the writing process will save you time in producing a high-quality product.

4. An outline will help you to present your point and supporting details in a logical way.

5. Most introductions include a thesis statement.

6. A conclusion may explain the significance of a thesis statement or point.

7. The order in which you choose to present your ideas will influence the impact that your writing has on your readers.

8. Narrations lend themselves to the importance method.

9. An argument may be presented effectively through more than one type of importance order.

10. After you write an outline, you should stick to it strictly when writing your rough draft.

WRITING ASSIGNMENTS

1. Academic Assignment: Visit American Memory at http://memory.loc.gov to learn about a significant historical event. Write a short essay in which you summarize an article about an historical event and explain the significance of it. Follow the format and guidelines in this chapter for creating an outline as part of the prewriting process. For additional information on organizing a paper, visit Bowling Green State University's Writing Lab Online at http://www.bgsu.edu/departments/writing-lab/how_to_effectively_o.html.

2. Journal Assignment: Explain everything that you have learned in this chapter: "How does a writer organize ideas?"

3. Creative Assignment: Visit America's Shrine to Music Museum at the University of South Dakota at http://www.usd.edu/smm/. Select an image that you like from the virtual tour, and describe it in a one-page essay. For tips on writing descriptions, visit Purdue University's Online Writing Lab at http://owl.english.purdue.edu/handouts/general/gl_describe.html. Follow the format and guidelines in this chapter for creating an outline as part of the prewriting process.

How does a writer write the first draft?

"Much of writing might be described as a mental pregnancy with successive difficult deliveries."

—J. B. Priestley

LEARNING OBJECTIVES

1. Learn what a rough draft is and why one should be written.
2. Learn what to focus on in a rough draft.
3. Learn what not to focus on in a rough draft.
4. Learn how and why a computer can help at this stage of the writing process.

PRE-READING QUESTIONS

1. Why should writers write a rough draft first?
2. What should writers focus on in the first draft?
3. What should writers not focus on in the first draft?
4. How can the outline help your first draft?
5. Do you prefer to handwrite or type your first draft? Why?

WHAT IS A ROUGH DRAFT AND WHY WRITE ONE?

Before we can answer these questions, let's reflect upon all that you have done in the prewriting stage of the writing process:

- Considered the purpose, audience, and tone (Chapter 3)
- Generated ideas (Chapter 4)
- Chosen and narrowed a topic (Chapter 5)
- Written a topic sentence or thesis statement (Chapter 5)
- Found and generated support (Chapter 6 to 7)
- Organized ideas (Chapter 8)

Now that you are finished with the prewriting stage, you can begin the writing stage of the writing process. The first step involves writing a rough draft, which takes advantage of all of your work in the prewriting stage as you write out your ideas from beginning to end in a first draft of your paper. If you have worked through the prewriting stage carefully and thoroughly, writing a rough draft will be quick and easy.

Writing a first draft has been compared to a dress rehearsal for a play. A lot of work has already been done, and now it's time to put it all together, to see how the parts combine to produce the whole. Of course, this is not the final performance, but it is an important step along the way because from a dress rehearsal a producer can see what changes or improvements need to be made. In the same way that a dress rehearsal is never perfect, nobody writes a perfect paper in the first draft, so don't try to write one.

WHAT SHOULD WRITERS FOCUS ON IN THE FIRST DRAFT?

1. **Build on the work that you have done already.** Since your previous step in the writing process involved organizing your ideas in an outline, now is the time to use it. During the first few years that I taught writing, several students submitted first

drafts that in no way resembled their outlines. When I asked them why this was the case, they explained that they didn't realize that there was a connection between the two. As a result, I now know that this connection between the outline and the first draft does not go without saying, so I explain to all of my students that the process of writing a first draft involves following an outline. Find your outline, and place it on your desk so that you can read it as you write or type your first draft. As you write, remember that your objective is to write out your paper from beginning to end by following your outline. This will allow you to develop ideas that support your point in an organized way, a process that produces effective writing.

2. Use the outline as a guide, not a straightjacket. This means that, as you write your first draft while looking at your outline, you may have insights about your subject, and these insights need a chance to emerge in your first draft. For example, if you remember a detail that will clarify your point, insert it. If you see that one of the ideas on your outline is a non sequitur, something illogical that doesn't follow, drop it. If you recognize that an example of a point would make your case much easier to believe, add it. In other words, the first draft should reflect your entire outline, but it should also reflect insights that you have as you write.

3. Acknowledge sources in your paper when, for example, you are summarizing or reacting to an article, as described in Chapter 7. If you are writing a summary, begin it with an introductory sentence that states the name of the author, the title of the reading, and the main point of the entire reading. In parentheses, add the name of the publication and the date. This is called citing your source. The first sentence of your summary might look like this: "In 'Never Cry Arctic Wolf' (*National Geographic,* July 7, 2001), Jennifer Gomez explains that wolves are not responsible for the declining numbers of caribou." When writing research papers in various college classes, acknowledge sources in a paper by following the Modern Language Association (MLA) format explained at 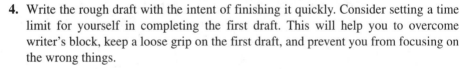http://webster.commnet.edu/mla.htm.

4. Write the rough draft with the intent of finishing it quickly. Consider setting a time limit for yourself in completing the first draft. This will help you to overcome writer's block, keep a loose grip on the first draft, and prevent you from focusing on the wrong things.

PRACTICE 1

1. *In which of the following paragraphs does the author follow the simple outline? Explain why you chose your answer on a separate piece of paper or on a computer.*

First Outline and Paragraph

I Narrowed Topic: Fun first date
   A. Topic Sentence: We had an exciting first date.
   B. Supporting Idea: Feelings

C. Supporting Idea: Double-date
D. Supporting Idea: My outfit
E. Supporting Idea: Dinner
F. Concluding Idea: Wonderful

My first date was wonderful while it lasted. I had a crush on Robby, my brother's friend. One day he called me to ask me out. I was nervous like a trembling leaf, but all my worries seemed to disappear when we were on the date. He took me to the Santa Monica Pier. It was wonderful! We had so much fun walking around and going on the rides. The night ended with a sweet kiss.

Adapted from Mirella Hernandez

Second Outline and Paragraph

I Narrowed Topic: Cause of Divorce
A. Topic Sentence: A common cause of divorce is ineffective communication.
B. Supporting Idea: Criticism
C. Supporting Idea: Anger
D. Supporting Idea: Screaming and swearing
E. Concluding Idea: May cause divorce

People get divorced for many reasons, but the most common cause of divorce is ineffective communication. Some people criticize their partners, but they do not recognize that they make many mistakes themselves. They do this when they get angry. Sometimes they will scream and swear at each other. People who do not talk through their problems may become angry and criticize their partners, which could lead to divorce.

Adapted from Marta Santana

2. *In the paragraph above that does follow the outline, find the detail that was added as "insight" into the rough draft and write it on a separate piece of paper or on a computer.*

PRACTICE 2

On a separate piece of paper or on a computer, write five topic sentences that combine the information in the table below. Follow the example in order to cite the source.

Title of Article	Title of Periodical	Date	Author	Thesis of Article
"Nuclear Power: Why Wait?"	*The Los Angeles Times*	February 2, 1998	Robert Radcliff	Americans should increase their reliance on nuclear power.

Example: In "Nuclear Power: Why Wait?" (*The Los Angeles Times,* July 2, 1998), Robert Radcliff explains why Americans should increase their reliance on nuclear power.

Title of Article	Title of Periodical	Date	Author	Thesis of Article
"Saving Alaska's Grizzly Bears Through Tourism"	*Western Wilderness*	January 10, 2001	Sarah Hilnholm	The increase in tourism has increased public appreciation for the grizzly bears.
"Olympic Runners"	*Sports Illustrated*	November 17, 1999	Randy De Leon	New diets and training methods are making today's Olympic runners faster than ever.
"Refugees Ravaged by War"	*Newsweek*	October 21, 2000	Audrey Brill	Children suffer the most in refugee camps.
"Human Rights: Who Enjoys Them?"	*Time*	June 3, 2002	Samuel Billion	Countries are ranked according to the rights and privileges they offer their citizens.
"What Have We Learned from Cloning Sheep?"	*The New England Journal of Medicine*	December 29, 2001	Dr. Wendy Scott	Cloning sheep has revealed essential information that may be used to clone other species.
"The Next Generation of Computers"	*Science and Technology*	July 26, 2001	Michael Uesugi	The next generation of computers will significantly change the work environment.

WHAT SHOULD WRITERS NOT FOCUS ON IN THE FIRST DRAFT?

1. Do not try to express ideas as you think they should read in their final form in polished writing. A preoccupation with perfection in the rough draft will generate a paralysis called writer's block.

2. Do not focus on spelling, grammar, punctuation, and errors. These are concerns during the revision process, which comes in later drafts. The first draft is supposed to

be rough and unpolished. Writers who focus on spelling, grammar, punctuation, and errors in the first draft don't realize that it will hurt them more than it will help them by creating a level of frustration tantamount to that experienced by a person who insists on learning to juggle five balls before learning how to juggle three balls.

3. Do not focus on yourself unnecessarily. Beginning writers are typically guided to write about themselves, their experiences, and their thoughts. As writing students advance, however, they will be challenged to shift the focus of their writing from themselves to a discussion of ideas. To accomplish this, place yourself in the background by writing in the third person; i.e., use *he, she, it, one,* or *they* instead of *I* (first person) or *you* (second person). Doing this will place the ideas in the foreground. Notice the difference in the following examples.
   - *I* understand that farmers enjoyed improved agriculture in Europe in the eighteenth-century because of the increase in cultivated land and enhanced yield per acre. (first person brings the writer to the foreground)
   - *You* understand that farmers enjoyed improved agriculture in Europe in the eighteenth-century because of the increase in cultivated land and enhanced yield per acre. (second person brings the reader to the foreground)
   - Farmers enjoyed improved agriculture in Europe in the eighteenth-century because *they* increased the cultivated land and enhanced the yield per acre. (third person brings the subject to the foreground)

PRACTICE 3

In order to avoid stopping to revise or edit your writing, attempt to write one paragraph on a separate piece of paper or on a computer that follows the outline below. To keep your pen moving (or your fingers typing), limit yourself to five minutes.

   I Narrowed Topic: Improving writing skills
     A. Topic Sentence: Improving writing skills involves receiving writing instruction, practicing writing, and obtaining feedback on papers.
     B. Supporting Idea: Receiving writing instruction
     C. Supporting Idea: Practicing writing
     D. Supporting Idea: Obtaining feedback on papers
     E. Concluding Idea: Effort required in process

PRACTICE 4

In the following paragraph, a student has made many references to himself. Rewrite the paragraph on a separate piece of paper or on a computer by shifting

from first person to third person. Doing this will place the subject in the foreground and the author in the background. Occasionally, a verb will have to change form to agree with a pronoun, as in the example below:

Example:

> First Person: I am relieved because the snake did not bite me.
>
> Third Person: **She is** relieved because the snake did not bite **her**.

The most incredible thing happened to me today while I was bowling. Before I went up to bowl, this pretty girl came up to me and gave me her phone number. She told me to call her if I wanted to do something, but I could not move or believe what the woman was doing. She wanted to go on a date with me. I am not the manly man that women like. I was so surprised; then, she gave me a hug and left. The next day I called her and took her out to dinner. She is the most amazing girl I have ever met. She is very smart; in fact, she is brilliant, and her looks are wonderful. I am in a tough situation now because I already have a girlfriend.

Adapted from Andy Abrahim.

HOW AND WHY CAN A COMPUTER HELP AT THIS STAGE OF THE WRITING PROCESS?

 Computers can help at each stage of the writing process: prewriting, writing, and rewriting. If you have done all of your prewriting with a pen or pencil, however, this is the time in which using a computer pays off the most (see Chapter 12 for a detailed explanation of how to use computers in the writing process). You will want to write and save your work on a computer because doing so will save you much time in the rewriting process.

First Draft Checklist

Do

1. Build on the foundation of your prewriting work.
2. Follow your outline as you write the first draft.
3. Allow insights that are not on your outline to be included in the first draft.
4. Acknowledge sources when applicable.
5. Remember that you want to quickly produce a complete rough draft.
6. Save your work on a disk or computer.

Do Not

1. Try to produce polished writing.
2. Focus on spelling, grammar, punctuation, and errors.
3. Focus on yourself unnecessarily.

GROUP WORK

1. As a group, find, read, and print (or copy) one short article in the library, on the Internet, or in your textbook. Create a topic sentences that includes the title of the article, the title of the periodical, the date, the author, and the thesis of the article. Follow the examples in this chapter.
2. As a group, select one outline for a paragraph that you created in Chapter 8 or create a new one now. Select one person to write or type the rough draft while other members of the group explain what to write. Follow the first draft checklist provided in this chapter.
3. As a group, select one outline for an essay that you created in Chapter 8 or create a new one now. Select one person to write or type the rough draft while other members of the group explain what to write. Follow the first draft checklist provided in this chapter.

TEST (TRUE/FALSE)

1. A rough draft is simply your ideas written out from beginning to end in a paper.
2. A rough draft should be written before the prewriting stage of the writing process.
3. As students write their rough drafts, they should be looking at their outlines.
4. The first draft should basically follow the outline.
5. Writers should never deviate from their outlines for any reason.
6. In a rough draft that summarizes an article, the writer should cite the source.
7. Rough drafts should be written perfectly and slowly.
8. Writers should check the spelling of all unknown words in the dictionary while writing the rough draft.
9. Writers should refer to themselves frequently in all types of writing so that the readers know who they really are.
10. Generally speaking, rough drafts should be written and saved on a computer.

WRITING ASSIGNMENTS

1. Academic Assignment: Visit fitnessonline at http://www.fitnessonline.com to learn about fitness programs. Create and explain an ideal personal fitness program. Begin by following the steps in the prewriting process. For assistance in overcoming writer's block, visit the Writers' Workshop at the University of Illinois at Urbana-Champaign at http://www.english.uiuc.edu/cws/wworkshop/tips/writersblock.htm.

2. Journal Assignment: Explain everything that you have learned in this chapter:"How does a writer write the first draft?"

3. Creative Assignment: Visit Corbis at http://corbis.com/ and find a professional photograph that you like. Create an outline that describes your photograph (see Chapter 8), and write a first draft by following your outline. For tips on writing descriptions, return to Purdue University's Online Writing Lab at http://owl.english.purdue.edu/handouts/general/gl_describe.html.

Chapter 10

How does a writer move smoothly from one idea to the next in sentences and paragraphs?

"It's not wise to violate rules until you know how to observe them."

—T. S. Eliot

LEARNING OBJECTIVES

1. Learn what transitions are.
2. Learn why transitions are needed.
3. Learn the types of transitions between sentences.
4. Learn where transitions are placed and how to punctuate them.
5. Learn the types of transitions between paragraphs.
6. Learn how to avoid making your writing worse by using transitions incorrectly.

PRE-READING QUESTIONS

1. Do you know how to drive a stick shift, a car with a manual transmission?
2. When driving a car with a manual transmission, what must you engage before shifting gears?
3. If you shift from first gear to second gear in a stick shift without engaging anything, what will happen?
4. When you want to shift from one idea to another idea in your writing, how do you write so that your readers experience a smooth transition from the first idea to the second idea?
5. Do you use the same technique to transition from one paragraph to the next as you would to transition from one sentence to the next?

WHAT ARE TRANSITIONS AND WHY ARE THEY NEEDED?

In writing, transitions are words, phrases, and sentences that function like the clutch on a manual transmission; i.e., they take readers smoothly from one idea to the next in sentences and paragraphs.

Transitions can also be understood by comparing them to signs. Imagine that you are driving to a ski resort on a highway. As you approach the ski lodge, you see a sign with a wiggly line and the words "next ten miles." This sign lets you know that you will be driving through a winding road for the next ten miles. As a consequence of seeing this sign, you understand that the terrain has changed. You may reduce your speed from sixty-five to forty-five miles per hour and proceed cautiously, especially if you have never driven this road before. In short, this sign has helped you to reach your destination.

In writing, transitions are like signposts in that they provide readers with important information about what lies ahead, and they help readers see relationships between ideas. They create coherence by echoing ideas that have already been discussed and announcing upcoming ideas, thus allowing readers to move smoothly from one idea to the next. Transitions are essential in your writing because most of your readers will be reading your writing for the first time, and they will need signposts to be able to follow your train of thought easily. Signposts will increase the likelihood of your readers understanding what you are trying to explain, agreeing with the point you are trying to make, and appreciating the way in which you have expressed yourself.

Notice how the following paragraph, which describes a process, includes transitions.

Would you like to know the secret on how to get all of the girls that you want? Well, here are a couple of steps that could get you a couple of phone numbers. *First*, although you may think that you are clean because you took a shower yesterday, take a shower before going on your expedition. *Second*, girls tend to pay much attention to how a guy dresses, so dressing up when hunting for girls is a must. Do not wear work uniforms; *in fact*, you should dress nicely. *Third*, smelling good is like a magnet for girls. When out on the prowl, wear cologne. If you do not have cologne, go to a place like a mall to spray yourself with cologne for free. *Fourth, after you look and smell good*, go to a place with lots of girls like the mall, parties, or low-rider car shows. Make a couple of rounds before talking to any one girl. This will help you to scope the whole scene. *Fifth*, when you do find a girl that you want to talk to, be polite, considerate, and charming. *Finally, at the end of the conversation*, ask her for her phone number. If you follow these instructions correctly, she will give you her true phone number. If you don't want to seem desperate, wait until the next day to call her and ask for a date. Who knows? Maybe you will hit it off and marry one of the girls that you meet by following these simple steps. Good luck!

—Adapted from Angel Ramirez

To see how transitions fit into the process of writing, recall the four steps of effective writing from Chapter 2:

1. Make a point.
2. Support the point.
3. Organize the ideas.
4. Present the ideas in error-free sentences.

Transitions, like the outline, help the writer to accomplish step three, *organize the ideas*.

Transitions are closely tied to the method of development or organization of your writing, and the transitions that you use will depend upon the way in which you have decided to organize your paper in your outline (see Chapter 8): by time, by space, or by importance.

WHAT TYPES OF TRANSITIONS CAN A WRITER USE BETWEEN SENTENCES?

- Transitional words and phrases
- Repeating key words (synonyms), ideas, and sentence patterns
- Using pronouns

Transitional Words and Phrases

Transitions tie together two ideas, indicated by arrows in the following example:

The origin of killer bees in South and North America has been traced. ← *First,* →
in 1957 these bees escaped from a Brazilian breeding program. ← *Then,* → they
proliferated throughout South and Central America.

Become acquainted with the transitional expressions listed in the table below. Realize that some transitional expressions may be used in more than one category. For example, *first, second, third* may be used to provide a smooth transition from one idea to the next in a paper with ideas organized by either time, space, or importance.

Transition Category	Method of Development (see Chapter 8)	Useful Transitional Words or Expressions	Example of Transition Used in a Sentence
To show sequence	The time method: narration, process	after, and then, as soon as, before, by then, eventually, ever since, finally, first, gradually, in the future, later, meanwhile, next, now, second, sometimes, soon, suddenly, the next day, then, until, when, whenever, while	She heard a branch break outside her tent. *Then,* she heard an animal breathing.
To show place	The space method: narration, description	above, adjacent to, around, below, beside, beyond, close, farther on, in, inside, in front, left, nearby, next to, opposite, out, outside, north (south, east, or west), on the opposite side of, over, right, through, left, under, where	The photograph shows three girls standing on a soccer field *next to* a referee. Two soccer balls are on the grass *in front* of them.
To show arguments	The importance method: argument, explanation, illustration, definition, classification, compare and contrast, problem and solution, cause and effect	one reason, another reason, furthermore, the main reason, the first reason, also, yet another reason, the biggest reason, therefore, first, second, third, most significantly, con-	The three strikes law has decreased the number of crimes committed by repeat offenders; *furthermore,* it has reduced the number of crimes committed by first-time offenders.

(continued)

Transition Category	Method of Development (see Chapter 8)	Useful Transitional Words or Expressions	Example of Transition Used in a Sentence
		sequently, naturally, another reason, besides that, the strongest reason, thus, undoubtedly, unquestionably	
To show addition	Any method	and, again, also, another, as well, besides, first, further, furthermore, in addition, moreover, next, once again, once more, second, too	*First*, find a poem that you like in the book. *Second*, reread it until you understand what the poet is trying to say.
To show examples	Any method	an example is, as, as an example, for example, for instance, in fact, one such, some examples are, specifically, such as, to illustrate	Jerry shows his drive to excel by the way that he works; *for example*, yesterday he wouldn't go home until he had responded to all of the customers' complaints.
To show similarities or comparisons	Any method	also, as, as if, as though, in the same manner, in the same way, like, likewise, similarly	*In the same way* that seat belts save lives in a car, helmets save lives on a motorcycle.
To show differences or contrasts	Any method	although, but, even so, even though, however, in contrast, nevertheless, nonetheless, on the contrary, on the one hand, on the other hand, otherwise, still, then again, though, unlike, while, yet	*A* students could be sitting anywhere in a class; *however*, several studies have shown that *A* students tend to sit in the front row.
To show conclusion	Any method	above all, again, as has been noted, as you have read, for these reasons, in brief, in conclusion, in fact, in other words, in short, in sum, in summary, of course, on the whole, that is, therefore, to be sure, to sum up	*In conclusion*, the more that people understand about the feeding, mating, and migration habits of the gray whale, the more likely they will be to want to preserve it.

WHERE ARE TRANSITIONAL EXPRESSIONS PLACED IN A SENTENCE, AND HOW ARE THEY PUNCTUATED?

Most transitional words or phrases interrupt the flow of a sentence and, therefore, must be set off with commas as non-essential elements. As a general rule, if the transition appears at the beginning or end of a sentence, only one comma is needed. If it appears in the middle of a sentence, two commas are needed. Notice the location of the commas in the following sentences:

> Each person in the family favors a different sport. *For example*, Jennifer prefers skiing.
> Each person in the family favors a different sport. Jennifer, *for example*, prefers skiing.
> Each person in the family favors a different sport. Jennifer prefers skiing, *for example*.

Transitions that show place typically require no punctuation:

> You will find the restroom *on the opposite side of* the gym.

PRACTICE 1

however	similarly	for instance	at the same time	for example

Insert the transitional words or expressions from the above table into the paragraph below. Include punctuation as needed:

About thirty years ago, adoption used to be a simple process. The country's conservative conventions influenced this policy. _____ the mother was often an unmarried woman who was to give up her son or daughter upon birth and relinquish all rights to ever see her child again. The father was often not granted access to the child _____. As social stigmas about illegitimacy, infertility, and having children out of wedlock changed, so did the laws relating to adoption. One driving force in these changes has been the fact that demand for children through adoption has increased while _____ the supply has decreased. _____ in 1970 about 90,000 children were adopted. In 1994 only about 50,000 were adopted while, according to some estimates, about two million infertile couples or individuals would like to adopt. Current laws on adoption vary from state to state, but all laws attempt to put the child's best interest first. People _____ disagree about what the best interest is, and disagreements have left some children as pawns in legal battles.

Source: "Adoption." Issues and Controversies, August 31, 2000. © 2001 Facts On File News Services

REPEATING KEY WORDS (SYNONYMS, ANTONYMS), IDEAS, AND SENTENCE PATTERNS

Repeating key words, ideas, and sentence patterns provides transitions from one idea to the next, as in the following example.

1. To everything there is a season, and a time to every purpose under the heaven:
2. A time to be born, and a time to die; a time to plant, and a time to pluck up that which is planted;
3. A time to kill, and a time to heal; a time to break down, and a time to build up;
4. A time to weep, and a time to laugh; a time to mourn, and a time to dance;
5. A time to cast away stones, and a time to gather stones together; a time to embrace, and a time to refrain from embracing;
6. A time to get, and a time to lose; a time to keep, and a time to cast away;
7. A time to rend, and a time to sew; a time to keep silence, and a time to speak;
8. A time to love, and a time to hate; a time of war, and a time of peace.

Ecclesiastes 3: 1–8

Why are these lines often quoted? Speakers and writers quote them because of their content and format. "*A time to*" appears in the first sentence and again four times in each succeeding verse. The repetition of these key words provides coherence, the glue that holds these ideas together.

Repeating key words or main ideas from previous sentences leads readers down a path in which an author is trying to develop an idea by reminding readers about what has previously been discussed and showing them the close connection to what will be discussed next.

Repeating certain sentence patterns also provides transitions for readers.

When a person is told what to do, the outcome may be negative.

When a person chooses what to do, the outcome may be positive.

Both sentences begin with similar dependent clauses, "When a person . . . ," and both sentences end with similar independent clauses, "The outcome may be. . . ." Using the same sentence pattern consecutively allows the readers to easily follow the narration.

PRACTICE 2

Underline key words, ideas, and sentence patterns that are repeated in the following paragraph.

Example:

The government is now distributing survival kits to aid victims of the hurricane. The survival kits contain food, water, and clothing.

1. Abraham Maslow described a process of reaching one's potential. He called the process self-actualization.
2. Self-actualization involves doing several things. The first thing that you must be willing to do is change.
3. Second, are you willing to take responsibility for your life? According to Maslow, you must also be willing to assume responsibility for every aspect of your life.
4. Furthermore, will you take risks? In other words, will you step out of your comfort zone to take some chances?
5. Finally, be honest. Be direct. This involves being willing to admit failure and assume responsibility for it.

Adapted from *Introduction to Psychology: Exploration and Application* by Dennis Coon

USING PRONOUNS

Using pronouns also provides transitions for readers. Pronouns refer back to nouns from previous sentences. Become familiar with the following list of pronouns because they can connect ideas between sentences through grammar.

This, these, that, he, she, it, they, some, one

Notice how a pronoun is used in the following example:

An avalanche started at 10:32 A.M. Within minutes, *it* had buried the Johnson cabin.

It is the pronoun used as a transition between the two sentences. *It* refers back to *avalanche*.
Avoid ambiguous references.

Incorrect: The dam broke and washed-out the bridge. Crews worked for six months to repair *it*.

Does *it* refer back to the broken dam or the washed-out bridge? Could *it* refer to both damaged structures?

Revised: The dam broke and washed out the bridge. Crews worked for six months to repair the *dam*.

Revised: The dam broke and washed out the bridge. Crews worked for six months to repair *them*.

PRACTICE 3

Underline the pronouns in the following paragraph and the nouns that they represent. Then draw an arrow from the pronouns to the nouns to which they refer. Write on a separate piece of paper or on a computer.

Example:

Hormones influence growth. They stimulate development in most regions of the body.

1. Jesse and Stephen were walking on the trails in the foothills when they saw a rattlesnake.
2. Jesse approached the snake. It coiled up and rattled its tail.
3. Stephen found two sticks. They were about five feet long.
4. Stephen held the head of the snake down with the sticks while Jesse grabbed it behind the head.
5. After Jesse and Stephen held the snake for a little while, they released it.

WHAT TYPES OF TRANSITIONS CAN BE USED BETWEEN PARAGRAPHS?

An essay has an introduction, a body, and a conclusion. Regardless of the length of the essay, a transition is required between each area of development to take the reader from one idea to the next and to show the relationship of the ideas.

Thesis Statement at End of Introductory Paragraph
Raising homing pigeons can be a fun hobby if you know something about building the cage, feeding the birds, and protecting them from predators.

This thesis statement clarifies that this essay will explain three aspects of raising homing pigeons.

Topic Sentence of First Body Paragraph

The first thing to know before buying pigeons is what kind of a *cage to build.*

First is a transition that clarifies which of the three ideas in the thesis statement will be discussed in this paragraph. The phrase *cage to build* repeats key words from the thesis statement.

Topic Sentence of Second Body Paragraph

After the cage is built, the *right kind of food* has to be provided.

The phrase *after the cage is built* is a transitional phrase that smoothly takes the reader from the first body paragraph that discussed building the cage to the second body paragraph that will discuss pigeon food. It also demonstrates the relationship between the two paragraphs; i.e., providing the proper food is considered only after the cage has been built. The phrase *right kind of food* is also a transition because it repeats key ideas from the thesis statement.

Topic Sentence of Third Body Paragraph

Finally, homing pigeons require *protection from predators.*

The word *finally* tells readers that this is the last idea discussed in the body of the paper, and *protection from predators* repeats key words from the thesis statement.

Thesis Restated at Beginning of Concluding Paragraph

Knowing something about building a pigeon cage, feeding these birds, and protecting them from predators will prepare anyone to enjoy raising homing pigeons.

The reworded thesis statement at the conclusion of the essay sends a signal that the essay is ending by reminding the reader of the topics explained in the paper.

PRACTICE 4

Create topic sentences that include transitions for the paragraphs in the following essay framework by following the example above. Refer to the transitions in the chart at the beginning of this chapter.

> **Thesis Statement at End of Introductory Paragraph**
> Learning to play the guitar involves picking the right instrument, learning the chords, and practicing consistently.

Topic Sentence of First Body Paragraph
_____
_____
_____

Topic Sentence of Second Body Paragraph
_____
_____
_____

Topic Sentence of Third Body Paragraph
_____
_____
_____

> **Thesis Restated at Beginning of Concluding Paragraph**
>
> _____
>
> _____
>
> _____

HOW CAN YOU AVOID MAKING YOUR WRITING WORSE BY USING TRANSITIONS INCORRECTLY?

Writers who are learning to use transitions can make their writing worse in two ways: first, they can use a transitional phrase or word with the wrong meaning, and second, they can use a transitional phrase or word with the wrong tone.

The Wrong Meaning

Below is an example of a sentence in which the author has selected a word with the wrong meaning:

> The Giant Pandas could not produce offspring at the zoo for two years; _consequently_, the female panda did give birth during the third year.

Consequently means _as a result_, so the use of it here confuses the reader. Notice the how the sentence reads with a different transitional word.

> The Giant Pandas could not produce offspring at the zoo for two years; _however_, the female panda did give birth during the third year.

However means _yet_ or _in spite of that_, so it helps the reader to see the relationship between the first and second sentences.

The Wrong Tone

Below is an example of a sentence in which the author has selected a word with the wrong tone:

> I'm writing you this letter just to thank you for helping me to move on Saturday; _moreover_, I want to thank you for bringing lunch.

Moreover means _also_, so the meaning is correct. _Moreover_, however, is too formal for a thank-you letter to a friend. The sentence sounds much better using another word:

I'm writing you this letter just to thank you for helping me to move on Saturday. *Also*, I want to thank you for bringing lunch.

PRACTICE 5

The transitional word in each sentence is used incorrectly. Cross out the incorrect transition, and replace it with one from the table below. Write on a piece of paper or on a computer.

consequently (as a result)	therefore (as a result)	furthermore (in addition)	moreover (in addition)	however (yet or in spite of that)

Example:

One-third of India's population lives in poverty; ~~however~~ that population is growing rapidly.

moreover

1. Traffic school can actually be enjoyable; therefore, some schools are run by intelligent comedians.
2. Some instructors show funny videos; eventually, these videos have a valuable point.
3. Instructors also provide important facts; moreover, students do not always remember the facts.
4. Students learn that most accidents occur in an intersection; nevertheless, drivers should cover their brakes and look both ways when they start to drive through one.
5. Traffic school usually lasts for eight hours; however, picking a school that is fun and informative is important.

GROUP WORK

1. As a group, provide an example sentence for each of the eight transition categories described in this chapter (*sequence, place, argument, addition, example, similarity, difference,* and *conclusion*). Example: (sequence) She heard a branch break outside her tent. *Then*, she heard an animal breathing.

2. As a group, select a process with which you are all familiar. Explain that process in one paragraph. Begin by selecting one person to write or type while other members of the group explain what to write. Then, generate a process through brainstorming, and create an outline to organize ideas. As you write the paragraph, use transitions as explained in this chapter.

3. Create nine sentences using one of the following pronouns in each sentence: *this, these, that, he, she, it, they, some, one*. Draw lines under the pronouns and the nouns to which they refer. Then draw an arrow from the pronoun to the noun to which it refers. Follow the example provided below.

Abraham Lincoln told stories because <u>he</u> wanted his audiences to understand his points.

TEST (TRUE/FALSE)

1. Transitions are like signposts.
2. Readers are more likely to understand writing that uses transitions than writing that does not use them.
3. Using transitions helps authors to organize ideas.
4. Transitions are not related to the method of development or the organization of a work of writing.
5. No transitional words may be used in more than one transitional category.
6. The transitional word *nevertheless* may be used to show contrast.
7. Most transitional words or phrases may only be placed at the end of a sentence.
8. Repeating key words, pronouns, and sentence patterns provides transitions between sentences for readers.
9. Repeating key words, pronouns, and sentence patterns provides transitions between paragraphs for readers.
10. All transitional words or expressions provide the appropriate tone for all writing situations.

WRITING ASSIGNMENTS

1. Academic Assignment: Visit Literacy Education Online at St. Cloud State University at http://leo.stcloudstate.edu/acadwrite/process.html to learn about process essays. Select a process with which you are all familiar. Explain that process in an essay. Begin by generating a process through brainstorming, and creating an outline to organize ideas. As you write the paragraph, use transitions as explained in this chapter. For assistance in using transitions, visit Harvard's Writing Center at http://www.fas.harvard.edu/~wricntr/documents/Transitions.html.

2. Journal Assignment: Explain everything that you have learned in this chapter: "How does a writer move smoothly from one idea to the next in sentences and paragraphs?"

3. Creative Assignment: Visit The Metropolitan Museum of Art at http://www.metmuseum.org/home.asp and find an image that you like. Create an outline that describes your image (see Chapter 8), and write a first draft by following your outline. Include transitional expressions that are appropriate to your method of development. For tips on writing descriptions, return to Purdue University's Online Writing Lab at http://owl.english.purdue.edu/handouts/general/gl_describe.html.

Chapter 11

How does a writer apply the writing process to the essay exam?

"To write simply is as difficult as to be good."

—Somerset Maugham

LEARNING OBJECTIVES

1. Learn what essay exams are.
2. Learn why essay exams are used.
3. Learn the unique challenges that essay exams impose.
4. Learn strategies for succeeding on essay exams.

PRE-READING QUESTIONS

1. Did you have to take an essay exam to be placed in your current English class?
2. Would you rather write an out-of-class essay or an in-class essay? Why?
3. How do you feel while you are taking an essay exam? What are the difficulties in writing in-class essays or essay exams?
4. What has been your strategy for success on essay exams?
5. How successful has your strategy been? What changes could strengthen it?

WHAT ARE ESSAY EXAMS?

Essay exams are in-class writing tests that require students to respond to a question or writing prompt during a specified amount of time. These exams may range in length from a short paragraph to a multi-paragraph essay. Sometimes students must take an essay exam to be placed in a college English class. Many college classes of all types require students to take essay exams on midterms and finals. Also, many universities now require students to pass an "exit exam" to graduate. In the workplace, employees often must communicate in writing in a specified time, such as a policeman writing a report at the scene of an accident. Since being able to write well under pressure will help you to be successful in these situations, we will explore why essay exams are used, challenges they impose, and strategies for succeeding on them.

WHY ARE ESSAY EXAMS USED?

Most students find taking essay exams more difficult than taking multiple-choice tests; however, many teachers prefer to use essay exams because they display more than a student's knowledge of a subject; they display a student's ability to think and write. For many, the ability to think clearly and logically and to express ideas in writing effectively remains a top priority of education. Some "exit exams," for example, require students to come to a testing site with no knowledge of the question or writing prompt beforehand. These essay exams are writing tests because they simply assess each student's ability to think and write. Essay exams, whether they are testing for writing ability, knowledge of subject matter, or both, carry a lot of weight, partly because teachers can be fairly confident that they are seeing a student's unassisted performance. For these reasons, essay exams will remain a part of education for some time.

Performing well on these tests, furthermore, will remain important for students. In a college class, a grade on an essay exam from a midterm or final can mean the difference between passing and not passing. The results of an "exit exam" can mean the difference between graduating and not graduating. Students who learn how to succeed on essay exams, then, will have a clear advantage over those who do not.

WHAT ARE THE UNIQUE CHALLENGES THAT ESSAY EXAMS IMPOSE?

Essay exams by nature impose several challenges. First, they must be completed in a short period of time. A writing process that might take ten to twelve hours to complete for an out-of-class essay might have to be abbreviated into one hour on an in-class essay. Second, essay exams usually afford no opportunities for assistance in the writing process. Students may not obtain feedback from teachers, tutors, peers, notes, computers, the library, or other resources. The time pressure and the lack of assistance often produce anxiety in students, particularly in those who are not prepared.

WHAT ARE STRATEGIES FOR SUCCEEDING ON ESSAY EXAMS?

Before exploring strategies for succeeding on essay exams, we can recall the four steps of effective writing since successful essay exam writing shares these elements.

1. Make a point
2. Support the point
3. Organize the ideas
4. Present the ideas in error-free sentences

Preparing for the Test

In preparing to produce effective writing on an essay exam, keep the following guidelines in mind:

1. Study in advance. Students who manage their time by preparing for an essay exam for a week before the test will do much better than students who cram the night before the exam. If the exam is designed to test your thinking and writing ability, consult your instructor to learn what writing characteristics he or she expects to see in good essay exams. If the exam is designed to test your knowledge of subject matter, anticipate the test by generating a half-dozen exam questions that could be on the test and writing out your answers to them.

2. Form a study group. The collective ability of a group typically exceeds the ability of an individual. Members of a group can discuss ideas, share notes, create outlines, and prepare practice questions and answers.

3. Read and study actively. Study and memorize the four steps of effective writing above and methods of organizing and presenting ideas (see Chapter 8) that are appropriate to your essay exam. Take notes as you read assigned chapters. Highlight, define, and memorize all key words or concepts in assigned readings.

4. Ask the teacher questions. How many exam questions will be given? How much time will be given to complete the exam? Also, after you review your notes and prepare for the test, take a few questions to your teacher about aspects of the subject that are not clear to you yet. Was the Bill of Rights part of the original Constitution? Did Hamlet regret killing Polonius?

5. Sleep and eat well before the test. Staying up "cramming" until 2 a.m. and eating just a candy bar for breakfast will diminish your ability to perform well. On the other hand, a good night's rest and a balanced meal will enhance your performance.

Taking the Test

While taking the test, keep the following guidelines in mind:

1. Track your time. Take about 15 percent of the allotted time to prepare, 70 percent of the time to write, and another 15 percent to proofread. Unfortunately, many students spend 95 percent of their time writing; that is a mistake. Planning and proofreading can mean the difference between a *C* and an *A*.

2. Read the entire test, and make sure that you understand it. If you do not understand the directions or the emphasis of a prompt, approach your teacher for clarification. Many essay exam questions or writing prompts will have one of the key words listed below, so make sure that you understand their meanings:

Essay Exam Key Words	What It Means
Define	Give the formal meaning of
Describe	Write a detailed account of
Illustrate	Make clear through examples
Explain	Make clear by giving details or reasons
Summarize	Give a brief overview of the main points
Trace	Describe the development of
Discuss	Objectively write about
Discuss the main stages of	Write about the steps in a process
Discuss the effects of	Write about the results of
Discuss the causes of	Write about the persons or things that brought about the result
Compare	Write about the likenesses or similarities of
Contrast	Write about the differences of
Prove	Show how something is true or a fact
Interpret	Give one's own understanding of the meaning of
Analyze	Examine the parts of something to better understand them and how they fit together
Evaluate	Determine the worth or quality of something after considering its strengths and weaknesses

Some essay exam questions, however, will not use one of these key words. When you find such a question, consider which of these words could be used as a substitute. For example, imagine that you received the following question on a writing prompt: What is the message in Frost's "The Road Not Taken?" This question is asking you to interpret this work, to give your own understanding of the meaning of the poem.

3. Sketch a simple list (see Chapter 4) or a simple outline (see Chapter 8) of ideas in the order that they come to your mind before starting the essay.

4. Prioritize the list (see Chapter 8). In other words, decide which ideas to present first, second, third, and so on.

5. Change the question or writing prompt to a topic sentence or thesis statement that includes the key ideas from your prioritized list in the order in which you want to present them, as in the following examples:

Essay Exam Question or Prompt	Topic Sentence or Thesis Statement
Define socialism.	Socialism is a theory of ownership, production, and distribution by the community as opposed to individuals.
Explain the purpose of the League of Nations.	The League of Nations was created to maintain world peace among nations through discussion and agreement.
Discuss an experience that you had while growing up that changed your perspective.	My parents' divorce when I was thirteen changed my perspective about my mom, my dad, and marriage itself.
Summarize the characteristics of the Romantic Movement	The main characteristics of the Romantic Movement were a rejection of neoclassicism through freedom of form, emphasis on creativity, and appreciation for the artist's personality.
Discuss Piaget's stages of human development.	Jean Piaget believed that children progress through four stages of cognitive development.
Compare the male-female relationships in James Joyce's "Eveline" and Ernest Hemingway's "Hills Like White Elephants."	The male-female relationships in Joyce's "Eveline" and Hemingway's "Hills Like White Elephants" are similar in that the couples display an inability to communicate effectively.

6. Support your position with specific details and examples (see Chapters 6 and 7).

7. Default to present tense (see Chapter 18).

8. Write using the five sentence-combining options (see Chapter 16).

9. Write legibly. Writing neatly requires effort and takes time. If your printing is neater than your handwriting, then print on the essay exam. Illegible writing vexes professors and lowers grades.

PRACTICE 1

Underline the essay exam key words in the following writing prompts. Refer to the key words and phrases in the table in this chapter.

Example: <u>Explain</u> the purpose of the NAACP.

1. Describe the events leading up to World War II.
2. Read the article below, and summarize it.
3. Discuss the effects of the computer in education.
4. Compare and contrast the foreign policies of the last two presidents.
5. Read the poem below, and evaluate its theme in relation to contemporary society.

PRACTICE 2

Match the following essay exam key words with their definitions by placing the letter of the definition on the blank line. The first one has been completed as an example.

Essay Exam Key Words	What It Means
1. Define <u>h</u>	a. Write about the steps in a process
2. Describe _____	b. Write about differences
3. Illustrate _____	c. Determine the worth or quality of something after considering its strengths and weaknesses
4. Explain _____	
5. Summarize _____	d. Give a brief overview of the main points
6. Trace _____	e. Make clear by giving details or reasons
7. Discuss _____	f. Show how something is true or a fact
8. Discuss the main stages of _____	g. Examine the parts of something to better understand them and how they fit together
9. Discuss the effects of _____	
10. Discuss the causes of _____	h. Give the formal meaning of
11. Compare _____	i. Write about the persons or things that brought about the result
12. Contrast _____	
13. Prove _____	j. Write about the results
14. Interpret _____	k. Give one's own understanding of the meaning
15. Analyze _____	l. Write a detailed account
16. Evaluate _____	m. Describe the development
	n. Write about the likenesses or similarities
	o. Objectively write about
	p. Make clear through examples

PRACTICE 3

Change the following essay exam questions or writing prompts to topic sentences or thesis statements on a separate piece of paper or on a computer.

Example: What is an important trait in a friend?

> To be a friend, a person must be trustworthy.

1. Discuss whether or not sex education should be taught in public schools.
2. Name someone whom you consider to be a hero or heroine, and explain why you so classify that person.
3. What do you believe are the chief reasons for student academic failure in college? Explain why.
4. Evaluate the use of capital punishment as a means of deterring criminals.
5. Compare the strengths of two good teachers whom you have had during your education.

PRACTICE 4

Decide whether or not the following thesis statements address the essay exam questions. Put a C for correct *when they answer the exam questions and a I for* incorrect *when they do not answer the exam questions. The first one has been completed as an example.*

Example: C̲ Define sharecropping.

Sharecropping involved laborers farming land and dividing the crop evenly with the
land owners.

1. _____ Explain one trait that is essential for parents to have to successfully raise a child.

   Love is an important trait for parents to have as they raise their children, meaning
   that they always have their child's best interest in mind.

2. _____ Compare depictions of a "deferred dream" in "Harlem" and "Island" by Langston Hughes.

   Langston Hughes wrote children's stories, short stories, and novels.

3. _____ Define photosynthesis.

   Photosynthesis involves the reactions of chemical compounds in the presence of
   light.

4. _____ Discuss how Abraham Lincoln won the Republican nomination in 1860.

   Abraham Lincoln's mother died when he was ten years old.

5. _____ Explain blood pressure in the circulation system of humans.

   The heart's contractions force blood to move through the entire circulatory system.

PROOFREADING YOUR ESSAY

When you have time to proofread an out-of-class essay, you check for all of the errors described in Part Three: Rewriting (Chapters 13–23). With so little time during an exam essay, you must focus your proofreading on a few main points. If you need to make a correction, put one line through the word or phrase, and write the correction above the words that have been crossed out. Do not attempt to rewrite the entire essay; you will probably not have time for that. Follow the general guidelines below:

1. Check for a topic sentence or thesis statement that addresses the writing prompt (see Chapter 5).
2. Check for lots of specific details (see Chapter 6).
3. Check for fragments and run-ons (see Chapters 15 and 16).
4. Check for omitted words (see Chapter 14).
5. Check for spelling errors (see Chapter 19).

Spelling, in particular, can be very challenging on essay exams. Remember not to use words that you probably cannot spell correctly like *rendezvous* when you know how to spell an alternative word like *meeting*. Also, do not attempt to use terms which you may have heard but which you do not yet understand like *onomatopoeia*. In other words, become aware of the words that you cannot now spell or use correctly, and avoid them on the essay exam. Finally, do not misspell any words that are on the essay exam handout; this includes words in the directions and writing prompt.

Below is an example of a student's essay exam question, list of ideas, ordering of ideas, underlined thesis statement, and response:

Essay exam prompt: Describe an experience that matured you.

bike race (1)

crash (2)

trophy (5)

stitches (3)

apology (4)

An experience that matured me was when I was racing bikes in a competition. Some kid cut me off. I fell, and the handlebars hit my head and I had to get stitches and stay in the hospital a couple of days. While in the hospital, the kid who I didn't know came to visit me and apologize. He brought with him the trophy he got from the race. He gave it to me and said, "It would have been yours if I hadn't been so greedy." We became good friends and are to this day. It matured me by helping me forgive him and learn that people don't always mean what they do. Sometimes they wish they would not have done it after the outcome.

Adapted from Kyle Johnson

PRACTICE 5

Proofread the following essay exam response by looking for a good topic sentence, plenty of support, fragments, run-ons, omitted words, and misspelled words. Find and fix five errors by inserting words and punctuation. Write on a separate piece of paper or on a computer. The first error has been corrected as an example.

Essay Exam Writing Prompt: Illustrate classical conditioning

experiments

Classical conditioning can be understood through Ivan Pavlov's ~~experiments~~. Pavlov studied the salivation of dogs in his laboratory in Russia. He attached a tube to a dog's mouth. (1) Ran from the dog's mouth to a device that measured the amount of saliva produced. (2) Pavlov then placed food in front of dog and measured the results. (3) At first, he noticed that dogs salivate when food presented. (4) With time, he noticed that dogs began salivating before the food was presented, finally, he noticed that the dogs began salivating just at the sight of Pavlov. (5) Pavlov realized that the dogs were learning to associate him with food, and this kind of learning is called clasical conditioning.

GROUP WORK

1. To reduce anxiety and increase chances of success, discuss and prioritize the three most helpful things that you can do before a test. Then discuss and prioritize the three most helpful things that you can do during a test.

2. Develop five essay exam questions about any subject. Use five different words or phrases from the "essay exam key words" table.

3. Answer one of the essay exam questions as a group; include a list of ideas, prioritize them, write a thesis statement, and compose a one-paragraph answer. Visit the Writing Center at Bowie State University at http://www.bowiestate.edu/academics/english/writingcenter/tips.htm for assistance with writing essay exams.

TEST (TRUE/FALSE)

1. An essay exam is a timed in-class writing test.
2. Essay exams are not a good measure of a student's knowledge of a subject.
3. Essay exams are a good measure of a student's ability to communicate in writing.
4. Essay exams may account for a large percentage of a student's grade in a class.
5. Time constraints and lack of resources during essay exams may produce anxiety in students.
6. Reading actively does not involve writing.
7. Students should ask teachers many questions before the test about material that will be covered.
8. If a student does not understand an essay exam question during a test, he or she should ask the teacher for clarification.
9. *Analyze* means "give one's own understanding of the meaning of" something.
10. When you proofread your essay exam, make sure that your response addresses the question.

WRITING ASSIGNMENTS

1. Academic Assignment: Visit The Writing Center at the University of North Carolina at Chapel Hill at http://www.unc.edu/depts/wcweb/handouts/essay-exams.html for advice on writing essay exams. Then respond to one of the following essay exam prompts that do not require advanced study or research. Follow the guidelines for taking essay exams in this chapter.
   a. Describe a positive experience that you have had some time during your education.

b. Discuss an important parenting trait and illustrate how a parent with this trait would behave in a specific situation.

c. Evaluate the following statement: success comes by working hard long after the initial enthusiasm of something passes.

For additional tips on writing essay exams, visit Sonoma State's Writing Center at http://www.sonoma.edu/programs/writingcenter/pdf_files/essay_exam.pdf.

2. Journal Assignment: Explain everything that you have learned in this chapter: "How does a writer apply the writing process to the essay exam?"

3. Creative Assignment: Visit the National Gallery of Art at http://www.nga.gov/home.htm and find an image that you like. Describe that image in a paragraph or short essay. To practice the skills required for success on essay exams, limit yourself to one page and one hour. Review the strategies in this chapter before you begin. For tips on writing descriptions, return to Purdue University's Online Writing Lab at http://owl.english.purdue.edu/handouts/general/gl_describe.html.

Chapter 12

How does a writer use a computer to write?

"How vain it is to sit down to write when you have not stood up to live!"

— Henry David Thoreau

LEARNING OBJECTIVES

1. Learn why computers are useful to writers.
2. Learn how to find a computer for writing.
3. Learn ways to use a computer in the writing process.
4. Learn strategies for coping with computer challenges.

PRE-READING QUESTIONS

1. Do you prefer writing with a pencil or a computer? Why?
2. Have you taken any computer classes yet? If so, which ones?
3. Where can you use a computer on campus?
4. How have you used a computer in the writing process?
5. What problems have you had while trying to use a computer?

WHY ARE COMPUTERS NEEDED?

Each year, computers become more and more a part of our lives, particularly in education. In writing, computers help us at every stage of the process, and they also save us time and produce legible documents. Experienced writers depend heavily upon their computers, and beginning writers should develop and apply basic computer skills in order to make the most of their educations and prepare to compete for employment. Specifically, students will benefit from learning to type at least thirty to sixty words per minute; this skill can be obtained in a keyboarding class. Students who desire the ability to operate a computer and manage files will benefit from an introductory computer class. Finally, students desiring basic skills in searching and downloading from the Internet will benefit from an introductory Internet class. Students who develop these computer skills early will benefit the most.

HOW CAN YOU FIND A COMPUTER FOR WRITING?

Of course, if you own your own computer or have access to one in your home, you are ready to write. Whether or not you have access to a computer at home, you should be familiar with your campus computer resources because your own computer may break down sometime and, at some point, you may want academic or technical assistance.

 Most campuses have three types of computer labs. Writing centers, the first type of lab, are the most helpful to writing students. Most colleges and universities have a writing center where students can use computers and obtain assistance in all aspects of using computers and writing papers. A second type of computer lab is your library lab. These computers probably will provide you with access to the library holdings (books, magazines, journals, etc.), word processing, and the Internet; however, academic and technical assistance may be limited. Finally, your campus probably provides several general-use computer labs. These will probably at least provide you with word processing and access to the Internet. Technical assistance will probably be available, but academic assistance may not.

PRACTICE 1

Visit a campus computer lab and obtain written answers to the following questions.

1. What are the hours of operation?
2. What software and hardware are available for writing?

3. Do all computers have access to the Internet?
4. Does the campus web page provide links to Online Writing Labs (OWLs)?
5. Must students provide their own printer paper?
6. Must a student bring a student ID to use a computer?
7. Is technical and academic assistance available while writing on computers in the lab?
8. Do computers provide access to library holdings for research?

WHAT ARE THE DIFFERENT WAYS TO USE A COMPUTER IN THE WRITING PROCESS?

A computer can be used at every step of the writing process, and the ways in which computers can assist writers increase every year with new software, hardware, and websites. Of course, not all computers are alike, and because word processing programs differ in features and names of features, consult the Help feature in your word processing program or your lab assistant with specific questions. Despite differences, computers share some common functions that will help writers throughout each step of the writing process.

PREWRITING

1. Writers generate ideas (see *listing, clustering, free writing, journal writing*, and *questioning* in Chapter 4) on a computer. Invention software also assists writers in generating ideas, and many writing centers come equipped with these products. Because generating ideas should happen quickly, the faster you can type, the more productive this stage of prewriting will be on a computer. If you type very slowly, consider generating your ideas with a pen and paper until your typing speed increases. Regardless of the method of generating ideas, never delete unused thoughts. They may prove to be valuable later in the writing process.

2. Writers narrow topics (see *clusters, flowcharts, circle diagrams, topic sentences*, and *thesis statements* in Chapter 5) through word processing and software programs.

3. Writers find specific information to support a thesis statement (see *sources of information* in Chapter 7) through the Internet and computers in the library. Specifically, words can be defined through online dictionaries, ideas can be explored through online encyclopedias, and subjects can be researched through online libraries.

4. Writers organize ideas (see *outline* in Chapter 8) in word processing programs. Writing an outline on a computer affords great flexibility. If, for example, a writer

completes an outline and, after reviewing it, wants to make a global revision by changing the order of the main ideas in the body, this can be accomplished in seconds by cutting and pasting, and without any additional writing. Also, writers can take various information from the Internet and insert it into a word processing document, toggling back and forth until the outline or draft is complete.

WRITING

1. Of course, writers write on computers. The **Help** feature will answer any questions that you have during the process of writing. As you begin to write, **Save** your document on the hard drive if you are at home and on a disk if you are borrowing a computer. If you do not save your document, you will lose it when you turn off your computer. As you **Save** your document, you will need to name it. Use a short name (some computers limit the number of characters that can be used in a file name) that makes sense to you, like "WolfD1" for a paper about an endangered species of wolves (draft #1) in your English class. You will also want to continue to **Save** your document every ten minutes or so to preserve changes as you write.

2. Writers format papers on a computer (see your instructor for specific formatting instructions). Generally, formatting features that you will want to become familiar with include **Page Setup** (set all margins at one inch), **Alignment** (center title and justify left all text), **Font Size** (do not try to compensate for a short paper by using large font; use twelve-point font), and **Line Spacing** (double space to allow room for editing and correcting marks). Indent each paragraph by hitting the **Tab** key or indenting five spaces. Leave two spaces after end punctuation (period, question mark, exclamation point) by using the **Space Bar**.

REWRITING

1. Writers save new drafts. Each time that you revise a draft, **Save** it under a new name like "WolfD2" for a paper about wolves (draft #2). Later, this will allow you to reconsider ideas that have been deleted from your most current draft. Students who do not **Save** their work will make new errors each time that they type a draft from scratch, so their writing will not necessarily improve from one draft to the next.

2. Writers move text around as needed by **Highlighting, Cutting,** and **Pasting** words.
3. Writers insert words by typing them in appropriate places.
4. Writers remove words by **Highlighting** them and using the **Delete** or **Backspace** key.

5. Writers check spelling by running the **Spell Check**. It will give you a list of words from the computer's dictionary that are close in spelling to the word that you misspelled. Select the correctly spelled word to replace the misspelled word. Also, run your **Grammar Check** after writing each draft. Neither your **Spell Check** nor your **Grammar Check** will catch all of the errors in your document, so you will need to proofread your work also.

6. Writers also use the **Thesaurus** and the **Find and Replace**. The **Thesaurus** allows students to use synonyms or a variety of words to discuss one idea, which improves the quality of writing by reducing repetition, such as with overly-used verbs. The **Find and Replace** feature allows students to locate overly-used or incorrectly-used words or phrases in a paper and replace them with precise language.

7. Writers often **Insert** graphics into their documents, such as images from the internet, clip art, word art, charts, graphs, tables, etc.

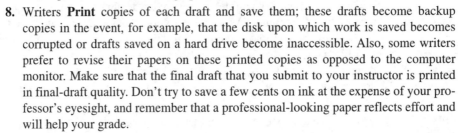
8. Writers **Print** copies of each draft and save them; these drafts become backup copies in the event, for example, that the disk upon which work is saved becomes corrupted or drafts saved on a hard drive become inaccessible. Also, some writers prefer to revise their papers on these printed copies as opposed to the computer monitor. Make sure that the final draft that you submit to your instructor is printed in final-draft quality. Don't try to save a few cents on ink at the expense of your professor's eyesight, and remember that a professional-looking paper reflects effort and will help your grade.

9. When writers have finished writing and saving a draft in a computer lab, they **Exit** the word processing program. This is particularly important because the next student to use the computer will have access to the work if the document and program are left open.

10. Writers use online writing labs (OWLs) throughout the writing process. They provide students with opportunities to obtain information through handouts, to ask questions about any aspect of writing, and to submit papers to online writing coaches for feedback.

11. Finally, writers communicate with their instructors. Most instructors make a point of responding to their e-mail on a regular basis, and you may find that this is an enjoyable and productive means of support throughout the writing process. Remember that no one knows exactly what your professor wants to see in student papers like your professor. Because your professor is monitoring your writing progress throughout the semester, he or she also has a unique perspective—that you cannot get from anyone else—about what you need to focus on to improve your writing.

PRACTICE 2

To generate some potential topics for journal writing, brainstorm a list of a dozen people who have been your best friends throughout your life (see listing *in Chapter 4) on a computer.*

PRACTICE 3

Initiate an online discussion with your instructor about writing by sending him or her a question through e-mail.

WHAT ARE STRATEGIES FOR COPING WITH COMPUTER CHALLENGES?

Man Shoots PC

An Issaquah, Washington, man apparently became frustrated with his personal computer, pulled out a gun and shot it. The computer, located in the man's home office, had four bullet holes in its hard drive and one in the monitor. Police evacuated the man's townhouse complex, contacted the irate PC owner by phone, and persuaded him to come out. "We don't know if it wouldn't boot up or what," says one of the police officers at the scene. (*St. Petersburg Times,* July 20, 1997)

Although computers make the writing process easier than it used to be without them, they also present some challenges. Anticipating these challenges and preparing for them can minimize their effects.

1. Losing a document on a computer or disk can occur for many reasons, like a computer crashing, a disk being damaged, a virus getting into your disk or hard drive, a document not being saved, a document being saved in the wrong place, etc. This frustrates writers because all of the work has to be redone. To avoid this problem, do the following:
   - Know the location where you **Save** the document.
   - **Save** the document in a second location as a back-up.
   - **Save** the document frequently as you write.
   - Store your floppy disk in a case to protect it.
   - **Print** a hard copy of the document as a back-up copy.
   - Install an anti-virus program on your computer.
   - Never open e-mail from an unfamiliar source.
   - Never download something from an unfamiliar source.
   - Make sure that the computers in which you insert your disks are virus free.

2. Not being able to open a document that was written and saved on another computer occurs because not all hardware and software are compatible. If, for example, you write your outline in ClarisWorks® on a Macintosh at your home and you try to open the document in Microsoft Word® on a PC in the computer lab at your college, you will not be able to do it because you are trying to open a document with the wrong software and the wrong hardware. To avoid this problem, keep the following in mind:
   - Plan on using the same computer throughout the writing process.
   - If you need to use more than one computer for writing—and I do not recommend it—check to see that the software and hardware are compatible *before* you start writing.

3. Having misspelled words (see *spelling* in Chapter 19) and incorrect sentences after you run your **Spell Check** and **Grammar Check** is another problem. Of course, your computer cannot correct misspelled words that are simply the wrong words, like when you type "The students left *there* school" and you mean "The students left *their* school." Your computer also cannot catch typographical errors, like when you write "*The* went to the park" and you mean "*He* went to the park." Neither your **Spell Check** nor your **Grammar Check** can correct all of your spelling and grammar errors. To remedy this problem, always proofread your papers carefully for all forms of errors after you run your **Spell Check** and **Grammar Check**.

4. Incorrect information on the Internet is a source of frustration for writers (see *Internet* in Chapter 7). To avoid misinformation in your papers, be selective in the material that you find on the Internet by using information from credible websites. As you search on the Internet, realize that not everything you read will be useful, accurate, or true. Because anyone can post almost anything on the Internet, the Internet is like a swap meet, where some items that you find suit your needs, and others are useless. Most of the material that you find on the Internet has not passed through the rigorous process of publication. For that reason, assess the credibility of each site as you consider the validity of its contents.

5. Finally, taking longer than expected is typical when beginning to use computers, particularly considering the learning curve involved in dealing with computer challenges, software, and hardware. For this reason, planning ahead pays off. Locate a computer on campus, and familiarize yourself with the software and hardware a week or two before an assignment is due. Better yet, take one of the computer classes recommended at the beginning of this chapter the semester before or while taking a class that is writing intensive.

PRACTICE 4

Read "Dreams" and do the following on a computer:

1. Type the poem on a computer.
2. Include your name and the date at the top left.
3. Bold and center the title and poet's name.
4. Double space entire document.
5. Justify left the poem.
6. Make all text twelve point font.
7. Run spell check.
8. Beneath the poem, insert any image of one of your dreams.
9. Name and save document on a disk.
10. Print document.

DREAMS BY LANGSTON HUGHES

Hold fast to dreams
For if dreams die
Life is a broken-winged bird
That cannot fly.

Hold fast to dreams
For when dreams go
Life is a barren field
Frozen with snow.

GROUP WORK

1. As a group, to become acquainted with general rules and guidelines of writing centers, visit the Writing Center at California State University at Northridge at http://www.csun.edu/~hflrc006/faq.html and summarize the answers to ten frequently asked questions (FAQs).

2. As a group, select one writing topic and visit Ohio State University's Writing Center at http://www.cstw.ohio-state.edu/tutor/invent3.htm to learn how to explore and narrow your topic. Plug your topic into the questions asked at this website, and record your answers.

3. As a group, take the quiz "Repairing Run-On Sentences" (1 of 172 quizzes) at Guide to Grammar and Writing at Capital Community Technical College at http://webster.commnet.edu/grammar/quizzes/runons_quiz.htm.

TEST (TRUE/FALSE)

1. Computers can save writers a lot of time.
2. A handwritten paper is easier to read than a typed paper.
3. Writing students should develop basic skills in keyboarding, computer operations, and surfing the Internet.
4. If you have a running computer at home, you do not need to know where the computer labs are on campus.
5. A writing center is the best type of computer lab on campus for writers.
6. If you type very slowly, you should use a computer to generate ideas.
7. You should **Save** your document every forty-five minutes or so.

8. You should not increase your font size to compensate for a short paper.

9. OWLS often allow students to ask tutors questions about writing and obtain feedback on papers.

10. Starting the writing process early on computers will improve the quality of the work.

WRITING ASSIGNMENTS

1. Academic Assignment: Visit the American Psychological Association at http://www.helping.apa.org to learn about a family problem. Then, analyze one family problem, its causes, and its effects. Visit Ohio State University's Writing Center at http://www.cstw.ohio-state.edu/tutor/invent3.htm to learn how to explore and narrow your topic.

2. Journal Assignment: Explain everything that you have learned in this chapter: "How does a writer use a computer to write?"

3. Creative Assignment: Visit the Smith College Museum of Art at http://www.smith.edu/artmuseum/ and find an image that you like. Describe that image in a paragraph or short essay. For tips on writing descriptions, return to Purdue University's Online Writing Lab at http://owl.english.purdue.edu/handouts/general/gl_describe.html.

Chapter 13

How does a writer improve a first draft?

"Success comes by working hard long after the initial enthusiasm of something passes."

— Anonymous

LEARNING OBJECTIVES

1. Learn what revision is.
2. Learn why revision is needed.
3. Learn who may revise a paper.
4. Learn how to revise a paper.

PRE-READING QUESTIONS

1. What is the point in revising a paper?
2. What do you think is involved in revising a paper?
3. What is difficult about revising a paper?
4. How many drafts of a paper do you typically write?
5. Do great writers produce perfect drafts on the first try?

WHAT IS REVISION?

Revision means *re-vision* or to *see again*. When we examine something for a second or third time, we may see things that we did not notice the first time. In writing, revision involves looking at a paper again and again, seeing new things each time, with an eye toward making changes of improvement. The process requires looking at the paper many times because we cannot perceive everything the first time that we examine something.

PRACTICE 1

 What do you see in Figure 13–1? Look at the figure again. Name the two images in Figure 13–1 on a separate piece of paper or on a computer.

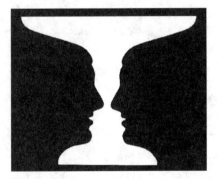

Figure 13–1

Figure 13–2

PRACTICE 2

What do you see in Figure 13–2? Look at the figure again. Name the two images in Figure 13–2 on a separate piece of paper or on a computer.

WHY IS REVISION NEEDED?

No first draft is perfect. The best writers revise; in fact, generally, advanced writers revise more than beginning writers. Some beginning writers believe that a great paper can be produced in one draft, and they see rewriting as an unnecessary chore. Experienced writers, on the other hand, see revision as an opportunity, one that they take every time that they write. Writers with this attitude will find an increase both in enjoyment in writing and in the quality of their work.

WHO REVISES WRITING?

A writer will always spend a significant part of the writing process revising the work; however, others should also be brought into the process. In an academic setting, peers in a writing class, tutors in a writing center, and writing coaches in an online writing lab can all be helpful in providing feedback during the revision stage of writing. Of course, a writer's writing instructor is the best source of feedback because of his or her experience and expertise.

HOW IS A PAPER REVISED?

Before any revision can be done, the writer needs to possess a little humility, the kind of humility that is required in order to apologize about a mistake. Humility is required in order to distance one's self effectively from one's paper, let go of one's ego, "see again" the work from a reader's perspective, and notice errors in one's own work. Writers with this attitude will be comfortable asking the following question: how can this work be improved to more effectively communicate to my readers? The writer assumes, then, that the first draft is imperfect.

Revision or seeing a paper again with the intent of improving it can be viewed as a two-step process. First, the writer will need to focus on global revisions. Second, the writer will need to focus on sentence-level editing. Global revision involves looking at the big picture, the content of the entire paper, what is being said. Perhaps entire paragraphs need to be moved to different sections of the paper. Perhaps an entire paragraph needs to be eliminated. Perhaps a section of the essay needs to be developed in order to make a point.

On the other hand, sentence-level editing involves looking at the small picture, the way in which the ideas in each sentence are expressed, how the ideas are being communicated. A sentence may have a misspelled word, or be a run-on sentence, or display lack of subject-verb agreement. In other words, revising involves modifying the content, and editing involves polishing the product. Although revision may be viewed as a two-step process, in practice the line between the two is often vague. For example, when a writer has finished revising and is involved in the editing process, he or she may "see" that a big change like adding an entire paragraph would make the paper quite a bit better.

The following checklist will guide writers to focus on global revisions first and sentence-level editing last in an attempt to produce effective writing:

REVISION CHECKLIST

Trait #1: Make a Point

Have you made a point in one topic sentence or thesis statement (see Chapter 5)?
Does the point fulfill the purpose of the paper or writing assignment (see Chapter 3)?
Is the topic sentence or thesis statement clear and accurate (see Chapter 5)?

Is the topic sentence or thesis statement strong, interesting, and effective (see Chapter 5)?

Are the point and tone appropriate for the audience (see Chapter 3)?

Does the introduction capture the reader's attention (see Chapter 8)?

Does the essay stick to the point throughout the paper (see Chapter 8)?

Does the conclusion drive home the point (see Chapter 8)?

Trait #2: Support the Point

Do all paragraphs support the point or thesis statement (see Chapter 6)?

Would the point be stronger if some sentences or paragraphs were eliminated (see Chapter 6)?

Would the point be stronger if some sentences or paragraphs were added (see Chapter 6)?

Do any sentences or paragraphs interrupt the flow of thought (see Chapter 10)?

Is a sufficient amount of specific, concrete details, support, facts, examples, illustrations, etc. used to develop each paragraph (see Chapter 6)?

In the essay, does each supporting paragraph have a topic sentence that supports the thesis statement (see Chapter 5)?

What are the strengths of the support (see Chapter 6)?

What are the weaknesses of the support (see Chapter 6)?

Trait #3: Organize the Ideas

Are the ideas in the paper organized according to a logical plan from an outline (see Chapter 8)?

What order for presenting ideas is being used (see Chapter 8)?

Does the essay have an introduction, a body, and a conclusion (see Chapter 8)?

Would the point be stronger if any of the paragraphs were rearranged (see Chapter 8)?

Would the point be stronger if any of the sentences were rearranged (see Chapter 8)?

Do any sentences in one paragraph belong in another paragraph (see Chapter 8)?

Do transitions lead the reader from one sentence to the next and from one paragraph to the next (see Chapter 10)?

Trait #4: Present Ideas in Error-Free Sentences

Have words been chosen well (see Chapter 14)?

Are sentences free of fragments (see Chapter 15)?

Are sentences free of run-ons (see Chapter 16)?

Do the subjects and verbs agree (see Chapter 17)?

Have ESL trouble spots (including incorrect verb use) been avoided (see Chapter 18)?
Have words been spelled correctly (see Chapter 19)?
Have capital letters been used as needed (see Chapter 20)?
Has parallel structure been employed (see Chapter 21)?
Has basic punctuation been used correctly (see Chapter 22)?
Has other punctuation been used correctly (see Chapter 23)?

Now that you know what to look for in the revision process, you are ready to consider the actual steps to take in rewriting a paper.

DIRECTIONS FOR USING THE REVISION CHECKLIST

1. Plan on spending half of the time in the writing process on revision. If, for example, you receive an assignment to turn in a paper in your English class in two weeks, write the paper during the first week in order to give yourself the entire second week for revision.

2. Distance yourself from the paper. Let the paper sit overnight, longer if possible, before reading it. When you do read it for the first time, imagine that you are the audience. Ask yourself the following question: What global changes could be made first? Keep a loose grip on the first draft; in other words, read it *expecting* to see ways in which the paper can be improved.

3. Read a double-spaced, hard copy of the paper *out loud* and *slowly.* This will help you to *see* more than if you read it quickly and silently.

4. Make global revisions first, sentence-level editing second for the same reason that a solid foundation is laid before a house is built. Sentence-level editing builds upon global revision.

5. Mark on the hard copy. Use circles, lines, and arrows to move blocks of text around. Cross out unwanted text with a single line. Insert text with a caret and new text above the line.

 6. After marking on a hard copy, make corrections on your computer, and save this next draft under a new name such as "WolfD2" for a second draft paper about wolves. This will allow you to revisit deleted ideas.

7. Check each one of your corrections by comparing the marked-up hard copy with the text on your monitor. Make additional changes on your computer if necessary and save the changes. Checking corrections is the most overlooked step in the process of rewriting; don't let it be for you because it reflects the extra effort and discipline that creates success.

8. Proofread the paper again by reading it backwards, i.e., from the end to the beginning. This will allow you to engage in sentence-level editing by considering each sentence out of context. Remember that revision involves *seeing again*, and it is im-

possible to see all aspects of the paper in one reading, particularly when reading it from beginning to end. All in all, proofread your paper ten times, answering the ten questions under Trait #4: Present Ideas in Error-Free Sentences.

9. Combine sentences to produce the sentence variety that is typical of mature, college-level writing (see Chapter 16)?

10. Ask peers, tutors, and your instructor to read your paper to give you additional feed-back.

PRACTICE 3

To develop the ability to make global revisions in essays, underline the item in each group that does not belong with the other items.

Example:

1. wood shot
2. iron shot
3. chip shot
4. <u>golf etiquette</u>
5. putting stroke

1.
   a. memory
   b. phone
   c. processor
   d. modem
   e. network

2.
   a. engine mount
   b. igniter
   c. radio
   d. rocket engine
   e. recovery system

3.
   a. tripod
   b. framing
   c. vacation
   d. lighting
   e. recording sound

4.
   a. tinfoil
   b. aircraft
   c. flight
   d. airfoil
   e. altitude indicator

5.
   a. trees
   b. newspaper
   c. pulp mill
   d. paper
   e. rocks

PRACTICE 4

 To develop the ability to engage in sentence-level editing in essays, answer the questions below to demonstrate that you understand how to use the revision checklist. Write on a separate piece of paper or on a computer.

Example:

> *Question:* How much time in the writing process is spent on revision?
> *Answer:* Half of the writing process is spent on revision.

1. How can you distance yourself from your paper?
2. Why read your paper out loud and slowly?
3. Why are global revisions made first?
4. How do you arrange to move text around on a hard copy?
5. Why should new drafts be saved under new names?
6. Why is checking corrections an important habit to develop in the writing process?
7. Why proofread your paper backwards, from end to beginning?
8. How many times should you proofread your paper?
9. Why combine sentences?
10. Why ask others to read your paper?

GROUP WORK

1. As a group, revise the following paragraph by focusing on global revisions. Draw a line through two sentences that do not support the topic sentence.

Dancing is way of expressing for me, and I love to dance. I always liked dancing when I was young; I was taught by my mother. (1) I used to just jump around when i was a young dancer. (2) Then, my mother taut me to dance with my sisters. My mom also taught me how to cook. (3) Although I were embarrassed to dance, I got used to it and danced with my mother and sisters. (4) As I grew older, I got less embarrassed about dancing in front of other people, now I can't stop dancing. (5) For me dancing is a great stress reliever. it takes all my problems away. Exercise also relieves stress. Dancing is a way to express yourself.

Adapted from Jerry Lopez

2. As a group, proofread the paragraph again by reading it backwards, i.e., from the end to the beginning. This will allow you to engage in sentence-level editing by considering each sentence out of context. Correct five errors.

3. As a group, visit the Campus Writing Center at the University of Michigan-Dearborn http://www.powa.org/revifrms.htm, and read and summarize in one paragraph one of their many points on revising writing.

TEST (TRUE/FALSE)

1. Revision means to "see again."
2. Professional writers do not need to revise their work.
3. Revision is an opportunity to improve writing.
4. Peers, tutors, writing coaches, instructors, and OWLs may provide feedback on a paper.
5. Humility does not help in the process of rewriting.
6. In the rewriting process, checking to make sure that a point is made comes before checking for run-on sentences.
7. In the rewriting process, checking for transitions comes before checking for support for a point.
8. Writers should plan on spending one-fourth of their time in the writing process on revision.
9. Papers should be read slowly and silently.
10. Checking corrections is important.

WRITING ASSIGNMENTS

1. Academic Assignment: Visit the U.S. Department of Labor at http://www.bls.gov/oco, and research a professional career that interests you. Compose a plan for entering this career. Include positive aspects of the profession, qualifications, job prospects, salary, functions and responsibilities, and professional organizations, associations, or licenses. For assistance with revision, visit the Online Writing Lab at Gallaudet University at http://depts.gallaudet.edu/englishworks/writing/checkwriting.html.

2. Journal Assignment: Explain everything that you have learned in this chapter: "How does a writer improve a first draft?"

3. Creative Assignment: Visit the Smithsonian Institute at http://www.si.edu/ and find an image that you like. Describe that image in a paragraph or short essay. For tips on writing descriptions, return to Purdue University's Online Writing Lab at http://owl.english.purdue.edu/handouts/general/gl_describe.html.

Chapter 14

Have words been chosen well?

"Vigorous writing is concise. A sentence should contain no unnecessary words, a paragraph no unnecessary sentences, for the same reason that a drawing should have no unnecessary lines and a machine no unnecessary parts."

—William Strunk, Jr.

LEARNING OBJECTIVES

1. Learn what choosing words well involves.
2. Learn why choosing words well is important.
3. Learn how to eliminate slang.
4. Learn how to eliminate clichés.
5. Learn how to eliminate sexist language.
6. Learn how to eliminate wordiness.
7. Learn how to add omitted words.

PRE-READING QUESTIONS

1. Have you ever read something that you couldn't understand? Why couldn't you understand it?
2. Is it appropriate to use slang in college papers?
3. What is a cliché?

4. When you are writing something, do you want to use the most or the least amount of words to communicate?

5. What is missing word from this sentence?

WHAT DOES CHOOSING WORDS WELL INVOLVE?

First, recall the four traits of effective writing:

Trait 1: Make a point.
Trait 2: Support the point.
Trait 3: Organize the ideas.
Trait 4: Present the ideas in error-free sentences.

Now that you have your first draft completed, and you have made global revisions, you can produce more effective writing by improving your word choice. In Chapter 6, you learned how to replace vague and general words with specific, concrete words. In this chapter, you will also learn that using the right words means replacing slang, clichés, sexist language, and wordy phrases with concise and direct language. It means communicating your point clearly, thoroughly, and briefly.

WHY IS CHOOSING WORDS WELL IMPORTANT?

As you read the two paragraphs below, ask yourself two questions. What is the author's point? Which of the two paragraphs demonstrates effective writing?

"If you're not the lead dog, the view never changes." I heard this Zig Ziglar quote when I was in high school; it took me twelve years of corporate life to understand it. Corporate decision makers are usually well-educated individuals making a lot of money. I, unlike many of my co-workers, did not acquire a college degree. I learned quite early that if you don't have a degree, you can't expect to advance; if you don't advance, you can't raise your salary. My wanting to advance in my corporate life, but lacking the education to do so, left me in an incredibly powerless position, and far behind the pack.

Adapted from Reneé Kammrad

A critical initiative beginning in 2000 will involve organizing our internal knowledge, best practices and innovations into an effective knowledge management system. Building upon our proven methodology for continuous quality improvement, Unicorp will combine resources to develop a corporate learning system. The system will assist our professionals in staying abreast of current company goals, objectives and strategies and will enable Unicorp as a whole to provide a higher level of customer service through the sharing of validated knowledge management processes.

http://www.westegg.com/jargon/ (2-26-02)

What makes one paragraph more effective at communicating than another?

Well-chosen words are easy to read, allowing the message to be communicated. On the other hand, poorly-chosen words confuse readers and call attention to themselves as mistakes. They cause the reader to question the writer's ability to communicate, distracting the reader from the writer's point, thus making for less effective writing. Choosing words well also means avoiding several specific categories of words.

HOW DOES A WRITER ELIMINATE SLANG?

Slang is specialized, informal communication understood only by a specific group and often used in oral communication with close friends.

Slang: Jerry won a gold medal; that's dope.
Revised: Jerry won a gold medal; that's fantastic.

Slang: Hey dude! Wassup?
Revised: Hi Mike. How are you doing?

Slang: That surfboard is so tight.
Revised: That surfboard is so nice.

In the last example, what is nice about the surfboard? The color? The size? The shape? The reader does not know because *nice* is vague and abstract. Slang terms and their translations are inherently vague and abstract. To produce good writing, *nice* needs to be replaced with specific and concrete language (see *Guidelines for Using Support* in Chapter 6).

Vague and abstract: That surfboard is so nice.
Revised: The shape of your tri-fin surfboard makes maneuvering on the waves easy.

In most written communication—specifically in college writing—slang is not appropriate or effective. If you notice slang in something that you have written, replace it with formal language that communicates your meaning precisely.

PRACTICE 1

Rewrite the sentences below by replacing slang with formal, precise communication. Write on a separate piece of paper or on a computer. If you do not know the definition of a slang term, consult College Slang Terms at California State Polytechnic University, Pomona at http://www.csupomona.edu/~jasanders/slang/top20.html.

Example:

> Slang: Tonight we'll just kick it.
> Revised: Tonight we will just sit around my living room, watch TV, and relax.

1. My homie and I are going to the beach tomorrow.
2. That movie was bad.
3. We were supposed to meet before the party, but they dissed us.
4. When he couldn't find his wallet, he started trippin'.
5. That was a sweet car.

HOW DOES A WRITER ELIMINATE CLICHÉS?

A cliché is a statement or phrase that has been worn-out by frequent use so that it no longer has originality or freshness. People grow tired of hearing clichés, and writers should replace them with specific, vital details. Notice the clichés in the following sentences.

> Cliché: Harry painted himself into a corner again.
> Revised: Harry's actions have placed him in a difficult position again.
>
> Cliché: The coach's words fell on deaf ears.
> Revised: The coach's words were ignored.
>
> Cliché: Computers are selling like hot cakes.
> Revised: Computers are selling quickly.

If you find any clichés in your writing, replace them with formal, precise communication.

PRACTICE 2

Rewrite the sentences below to replace all clichés with formal, precise communication. Write on a separate piece of paper or on a computer.

Example:

> Cliché: Why are you beating around the bush?
> Revised: Why are you not getting to the point?

1. My boss was obviously having a bad hair day.
2. He will fight the issue in court, and he believes that it ain't over till the fat lady sings.
3. The mayor thought that he could kill two birds with one stone with his speech.
4. The young woman finally saw the light.
5. My friend handed back my essay and suggested that I trim the fat.
6. She worked like a dog.
7. Don't look a gift horse in the mouth.
8. Last but not least, we have Mike.
9. It goes without saying that most kids love to swim.
10. The team was tickled to death about the victory.

HOW DOES A WRITER ELIMINATE SEXIST LANGUAGE?

Language communicates gender, and sexist language demeans men or women—historically women—as in the following examples:

> Sexist Language: When an <u>employee</u> does *his* job well at Furniture Warehouse, *he* will earn a raise.

His and *he* refer to *employee*, but some of the employees at Furniture Warehouse are women, and they earn raises when they do their jobs well also. The sentence does not communicate that fact, which will offend some readers. The sentence can be rewritten to communicate the idea more accurately.

> Revised to refer to either sex: When an employee does *his* or *her* job well at Furniture Warehouse, *he* or *she* will earn a raise.

Although the revised sentence now includes women, some readers will view the construction as clumsy, particularly if *he/she* and *his/her* are used frequently. Furthermore, this construction could still be considered sexist if the *he* and the *his* always precede the *she* and the *hers*.

An alternative that will work in many situations is to change a singular noun like *employee* to a plural noun like *employees*, allowing the writer to use *they* and *their*:

> Revised to refer to both sexes: When employees do *their* jobs well at Furniture Warehouse, *they* will earn raises.

Another option is to reword the sentence so that the problem does not arise:

> Revised to refer to neither sex: A hard-working employee at Furniture Warehouse will earn a raise.

When you come across sexist language with indefinite pronouns (see *indefinite pronouns* in Chapter 17), rewrite the sentence by replacing the indefinite pronoun with a plural noun.

> Sexist Language: When <u>someone</u> does *his* job well at Furniture Warehouse, *he* will earn a raise.

> Revised to eliminate the indefinite pronoun: When <u>employees</u> do *their* jobs well at Furniture Warehouse, *they* will earn raises.

Writers should also be aware of sexist terms or phrases that refer to groups that do not include women. These terms promote sexist stereotypes and should be replaced with non-sexist terms:

Sexist Terms	Non-sexist Terms
Best man for the job	Best person for the job
Businessman or businesswoman	Business executive
Chairman	Chairperson
Clergyman	Minister
Congressman or congresswoman	Member of congress
Fireman	Firefighter
Mailman	Mail carrier
Man-hours	Work-hours
Mankind	People
Policeman or policewoman	Police officer
Salesman	Salesperson
Workman	Worker
Waiter or waitress	Food server

For additional information on avoiding sexist language, see the "Guidelines for Nonsexist Use of Language" by the National Council of Teachers of English at http://www.ncte.org/positions/nonsex.html.

PRACTICE 3

Rewrite the sentences below to replace all sexist language with non-sexist language. Write on a separate piece of paper or on a computer.

Example:

> Sexist: War has a devastating effect on mankind.
> Revised: War has a devastating effect on humanity.

1. Education should be available to the common man.
2. The fireman parked his truck at the park.
3. The average citizen will cast his vote against raising taxes.
4. Give each customer her change quickly.
5. When a swimmer asks his coach for advice, he usually gets it.
6. A student's attitude will determine his future.
7. When each person carries his weight, the work will end quickly.
8. Each speaker explained his views.
9. The job will take twenty man-hours.
10. Everyone should express his opinion.

HOW DOES A WRITER ELIMINATE WORDINESS?

Wordiness involves using more words than are needed to communicate a point effectively, and it can be broken into three categories: redundant language, flowery language, and wordy language.

Redundant Language

In Chapter 10, we discussed the fact that repetition may provide a needed transition for the reader in following a writer's ideas from one sentence to the next or from one paragraph to the next. Such repetition is positive and serves a purpose in effective writing. When repetition is overly used or serves no purpose, it becomes redundant:

Redundant: The policeman pulled us over to give us a ticket. We had to pull over so he could write us up.

Revised: The policeman pulled us over to give us a ticket.

Notice how the second sentence provides no new information; it is just saying the same message using different words. This is redundant, and it annoys the readers by wasting their time since the entire second sentence is unnecessary. When you see redundancy in your writing, delete it.

Flowery Language

Flowery language appears when writers overly use adjectives and adverbs. To avoid this problem, focus on nouns and verbs, not their assistants, adjectives and adverbs. Notice how the flowery language in the following example has been revised:

Flowery: A *dozen, somber* people listened *intently* to the *horrific, tall* tale of the *elderly* gentleman.

Revised: The jury concentrated on the testimony of the witness.

When you notice flowery language in your writing, decrease your use of adjectives and adverbs, and focus on nouns and verbs.

Wordy Language

Wordy language simply involves using more words than are needed to communicate an idea effectively.

Incorrect: The fact of the matter is that at this point in time he is a man who loves computers due to the fact that he grew up playing computer games.

Revised: Now he loves computers because he grew up playing computer games.

Replace wordy language with concise language, as in the table below:

Wordy (stuffy, inflated)	Concise (short, edited)
A large number of	Many
Along the lines of	Like
As a matter of fact	In fact
As a result of	Because
At this point in time	Now
Blue in color	Blue

Wordy (stuffy, inflated)	Concise (short, edited)
Due to the fact that	Because
He is a man who	He
In order to	To
In spite of the fact that	Although
In the event that	If
In the neighborhood of	About
In this day and age	Today
In this paper I will show that Mr. Hays is responsible for Neil's death.	Mr. Hays is responsible for Neil's death. (*just make your point*)
Large in size	Large
Repeat again	Repeat
Six in number	Six
The fact of the matter is that escape was impossible.	Escape was impossible. (*just make your point*)
The reason why is that	Because
Until such time as	Until

PRACTICE 4

Rewrite the sentences below to replace redundant, flowery, and wordy language with concise language. Write on a separate piece of paper or on a computer.

Example:

> Redundant and Wordy: At this point in time, compare the gasoline engine to the diesel engine by looking at the similarities between each type of engine.
> Revised: Now compare the similarities of the gasoline engine and the diesel engine.

1. Playing sports may help someone to lose weight, and playing sports burns calories.
2. Plant your garden in the spring. March is a good time to put most seeds in the ground.
3. Psychologists have studied human behavior, so they have some understanding about how people behave.
4. Two beautiful birds fly annually vast distances to visit their brisk winter feeding grounds.
5. Job-related issues were talked about extensively at the three-day conference in sunny San Diego.
6. Intelligent communication with smart dogs will successfully result in a mutually-beneficial relationship between content dog and pleased dog owner.

7. The fact of the matter is that snowboards are popular due to the fact that they are fun in this day and age.

8. In this paper I will show that at this point in time domestic violence has increased as a result of poverty.

9. In the neighborhood of two thousand sea turtles were drowned due to the fact that fishing nets trapped them.

10. As a result of the length of the course, many skiers at this point in time are struggling in order to finish.

HOW DOES A WRITER ADD OMITTED WORDS?

Seeing where words have been omitted is simply a matter of proofreading, and it is necessary because missing words in sentences annoy and confuse readers. Words that are often left out of sentences include: *a, an, the, of,* and *to*.

PRACTICE 5

Proofread the paragraph below from Always Running *by Richard Rodriguez for omitted words (a, an, the, of, to), and insert them as you rewrite the paragraph on a separate piece of paper or on a computer.*

(1) But "family" is a farce among propertyless and disenfranchised. (2) Too many families are wrenched apart, as even children are forced supplement meager incomes. Family can only really exist among those who can afford one. (3) In increasing number of homeless, poor, and working poor families, the things that people must do to survive undermines most family structures. (4) At a home for troubled youth on Chicago's South Side, for example, I met 13-year-old boy who was removed from his parents after police found him selling chewing gum at bars and restaurants without a peddler's license. (5) I recall at the age nine my mother walking me to the door, and, in effect, saying: Now go forth and work. (p. 250)

GROUP WORK

1. Visit California State Polytechnic University, Pomona at http://www.csupomona.edu/~jasanders/slang/top20.html to see slang words frequently-used on college campuses. Select five slang terms, create original sentences using the slang terms, and then rewrite those five sentences to eliminate the slang.

2. As a group, generate five sentences of clichés not used in this chapter; then, rewrite those five sentences to eliminate the clichés.

3. As a group, generate three sentences with sexist language; then, rewrite those three sentences with non-sexist language.

TEST (TRUE/FALSE)

1. Slang may distract your readers from your point, making your writing less effective.
2. Saying, "Thanks, dude" is an example of a cliché.
3. "The coach was as sick as a dog" is an example of slang.
4. "When anyone earns an *A* in class, the teacher gives him a candy" is sexist.
5. There is only one way to revise a sexist sentence.
6. "Gentlemen of the jury" is a sexist phrase when the jury contains women.
7. Redundant language is language in which an idea is repeated needlessly.
8. Flowery language relies too heavily upon adjectives and adverbs.
9. Replacing "in the neighborhood of" with "about" makes writing more concise.
10. "Too" is a word that is frequently omitted.

WRITING ASSIGNMENTS

1. Academic Assignment: Visit the Rock and Roll Hall of Fame and Museum at http://www.rockhall.com, and examine the challenges and success of one rock band or musical group in an essay. Begin by researching the group of your choice. For assistance with avoiding clichés, visit the University of Richmond at http://www.csupomona.edu/~jasanders/slang/top20.html. Visit the Writing Center at Hamilton College at http://www.hamilton.edu/ACADEMIC/resource/wc/AlternToSexistLang.html for assistance with avoiding sexist language.

2. Journal Assignment: Explain everything that you have learned in this chapter: "Have words been chosen well?"

3. Creative Assignment: Visit the University of Notre Dame's Snite Museum of Art at http://www.nd.edu/~sniteart/97/main3.html and find an image that you like. Describe that image in a paragraph or short essay. For tips on writing descriptions, return to Purdue University's Online Writing Lab at http://owl.english.purdue.edu/handouts/general/gl_describe.html.

Chapter 15

Are sentences free of fragments?

"I've been to a lot of places and done a lot of things, but writing was always first. It's a kind of pain I can't do without."

— Robert Penn Warren

LEARNING OBJECTIVES

1. Learn what a sentence is.
2. Learn what fragment sentences are and why they should be eliminated.
3. Learn the four types of fragment sentences.
4. Learn two ways to correct fragment sentences.
5. Learn how to recognize and correct fragments in your own writing.
6. Learn why and when professional writers sometimes use fragments.

PRE-READING QUESTIONS

1. What do you think a fragment is?
2. Would you be content with a fragment of a gold cup if the entire cup were available to you?
3. Which of the following sentences is a fragment?
   a. Without going to college before entering the workforce.
   b. Jack ran home.
4. What is the consequence of writing in sentence fragments?
5. How do you fix a fragment?

WHAT IS A SENTENCE?

Independent Clauses

To understand what a fragment is, writers must understand what a sentence is. The sentence is the basic unit for expressing ideas in English. Each simple sentence is made up of at least two smaller parts, a subject and a verb, which combine to express one idea, and that sentence can stand alone. "Jesus wept," the shortest verse in the Bible (John 11:35), provides an example of a sentence in its simplest form. It contains a subject and a verb. Since it also expresses an idea and can stand alone, it qualifies as a complete sentence or independent clause.

In order to be able to tell if a group of words is actually a sentence, writers need to be able to see subjects and verbs in sentences. To find the subject, ask the following question: who or what is the sentence about? In the example from the Bible, the sentence is about Jesus, so *Jesus* is the subject. To find the verb, ask the following question: what is the sentence saying about the subject? In the example, the sentence is telling the readers that the subject wept, so *wept* is the verb.

Independent clause: Jesus (subject) wept (verb).

Notice that the subject came first, the verb came second, and that they were right next to each other; that is often the case, even in longer sentences. Of course, not all sentences are this easy to analyze. Some sentences have more than one subject:

Independent clause: *John* and *Erica* ran across the field.

Some sentences have more than one verb:

Independent clause: John *ran* across the field and *climbed* the bleachers.

Some sentences have more than one subject and more than one verb:

John and *Erica* *ran* across the field and *climbed* the bleachers.

Of course, sentences can be combined and become more complicated still (see *compound sentences* and *complex sentences* in Chapter 16).

Furthermore, verbs come in two forms: active verbs and linking verbs. Active verbs show action, as their name suggests:

Independent clause: *John* *ran* across the field.

Running across a field shows action.

Linking verbs, on the other hand, connect or link the subject of a sentence with a descriptive word or words:

Independent clause: John _is_ honest.

_Is_ connects _John_, the subject, to _honest_, a descriptive word. Forms of _be_ are often linking verbs: _be, am, is, are, was, were, being, been, will be, has been._ Other words like _act, appear, become, feel, get, grow, look, make, prove, remain, seem, smell, sound_, and _taste_ also serve as linking verbs when they connect or link the subject of a sentence with a descriptive word or words.

Independent clause: Amanda _appears_ happy.

You need to understand the two verb forms so that you can determine if a sentence has both a subject and a verb and can qualify as a complete sentence, an independent clause.

PRACTICE 1

Underline the subject once and the verb twice in the following sentences. More than one subject and verb may exist. Verbs may be action verbs or linking verbs.

1. Mark skated across the rink.

2. The microphone rested on the table.

3. Poisonous plants lined the path.

4. Circles and squares are on the cover of the book.

5. I visited a chiropractor and a physician.

6. Plants and animals of all types live in the forest.

7. He washed, ironed, and pressed his clothes.

8. Indian artifacts and Indian games are at the museum.

9. Jason, Patricia, and Claudia found, caught, and labeled the insects.

10. The girl appears happy and seems intelligent.

When a student of writing looks at a sentence, he or she sometimes mistakenly thinks that the subject is in a prepositional phrase. Since subjects and verbs are never in prepositional phrases, writers need to be able to spot them so that they can look elsewhere to find the subject and the verb.

A prepositional phrase is a group of words in a sentence that starts with a preposition and answers one of three questions: What? When? or Where? In other words, prepositional phrases provide more information about the idea being expressed in the sentence by showing relationships of type, time, and space.

Find the prepositional phrase in the following sentence:

John rode his bike through the park.

Where did John ride his bike? He rode his bike *through the park*. In other words, *through the park* is a prepositional phrase that describes the spatial relationship of John and the park. Notice the prepositions in the table below.

Common Prepositions

About	Behind	During	Of	Till (Until)
Above	Below	Except	Off	To
Across	Beneath	For	On	Toward
After	Beside	From	Onto	Under
Against	Besides	In	Out	Unfit
Among	Between	Inside	Outside	Up
Around	Beyond	Into	Over	Upon
At	By	Like	Through	With
Before	Down	Near	Throughout	Without

PRACTICE 2

First, cross out prepositional phrases so that you may easily find the subjects and verbs. Then, underline the subject once and the verb twice. More than one subject and verb may exist. Verbs may be action verbs or linking verbs.

1. The stars in the sky are bright at night in the desert.

2. The heart pumps blood throughout the body.

3. The crew performs routine maintenance on the craft at the airport.

4. In the spring track events are held at the stadium near the gym.

5. In France nuclear power plants produce much energy.

6. Vinyl and rubber are used extensively in the automotive industry.

7. Hiking in the mountains fifteen miles each day conditions the legs.

8. Training, salary, and working conditions will be discussed during the conference.

9. The restroom for the fitness center is on the first floor of the gym.

10. The snow fell throughout each day from the beginning of the week until the end of the week.

Now that you understand that a sentence has a subject, a verb, and can stand alone to express an idea, do not break sentences part.

WHAT ARE FRAGMENT SENTENCES, AND WHY SHOULD THEY BE ELIMINATED?

A fragment is a broken, detached part of something; it's incomplete. A sentence fragment is a part of a sentence that is masquerading as a complete sentence. In other words, it is less than a sentence because something is missing; however, it is punctuated as if it were a complete sentence, starting with a capital letter and probably ending with a period.

Imagine that a friend walked up to you and said, "To the beach." That's it, no more, no less, just, "To the beach." How would you respond to that? You might lean forward, putting your hand to your ear, saying, "Excuse me?" or "What did you say?" or "What about the beach?" You might guess about your friend's intention: "Did you go to the beach yesterday?" or "Are you asking me if I want to go to the beach now?" The reason that you would do and say these things is that your friend spoke in a fragment, an incomplete sentence that lacks enough information to communicate effectively.

Beginning students of writing typically write a few fragment sentences in their first drafts because they are focusing on expressing ideas—and rightly so. The writer's task, then, is to find and correct fragments in the revision process so that the writing does not confuse, frustrate, or irritate the reader.

WHAT ARE THE FOUR TYPES OF FRAGMENTS, AND HOW DO WRITERS CORRECT THEM?

1. **Fragment sentence with a missing subject.**

   Consider the following example:

   Example: <u>Mike works</u> hard in school. <u>Is</u> a good student.

   The reader lacks information, and the following question needs to be answered: who or what is the sentence about? If the sentence is about Mike, then Mike is the subject of the sentence. Even though the reader could probably guess that the sentence is about Mike, a pronoun like *he* must be inserted into the fragment for it to become a sentence and to reduce potential confusion for the reader. Two main methods of correcting fragments exist:
   1. Change the fragment into a dependent clause.
   2. Incorporating the fragment into a nearby sentence.

   Revised with method 1: <u>Mike works</u> hard in school. <u>He is</u> a good student.

   Or, the two sentences can be combined using one subject and two verbs.

   Revised with method 2: <u>Mike works</u> hard in school and <u>is</u> a good student.

2. **Fragment sentence with a missing verb.**

   Consider the following example:

   Example: <u>Clara</u> and <u>Sheryl eating</u> healthy foods. <u>They have lost</u> 10 pounds.

   The reader lacks information, and the following question needs to be answered: what is the sentence saying about Clara and Sheryl? If the sentence is saying that Clara and Sheryl eat healthy foods, then the verb *are* needs to be added.

   Revised with method 1: <u>Clara</u> and <u>Sheryl are eating</u> healthy foods. <u>They have lost</u> 10 pounds.

   Or, the fragment can be attached to the sentence in a couple of ways: first, by attaching it with a comma **before** the sentence.

   Revised with method 2: <u>Eating</u> healthy foods at work, <u>Clara</u> and <u>Sheryl have lost</u> 10 pounds.   insert comma ↗

   Or, by attaching the fragment **after** the sentence.

   Revised with alternative method 2: <u>Clara</u> and <u>Sheryl have lost</u> 10 pounds by eating healthy foods at work.

3. **Fragment sentence with a missing subject and verb.**

   Consider the following four types of fragments with missing subjects and verbs. The first type is the **prepositional phrase fragment sentence**.

Example: The <u>monitor</u> <u>connects</u> to the hard drive. At the back of the computer.

The reader lacks information when reading the fragment by itself, and the following question needs to be answered: who or what is the sentence about? and what is the sentence saying about the subject?

Revised with method 1: The <u>monitor</u> <u>connects</u> to the hard drive. <u>It</u> <u>attaches</u> at the back of the computer.

Revised with method 2: The <u>monitor</u> <u>connects</u> to the hard drive at the back of the computer.

The second type is the **ing-fragment sentence**. This type of phrase starts with a verb + ing.

Example: The <u>firefighter</u> <u>saw</u> the accident. Running down the street.

The reader lacks information when reading the fragment by itself, and the following question needs to be answered: who or what is the sentence about? and what is the sentence saying about the subject? This can be corrected by adding a subject and a verb.

Revised with method 1: The <u>firefighter</u> <u>saw</u> the accident. <u>He</u> <u>was</u> running down the street.

This can also be corrected by joining the fragment to the sentence. Place the fragment before the subject, and set it off with a comma.

Revised with method 2: Running down the street, the <u>firefighter</u> <u>saw</u> the accident.
        insert comma ↗

When using the second method in this situation, make sure that the subject of the sentence is also the subject of the ing-fragment.

Incorrect use of method 2: Running down the street, the <u>accident</u> <u>was seen</u> by the firefighter.

Who or what is doing the running? The sentence above states that the accident is doing the running. This error is called a dangling modifier. To correct this problem, the subject of the ing-fragment needs to appear first as the subject of the sentence.

Revised with method 2: Running down the street, the <u>firefighter</u> <u>saw</u> the accident.
        insert comma ↗

The third type is the **to-fragment sentence**. This type of phrase starts with *to* + a verb.

Example: The <u>girl</u> <u>ran</u> down to the dock. To jump into the lake.

The reader lacks information when reading the fragment by itself, and the following question needs to be answered: who or what is the sentence about? and what is the sentence saying about the subject? This can be corrected by adding a subject and a verb.

Revised with method 1: The <u>girl</u> <u>ran</u> down to the dock. <u>She</u> <u>jumped</u> into the lake.

Revised with method 2: The <u>girl</u> <u>ran</u> down to the dock to jump into the lake.

The fragment may also be placed in front of the sentence and set off with a comma because it is introductory material.

Revised with alternative method 2: To jump into the lake, the <u>girl</u> <u>ran</u> down to the dock.
insert comma ↗

The fourth type is the **added-detail fragment sentence**, which includes examples, explanations, lists, etc. This type of phrase may start with any one of the words below.

Words that Commonly begin Added-Detail Phrases

About	Except	Like	Such as
Also	For example	Mainly	That is
Among	For instance	Namely	Without
And	From	Not even	
But	In addition	Or	
Especially	Including	Particularly	

Example 1: The <u>clerks</u> <u>check</u> items quickly. Especially at the end of their shifts.

The reader lacks information when reading the fragment by itself, and the following question needs to be answered: who or what is the sentence about? and what is the sentence saying about the subject? As you can see from the following examples, method 1 is redundant, so method number 2 is preferred.

Revised with method 1: The <u>clerks</u> <u>check</u> items quickly. <u>They</u> <u>check</u> items quickly, especially at the end of their shifts.

Revised with method 2: The <u>clerks</u> <u>check</u> items quickly, especially at the end of their shifts.
insert comma ↗

Example 2: <u>Amanda</u> <u>bought</u> new clothes for her daughter. One t-shirt, two dresses, two pairs of jeans, and three pairs of shoes.

The reader lacks information when reading the fragment by itself, and the following question needs to be answered: who or what is the sentence about? and what is the sentence saying about the subject? Again, as you can see from the following corrections, method 1 is redundant, so method 2 is preferred.

Revised with method 1: <u>Amanda</u> <u>bought</u> new clothes for her daughter. She bought one t-shirt, two dresses, two pairs of jeans, and three pairs of shoes.

Revised with method 2: <u>Amanda</u> <u>bought</u> new clothes for her daughter: one t-shirt, two dresses, two pairs of jeans, and three pairs of shoes.
insert colon before list ↗

PRACTICE 3

Read the sentences pairs below, and revise the one that is a fragment using one of the methods described in this chapter. Write on a separate piece of paper or on a computer.

1. We painted the birdhouse white. Keeps the birds cool in the summer.
2. The servant bowed. He showing reverence for the king.
3. They ate nutritious foods. During breakfast, lunch, and dinner.
4. Walking through the park. A flock of doves was seen by a couple.
5. The seagulls surrounded the fish. Squawking the entire time.
6. The family raised enough money. To take a vacation to Hawaii.
7. To lose weight. He ran three miles per day.
8. The laborers work hard every day. Except for Larry.
9. She hates eating vegetables. Especially broccoli.
10. He reads everything he can find. Such as books, magazines, newspapers, etc.

   4. Fragment sentence that is a dependent clause.

Relative Clauses

A dependent clause that begins with a relative pronoun is a relative clause. Relative clauses have both a relative pronoun and a verb; however, they cannot stand alone.

Chart of Relative Pronouns

That	Which	Who (Whom, Whose)

Incorrect: <u>Kathy</u> <u>loves</u> her first-place medal. *Which* <u>is</u> *gold.*

Which makes the second word group a fragment. The relative clause can either be separated from the first sentence or combined to it. If it is combined to it, it may appear in the middle or at the end of the independent clause.

Revised with method 1: <u>Kathy</u> <u>loves</u> her first-place medal. <u>It</u> <u>is</u> gold.

Revised with method 2: <u>Kathy</u> <u>loves</u> her first-place medal, *which* <u>is</u> gold.
                                                        insert comma ➚

Revised with method 2: <u>Kathy</u> <u>loves</u> her first-place medal, *which* <u>is</u> gold,
more than the other medals.
                                                   insert two commas ➚

To use a relative clause correctly, do the following:

- Identify the word to which *that, which,* or *who* refers.
- Place the relative pronoun immediately next to the word that it is modifying.
- Make sure that the verb agrees with the relative pronoun (relative pronouns may be either singular or plural).
- Set off non-essential (nonrestrictive) relative clauses with commas.

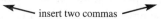

Incorrect: <u>Dr. Volt</u> <u>conducted</u> the experiment. W<u>ho</u> <u>are</u> *about to retire.*

Revised: <u>Dr. Volt</u>, *who* (singular) *is about to retire*, <u>conducted</u> the experiment.

insert two commas

Relative clauses that are essential (restrictive) to the meaning of the sentence require no commas. In other words, the relative clause that identifies a person or thing by distinguishing it from other people or things is not set off with commas.

Incorrect: Cars, *that have a solar panel,* require no gas.

Revised: Cars *that have a solar panel* require no gas.

The relative clause *that have a solar panel* is essential because one would not say, "Cars require no gas." Since that information is essential to understanding the sentence, commas do not set off the relative clause.

Set off relative clauses that are not essential to the meaning of the sentence (non-restrictive) with commas.

Incorrect: Jasmine's mother *who lives in Michigan* will visit us this summer.

Revised: Jasmine's mother, *who lives in Michigan*, will visit us this summer.

insert commas

The relative clause *who lives in Michigan* is not essential to the meaning of the sentence since the reader understands without the relative clause exactly who will be visiting during the summer (Jasmine's mother). As a result, commas set off the relative clause.

That is often used in restrictive clauses while *which* and *who* are often used in non-restrictive clauses.

Notice that *who* refers to people, *which* refers to things, and *that* refers to either people or things.

PRACTICE 4

Read the sentence pairs below, and revise the one that is a fragment using one of the methods described in this chapter. Write on a separate piece of paper or on a computer.

1. The man gave me a brochure. Who is standing behind the counter.
2. Our minister welcomed us. Who wore a black robe.
3. The first advertisement was distasteful. Which interrupted our show.
4. That were on the second shelf. The books fell onto us.
5. Which I have had for ten years. My only flashlight stopped working.

Subordinate Clauses

A second type of dependent clause is a subordinate clause, and it begins with a subordinate conjunction. Subordinate clauses have both a subject and a verb; however, they—like relative clauses—cannot stand alone.

Chart of Subordinate Conjunctions

After	As soon as	Ever since	Once	Though	Whenever
After all	As though	How	Provided that	Till	Where
Afterward	Because	If	Rather than	Unless	Whereas
Although	Before	In order that	Since	Until	Wherever
As	Even though	Just as	So	What	Whether
As if	Even if	Just as if	So that	Whatever	While
As long as	Even since	Now that	Than	When	Why

Example: The artist received a scholarship. Because she draws beautiful images.

Because makes the second word group a fragment. Since the fragment describes the reason for the scholarship, it begs to be connected to the preceding sentence, so correction method 2 is better than method 1.

Revised with method 1: The artist received a scholarship. She draws beautiful images.

Revised with method 2: The artist received a scholarship because she draws beautiful images.

The fragment may also be connected before the adjacent sentence, but a comma must be inserted (see Chapter 16).

Revised with alternative method 2: Because the artist draws beautiful images, she received a scholarship.   insert comma ↗

PRACTICE 5

Read the sentence pairs below, and revise the one that is a fragment using one of the methods described in this chapter. Write on a separate piece of paper or on a computer.

1. Because she drives quickly. She gets a ticket every month or two.
2. The parents paid the babysitter. When they came home.
3. While attending school. He works at a restaurant.
4. The pioneers walked long distances. Since cars were not available.
5. The crowd went crazy. After Joe hit a grand slam.

Summary

The following table summarizes correcting fragments by providing examples, comments, and corrections of the four main types of fragments.

Correcting Fragment Sentences

Type of Fragment	Example	Comment	Correction
Missing Subject	John loves to jog on the sand. Runs at the beach.	Who runs at the beach? Add a subject to correct the fragment, or attach the fragment to a sentence.	Method 1 (change the fragment into a complete sentence): John loves to jog on the sand. He runs at the beach.
			Method 2 (attach the fragment to another sentence): John loves to jog on the sand at the beach.
Missing Verb	I will meet you there. Jennifer's house behind the park.	What is the sentence saying about the house? Explain that the house exists behind the park by adding a verb, or attach the fragment to a sentence.	Method 1 (change the fragment into a complete sentence): I will meet you there. Jennifer's house is behind the park.
			Method 2 (attach the fragment to another sentence): I will meet you at Jennifer's house behind the park.

(continued)

Correcting Fragment Sentences (*continued*)

Type of Fragment	Example	Comment	Correction
Missing Subject and Verb	<u>Carmen</u> <u>runs</u> every day. Over the hill.	Who or what is the sentence about? What is the sentence saying about the subject? Add a subject and verb, or attach the fragment to a sentence.	Method 1 (change the fragment into a complete sentence): <u>Carmen</u> <u>runs</u> every day. <u>He</u> <u>jogs</u> over the hill. Method 2 (attach the fragment to another sentence): <u>Carmen</u> <u>runs</u> every day over the hill.
Dependent Clause	Because <u>Leslie</u> <u>crashed</u> her car. <u>She</u> <u>needs</u> a new one.	What is the consequence of the car crash? Drop the dependent word (*because*) from the fragment, or attach the fragment to a sentence (see Chapter 16).	Method 1 (change the fragment into a complete sentence): <u>Leslie</u> <u>crashed</u> her car. <u>She</u> <u>needs</u> a new one. Method 2 (attach the fragment to another sentence): Because <u>Leslie</u> <u>crashed</u> her car, <u>she</u> <u>needs</u> a new one.

HOW DO WRITERS RECOGNIZE AND CORRECT FRAGMENTS IN THEIR OWN WRITING?

With practice, recognizing and correcting fragments will become second nature. Until then, use the following guidelines to develop this ability.

Guidelines for recognizing fragments in your own writing.

1. Read your paper aloud from end to beginning. This will cause each fragment to stand out because you are reading each word group in isolation, not with related ideas. Reading aloud will also help you to develop the ability to hear an incomplete sentence. Does each sentence make sense when it stands alone?

2. Identify the subject and verb in each sentence. By asking yourself two questions (who or what is the sentence about? and what is the sentence saying about the subject?) you will be able to determine if each sentence has a subject and verb. Put one line under each subject, two lines under each verb, and cross out any prepositional phrases that might confuse you. ESL Warning: English does not allow the subject or the verb to be missing, as is the case in some languages. An exception to this would be in commands: Do not enter!

3. Be suspicious of all short sentences. Although a sentence may only consist of two words, many short sentences in student writing turn out to be incomplete sentences.

4. Double check all sentences beginning with a relative pronoun or a subordinating conjunction. Is the dependent word group attached to an independent word group. In other words, can each word group stand alone?

5. Computer warning: Remember that grammar checks will catch many fragments, but they will miss some and incorrectly label some good sentences as fragments. As a result, you must also check each sentence yourself.

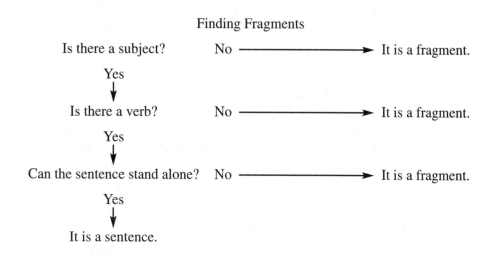

Finding Fragments

Is there a subject?	No ⟶	It is a fragment.
Yes ↓		
Is there a verb?	No ⟶	It is a fragment.
Yes ↓		
Can the sentence stand alone?	No ⟶	It is a fragment.
Yes ↓		
It is a sentence.		

Correcting Fragments

Method 1	Method 2
Change the fragment into a dependent clause.	Incorporating the fragment into a nearby sentence.

WHY AND WHEN DO PROFESSIONAL WRITERS USE FRAGMENTS?

You should realize that professional writers will occasionally use fragments in their writing, and you may notice fragments used sparingly in published works like books and magazines. These fragments, however, are written intentionally for effect, typically in descriptive or narrative writing, particularly in dialogue. Students of writing should develop the ability to see and correct fragments before they attempt to use them in their writing. Certainly, avoid fragments in all formal and academic writing.

GROUP WORK

1. As a group, show that you understand fragments by creating one example of each of the four main types of fragments; then, correct each fragment with one of the methods described in this chapter.

2. As a group, create three sentences with relative clauses and three sentences with subordinate clauses. Review dependent clauses in this chapter to avoid writing fragments.

3. As a group, visit Capital Community College at http://webster.commnet. edu/cgi-shl/quiz.pl/fragments_add1.htm?cgi_quiz_form=1 and take their online quiz on fragments.

TEST (TRUE/FALSE)

1. Each simple sentence is made up of at least two smaller parts, a subject and a verb, which combine to express one idea, and that sentence can stand alone.
2. An independent clause may have more than one subject and verb.
3. Linking verbs show action.
4. *Against* is a preposition.
5. A sentence without a subject is a fragment.
6. A fragment may be changed into a dependent clause.
7. A fragment cannot be incorporated into a nearby sentence.
8. A fragment may have a missing subject and verb.
9. Set off non-essential (nonrestrictive) relative clauses with commas.
10. Subordinate clauses have both a subject and a verb and can stand alone.

WRITING ASSIGNMENTS

1. Visit Amnesty International at http://web.amnesty.org/web/wwa.nsf, and read about three prisoners of conscience; then, write a letter on behalf of a prisoner of conscience to the appropriate political leader in which you propose a solution to the problem. Read the letter-writing guide at http:// www.amnesty.org/actnow/wwa/letguide.htm before beginning to write. After completing the letter, proofread it for fragments.

2. Journal Assignment: Explain everything that you have learned in this chapter: "Are sentences free of fragments?"

3. Creative Assignment: Visit the Saint Louis Art Museum at http://www. slam.org/ and find an image that you like in the Collections. Describe that image in a paragraph or short essay. For tips on writing descriptions, return to Purdue University's Online Writing Lab at http://owl.english.purdue.edu/ handouts/general/gl_describe.html.

Chapter 16

Are sentences free of run-ons?

"A writer is somebody for whom writing is more difficult than it is for other people."

—Thomas Mann

LEARNING OBJECTIVES

1. Learn what run-on sentences are and why they should be corrected.
2. Learn the two types of run-on sentences.
3. Learn six ways to correct run-on sentences.
4. Learn how to recognize and correct run-on sentences in your own writing.

PRE-READING QUESTIONS

1. What do you think a run-on sentence is?
2. Which of the following sentences is a run-on sentence?
   a. She completed her résumé it reflected a lot of experience.
   b. He met with his counselor in the office behind the administration building.
3. What is the consequence of writing in run-on sentences?
4. How does a writer fix a run-on sentence?
5. Have you ever run a red light?

WHAT ARE RUN-ON SENTENCES, AND WHY SHOULD THEY BE CORRECTED?

In the last chapter, you learned that each simple sentence is made up of at least two smaller parts, a subject and a verb, which combine to express one idea, and that sentence or independent clause can stand alone.

Independent Clause: The <u>pyramid</u> <u>rose</u> above the forest.

In the last chapter, you also learned that a fragment is too little of a sentence. In this chapter, you will learn that a run-on sentence is the opposite of a fragment: it's too much of a sentence. A run-on sentence is two or more sentences that are punctuated as one sentence, starting with a capital letter and probably ending with a period. As a result, the reader may not be able to tell where one sentence ends and the next one begins. In other words, think of a run-on sentence as a car running a red light. The writer is not stopping as needed, and the consequences could be unpleasant.

Run-ons, like fragments, are serious writing mistakes because they force the reader to do the writer's work of organizing the ideas by sorting out where one idea stops and the next one starts. When readers read enough of a work to see that the writer cannot control the sentence, they tire of the work and stop reading. As an example of this, read the paragraph that follows about Gene Cernan's experience working in space, taken from Alan Shepard's *Moon Shot: The Inside Story of America's Race to the Moon*:

> Trouble remained his constant companion the job demanded more than just slipping into simple straps he needed to make electrical connections and he found that every move was more time-consuming that [sic] he had counted on when he seemed to have a job under control he floated helplessly from the spacecraft there was no way he could maintain a solid body position there were a few footholds and handholds there but they were woefully inadequate he needed positions that would allow him to use leverage. Soon he was severely overworking his own chest pack which circulated oxygen through his suit and also removed excessive moisture from his body he perspired fog collected inside his helmet visor and froze and he endured excessive heat perspiration and ice all at the same time he was barely able to see through the visor a potentially lethal situation for a man turning like a bloated rag doll in vacuum several feet from the security of his spaceship cabin. (pp. 187–188)

Because the information above has been presented in two run-on sentences, the reader struggles to decipher where ideas start and stop. As a result, effective communication has not taken place.

Now read the same paragraph with the correct punctuation. What difference do you notice as you read?

Trouble remained his constant companion. The job demanded more than just slipping into simple straps. He needed to make electrical connections, and he found that every move was more time-consuming that [sic] he had counted on. When he seemed to have a job under control, he floated helplessly from the spacecraft. There was no way he could maintain a solid body position. There were a few footholds and handholds there, but they were woefully inadequate. He needed positions that would allow him to use leverage. Soon he was severely overworking his own chest pack, which circulated oxygen through his suit and also removed excessive moisture from his body. He perspired. Fog collected inside his helmet visor and froze, and he endured excessive heat, perspiration, and ice all at the same time. He was barely able to see through the visor, a potentially lethal situation for a man turning like a bloated rag doll in vacuum several feet from the security of his spaceship cabin. (pp. 187–188)

Clearly, learning to identify and correct run-on sentences is an important skill to acquire.

WHAT ARE THE TWO TYPES OF RUN-ONS AND THE SIX WAYS TO CORRECT THEM?

The following table explains the two types of run-on sentences:

Run-On Sentences

Type of Run-On	Example	Comment
Fused Sentence: two sentences set side by side.	John made a basket he is a good basketball player.	These fused sentences require the reader to figure out where the first sentence ends and the second one starts. Two sentences may not be joined in this way.
Comma Splice: two sentences set side by side and joined with a comma.	John made a basket, he is a good basketball player.	Although the comma marks where the first sentence ends, two sentences may not be joined in this way either.

Now that you understand the two types of run-ons, consider the following main methods of correcting a run-on sentence.

1. **Fix a run-on sentence by separating it**
   This method of fixing run-on sentences involves separating two sentences with a period (or a question mark or an exclamation point) and starting the second sentence with a capital letter.

   Fused Sentence: John made a basket he is a good basketball player.

   Revised: John made a basket. He is a good basketball player.

PRACTICE 1

Read each sentence aloud to "hear" a natural pause where the comma splice or fused sentence should be separated by using a period and a capital letter. Then, rewrite the sentences correctly. Underline subjects once and verbs twice. Write on a separate piece of paper or on a computer.

Example:

> Fused Sentence: Mike listens to the radio daily he loves music.
> Revised: Mike listens to the radio daily. He loves music.

1. The portrait hung on the wall, it had a mahogany frame.
2. She wanted to know about job prospects she researched her career.
3. He studied world religions each one taught him something new.
4. The gear broke after two miles, the car was twenty-five years old.
5. The car could not be salvaged they hauled it to the junkyard.
6. Writing a history may be difficult it will require research and time.
7. She borrowed ten thousand dollars to buy a car her payments continued for ten years.
8. Gas prices have risen they doubled this month.
9. Ants multiply in the spring they may even come into your home.
10. The tree orchard is old most of the trees no longer bear fruit.

   2. Fix a run-on sentence by combining sentences

Sentence-Combining Option 1

Combine the two sentences with a comma and a coordinating conjunction (*and, but, for, nor, or, so,* and *yet*) to create a compound sentence.

> Fused Sentence: John made a basket he is a good basketball player.
> Revised: John made a basket, and he is a good basketball player.

The coordinating conjunctions have been defined below:

Coordinating Conjunctions

*Coordinating Conjunctions	Meaning	Example
and	in addition	A driver threw a cigarette out the window, and brush caught on fire along the road.
but	however	The motorcycle hit the side of the car, but no one was injured.
for	because	He has two jobs, for he wants to get out of debt.
**nor	indicates a second negative statement	Jerry does not like snakes, nor does he like spiders.

*Coordinating Conjunctions	Meaning	Example
or	indicates alternatives	She will study philosophy, or she will study sociology.
so (may use *and so*)	as a result	She wants to become a lawyer, so she is earning A's and B's in high school.
yet (may use *and yet*)	however	His major is economics, yet he prefers taking classes in history.

*The acronym **FANBOYS** may help you to remember the seven coordinating conjunctions.
**Notice that when an independent clause begins with *nor*, the subject-verb order is reversed.

PRACTICE 2

Read each sentence aloud to "hear" a natural pause between clauses. Then, rewrite the sentences correctly using the first sentence-combining option. Use a different coordinating conjunction in each sentence. Write on a separate piece of paper or on a computer.

Example:

> Fused Sentence: I will listen to you please tell me what happened.
> Revised: I will listen to you, so please tell me what happened.

1. She threw out all of her clothes some of them were in good shape.
2. They fired me I protested in a letter to the manager.
3. The crime instilled rage in the victim he lost his entire savings.
4. She will take algebra she will take history.
5. He has high grades he did not get into Harvard.

Sentence-Combining Option 2

Combine the two sentences with a semicolon to create a compound sentence.

> Fused Sentence: John made a basket he is a good basketball player.
> Revised: John made a basket; he is a good basketball player.

PRACTICE 3

Read each sentence aloud to "hear" a natural pause between clauses. Then, rewrite the sentences correctly using the second sentence-combining option. Write on a separate piece of paper or on a computer.

Example:

> Fused Sentence: Paul works as a computer technician he loves it.
> Revised: Paul works as a computer technician; he loves it.

1. Dianna is an optimist she believes that everything will work out.
2. They watch movies in the evening the movies are free.
3. Family night is a ritual they go out for ice cream.
4. She plays the piano and the violin she wants to play the guitar.
5. The gas stove exploded flames burned my hands.

Sentence-Combining Option 3

Combine the two sentences with a semicolon, a conjunctive adverb (*consequently, furthermore, however, in fact, indeed, moreover, nevertheless, then,* and *therefore*), and a comma to create a compound sentence.

> Fused Sentence: John made a basket he is a good basketball player.
> Revised: John made a basket; in fact, he is a good basketball player.

Common Conjunctive Adverbs or Transitional Expressions

Conjunctive Adverbs	Meaning	Example
consequently	as a result	The business expenses exceeded the income for two years; consequently, the company went bankrupt.
furthermore	in addition	She supported her point with convincing evidence; furthermore, she addressed everyone's concerns.
however	in contrast	The crew cleared debris all morning; however, the road was still not clear by the afternoon.
in fact	in reality	Elinore loves taking pictures as a hobby; in fact, she wants to pursue a career as a wildlife photographer.
indeed	certainly	Two warning lights came on; indeed, the pilots became concerned.
moreover	in addition	Spot-billed pelicans need legal protection; in addition, they need sanctuaries.
nevertheless	in contrast	Fierce winds swept across the sand dunes; nevertheless, the camels pressed on.
then	after that	The wall fell; then, the neighbors started talking.
therefore	as a result	The soldier saved fourteen lives; therefore, the military awarded him a medal of honor.

Additional conjunctive adverbs and transitional expressions include the following: *accordingly, also, at least, besides, certainly, finally, for example, hence, instead, likewise, meanwhile, no doubt, nonetheless, of course, on the other hand, otherwise, perhaps, similarly, still,* and *thus*.

PRACTICE 4

Read each sentence aloud to "hear" a natural pause between clauses. Then, rewrite the sentences correctly using the third sentence-combining option. Write on a separate piece of paper or on a computer. Use a different conjunctive adverb or transitional expression in each sentence.

Example:

> Fused Sentence: Five screws held the mirror on it came off easily.
>
> Revised: Five screws held the mirror on; however, it came off easily.

1. She passed her final exam she earned an *A* in the class.
2. They reduced their expenses they raised their income.
3. The crew tracked the tiger they never found it.
4. The laboratory report produced nothing investigators found no other evidence.
5. A candidate won the election is over.

Sentence-Combining Option 4

Combine the two sentences with a subordinating conjunction (*after, although, as, because, before, if, since, unless, until, when, whereas,* and *while*) to create a complex sentence.

> Fused Sentence: John made a basket he is a good basketball player.
>
> Revised: John made a basket because he is a good basketball player.

Common Subordinating Conjunctions

Subordinating Conjunctions	Meaning	Example
after	next	Teresa paid her taxes after she balanced her budget.
although	in spite of the fact that	The morning remained calm although a breeze swept through camp in the afternoon.
as (as if)	equally, while	The entrepreneur studied the market as the stocks plummeted.
because	for the reason or cause that	He paints rural settings because he prefers to depict tranquil scenes.
before	in advance, prior to	The sailors signaled for help before the mast broke.
if	on condition that	The work can be done if we upgrade the computers.

(continued)

Common Subordinating Conjunctions (*continued*)

Subordinating Conjunctions	Meaning	Example
since	from then until now, because	The <u>population</u> <u>has doubled</u> since <u>poachers</u> <u>have been prosecuted</u>.
unless	except if	The <u>people</u> <u>will be</u> safe unless the <u>hurricane</u> <u>moves</u> west.
until	up to the time of	The <u>company</u> <u>produced</u> a profit until the <u>cost</u> of raw materials <u>soared</u>.
when (whenever)	at the time that	The main <u>character</u> <u>suffered</u> a series of health problems when her <u>son</u> <u>died</u>.
whereas	but on the other hand	The white <u>bars</u> <u>are</u> horizontal whereas the black <u>bars</u> <u>are</u> vertical.
while	during or through the time that	The <u>band</u> <u>played</u> while the <u>flags</u> <u>rose</u>.

Additional subordinating conjunctions and dependent words include the following: *afterward, even though, even if, even though, even since, ever since, how, in order that, just as, just as if, now that, once, provided that, rather than, so, so that, than, that, though, till, what, whatever, where, wherever, whether, which, whichever, who, whoever, whom, whomever, whose, why.* See Chapter 15 for a discussion of subordination with relative pronouns like *that, which,* and *who.*

PRACTICE 5

Read each sentence aloud to "hear" a natural pause between clauses. Then, rewrite the sentences correctly using the fourth sentence-combining option. Write on a separate piece of paper or on a computer. Use a different subordinating conjunction in each sentence.

Example:

> Fused Sentence: He took off his shoes he came home.
> Revised: He took off his shoes when he came home.

1. The police examined the fingerprints they arrived.
2. They put the tools in the bin they finished the work.
3. She stayed home from the concert she had no money.
4. The horses crossed the river it was deep.
5. Carrots are orange strawberries are red.

Sentence-Combining Option 5

Combine the two sentences by starting with a subordinating conjunction (*after, although, as, because, before, if, since, unless, until, when, whereas,* and *while*) and inserting a comma between the clauses to create a complex sentence.

> Fused Sentence: John made a basket he is a good basketball player.
> Revised: Because John is a good basketball player, he made a basket.
>   insert comma ➚

The following table shows the relationship between sentence-combining options 4 and 5.

Common Subordinating Conjunctions

Subordinating Conjunctions	Meaning	Example
after	next	Option #4: <u>Teresa</u> <u>paid</u> her taxes after <u>she</u> <u>balanced</u> her budget.
		Option #5: After <u>Teresa</u> <u>balanced</u> her budget, <u>she</u> <u>paid</u> her taxes.
although	in spite of the fact that	Option #4: The <u>morning</u> <u>remained</u> calm although a <u>breeze</u> <u>swept</u> through camp in the afternoon.
		Option #5: Although a <u>breeze</u> <u>swept</u> through camp in the afternoon, the <u>morning</u> <u>remained</u> calm.
as (as if)	equally, while	Option #4: The <u>entrepreneur</u> <u>studied</u> the market as <u>stocks</u> <u>plummeted</u>.
		Option #5: As <u>stocks</u> <u>plummeted</u>, the <u>entrepreneur</u> <u>studied</u> the market.
because	for the reason or cause that	Option #4: <u>He</u> <u>paints</u> rural settings because <u>he</u> <u>prefers</u> to depict tranquil scenes.
		Option #5: Because <u>he</u> <u>prefers</u> to depict tranquil scenes, <u>he</u> <u>paints</u> rural settings.
before	in advance, prior to	Option #4: The <u>sailors</u> <u>signaled</u> for help before the <u>mast</u> <u>broke</u>.
		Option #5: Before the <u>mast</u> <u>broke</u>, the <u>sailors</u> <u>signaled</u> for help.
if	on condition that	Option #4: The <u>work</u> <u>can be done</u> if <u>we</u> <u>upgrade</u> the computers.
		Option #5: If <u>we</u> <u>upgrade</u> the computers, the <u>work</u> <u>can be done</u>.
since	from then until now, because	Option #4: The <u>population</u> <u>has doubled</u> since <u>poachers</u> <u>have been prosecuted</u>.
		Option #5: Since <u>poachers</u> <u>have been prosecuted</u>, the <u>population</u> <u>has doubled</u>.
unless	except if	Option #4: The <u>people</u> <u>will be</u> safe unless the <u>hurricane</u> <u>moves</u> west.

(continued)

Common Subordinating Conjunctions (*continued*)

Subordinating Conjunctions	Meaning	Example
		Option #5: Unless the <u>hurricane</u> <u>moves</u> west, the <u>people</u> <u>will be</u> safe.
until	up to the time of	Option #4: The <u>company</u> <u>produced</u> a profit until the <u>cost</u> of raw materials <u>soared</u>.
		Option #5: Until the <u>cost</u> of raw materials <u>soared</u>, the <u>company</u> <u>produced</u> a profit.
when (whenever)	at the time that	Option #4: The main <u>character</u> <u>suffered</u> a series of health problems when her <u>son</u> <u>died</u>.
		Option #5: When the main character's <u>son</u> <u>died</u>, <u>she</u> <u>suffered</u> a series of health problems.
whereas	but on the other hand	Option #4: The white <u>bars</u> <u>are</u> horizontal whereas the black <u>bars</u> <u>are</u> vertical.
		Option #5: Whereas the black <u>bars</u> <u>are</u> vertical, the white <u>bars</u> <u>are</u> horizontal.
while	during or through the time that	Option #4: The <u>band</u> <u>played</u> while the <u>flags</u> <u>rose</u>. Option #5: While the <u>flags</u> <u>rose</u>, the <u>band</u> <u>played</u>.

Additional subordinating conjunctions and dependent words include the following: *afterward, even though, even if, even though, even since, ever since, how, in order that, just as, just as if, now that, once, provided that, rather than, so, so that, than, that, though, till, what, whatever, where, wherever, whether, which, whichever, who, whoever, whom, whomever, whose, why.* See Chapter 15 for a discussion of subordination with relative pronouns like *that, which,* and *who.*

PRACTICE 6

Read each sentence aloud to "hear" a natural pause between clauses. Then, rewrite the sentences correctly using the fifth sentence-combining option. Write on a separate piece of paper or on a computer. Use a different subordinating conjunction in each sentence.

Example:

> Fused Sentence: The faucet leaks it must be repaired.
> Revised: Because the faucet leaks, it must be repaired.

1. She wins the election she will stay in office for four years.
2. He went to school he worked part time.
3. They were trained they worked on a locomotive.
4. Dania took over Stacy led the discussion
5. Prices have risen houses are not affordable.

Summary of Correcting Run-On Sentences

Method	Example	Comment
1. Separate the two sentences with a period.	John <u>made</u> a basket. <u>He</u> <u>is</u> a good basketball player.	Use two separate sentences for two separate ideas.
2. Combine the two sentences with a comma and a conjunction.	John <u>made</u> a basket, and <u>he</u> <u>is</u> a good basketball player.	Use this method when the two ideas are closely related.
3. Combine the two sentences with a semicolon.	John <u>made</u> a basket; <u>he</u> <u>is</u> a good basketball player.	Use this method when the two ideas are closely related.
4. Combine the two sentences with a semicolon, a conjunctive adverb, and a comma.	John <u>made</u> a basket; indeed, <u>he</u> <u>is</u> a good basketball player.	Use this method when the two ideas are closely related.
5. Combine the two sentences with a subordinating conjunction.	John <u>made</u> a basket because <u>he</u> <u>is</u> a good basketball player.	Use this method when the first idea is more important than the second idea.
6. Combine the two sentences by starting with a subordinating conjunction and inserting a comma between the clauses.	Because <u>John</u> <u>is</u> a good basketball player, <u>he</u> <u>made</u> a basket.	Use this method when the second idea is more important than the first idea.

HOW DO WRITERS RECOGNIZE AND CORRECT RUN-ONS IN THEIR OWN WRITING?

With practice, recognizing and correcting run-ons will become second nature. Eventually, you will be able to avoid writing them. Until then, use the following guidelines to develop this ability.

Guidelines for recognizing run-on sentences in your own writing.

1. Read your paper aloud from end to beginning. This will cause each run-on to stand out because you are reading each word group in isolation, not with related ideas. Reading aloud will also help you to develop the ability to hear run-on sentences. You will hear a pause in your voice at the end of each clause. If you hear a pause in your voice in the middle of a sentence, check the sentence closely.

2. Identify the subject and verb in each sentence. By asking yourself two questions (who or what is the sentence about? and what is the sentence saying about the subject?), you will be able to determine if each sentence has a subject and verb. Put one line under each subject, two lines under each verb, and cross out any prepositional phrases that might confuse you. If you see more than one subject-verb set, you may be looking at a run-on sentence.

3. Be suspicious of all long sentences. Although long sentences are not always run-ons, many of them will turn out to be so.

4. Check for the following words within a sentence because they often start new sentences: *I, you, he, she, it, we, they, there, this, that, now, then, next, therefore, in fact.*)

5. Check all commas; are they used correctly? Can you find a subject and a verb on both sides of the comma? Never separate two sentences with a comma alone. ESL Warning: English does not allow a comma to separate sentences as is the case with some languages.

 6. Computer warning: remember that grammar checks will catch many run-ons, but they will miss some and incorrectly label some good sentences as run-ons. As a result, you must also check each sentence yourself.

Finding Run-Ons

After you read each sentence aloud, ask the following questions:

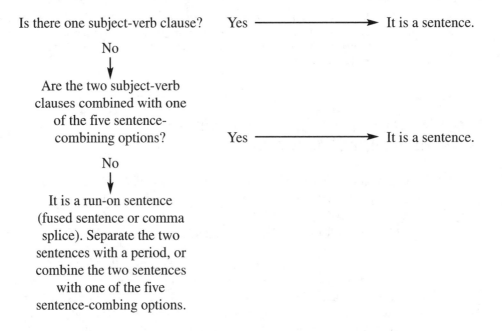

Is there one subject-verb clause?   Yes ──────────► It is a sentence.

No
↓

Are the two subject-verb clauses combined with one of the five sentence-combining options?   Yes ──────────► It is a sentence.

No
↓

It is a run-on sentence (fused sentence or comma splice). Separate the two sentences with a period, or combine the two sentences with one of the five sentence-combing options.

GROUP WORK

1. As a group, show that you understand run-ons sentences and how to fix them by creating five comma splices or fused sentences. Then rewrite the run-on sentences by separating them with a period and a capital letter.

2. As a group, show that you understand run-ons sentences and how to fix them by creating one comma splice or fused sentence. Then correct the

run-on sentence by using each of the five sentence-combining options described in this chapter.

3. As a group, visit Capital Community College at http://webster.commnet. edu/grammar/quizzes/runons_quiz.htm and take the Repairing Run-On Sentence quiz.

TEST (TRUE/FALSE)

1. A sentence or independent clause has a subject, a verb, an idea, and it can stand alone.

2. A fused sentence is two sentences placed side by side; they have been joined incorrectly.

3. A comma splice is two sentences joined by a comma only; they have been joined incorrectly.

4. A run-on is too little of a sentence.

5. Run-on sentences force the reader to organize the ideas by sorting out where one idea ends and the next one starts.

6. Run-on sentences may be corrected by separating independent clauses with a period and a capital letter.

7. Sentence-combining option one involves joining ideas with a comma and a semicolon and a coordinating conjunction.

8. *Therefore* is a subordinating conjunction for sentence-combining option four and five.

9. When proofreading a paper aloud, listen for a pause in the middle of a sentence to try to find run-on sentences.

10. Grammar checkers on a computer will find and correct all of your run-on sentences for you.

WRITING ASSIGNMENTS

1. Academic Assignment: Visit the writing center at Hamilton College to learn about persvasive essays at http://www.hamilton.edu/academic/Resource/ wc/effective.essays.html. Then, create a plan to persuade people to do something. Articulate your plan in a short essay. When you are finished, proofread your essay for run-on sentences. For assistance in finding and correcting run-on sentences, visit The Writing Center at The University of North Carolina at Chapel Hill at http://www.unc.edu/depts/wcweb/handouts/fragments.html.

2. Journal Assignment: Explain everything that you have learned in this chapter: "Are sentences free of run-ons?"

3. Creative Assignment: Visit the Stowitts Museum and Library at http://www.stowitts.org/ and find an image that you like in the Exhibitions. Describe that image in a paragraph or short essay. For tips on writing descriptions, return to Purdue University's Online Writing Lab at http://owl.english.purdue.edu/handouts/general/gl_describe.html.

Do subjects and verbs agree?

"Great writers leave us not just their works, but a way of looking at things."

—Elizabeth Janeway

LEARNING OBJECTIVES

1. Learn what subject-verb agreement is and why it is important.
2. Learn the subject-verb agreement rules.
3. Learn what a writer must know in order to address difficult situations in subject-verb agreement.
4. Learn how to recognize subject-verb disagreement in your own writing.

PRE-READING QUESTIONS

1. How would a marriage work without agreement?
2. What do you think subject-verb agreement is?
3. Determine which of the two sentences is correct? Why is it correct?
   a. The cheetahs runs quickly.
   b. The cheetah runs quickly.
4. How do you know if you are looking at a sentence with subject-verb disagreement?
5. What is the consequence of having subject-verb disagreement in your writing?

WHAT IS SUBJECT-VERB AGREEMENT, AND WHY IS IT IMPORTANT?

To understand what subject-verb agreement is, writers must remember how to find the two main parts of a sentence, the subject and the verb.

To locate the subject of any sentence, ask who or what is the sentence about.

Merian estimated the company's value.

The sentence is about Merian, so *Merian* is the subject.

To locate the verb of any sentence, ask what is the sentence saying about the subject.

Merian estimated the company's value.

The sentence is saying that Merian estimated something, so *estimated* is the verb.

Now that you recall how to identify subjects and verbs in sentences, you can consider the significance of subject-verb agreement.

Subject-verb disagreement is a serious writing mistake, particularly in formal writing situations like the classroom and the workplace. Read the corrupted version of the last paragraph of Steven Callahan's book *Adrift: Seventy-Six Days Lost at Sea* to see the consequences of subject-verb disagreement:

> The accident have left me with a sense of loss and a lingering fear, but I has chosen to learn from this crisis rather than let it overcome me. Each of us are lucky if we must face only one serious crisis in our lives. And in those times when I feels alone and desperate, I takes comfort in the silent company of those who has suffered greater ordeals, and survived. (p. 344)

Effective communication has not taken place, obviously. The reader is annoyed by the s-v disagreement. Notice the improvement in the correct version.

> The accident has left me with a sense of loss and a lingering fear, but I have chosen to learn from this crisis rather than let it overcome me. Each of us is lucky if we must face only one serious crisis in our lives. And in those times when I feel alone and desperate, I take comfort in the silent company of those who have suffered greater ordeals, and survived. (p. 344)

Now let's consider how s-v agreement works.

The subject of a sentence is a person, place, or thing, and the writer of the sentence needs to know how many subjects are being discussed. If only one item is being discussed, then the subject of that sentence is singular. If more than one item is being discussed, then the subject of that sentence is plural. For example, consider the following sentence:

The girl runs quickly. (singular subject because only one girl is being discussed)

At this point, by asking yourself who or what is the sentence about, you should be able to identify *girl* as the subject. You should also be able to identify *girl* as a singular subject since *girl* refers to just one young female.

By asking yourself what the sentence is saying about the subject, you should be able to identify *runs* as the verb. If the subject of a sentence is singular, the verb must also be singular to match or be in agreement in number with the singular subject. The number of the subject determines the number of the verb, and subjects and verbs must agree in number (singular or plural). Notice that the singular form of most present tense verbs ends in *–s* or *–es* (*runs*).

In the next sentence, however, you can see that the subject is plural.

The girls run quickly. (plural subject because more than one girl is being discussed)

Notice that in most cases a subject is made plural by adding an *–s* to the end of the word (*girls*).

Consider the fact that in the first sentence (singular), an *–s* is attached to the verb (*runs*); in the second sentence (plural) an *–s* is attached to subject (*girls*). Typically, then, in present tense, the *–s* is attached to either the subject (if it is plural) or the verb (if it is singular) to make them agree.

Typically, the *–s* is never attached to both the subject and the verb:

Incorrect: The girls runs quickly.

Typically, the *–s* is also never omitted from both the subject and the verb:

Incorrect: The girl run quickly.

Native speakers of English have developed an ear for s-v agreement and only get confused in certain tricky situations. People who are learning English as a second language and people who hear non-standard English in their communities may need to review s-v agreement.

WHAT ARE THE SUBJECT-VERB AGREEMENT RULES?

Subject-Verb Agreement (present tense forms of *eat*, a typical verb)

	Singular		Plural	
First Person	I	eat	we	eat
Example	I eat salad.		Jerry and I (the same as we) eat hot dogs.	
Second Person	you	eat	you	eat
Example	You eat your vegetables.		You (more than one) eat your vegetables.	
Third Person	he/she/it	eats	they	eat
Example	1. Kevin (the same as he) eats hamburgers. 2. Melissa (the same as she) eats pizza. 3. The dog (the same as it) eats bones.		Carol and Ryan (the same as they) eat their vegetables.	

Since most subject-verb agreement problems occur in the present tense, notice that all of the verb forms in the chart above are identical, except for the third person singular, which takes an –*s* on the verb.

WHAT MUST A WRITER KNOW IN ORDER TO ADDRESS DIFFICULT SITUATIONS IN SUBJECT-VERB AGREEMENT?

Writers often make mistakes in subject-verb agreement in the following ten difficult situations.

> **1. *Be, do,* and *have* are irregular verbs, so their forms need to be memorized.**

The simple present tense forms of *be, do,* and *have* are below:

Subject-Verb Agreement (present tense forms of *be*, an irregular verb)

	Singular		Plural	
First Person	I	am	we	are
Example	I am here.		Jerry and I (the same as we) are here.	
Second Person	you	are	you	are
Example	You are here.		You (more than one) are here.	
Third Person	he/she/it	is	they	are
Example	He is here.		Carol and Ryan (the same as they) are here.	

Subject-Verb Agreement (present tense forms of *do*, an irregular verb)

	Singular		Plural	
First Person	I	do	we	do
Example	I <u>do</u> homework after dinner.		Jerry and I (the same as we) <u>do</u> homework after dinner.	
Second Person	you	do	you	do
Example	You <u>do</u> homework after dinner.		You (more than one) <u>do</u> homework after dinner.	
Third Person	he/she/it	does	they	do
Example	He <u>does</u> homework after dinner.		Carol and Ryan (the same as they) <u>do</u> homework after dinner.	

Subject-Verb Agreement (present tense forms of *have*, an irregular verb)

	Singular		Plural	
First Person	I	have	we	have
Example	I <u>have</u> friends.		Jerry and I (the same as we) <u>have</u> friends.	
Second Person	you	have	you	have
Example	You <u>have</u> friends.		You (more than one) <u>have</u> friends.	
Third Person	he/she/it	has	they	have
Example	1. Kevin (the same as he) <u>has</u> friends. 2. Melissa (the same as she) <u>has</u> friends. 3. The <u>dog</u> (the same as it) <u>has</u> friends.		Carol and Ryan (the same as they) <u>have</u> friends.	

One verb requires agreement in the past tense: *be*.

Subject-Verb Agreement (past tense forms of *be*, an irregular verb)

	Singular		Plural	
First Person	I	was	we	were
Example	I <u>was</u> there.		Jerry and I (the same as we) <u>were</u> there.	
Second Person	you	were	you	were
Example	You <u>were</u> there.		You (more than one) <u>were</u> there.	

(continued)

Subject-Verb Agreement (past tense forms of *be*, an irregular verb) (*continued*)

	Singular		Plural	
Third Person	he/she/it	was	they	were
Example	1. <u>Kevin</u> (the same as he) <u>was</u> there. 2. <u>Melissa</u> (the same as she) <u>was</u> there. 3. The <u>dog</u> (the same as it) <u>was</u> there.		<u>Carol</u> and <u>Ryan</u> (the same as they) <u>were</u> there.	

2. **Subject-verb agreement is not affected by words that come between the subject and the verb.** Students may find subject-verb agreement difficult when groups of words like prepositional phrases or dependent clauses come between the subject and the verb.

Prepositional phrases

Prepositional phrases typically begin with one of the words in the table below. In Chapter 15, you learned that the subject and the verb of a sentence are never found in a prepositional phrase. Cross out prepositional phrases in a sentence to be able to identify the subject and verb. Once you have identified the subject, make sure that it agrees with the verb.

Common Prepositions

About	Behind	During	Of	Till
Above	Below	Except	Off	To
Across	Beneath	For	On	Toward
After	Beside	From	Onto	Under
Against	Besides	In	Out	Unfit
Among	Between	Inside	Outside	Up
Around	Beyond	Into	Over	Upon
At	By	Like	Through	With
Before	Down	Near	Throughout	Without

Incorrect: The <u>monkey</u> ~~with the sticks~~ <u>eat</u> bananas.

Don't be confused by the prepositional phrase between the subject and the verb. Which is the subject of the sentence: *monkey* or *sticks*?

1. The <u>monkey</u> . . . <u>eats</u> bananas.
2. The <u>sticks</u> . . . <u>eat</u> bananas.

Obviously, *monkey* has to be the subject of the sentence, and *monkey* is singular. The verb, then, must also be singular.

Revised: The <u>monkey</u> ~~with the sticks~~ <u>eats</u> bananas.

PRACTICE 1

Cross out all prepositional phrases. Then, underline the subjects once and the correct verbs twice in each sentence. Write on a separate piece of paper or on a computer.

Example: The horses in the barn (is, are) ready to run.

The <u>horses</u> ~~in the barn~~ <u>are</u> ready to run.

1. The man in the red suit on the table (is, are) a clown.
2. The stones in the stream (appears, appear) black.
3. The cabinet above the counter (has, have) a broken door.
4. For your information, communication throughout the world (does, do) improve each year.
5. Ants on the rim of the glass (scares, scare) the guests at the party.

Relative Clauses

A relative clause, like a prepositional phrase, may come between subjects and verbs in sentences and they typically start with *that, which,* or *who (whose, whom)*. The main subject and verb of a sentence are never found within a relative clause; therefore, cross out relative clauses.

Incorrect: The alligator that has gray spots eat big fish.

Don't be confused by the relative clause between the subject and the verb. Which is the subject of the sentence: *alligator* or *spots?*

The <u>alligator</u> . . . <u>eats</u> big fish.
The <u>spots</u> . . . <u>eat</u> big fish.

Obviously, *alligator* has to be the subject of the sentence, and *alligator* is singular because we are only talking about one animal. The verb, then, must also be singular.

Revised: The <u>alligator</u> ~~that has gray spots~~ <u>eats</u> big fish.

PRACTICE 2

Cross out all relative clauses. Then, underline the subjects once and the correct verbs twice in each sentence. Write on a separate piece of paper or on a computer. Notice that some relative clauses may have prepositional phrases in them.

Example: The stamps that are on the table (is, are) valuable.

The <u>stamps</u> ~~that are on the table~~ <u>are</u> valuable.

1. The detention facility that is on the edge of town (needs, need) refurbishing.
2. The fireplace, which rests on a ledge, (provides, provide) warmth in the winter.
3. The region that was examined (appears, appear) suitable for building.
4. The woman who is on the edge of the cliff (has, have) a good view of the horizon.
5. For the passengers, the ride, which is supposed to be short, (seems, seem) to take hours.

Now take a closer look at the example above. Focus on the relative clause *that has gray spots*.

The <u>alligator</u> *that has gray spots* <u>eats</u> big fish.

First, notice that the relative clause cannot stand alone. If you walk up to someone and say, "That has gray spots," the listener would look at you like you are crazy because the relative clause is a fragment. In other words, you have provided too little information. The listener might lean forward and say, "Excuse me?" or "What did you say?" hoping that you would finish your sentence and make sense. Notice that although "that has gray spots" is a fragment, it does have a subject and a verb, and they must agree in number also. *Who, which*, and *that* are often the subjects of relative clauses, and they may be singular or plural. They typically represent, and must agree in number with, the closest preceding noun.

The <u>alligator</u> *that* <u>has</u> gray spots <u>eats</u> big fish. (*that* is singular, so it must take a singular verb, *has*)

In the example above *alligator* agrees with *eats* and *that* (referring to the alligator) agrees with *has*. Really, we are looking at a sentence embedded within a sentence or two sentences.

1. The <u>alligator</u> <u>eats</u> big fish. (the outer sentence)
2. The <u>alligator</u> <u>has</u> gray spots. (the inner sentence)

These two sentences have been combined, and both subject-verb pairs are in agreement (see Chapter 15 for more information on relative clauses, including punctuating them).

PRACTICE 3

Double underline the correct form of the verb in the relative clause. Identify the relative pronoun as singular or plural. Write on a separate piece of paper or on a computer.

Example: Donavon, who (is, are) sitting, will play next.

Donovan, who is sitting, will play next. (singular)

1. The students who (is, are) in the class discussed the final exam.
2. The truck that (has, have) big tires will win the race.
3. The games, which (begins, begin) in the afternoon, are for everyone.
4. In the evening, the sun, which (looks, look) red, sets around 6:30 p.m.
5. The white yacht, which (is, are) more than one hundred feet long, left before dawn.

3. Subjects joined by *and* take a plural verb. The *and* causes the verb to be plural.

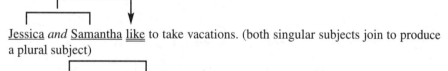

<u>Jessica</u> *and* <u>Samantha</u> <u>like</u> to take vacations. (both singular subjects join to produce a plural subject)

<u>Jessica</u> *and* the <u>Johnsons</u> <u>like</u> to take vacations. (one singular and one plural subject join to produce a plural subject)

The <u>Johnsons</u> *and* <u>Jessica</u> <u>like</u> to take vacations. (one plural and one singular subject join to produce a plural subject)

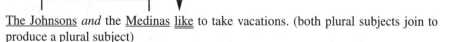

The <u>Johnsons</u> *and* the <u>Medinas</u> <u>like</u> to take vacations. (both plural subjects join to produce a plural subject)

Three exceptions exist. First, when the subjects combine to name one unit, the subject is singular.

Your <u>cake</u> *and* <u>ice cream</u> <u>is</u> on the table.

Second, when the subjects both refer to the same thing, the subject is singular.

His <u>brother</u> and <u>friend</u> <u>has</u> arrived.

Third, when the subjects are preceded by a word like *each* or *every,* use a singular verb. See the list of common singular indefinite pronouns later in this chapter.

Revised: <u>Each</u> girl *and* boy <u>plays</u> during recess.

4. **With subjects joined by *or* or *nor,* the verb agrees with the nearer subject**.

<u>Kyle</u> or <u>Peter</u> <u>mows</u> the lawn each Saturday. (*Peter* is singular and nearer the verb)

The <u>girls</u> *or* <u>Peter</u> <u>mows</u> the lawn each Saturday. (*Peter* is singular and nearer the verb)

Neither <u>Peter</u> *nor* the <u>girls</u> <u>mow</u> the lawn each Saturday. (*Girls* is plural and nearer the verb)

PRACTICE 4

Double underline the correct form of the verb. Identify the subject as singular or plural. Write on a separate piece of paper or on a computer.

Example: The earrings or the bracelet (has, have) been stolen.

The earrings or the bracelet <u>has</u> been stolen. (singular)

1. A résumé and an application (is, are) required.
2. Her husband and lover (remains, remain) faithful.
3. A mountain lion or a cougar (has, have) appeared on the trail.
4. Cookies or brownies (was, were) served for dessert.
5. Neither the employees nor the manager (knows, know) the cause of the malfunction.

5. **Some subjects do not form a plural by adding *–s* or *–es*.** In fact, some subjects have the same form for both the singular and the plural form. Becoming familiar

with the words in the chart below will help you to avoid subject-verb disagreement. See Chapter 19 for more information about plurals.

Nouns with Unusual Plurals

Singular	Plural
Antenna	Antennae
Child	Children
Crisis	Crises
Criterion	Criteria
Curriculum	Curricula
Datum	Data
Deer	Deer
Fish	Fish
Foot	Feet
Goose	Geese
He, she, it	They
Louse	Lice
Man	Men
Medium	Media
Moose	Moose
Mouse	Mice
Person	People
Salmon	Salmon
Sheep	Sheep
Species	Species
Trout	Trout
Woman	Women

Incorrect: Three <u>deers</u> <u>crossed</u> the road.

Revised: Three <u>deer</u> (–*s* is not added to form the plural) <u>crossed</u> the road.

A few nouns end in –*s,* but they may refer to just one item. These words take a plural verb.

Single Items That Take Plural Verbs

Eyeglasses	Fireworks	Riches	Trousers
Clothes	Jeans	Scissors	

Incorrect: My <u>eyeglasses</u> <u>looks</u> cracked.

Revised: My <u>eyeglasses</u> <u>look</u> cracked. (singular subject that takes a plural verb)

A few words end in –*s*, but they typically refer to just one item:

Common Singular Words (that end in –*s*)

Civics	Ethics	Measles	News	Politics
Economics	Mathematics	Mumps	Physics	Statistics

Incorrect: <u>News</u> <u>travel</u> quickly.

Revised: <u>News</u> <u>travels</u> quickly. (singular subject that ends in –*s*)

The –*s* rule does not apply to sentences with these words as the subject. When these words are used as the subjects of sentences, they typically take singular verbs.

6. **Collective nouns are typically singular.** They name a group of people or things and emphasize the group as one unit.

Common Collective Nouns

Army	Corporation	Gang	Panel
Audience	Crew	Government	Public
Board	Crowd	Group	School
Class	Department	Herd	Society
College	Enemy	Jury	Team
Committee	Faculty	Majority	Tribe
Community	Family	Minority	Troop
Company	Firm	Office	World
Congregation	Flock	Orchestra	

These words are singular in form, but they represent a group of individuals or items. Typically, they call for the singular form of a verb. If you want to emphasize the members or items of the body, then use the plural form of the verb.

Incorrect: The <u>family</u> <u>are</u> here.

Revised (as one unit): The <u>family</u> <u>is</u> here.

Revised (as individuals): The <u>family</u> <u>are</u> here to discuss their opinions.

7. **Some indefinite pronouns are singular, some are plural, and some may be used as either singular or plural.** Consider the indefinite pronouns in the following charts:

Common Singular Indefinite Pronouns

-one words	-body words	-thing words	other words	
Anyone	Anybody	Anything	Another	Much
Each one	Everybody	Everything	Each	Neither
Everyone	Nobody	Nothing	Either	Other
No one	Somebody	Something	Every	
One			Little	
Someone			Many	

Incorrect: <u>Everyone love</u> baseball.

Revised: <u>Everyone loves</u> baseball.

Common Plural Indefinite Pronouns

Both	Many	Several
Few	Others	

Incorrect: <u>Few</u> of the people <u>enjoys</u> skydiving.

Revised: <u>Few</u> of the people <u>enjoy</u> skydiving.

Some indefinite pronouns are singular or plural depending upon the noun or pronoun to which they refer:

**Common Singular or Plural Indefinite
Pronouns (based on how they are used)**

All	More	None	Such
Any	Most	Some	

When the sentence indicates *how much*, a singular verb is needed.

Singular: <u>Some</u> of the food <u>is</u> bad. (singular)

When the sentence indicates *how many*, a plural verb is needed.

Plural: <u>Some</u> of the donuts <u>are</u> bad. (plural)

PRACTICE 5

Choose the correct form of the verb to match the subject.

Example: Anyone (is, are) welcome to attend the party.

Anyone is welcome to attend the party.

1. Three (geese, gooses) walked across the road.
2. The army (fight, fights) to win the conflict.
3. Everyone (supports, support) his or her leader.
4. Both of the dogs (attacks, attack) at once.
5. Most of the milk (is, are) gone.

8. **Subjects and verbs must agree even when the verb comes before the subject**. In English, the subject usually comes before the verb in a sentence, but in a few special cases, the order is reversed.

In Questions

In questions, the verb may come before the subject.

Is Mike already six feet tall? (The verb comes before the subject.)
Has Patricia been in college for three years now? (Part of the verb is in front of the subject, and part of the verb is after the subject.)

When a sentence begins with a question word like *who, what, why, where, when,* look for the subject and verb later in the sentence.

What does Kathy want? (A question word is in front, part of the verb is before the subject, and part of the verb is after the subject.)

Notice that you may easily identify the subjects and verbs by answering the questions. This will usually put the subjects before the verbs.

Mike is already six feet tall. (The subject is now before the verb.)
Patricia has been in college for three years now. (The subject is now before the verbs.)
Kathy does want a house on the beach. (The subject is now before the verbs.)

In sentences beginning with *here* or *there*

Here and *there* are never subjects.

Here is my exam. (singular subject that comes after the verb)
There are the people. (plural subject that comes after the verb)

In unusual sentence patterns

Occasionally, a writer will put the verb before the subject for emphasis.

In the corner <u>sits</u> <u>Dr. Schooner</u>. (singular subject that comes after the verb)
On the walls <u>hang</u> <u>portraits</u>. (plural subject that comes after the verb)

Of course, the sentences may be rewritten with the subject first.

<u>Dr. Schooner</u> <u>sits</u> in the corner.
<u>Portraits</u> <u>hang</u> on the walls.

Remember that even when the verb comes before the subject—in questions, in sentences that begin with *here* or *there*, and in rare sentence patterns—the subject and verb must still agree in number (singular or plural).

9. **Amounts of money, distances, and measurements use a singular verb when a unit is meant, a plural verb when items are considered separately**.

<u>One-half</u> of the lawn <u>was</u> mowed yesterday. (singular subject takes a singular verb)
<u>Six</u> of the lawns <u>were</u> mowed yesterday. (plural subject takes a plural verb)

Also, *number* takes a singular verb when it is preceded by *the*, and it takes a plural verb when it is preceded by *a*.

The <u>number</u> of new books <u>is</u> ten. (singular subject takes a singular verb)
A <u>number</u> of new books <u>were</u> purchased. (plural subject takes a plural verb)

10. **Titles of books, plays, short stories, poems, essays, words used as words, and names of businesses take a singular verb**.

<u>*A Tale of Two Cities*</u> <u>is</u> an interesting book.
"O Captain! My Captain!" is a popular poem.

PRACTICE 6

Choose the correct form of the verb.

Example: *To Kill a Mockingbird* (deals, deal) with discrimination.

   To Kill a Mockingbird **deals** with discrimination.

1. How old (is, are) Susana?
2. Here (sits, sit) my children.

3. The total number of students (is, are) twenty-five.
4. "Fog" (uses, use) personification.
5. *Receive* and *embarrass* (is, are) often misspelled.

HOW DO WRITERS RECOGNIZE SUBJECT-VERB DISAGREEMENT IN THEIR OWN WRITING?

First, identify the subject and verb in each sentence. Remember that the subject determines the form of the verb.

Second, review and understand the rule explained at the beginning of this chapter about placing the *–s* on either the subject or the verb in present tense sentences to create subject-verb agreement. Make sure that the subject and verb sound right together by reading each sentence aloud.

Third, review and understand the ten guidelines that help beginning writers with typical subject-verb agreement problems. Check this chapter for any situations about which you feel unsure. Then make any necessary changes in agreement. The guidelines are summarized below:

1. *Be, do*, and *have* are irregular verbs, so their forms need to be memorized.
2. Subject-verb agreement is not affected by words that come between the subject and the verb.
3. Subjects joined by *and* take a plural verb.
4. With subjects joined by *or* or *nor,* the verb agrees with the nearer subject.
5. Some subjects do not form a plural by adding *–s* or *–es* (see plurals in Chapter 19 for more details).
6. Collective nouns are typically singular.
7. Some indefinite pronouns are singular, some are plural, and some may be used as either singular or plural.
8. Subjects and verbs must agree even when the verb comes before the subject.
9. Amounts of money, distances, and measurements use a singular verb when a unit is meant, a plural verb when items are considered separately.
10. Titles of books, plays, short stories, poems, essays, words used as words, and names of businesses take a singular verb.

GROUP WORK

1. As a group, create five sentences. Underline the subjects once and the verbs twice. Then, label the subjects as singular or plural, and make sure that the verbs agree with the subjects.

2. As a group, write five questions using *who, what, why, where, when*. Underline the subjects once and the verbs twice. Then, label the subjects as singular or plural, and make sure that the verbs agree with the subjects.

3. Visit Capital Community College at http://webster.commnet.edu/cgi-shl/quiz.pl/sv_agr_quiz.htm and take the quiz on subject-verb agreement.

TEST (TRUE/FALSE)

1. To be able to check subject-verb agreement, a writer must be able to identify correctly the subject(s) and verb(s) in each sentence.
2. The subject is who or what the sentence is about.
3. The verb is what the sentence is saying about the subject.
4. The subject does not determine the form of the verb.
5. In a typical present tense sentence, a writer will place an *–s* on either the subject or the verb, but not both, to create subject-verb agreement.
6. *Last year, he were happy* is a correct sentence.
7. *In the park* can never be the subject of a sentence because it is a prepositional phrase.
8. *Mary and the girls love video games* is a sentence with subject-verb agreement.
9. The plural of *sheep* is *sheeps*.
10. *Everyone* is plural because it refers to more than one person.

WRITING ASSIGNMENTS

1. Academic Assignment: Visit Southwest Texas State University at http://www.admission.swt.edu/_undergrad/admin_essay_require.htm to learn about requirements for an admissions essay. Then, compose an essay for admission to a university. First, discuss what experiences in your past have made you unique. Second, discuss what current talents, attitudes, or values you would bring to the college. Third, discuss your future career or the kind of person you want to become after you earn a degree. For assistance on making subjects and verbs agree, visit Purdue University's Online Writing Lab at http://owl.english.purdue.edu/handouts/esl/eslsubverb.html.

2. Journal Assignment: Explain everything that you have learned in this chapter: "Do subjects and verbs agree?"

3. Creative Assignment: Visit the Tampa Museum of Art at http://www.tampagov.net/dept_Museum/, and find an image that you like in the Collections. Describe that image in a paragraph or short essay. For tips on writing descriptions, return to Purdue University's Online Writing Lab at http://owl.english.purdue.edu/handouts/general/gl_describe.html.

Have ESL trouble spots been avoided?

"Most writers enjoy two periods of happiness—when a glorious idea comes to mind and, secondly, when a last page has been written and you haven't had time to know how much better it ought to be."

— J. B. Priestley

LEARNING OBJECTIVES

1. Learn the advantages of knowing two languages and why ESL trouble spots should be addressed.
2. Learn how to make a point.
3. Learn how to use articles correctly.
4. Learn the twelve tenses of verbs.
5. Learn how to avoid common trouble spots with verbs.
   a. Irregular Verbs
   b. Troublesome irregular verbs
   c. Gerunds and infinitives
   d. Progressives
   e. Modals
   f. Subjunctive mood
   g. Tense shifts
   h. Passive and active voice
6. Learn how to avoid repeating subjects.

7. Learn how to start sentences with *here* and *there*.
8. Learn how to start sentences with *it*.
9. Learn how to use adjectives.
    a. Word order with adjectives
    b. Punctuating adjectives
    c. Using present and past participles as adjectives
10. Learn how to avoid using double negatives.
11. Learn how to create questions.
12. Learn how to use prepositions to show time and place.
13. Learn how to use pronouns like *I* and *me*.

PRE-READING QUESTIONS

1. Are you aware of any cultures in which people typically do not communicate by making a point directly?
2. Is the following sentence correct? A wealth can provide many opportunities.
3. Chose the correct word in parentheses: Please (lie, lay) the book on the table.
4. Is the following sentence correct? Nobody cannot read the book.
5. Why do we say that we need a ride *on* a plane when, in fact, we need a ride *in* a plane?

WHAT ARE THE ADVANTAGES OF KNOWING TWO LANGUAGES, AND WHY SHOULD ESL TROUBLE SPOTS BE ADDRESSED?

Knowing more than one language is an asset because it allows you to communicate with people from different cultures or groups, and it provides you with a broader perspective of the world. In fact, your skills with two or more languages may open doors for you in your education, business, or community. If you communicate in two or more languages, you are already aware of some differences in the ways that words are connected to form sentences. Now, you will want to make sure that you gain skills in each area in this chapter so that you can capitalize on the benefits of being bilingual by being able to produce effective writing in English, which involves being able to do the following:

1. Make a point.
2. Support the point.
3. Organize the ideas.
4. Present the ideas in error-free sentences.

To help you write error-free sentences, this chapter covers several trouble spots for ESL students, but many other important areas are covered in other chapters because they are also trouble spots for native English speakers. They include the following areas:

- Focus on one point and support it (Chapters 5 and 6).
- Do not omit subjects or verbs from sentences (Chapter 15).
- Do not write in run-on sentences (Chapter 16).
- Make subjects and verbs agree in number (Chapter 17).
- Learn the irregular forms of *be, do*, and *have* (Chapter 17).
- Learn the most commonly misspelled and confused words (Chapter 19).
- Use capital letters correctly (Chapter 20).
- Punctuate sentences correctly (Chapters 22 and 23).

HOW DOES A WRITER MAKE A POINT?

In some cultures, communication meanders back and forth, like switchbacks on a mountainous trail that leads to a lake. In North America, however, direct, clear communication is valued, like the path that a bird might take to get to that same lake. After you state your point in your topic sentence or thesis (discussed in Chapter 5), support that point with facts, examples, explanations (discussed in Chapter 6), and do not deviate from your point.

Proofread each paragraph and essay to see that you have made and supported a point. If you can find any sentence that does not support your point, you have located a digression, a place where you have wandered away from your point. In English, effective writing avoids digressions, so delete the digression from your writing.

The best way to prevent digressions in the first place is to create an outline (see Chapter 8). Once the outline has been created, stick to it when writing the first draft (see Chapter 9). If you notice a tendency to digress from your point in your communication, work against this tendency by creating a well-focused outline and forcing yourself to stick with it as you write your first draft.

HOW DOES A WRITER USE ARTICLES CORRECTLY?

We have three articles: *a, an*, and *the*. Determining when to use an article and when not to use an article can be very difficult. Even when writers know that an article is required, determining which one of the three is called for can be a challenge.

Articles signal that a noun (person, place, or thing) is coming in a sentence. Notice the four nouns in the following sentence: *rain, man, sandwich,* and *apple.*

<u>*Rain*</u> <u>fell</u> on the *man* eating a *sandwich* and an *apple.*

Why does nothing precede *rain, the* precede *man, a* precede sandwich, and *an* precede *apple?* The following chart summarizes when and how to use articles, and an explanation follows.

How to Use Articles

#	Count Nouns	Example
1	Singular: Identity known	(the)
		I like *the* video that you recommended.
2	Singular: Identity unknown	(a or an)
		I want to rent *a* video tonight.
		I just met *an* honorable man.
3	Plural: Identity known	(the)
		I liked *the* videos that we saw last week.
4	Plural: Identity unknown or a general category	(no article)
		I like to watch videos.

	Noncount Nouns	Example
5	Singular: Identity Known	(the)
		Please pass me *the* water in the pitcher.
6	Identity unknown or a general category	(no article)
		Water covers 70 percent of the earth.

Explanation of the examples

1. In the first example, *video* is the noun (person, place, or thing).

   I like *the* video that you recommended.

   Since videos can be counted, it is a count noun. Since one video is being discussed, it is singular (one item). Since the identity of the video is known (the video that you recommended), *the* is the article that precedes *video.*

   When is the identity of a noun known?

   • The noun has been mentioned previously
   • The sentence clarifies its identity
   • The noun is modified by a word like *best*, which identifies the noun
   • The noun describes a specific person, place, or thing

      A dog ran into the street. Then a truck hit the dog's back leg.

A is used in the first sentence before *dog* because the dog's identity is not known to the reader. *The* is used in the second sentence before dog because now the reader knows which dog is being discussed (the dog that was mentioned in the first sentence).

2. In the second example, *video* is still the count noun, and it is still singular.

    I want to rent *a* video tonight.

    However, since we do not know which video is being discussed, the video's identity is unknown. As a result, *a*, not *the*, is the article that appears before *video*.

    Notice that *an* is used before words that begin with a vowel (an animal, an elephant, an infant, an orange, an uncle) or a vowel sound (an hour). Notice also that a word like an adjective (honorable) may come between the article and the noun (an honorable man), and in these cases the adjective determines whether *a* or *an* is used. Since *honorable* starts with a vowel sound, *an* is used. Warning: words beginning with *h* can have either a consonant sound (a hand) or a vowel sound (an hour) when the *h* is silent.

3. In the third example, *videos* is still the count noun, but now it is plural (more than one).

    I liked *the* videos that we saw last week.

    Since we do know which videos are being discussed (the videos that we saw last week), the identity of the videos is known. As a result, *the* is the article that appears before *videos*.

4. In the fourth example, *videos* is still the plural count noun.

    I like to watch videos.

    In this case, however, since we do not know which videos are being discussed (just a general category), the identity of the videos is unknown. Consequently, no article is used before *videos*.

5. In the fifth example, *water* is the noun.

    Please pass me *the* water in the pitcher.

    Since *water* cannot be counted, it is a noncount noun. Noncount nouns are always singular. Since the identity of the water is known (*the* water in the pitcher), *the* is the article that precedes *water*.

6. In the sixth example, *water* is still the noncount noun, and remember that noncount nouns are always singular.

    Water covers 70 percent of the earth.

    Since the identity of the water is unknown (a general category), no article precedes *water*.

A CLOSER LOOK AT NONCOUNT NOUNS

Count nouns are easy to understand because they include any person, place, or thing that can be counted: book, chair, hamburger, hammer, shirt, etc.

Noncount nouns can create trouble spots, so writers should become familiar with the words in the following categories.

Common Noncount Nouns: Activities

Jogging	Golf
Thinking	Hoping
Wondering	Sleep

Common Noncount Nouns: Food and Drink

Bacon	Cauliflower	Corn	Meat	Spaghetti
Beef	Cereal	Flour	Pasta	Water
Bread	Cheese	Fruit	Pie	Wine
Broccoli	Chicken	Ice cream	Rice	Yogurt
Butter	Chocolate	Lemonade	Salt	
Cabbage	Coffee	Lettuce	Spinach	
Candy	Cream	Milk	Sugar	
Celery	Fish	Oil	Tea	

Common Noncount Nouns: Nonfood Substances

Air	Dirt	Paper	Sleet	Straw
Bleach	Firewood	Petroleum	Smoke	Wood
Carbon dioxide	Gasoline	Plastic	Snow	Wool
Cat littler	Gold	Rain	Soap	
Cement	Kerosene	Sawdust	Steam	
Coal	Oxygen	Silver	Steel	

Common Noncount Nouns: Abstractions and Emotions

Advice	Embarrassment	Honesty	Love	Truth
Anger	Employment	Information	Poverty	Warmth
Beauty	Fun	Intelligence	Satisfaction	Wealth
Confidence	Happiness	Justice	Tenderness	
Courage	Health	Knowledge	Time	

Other Noncount Nouns

Arithmetic	Geology	Luggage	Research	Weather
Baggage	Gravity	Lumber	Room	Work
Biology	History	Machinery	Rust	
Cash	Homework	Mail	Scenery	
Clothing	Italian	Money	Traffic	
Equipment	Jewelry	News	Trash	
Experience	Korean	Poetry	Transportation	
Furniture	Lightning	Pollution	Violence	

Warning: remember that noncount nouns do not have plural forms, and they should not be used with numbers or words suggesting plurality (such as several, many, a few, a couple of, a number of).

Incorrect: I would like two corns.

Incorrect: Do you have a couple of monies?

Revised: I would like two ears of corn.

Revised: Do you have any money?

To communicate a specific amount with noncount nouns, you may precede a noncount noun with one of the words or phrases below.

Specific Amounts of Noncount Nouns

Qualifier	Noncount Nouns
Any	Mail, gasoline
A bottle of	Water, vinegar
A carton of	Ice cream, milk, yogurt
An ear of	Corn
A great deal of	Hope, wealth
A head of	Cabbage, lettuce
A little	Rust, rain
Less	Sugar, trash
A loaf of	Bread
Much	Information, rich
More	Traffic, advice
A piece of	Meat, furniture, advice
Plenty of	Time, cash
A pound of	Butter, sugar
A quart of	Milk, ice cream
Some	Sleep, news
A slice of	Bread, bacon

Notice in the chart above that *a* precedes *bottle* because bottles can be counted, but water cannot. Also, be aware that a few nouns can be used as count or noncount nouns.

Count: John caught a fish at the lake. (refers to a particular fish)

Noncount: Are you hungry for fish? (refers to fish in general)

Proper Nouns

Do not use *the* with most proper nouns. *The* is not used with most singular proper nouns (Alaminos Street, Lake Isabella), but *the* is used with plural proper nouns (the United Nations, the Florida Keys).

Many students find geographical names difficult because many exceptions to the rules exist. When you are in doubt, consult the chart below:

When to Omit *The* in Geographical Names

Streets, squares, parks	Central Park
Cities, states, counties	Orange County
Most countries	Norway
Continents	South America
Bays, single lakes	Newport Bay
Single mountains, islands	Catalina Island

When to Use *The* in Geographical Names

United countries	the United States
Large regions, deserts	the West Coast
Peninsulas	the Newport Peninsula
Oceans, seas, gulfs	the Gulf of Mexico
Canals and rivers	the Nile
Mountain ranges	the Alps
Groups of islands	the Galápagos Islands

Summary of articles

Use *a* (*an*) in the following situation:

- With singular count nouns whose identity is unknown. (*a* car, *an* orange)

Use *the* in the following situations:

- With singular count nouns whose identity is known (*the* best car, *the* car with the blue stripe).
- With plural count nouns whose identity is known (*the* largest airplanes, *the* airplanes that are used for spy missions).
- With noncount nouns (always singular) whose identity is known (*the* girl's courage helped her to survive).

Use no article in the following situations:

- With plural count nouns whose identity is unknown or a general category (we love athletes).
- With noncount nouns (always singular) whose identity is unknown or a general category (smoke always rises).

PRACTICE 1

Underline the correct word or words in parentheses.

Example: She enjoys (music, a music).

　　　　She enjoys <u>music</u>.

1. She took (train, a train) home last week.
2. (Tires, The tires) on the car were new.
3. (Jogging, The jogging) burns calories.
4. (Happiness, The happiness) comes from within.
5. She moved to (Rocky Mountains, the Rocky Mountains).

WHAT ARE THE TWELVE TENSES OF VERBS?

To understand the tenses of verbs, you must first understand the two main types of verbs and how they are found in a sentence.

Action and Linking Verbs

To find the verb, ask the following question: what is the sentence saying about the subject? Most verbs show action.

Example: The <u>quail</u> <u>ran</u> across the street.

This sentence explains that the quail (the subject) ran, so *ran* is the verb, and the verb shows action.

In some sentences, the verb does not show action; instead, it describes or names the subject or shows a state of existence:

Example: Jessica is happy.
Example: Jessica looks happy.

Is is a *linking verb* because it links or connects *happy* to *Jessica*. Linking verbs are usually forms of *be*: *be, am, is, are, was, were, being, been, will be, has been*. Other words like *act, appear, become, feel, get, grow, look, make, prove, remain, seem, smell, sound*, and *taste* are also linking verbs when they serve the same function.

Twelve Tenses

The tense of a verb indicates time. Some languages, like Chinese, have no tenses; however, the English language has a complex system of tenses to indicate time in a sentence.

Simple Tenses

1. Present	I, you, we, they eat apples.
	He/she/it eats apples.
2. Past	I, you, he/she/it, we, they ate apples.
3. Future	I, you, he/she/it, we, they will eat apples.

Simple Tenses Explained

Tense (verb forms)	Time Line	Explanation of Time
Present:		Present, and it may imply a continuation from past to future.
I <u>eat</u> apples. She <u>eats</u> apples.	past ——— xxx ——— future now	
Past:		Past
I <u>ate</u> apples.	past — xxx ——— future now	
Future: (*will* followed by present tense verb)	past ——— xxx — future now	Future
I <u>will eat</u> apples.		

Perfect Tenses

4. Present Perfect	I, you, we, they have eaten apples.
	He/she/it has eaten apples.
5. Past Perfect	I, you, he/she/it, we, they had eaten apples.
6. Future Perfect	I, you, he/she/it, we, they will have eaten apples.

Perfect Tenses Explained

Tense (verb forms)	Time Line	Explanation of Time
Present Perfect: (*have* or *has* followed by past participle)	past ——xxx—— future now	Completed recently in the past, and may continue into the present.
I <u>have eaten</u> apples. She <u>has eaten</u> apples.		
Past Perfect: (*had* followed by past participle)	apple lunch past —x y—— future now	Prior to a specific time in the past.
I <u>had eaten</u> an apple before lunch.		
Future Perfect: (*will have* followed by past participle) I <u>will have eaten</u> an apple before dinner.	apple dinner past ———x y— future now	At a time prior to a specific time in the future.

Progressive Tenses

7. Present Progressive	I am eating apples. He/she/it is eating apples. You, we, they are eating apples.	
8. Past Progressive	I, he/she/it, was eating apples. You, we, they were eating apples.	
9. Future Progressive	I, you, he/she/it, we, they will be eating apples.	

Progressive Tenses Explained

Tense (verb forms)	Time Line	Explanation of Time
Present Progressive: (*am, is,* or *are* plus verb + ing ending)	past ——xxx—— future now	In progress now.
I <u>am eating</u> an apple. He <u>is eating</u> an apple. They <u>are eating</u> apples.		

(continued)

Progressive Tenses Explained (*continued*)

Tense (verb forms)	Time Line	Explanation of Time
Past Progressive: (*was* or *were* followed by verb + ing ending) I <u>was eating</u> an apple. They <u>were eating</u> apples.	past ——— x̶x̶x̶ ——— future now	In progress in the past.
Future Progressive: (*will be* followed by verb + ing ending) I <u>will be eating</u> an apple.	past ——— x̶x̶x̶ ——— future now	In progress in the future.

Perfect Progressive Tenses

10. Present Perfect Progressive	I, you, we, they have been eating apples. He/she/it has been eating apples.
11. Past Perfect Progressive	I, you, he/she/it, we, they had been eating apples.
12. Future Perfect Progressive	I, you, he/she/it, we, they will have been eating apples.

Perfect Progressive Tenses Explained

Tense (verb forms)	Time Line	Explanation of Time
Present Perfect Progressive: (*have been* or *has been* plus verb + ing ending) I <u>have been eating</u> an apple. He <u>has been eating</u> an apple.	past ——— x̶x̶x̶ ——— future now	In progress up to now.
Past Perfect Progressive: (*had been* followed by verb + ing ending) I <u>had been eating</u> an apple when I bit into a worm.	apple worm ↘ ↓ past ——— x̶ y̶ ——— future now	In progress before another event in the past.

Tense (verb forms)	Time Line	Explanation of Time
Future Perfect Progressive: (*will have been* followed by verb + ing ending)	apple sunset past —— x y —— future now	In progress before another event in the future.
By sunset, I <u>will have been eating</u> an apple for twenty minutes.		

Warning: notice that most mental activity verbs, like *believe,* are not used with progressive forms.

HOW DOES A WRITER AVOID COMMON TROUBLE SPOTS WITH VERBS?

Irregular Verbs

Each main verb has five forms, and these forms can be used to create all twelve tenses. *Be* is an exception; it has eight forms—*be, am, is, are, was, were, being, been.* Most verbs have regular forms, like *walk.* The *-s* form is created by adding *-s* to the base form. The past and the past participle are formed by adding *-d* or *-ed* to the base form. The present participle is formed by adding *-ing* to the base form. Some verbs have irregular forms, like *eat.* Irregular verbs give everyone trouble.

Forms of Verbs

Base	-S Form	Past	Past Participle	Present Participle
Walk	Walks	Walked	Walked	Walking
Eat	Eats	Ate	Eaten	Eating

Sometimes people use irregular verbs incorrectly because they don't know the correct forms to use. For example, someone might say the following:

Incorrect: I seen a bird.
Revised: I saw a bird. (past tense)
Revised: I have seen a bird. (present perfect)

ar verbs have unique forms in the past tense and the past participle.
and the present participle form of irregular verbs are not listed in the
because their forms are predictable.

Common Irregular Verbs

Base Form	Past Tense	Past Participle (used after *have, has, had* or with a form of *be* to create the passive voice)
Arise	Arose	Arisen
Awake	Awoke, awaked	Awoke, awaked
Be (am/are/is)	Was/were	Been
Bear	Bore	Borne, born
Beat	Beat	Beaten
Become	Became	Become
Begin	Began	Begun
Bend	Bent	Bent
Bind	Bound	Bound
Bite	Bit	Bitten, bit
Bleed	Bled	Bled
Blow	Blew	Blown
Break	Broke	Broken
Bring	Brought	Brought
Build	Built	Built
Burn	Burned, burnt	Burned, burnt
Burst	Burst	Burst
Buy	Bought	Bought
Cast	Cast	Cast
Catch	Caught	Caught
Choose	Chose	Chosen
Cling	Clung	Clung
Come	Came	Come
Cost	Cost	Cost
Creep	Crept	Crept
Cut	Cut	Cut
Deal	Dealt	Dealt
Dig	Dug	Dug
Dive	Dived, dove	Dived
Do/does	Did	Done
Draw	Drew	Drawn
Dream	Dreamed, dreamt	Dreamed, dreamt
Drink	Drank	Drunk

Base Form	Past Tense	Past Participle (used after *have, has, had* or with a form of *be* to create the passive voice)
Drive	Drove	Driven
Eat	Ate	Eaten
Fall	Fell	Fallen
Feed	Fed	Fed
Feel	Felt	Felt
Fight	Fought	Fought
Find	Found	Found
Flee	Fled	Fled
Fling	Flung	Flung
Fly	Flew	Flown
Forbid	Forbade, forbad	Forbidden
Forget	Forgot	Forgotten, forgot
Freeze	Froze	Frozen
Get	Got	Got, gotten
Give	Gave	Given
Go/goes	Went	Gone (not *had went*)
Grind	Ground	Ground
Grow	Grew	Grown
Hang (suspend)	Hung	Hung
Hang (execute)	Hanged	Hanged
Have/has	Had	Had
Hear	Heard	Heard
Hide	Hid	Hidden, hid
Hold	Held	Held
Hurt	Hurt	Hurt
Keep	Kept	Kept
Kneel	Knelt, kneeled	Knelt, kneeled
Knit	Knit, knitted	Knit, knitted
Know	Knew	Known
Lay	Laid	Laid
Lead	Led	Led
Leap	Leaped, leapt	Leaped, leapt
Leave	Left	Left
Lend	Lent	Lent
Let	Let	Let
Lie	Lay	Lain
Light	Lighted, lit	Lighted, lit

(*continued*)

Common Irregular Verbs (*continued*)

Base Form	Past Tense	Past Participle (used after *have, has, had* or with a form of *be* to create the passive voice)
Lose	Lost	Lost
Make	Made	Made
Mean	Meant	Meant
Meet	Met	Met
Mistake	Mistook	Mistaken
Pay	Paid	Paid
Plead	Pleaded, pled	Pleaded, pled
Prove	Proved	Proved, proven
Put	Put	Put
Quit	Quit	Quit
Raise	Raised	Raised
Read	Read	Read
Rid	Rid	Rid
Ride	Rode	Ridden
Ring	Rang	Rung
Rise	Rose	Risen
Run	Ran	Run
Say	Said	Said
See	Saw	Seen
Seek	Sought	Sought
Sell	Sold	Sold
Send	Sent	Sent
Set	Set	Set
Sew	Sewed	Sewn, sewed
Shake	Shook	Shaken
Shine (radiate light)	Shone, shined	Shone, shined
Shine (polish)	Shined	Shined
Shoot	Shot	Shot
Show	Showed	Shown, showed
Shrink	Shrank, shrunk	Shrunk, shrunken
Shut	Shut	Shut
Sing	Sang, sung	Sung
Sink	Sank	Sunk
Sit	Sat	Sat
Sleep	Slept	Slept
Slide	Slid	Slid
Sling	Slung	Slung

Base Form	Past Tense	Past Participle (used after *have, has, had* or with a form of *be* to create the passive voice)
Slink	Slunk, slinked	Slunk, slinked
Sow	Sowed	Sown, sowed
Speak	Spoke	Spoken
Speed	Sped, speeded	Sped, speeded
Spend	Spent	Spent
Spin	Spun	Spun
Spit	Spit, spat	Spit, spat
Spring	Sprang, sprung	Sprung
Stand	Stood	Stood
Steal	Stole	Stolen
Stick	Stuck	Stuck
Sting	Stung	Stung
Stink	Stank, stunk	Stunk
Stride	Strode	Stridden
Strike	Struck	Struck, stricken
String	Strung	Strung
Strive	Strived, strove	Striven, strived
Swear	Swore	Sworn
Sweat	Sweat, sweated	Sweat, sweated
Swell	Swelled	Swelled, swollen
Swim	Swam	Swum
Swing	Swung	Swung
Take	Took	Taken
Teach	Taught	Taught
Tear	Tore	Torn
Tell	Told	Told
Think	Thought	Thought
Throw	Threw	Thrown
Understand	Understood	Understood
Wake	Woke, waked	Woken, waked, woke
Wear	Wore	Worn
Weave (make cloth)	Wove, weaved	Woven, weaved
Weep	Wept	Wept
Win	Won	Won
Wind	Wound	Wound
Wring	Wrung	Wrung
Write	Wrote	Written

Any dictionary will also provide the forms of irregular verbs, so writers may consult one or the table above when in doubt about the correct form of an irregular verb.

PRACTICE 2

Insert the correct form of the verbs on the blanks to create the tense that is called for. Check the table of Common Irregular Verbs for past participles as needed. Write on a separate piece of paper or on a computer.

Example: He (walk) _____ one mile each day. (simple present tense).

   He walks one mile each day.

1. They (grow) _____ vegetables each summer (simple present tense).
2. The light (change) _____ in the evening (simple past tense).
3. Your physician (prescribe) _____ drugs (simple future tense).
4. The governor (balance) _____ the budget (perfect present tense).
5. The students (see) _____ the movie (perfect past tense).
6. The worker (dig) _____ a pit (perfect future tense).
7. The lawyer (ask) _____ questions (present progressive).
8. The two fish (swim) _____ in the stream (past progressive).
9. The business (prosper) _____ in the community next year (future progressive).
10. Linda (study) _____ marine biology for two years (present perfect progressive).
11. The chef (bake) _____ the cake when the fire started (past perfect progressive).
12. By next January, the director (produce) _____ a movie for three months (future perfect progressive).

Troublesome Irregular Verbs

In Chapter 17, you learned about the irregular forms of *be, do,* and *have.* Four sets of additional verbs from the chart above can also prove challenging: lie/lay, sit/set, rise/raise, and shine/shine. Notice that the second word in each set takes an object.

Troublesome Irregular Verbs

Present Tense	Past Tense	Past Participle (follows *has, have* or *had*)
Lie (to rest or recline)	Lay	Lain
Lay (to put **something** down)	Laid	Laid

To Lie

Jennifer *lies* in her hammock.
Yesterday she *lay* in her hammock.
She has *lain* in her hammock all afternoon.

To Lay (objects are in bold)

Please *lay* the **plates** on the table.
Yesterday Mike *laid* the **plates** on the table.
He has *laid* the **plates** on the table.

Lie and lay are particularly confusing because the past tense of *lie* is the same as the present tense of *lay*. As a result, the context of the sentence must clarify the author's intention.

Troublesome Irregular Verbs

Present Tense	Past Tense	Past Participle (follows *has, have* or *had*)
Sit (to take a seat or rest)	Sat	Sat
Set (to put or to place something)	Set	Set

To Sit

Grandma *sits* in a rocking chair.
Yesterday she *sat* down in a rocking chair.
She has *sat* in her rocking chair since breakfast.

To Set (objects are in bold)

Gerald *set* the **silverware** on the table.
Yesterday he *set* the **silverware** on the table.
The kids have *set* the **silverware** on the table.

Troublesome Irregular Verbs

Present Tense	Past Tense	Past Participle (follows *has, have* or *had*)
Rise (to get up or to move up)	Rose	Risen
Raise (to lift up or increase something) *Raise* is a verb with regular endings.	Raised	Raised

To Rise

Chickens *rise* early.

Yesterday the chickens *rose* very early.

By 5:00 A.M. last Saturday, the chickens had *risen*.

To Raise (objects are in bold)

Soldiers *raise* the **flag** every morning.

They *raised* the **flag** before breakfast.

They have *raised* the **flag** every day for ten years.

Troublesome Irregular Verbs

Present Tense	Past Tense	Past Participle (follows *has, have* or *had*)
Shine (to radiate light)	Shone, shined	Shone, shined
Shine (to polish something)	Shined	Shined

To Shine

The sun *shines* in the summer.

Yesterday the sun *shone* all day.

The sun has *shone* all morning.

To Shine (objects are in bold)

Officer Martin *shines* her **shoes** each night.

She *shined* her **shoes** yesterday.

She has *shined* her **shoes** daily since joining the force.

PRACTICE 3

Choose the correct form of the verb.

Example: Gary (lay, laid) the body in the grave yesterday.

Gary **laid** the body in the grave yesterday.

1. The dog (lay, laid) on the grass last night.
2. Chris has (lay, lain) on his bed.
3. Hector and Carlos (sat, set) in the front of the room.

4. Kerri (rises, raises) at 5:00 A.M. for work.
5. The stars have (shine, shone) all night.

Gerunds and Infinitives

A gerund is a verb form that ends in -*ing*. An infinitive is the base verb form preceded by *to*. Neither gerunds nor infinitives can serve as the main verb of a sentence.

Gerund: I <u>love</u> swimming.
Infinitive: I <u>love</u> to swim.

Basically, both of the sentences above communicate the same idea, and both sentences are correct. Some verbs can be followed by either a gerund or an infinitive. However, some verbs can be followed only by a gerund while other verbs can be followed only by an infinitive. Becoming familiar with these verbs will help you to write correctly.

Below are some verbs that can be followed by either a gerund or an infinitive:

Verb + Gerund or Infinitive

Begin	Forget	Love	Start
Can't stand	Hate	Prefer	Stop
Continue	Like	Remember	Try

Sometimes the meaning is about the same with a gerund or an infinitive.

Gerund: I hate eating broccoli.
Infinitive: I hate to eat broccoli.

At other times, the meaning changes, like with *forget, remember*, and *stop*.

Gerund: The children stopped eating. (This means that the children quit eating.)
Infinitive: The children stopped to eat. (This means that the children started eating.)

Below are verbs that can be followed only by a gerund, not an infinitive.

Verb + Gerund (not an infinitive)

Admit	Consider	Finish	Postpone	Suggest
Apologize for	Deny	Imagine	Practice	Suspect of
Appreciate	Discuss	Insist on	Put off	Talk about
Approve of	Dislike	Keep	Quit	Thank for
				(*continued*)

Verb + Gerund (not an infinitive) (*continued*)

Avoid	Enjoy	Look forward to	Recall	Think about
Be used to	Escape	Finish	Resist	Tolerate
Believe in	Feel like	Miss	Risk	

Incorrect: James finished to run the race.

Revised: James finished running the race.

Below are verbs that can be followed only by an infinitive, not a gerund.

Verb + Infinitive (not a gerund)

Agree	Claim	Hope	Plan	Want
Ask	Decide	Manage	Pretend	Wish
Arrange	Expect	Mean	Promise	
Beg	Fail	Need	Refuse	
Choose	Have	Offer	Wait	

Incorrect: Roberto decided walking home.

Revised: Roberto decided to walk home.

With some verbs, a noun or pronoun must come between the verb and the infinitive:

Verb + Noun (or pronoun) + Infinitive (not a gerund)

Advise	Convince	Instruct	Require
Allow	Encourage	Order	Tell
Cause	Force	Persuade	Urge
Command	Have	Remind	Warn

Incorrect: Patricia encouraged *the kids* throwing their trash away.

Revised: Patricia encouraged *the kids* to throw their trash away.

With other verbs, a noun or a pronoun may or may not come between the verb and the infinitive:

Verb + Optional Noun (or pronoun) + Infinitive (not a gerund)

Ask	Expect	Need	Promise	Want	Would like

Incorrect: The driver needs using a map.

Revised: The driver needs the navigator to use a map.

Revised: The driver needs to use a map.

With a few verbs, a noun or a pronoun will come between the verb and the infinitive but the *to* is omitted from the infinitive:

Verb + Noun (or pronoun) + Unmarked Infinitive (not a gerund)		
Have (cause)	Let (allow)	Make (force)

Incorrect: The pilot makes me wearing a seatbelt.

Incorrect: The pilot makes me to wear a seatbelt.

Revised: The pilot makes me wear a seatbelt.

PRACTICE 4

Choose the correct form of the verb.

Example: I finished (running, to run) a mile.

I finished **running** a mile.

1. I suggest (practicing, to practice) for thirty minutes daily.
2. I plan (attending, to attend) the party.
3. Miguel advised me (taking, to take) three classes.
4. The instructor let me (knowing, to know, know) that I passed.
5. The couple agreed (going, to go) on a vacation.

Progressives

Progressive tenses use a form of *be* plus a verb with an *–ing* ending. They communicate a continuing activity.

Example: I am running.

Some verbs, however, are not normally used to create the progressive tense. These verbs typically indicate sensing or a state of being:

Common Verbs Not Normally Used in the Progressive

Agree	Have	Look	Possess	Understand
Appear	Hear	Love	See	Want
Believe	Imagine	Mean	Seem	Weight
Belong	Include	Need	Smell	Wish
Contain	Know	Own	Taste	
Cost	Like	Prefer	Think	

Incorrect: They are belonging to the organization.

Revised: They belong to the organization.

PRACTICE 5

 Change the verb forms to avoid the progressive. Write on a separate piece of paper or on a computer.

Example: Zaira was smelling the flowers.

Zaira **smelled** the flowers.

1. The hotel is costing two hundred dollars per night.
2. The counselor is understanding the problem.
3. Pam and Greg are knowing the truth.
4. They are preferring to dance.
5. The jars were containing peaches.

Modals

Modals are helping verbs that express relationships like permission, ability, possibility, etc. They are never the main verb in a sentence. They are used before the main verbs in sentences. When a modal is used before a main verb in a sentence, the main verb must take its base form.

Modals

Can	May	Will	Should
Could	Might	Shall	Would
	Must		

Incorrect: Jasmine *should* keeps her promise.

Incorrect: Jasmine *should* to keep her promise.

Revised: Jasmine *should* keep her promise.

PRACTICE 6

Change the main verb to its base form. Write on a separate piece of paper or on a computer.

Example: Rommel may singing in the concert.

Rommel may **sing** in the concert.

1. The pedigree chart will tracks her ancestors.
2. Wax could melting in the sun.
3. Pollution should being reduced.
4. The sun shall sets in two hours.
5. I will meeting you at the park.

Subjunctive Mood

Mood is the aspect of a verb that indicates the manner in which an idea is expressed. Three moods exist in English: The indicative mood, the imperative mood, and the subjunctive mood. The indicative mood expresses opinions, facts, and questions. It is used much more frequently than the other two and is created as explained under the Twelve Tenses head above. The imperative mood expresses a command or request and takes the base form of the verb. The subjunctive expresses statements, wishes, or requests that are contrary to fact. It gives everyone trouble, so how and when to use it requires some explanation.

Indicative: You are the president. (statement)
Imperative: Be the president. (request or command)
Subjunctive: If you *were* (not *was*) the president, you could lower taxes. (statement or wish contrary to fact)

Forms of the subjunctive

In the subjunctive mood, present tense verbs use the base form always.

Subjunctive: I suggested that he take (not *takes*) a second look at the car.
Subjunctive: She insists that he drive (not *drives*) safely.

In the subjunctive mood, there is only one form of *be* in the past tense: *were* (never *was*). The subjunctive mood in the past tense for all other verbs is the same as for the indicative mood.

Subjunctive: If he were (not *was*) a pilot, he could travel the world.
Subjunctive: If I were (not *was*) to travel to Mars, I would look for new life forms.

When to use the subjunctive

The subjunctive mood was used extensively in earlier English. Now, you just need to know how to use it in the following situations:

1. In contrary-to-fact clauses beginning with *if, as if,* or *as though:*

   Incorrect: *If* he was a millionaire, he would never work.
   Revised: *If* he were a millionaire, he would never work.

   Incorrect: He would never work *if* he was a millionaire.
   Revised: He would never work *if* he were a millionaire.

   Only use the subjunctive in statements that are contrary to fact; do not use it in statements that communicate conditions that exist or may exist.

   Incorrect: The fighter talked as though he were dangerous.

   Revised: The fighter talked as though he was dangerous.

   The fighter was, in fact, dangerous (and probably still is), so the subjunctive should not be used.

2. In contrary-to-fact clauses expressing a wish:

   Incorrect: I wish that my car was newer.

   Revised: I wish that my car were newer.

3. In contrary-to-fact clauses expressing a request that start with *that* following such verbs as *ask, insist, recommend, request,* and *suggest:*

   Incorrect: His father recommends that he attends college.

   Revised: His father recommends that he attend college.

PRACTICE 7

Correct the form of the verb. Write on a separate piece of paper or on a computer.

Example: I recommend that she takes piano lessons this summer.

   I recommend that she **take** piano lessons this summer.

1. If I was preparing for the Olympics, I would train all the time.
2. If he was programming the computers, we would not have problems now.
3. They wish that I was punctual.
4. The officer insists that the driver not moves.
5. The judge asks that he tells the truth.

Tense Shifts

Now that you are familiar with different forms of verbs, read the following corrupted version of a passage from *To Kill a Mockingbird* by Harper Lee in which Atticus explains courage to Jem:

> I wanted you to see something about her—I want you to see what real courage was, instead of getting the idea that courage is a man with a gun in his hand. It was when you know you were licked before you begin but you began anyway and you saw it through no matter what. You rarely won, but sometimes you do.

Did you notice the unnecessary shifting in tense when you read the passage? This distracts readers from the message that the writer is trying to communicate. Try to maintain consistent verb tenses. When you are telling a story, you may want to be in the past tense because the stories that we tell have happened in the past, so it makes sense to indicate that with the tense by adding a *–d* or *–ed* to regular verbs and by checking the past-tense verb forms of irregular verbs in the table above. Notice how the passage sounds when verb tenses do not shift needlessly.

> I wanted you to see something about her—I wanted you to see what real courage is, instead of getting the idea that courage is a man with a gun in his hand. It's when you know you're licked before you begin but you begin anyway and you see it through no matter what. You rarely win, but sometimes you do. (p. 116)

When writing in college, default to the present tense. When you need to shift to the past tense, do so with the intention of returning to the present tense after referring to an event in the past.

Regardless of the tense that you choose to write in, begin with a tense in mind, strive for consistency in verb tense, and avoid needless shifts in tense that will distract the reader.

PRACTICE 8

In the following corrupted version of a passage about love from The Road Less Traveled *by M. Scott Peck (p. 91), change the verbs from past tense to present tense. Write on a separate piece of paper or on a computer. You will need to change more than one verb in each sentence.*

Example: Love was difficult to analyze.

      Love is difficult to analyze.

1. The myth of romantic love told us that for every young man in the world there was a young woman who was "meant for him," and vice versa.
2. Moreover, the myth implied that there was only one man meant for a woman and only one women for a man, and this was predetermined "in the stars."
3. When we met the person for whom we are intended, recognition came through the fact that we fell in love.
4. Since the match was perfect, we will then be able to satisfy all of each other's needs forever and ever, and lived happily forever after in perfect union and harmony.
5. If we did not satisfy each other's needs, then we misread the stars, and we lived unhappily, or get a divorce.

Passive and Active Voice

Active voice involves the subject of the sentence performing the action of a verb.

      Example: <u>John</u> <u>threw</u> the ball.

This sentence shows John performing the action of throwing a ball. Passive voice, on the other hand, involves the subject of the sentence receiving the action of the verb.

      Example: The <u>ball</u> <u>was thrown</u> by John.

Notice that the passive voice involves a form of the verb *be (was)* plus a past participle (thrown) of the main verb.

      Which sentence do you think is more vivid and concise? Most writing is more effective when the verbs are in active voice, so default to active voice. Occasionally, you will want to use passive voice, for example, when the performer of the action is unknown or less important than the receiver of the action.

      Example: The <u>glass</u> <u>was broken</u> by one of the kids.

Since no one knows which kid broke the glass, the passive voice is appropriate.

PRACTICE 9

 Change the following sentences from passive to active voice. Write on a separate piece of paper or on a computer.

Example: The barn was burned by the fire.

      The fire burned the barn.

1. The desert sand was blown by the wind.
2. The rocks were polished by the river.
3. The magazine was read by Miguel.
4. The rockets were prepared and launched by the crew.
5. The snowboard was waxed by Phillip.

How does a writer avoid repeating subjects?

Some languages allow subjects to be repeated in sentences; English, however, does not. Avoid repeating a subject in a sentence by following it with a pronoun.

Incorrect: My <u>mom</u> she <u>is</u> a wonderful lady.
Revised: My <u>mom</u> <u>is</u> a wonderful lady.

Even if words come between the subject and the pronoun, do not repeat a subject in a sentence.

Incorrect: My <u>mom</u>, who treats everyone like an angel, she <u>is</u> a wonderful lady.
Revised: My <u>mom</u>, who treats everyone like an angel, <u>is</u> a wonderful lady.

PRACTICE 10

Rewrite the following sentences so that the subject is not repeated. Write on a separate piece of paper or on a computer.

Example: The car it is very expensive.

The car is very expensive.

1. The trees they are beautiful this time of year.
2. The anchor that is on the left side it is heavy.
3. Ice skating it is good exercise.
4. The clown who is juggling he is talented.
5. My essay, which discusses voter turnout, it earned an *A*.

How does a writer start sentences with *here* and *there*?

Some sentences start with *here* and *there*. Remember that a sentence contains a subject and a verb, and that typically the subject comes before the verb. In sentences that begin with *here* or *there*, however, the subject comes after the verb, and *here* or *there* is never the subject. Also, beginning these sentences with *here* or *there* is required, not optional.

> Incorrect: <u>Are</u> my <u>friends</u>.
> Incorrect: <u>Is</u> the <u>ball</u> in the yard.

Notice that the verbs agree with the subjects that follow them.

> Revised: Here <u>are</u> my <u>friends</u>.   Or: My <u>friends</u> <u>are</u> here.
> Revised: There <u>is</u> a <u>ball</u> in the yard.   Or: A <u>ball</u> <u>is</u> in the yard.

PRACTICE 11

Rewrite the following sentences so that they begin with here *or* there. *Make sure that the subjects and verbs agree. Write on a separate piece of paper or on a computer.*

Example: Is the balloons for the party.

> Here are the balloons for the party.

1. Is the information that you requested.
2. Are road hazard signs.
3. Was seven people in attendance.
4. Is my keys.
5. Come the bride.

HOW DOES A WRITER START SENTENCES WITH *IT*?

Some sentences start with *it*. Sometimes *it* functions like *here* and *there*; in other words, *it* starts sentences in which the subjects follow the verbs. In these cases, *it* is never the subject, and beginning these sentences with *it* is required, not optional:

> Incorrect: <u>is</u> enjoyable <u>to run</u>.
> Revised: It <u>is</u> enjoyable <u>to run</u>.   Or: <u>To run</u> <u>is</u> enjoyable.

At other times, however, *it* serves as the subject of the sentence. These situations usually involve a description of the weather, time, distance, or environment. In these cases, beginning the sentence with *it* is also required, not optional:

> <u>It</u> <u>is</u> cloudy in the morning at the beach.
> <u>It</u> <u>is</u> 8:00 A.M.

It <u>is</u> 150 miles to Miami.

It <u>looked</u> crowded in the restaurant on Saturday night.

PRACTICE 12

 Rewrite the following sentences so that they begin with it. *Make sure that the subjects and verbs agree. Write on a separate piece of paper or on a computer.*

Example: Are a windmill.

It is a windmill.

1. Is pleasant to walk on the beach.
2. Is 3:00 P.M.
3. Appears windy this afternoon.
4. Were a rainy day.
5. Seem like a ghost.

HOW DOES A WRITER USE ADJECTIVES?

WORD ORDER WITH ADJECTIVES

An adjective describes a noun or pronoun, and adjectives usually come before the nouns or pronouns that they describe or after linking verbs (forms of *be* like *is, was*) or after sense verbs (like *look, seem*).

Incorrect: Carmel wore a necklace red.

Revised: Carmel wore a red necklace.

Revised: Carmel's necklace was red.

Revised: Carmel's necklace looks red.

When more than one adjective describes a noun or pronoun in English, they should follow the conventional order described in the table below:

Order of Adjectives

1	Article or other noun marker	a, an, the, Jerry's, this, four, your
2	Judgment	attractive, delicious, intelligent, rude
3	Size	large, tall, little, small

(continued)

Order of Adjectives (*continued*)

4	Shape	long, round, square, fat, oval
5	Age	ancient, old, young, youthful
6	Color	red, blue, green, white
7	Nationality	Norwegian, Greek, Thai, Ethiopian, American
8	Religion	Catholic, Jewish, Mormon, Muslim
9	Material	paper, plastic, fur, wood, marble
10	Noun Used as an Adjective	tree (as in tree house), book (as in book report)
11	The Noun Modified	woman, teacher, bike, park, monkey

In addition to remembering the correct order for adjectives, limit the number that you use to two or three between the article or noun marker and the noun or pronoun:

> Incorrect: I own a red old small beautiful bike.
> Revised: I own a beautiful red bike.

Punctuating Adjectives

When two or more adjectives modify a noun or pronoun, the adjectives may be either coordinate or cumulative. When several adjectives each modify a noun separately, they are coordinate. You may test for coordinate adjectives by asking the following questions:

- Can the adjectives be joined by *and*?
- Can the adjectives be placed in any order?

If the answer is yes to these questions, then they are coordinate (each adjective modifies the noun separately), and a comma is needed between each adjective.

> Example: My mother is a *warm, intelligent, happy* person.
> Test #1: My mother is a *warm* and *intelligent* and *happy* person. (This sounds okay.)
> Test #2: My mother is a *happy, intelligent, warm* person. (This sounds okay.)

Since the answer to both questions is yes, the adjectives are coordinate, and a comma is required between each adjective. Notice that no comma is used between the last adjective and the noun.

Incorrect: My mother is a *warm intelligent happy* person. (Use commas to separate coordinate adjectives.)

Incorrect: My mother is a *warm, intelligent, happy,* person. (Do not use a comma to separate the last adjective and the noun or pronoun.)

Revised: My mother is a *warm, intelligent, happy* person.

If the answer to either of these questions is no, then the adjectives are cumulative, and no comma is needed. Instead, use the correct order of adjectives by consulting the table above.

Example: My mother is a pleasant small Irish person.

Test #1: My mother is a pleasant and small and Irish person. (This does not sound okay.)

Test #2: My mother is an Irish small pleasant person. (This does not sound okay.)

Since the answer to the two questions is no, they are cumulative, and no comma is used:

Incorrect: My mother is a pleasant, small, Irish person. (Do not use commas to separate cumulative adjectives.)

Revised: My mother is a pleasant small Irish person.

Notice that each adjective modifies the noun and all adjectives closer to the noun.

Irish modifies *person.*
Small modifies *Irish person.*
Pleasant modifies *small Irish person.*

PRACTICE 13

Create sentences using the nouns and adjectives below, and put the adjectives in the correct order. If the adjectives are coordinate, insert commas as needed. Write on a separate piece of paper or on a computer.

Example: hair (long, black)

She has long black hair.

1. bike (red, new, beautiful)
2. desk (wood, brown, oval)

3. woman (friendly, cheerful)
4. book (old, big)
5. man (outgoing, positive)

Using Present and Past Participles as Adjectives

The present participle is a verb that ends in *–ing*, and the past participle is a verb that typically ends in *–ed, –d, –en, –n,* or *–t.* Both forms of the participle may be used as an adjective to modify a noun or pronoun.

Present participle: caring person
Past participle: stolen car

They may come before the nouns that they modify, or they may follow linking verbs and describe the subject of the sentence.

Present participle: Tanesha is a loving mother.

Present participle: Tanesha is loving.

Notice that a present participle describes a noun that is causing or stimulating an experience. Tanesha is treating her children with love, so she is causing her children to have positive experiences. Therefore, the present participle *loving* is used to describe her.

Past participle: Tam is driving a stolen truck. Tam's truck was stolen.

Notice that a past participle describes a noun that is undergoing an experience. Perhaps the truck was hot-wired and taken from its owner, so the truck was undergoing the experience. Therefore, the past participle *stolen* is used to describe it. Below are additional examples of present and past participles used as adjectives:

Present participle: We saw a boring movie. (The movie caused the boredom, so *boring* is used.)
Past participle: We were bored during the movie. (We underwent the experience, so *bored* is used.)

Several sets of participles that describe mental states often cause trouble for nonnative speakers of English.

Participles Describing Mental States

Annoying/annoyed	Fascinating/fascinated
Boring/bored	Frightening/frightened
Confusing/confused	Satisfying/satisfied
Depressing/depressed	Surprising/surprised
Exciting/excited	Tiring/tired
Exhausting/exhausted	

Present participle: The job is tiring. (The job caused the fatigue, so *tiring* is used.)

Past Participle: After work, he is a tired man. (He underwent the experience, so *tired* is used.)

When you want to use one of these words in your writing, check to make sure that you are using it correctly.

PRACTICE 14

Correct the past and present participles in the following sentences when they are used incorrectly. Write on a separate piece of paper or on a computer.

Example: Jorge was surprising by the attack.

Jorge was surprised by the attack.

1. We saw a depressed movie.
2. That meal was satisfying.
3. Here comes an exhausting runner.
4. Brem is annoying by procrastinators.
5. The book was fascinating.

HOW DOES A WRITER AVOID USING DOUBLE NEGATIVES?

Double negatives should always be avoided in English. A negative statement can usually be created by using only one of the following words:

Words that Lead to Negative Statements

Neither	Nobody	Not
Never	None	Nothing
No	No one	Nowhere

Incorrect: The employee will not earn no bonus this year. (Avoid two negatives.)

Revised: The employee will not earn a bonus this year.

Revised: The employee will earn no bonus this year.

Notice that two negatives create a positive, and if a positive statement is desired, simply omit both negatives.

Incorrect: Mark did not catch no fish. (This means that he did catch fish.)

Revised: Mark caught fish. (Use a positive statement when a positive statement is desired.)

Revised: Mark caught nothing. (Use one negative when a negative statement is desired.)

Be careful when you use a contraction that ends in –n't (not). Remember to still use just one negative to create a negative statement.

Negative Contractions

can't = can not	shouldn't = should not
couldn't = could not	won't = will not
don't = do not	wouldn't = would not

Incorrect: Hazel **couldn't** find no money. (Avoid two negatives.)

Revised: Hazel **couldn't** find any money. (Use one negative when a negative statement is desired.)

Remember that some words become negative when a prefix like *un-* (unhappy) or *non-* (nonsense) is added.

Incorrect: The lawyer was not unsympathetic. (Avoid two negatives.)

Revised: The lawyer was sympathetic. (Use a positive statement when a positive statement is desired.)

Revised: The lawyer was unsympathetic. (Use one negative when a negative statement is desired.)

Barely, hardly, and *scarcely* are considered negatives in English, so they should not be used in conjunction with another negative.

Incorrect: She is so sick that she **can't hardly** speak. (Avoid two negatives.)

Revised: She is so sick that she can **hardly** speak. (Use one negative when a negative statement is desired.)

When creating a negative statement with the word *not, not* will come after the first helping verb in the sentence. If a helping verb is not in the sentence, insert a form of *do* to make the statement negative:

Positive: Christy will fly a kite.
Negative: Christy will not fly a kite.

Positive: Christy loves her kite.
Negative: Christy **does** not love her kite.

Notice that *loves* changed to *love* (the base form) after inserting *does* in the negative statement.

PRACTICE 15

Correct the double negatives in the following sentences. Write on a separate piece of paper or on a computer.

Example: The boat did not have no gasoline.

The boat did not have any gasoline.

1. The guide never left no one behind.
2. None of the nurses have nothing to say.
3. Patty can't find no pen.
4. Jim-bob can't hardly read a lick.
5. Little Tim don't barely walk.

HOW DOES A WRITER CREATE QUESTIONS?

To know how to create a question in English, understand how to change a statement into a question. To change a statement into a question, move the helping verb from its position after the subject to before it. Then, of course, replace the period with a question mark.

Statement: Samantha will eat a hamburger.
Question: Will Samantha eat a hamburger?

Statement: James is frustrated.
Question: Is James frustrated?

If there is no helping verb or form of *be* in the statement, insert a form of *do* before the subject to create a question.

> Statement: You won the race.
> Question: Did you win the race?

Notice that *won* changed to its base form (*win*) when *did* was added.

PRACTICE 16

Change the following statements into questions. Write on a separate piece of paper or on a computer.

Example: Pathology deals with the nature of disease.

> Does pathology deal with the nature of disease?

1. Auto accidents can cause spinal injuries.
2. A chipmunk darts around quickly.
3. The Magna Carta guaranteed certain rights.
4. Deciduous trees lose their leaves in the fall.
5. Centipedes and spiders are different.

HOW DOES A WRITER USE PREPOSITIONS TO SHOW TIME AND PLACE?

Prepositions were discussed in detail in Chapter 15, and their use can prove troublesome to nonnative speakers of English because their uses are idiomatic, not logical. In other words, there may be no logical or grammatical explanation for the use of certain groups of words involving prepositions, except that these combinations of words are always used the same way in English. These idiomatic expressions must be learned gradually through experience with the language. Prepositions that show time and place can be particularly troublesome.

Prepositions that Show Time

Preposition	Explanation	Example
at	at a specific time	meet at 8:30, at sunrise, at midnight
by	by a specific time	eat by 5:00, by the end of the week, by spring break
in	in a period of time	finished in an hour, in the afternoon, in July, in 1985
on	on a specific day	talk on my lunch break, on Tuesday, on July 4th

Prepositions that Show Place

Preposition	Explanation	Example
at	at a location	walk at the park, sit at the table, shoot at the target
by	by a landmark	stand by the wall, sit by the fountain, run by the river
in	in a location/space	park in the driveway, think in my room, eat in the kitchen
on	on a surface/ electronic medium	sit on the floor, parade on Broadway, surf on the Internet, type on a computer

PRACTICE 17

Choose the correct prepositions from the table above for the sentences below.

Example: I will meet you _____ the cafeteria tomorrow for lunch.

> I will meet you **in** the cafeteria tomorrow for lunch.

1. I will see you at my house _____ 5:00 P.M.
2. Shall I type the essay _____ my computer?
3. Please call me _____ an hour.
4. The statue stands _____ the parking lot.
5. We wrote letters _____ Tuesday.

HOW DOES A WRITER USE PRONOUNS LIKE *I* AND *ME*?

Pronouns change their forms based on the roles that they take in sentences. Notice the types of pronouns in the table below:

	Subject Pronouns	Object Pronouns	Possessive Pronouns
Singular	I	me	my
	you	you	your
	he/she/it	him/her/it	his/her/its
Plural	we	us	our
	you	you	your
	they	them	their

A few rules will help you to use pronouns correctly.

1. Use subject pronouns as subjects of verbs.

> *I* am going on a break now. (*I* is the subject of *am going.*)
>
> *They* organized the event. (*They* is the subject of *organized.*)

Even when the subject is compound, use a subject pronoun.

> Incorrect: Jessica and me went to the movies.
>
> Revised: Jessica and I went to the movies. (*Jessica* and *I* are the subjects of *went.*)

To help you know which pronoun to use, try each pronoun by itself in the sentence.

> Incorrect: Me went to the movies. (*Me* doesn't sound right.)
>
> Revised: I went to the movies. (*I* sounds right.)

Common courtesy dictates that we allow others to precede us.

> Incorrect: I and Jessica went to the movies.
>
> Revised: Jessica and I went to the movies.

2. Use subject pronouns after forms of *be* (*be, am, is, are, was, were, being, been, will be, has been*).

> It is I who wrote the note.
>
> It is she on the phone.

These examples may sound stilted because this rule is infrequently followed in conversation; however, it is still used in writing. If you prefer to avoid the issue, rewrite the sentence.

> I am the one who wrote the note.
>
> She is on the phone.

3. Use subject pronouns after *than* or *as* when a verb is implied after the pronoun.

> Incorrect: Jerry runs as fast as me.
>
> Revised: Jerry runs as fast as I (run). (*Run* is understood after *I.*)
>
> Incorrect: The elephants are stronger than us.
>
> Revised: The elephants are stronger than we (are). (*Are* is understood after *we.*)

Of course, use an object pronoun after *than* or *as* when a verb is not implied after the pronoun.

> The server gave more dessert to you than me.
>
> The victory means a lot to you as well as me.

4. Use object pronouns as objects of verbs and prepositions.

> Donavon is chasing him. (*Him* is the object of *is chasing.*)
>
> Araceli held the door for me. (*Me* is the object of *for.*)

Even when the object is compound, use an object pronoun.

> Araceli held the door for Kerri and me. (*Kerri* and *me* are the objects of *for.*)

To help you know which pronoun to use, try each pronoun by itself in the sentence.

> Incorrect: Araceli held the door for I. (*I* doesn't sound right.)

Revised: Araceli held the door for me. (*Me* sounds right.)

Common courtesy dictates that we allow others to precede us.

Incorrect: Araceli held the door for me and Kerri.

Revised: Araceli held the door for Kerri and me.

5. Use possessive pronouns to indicate ownership.

My car is red.

The players practice on their field.

PRACTICE 18

Choose the correct pronoun for each sentence.

Example: He gave a dollar to (I, me).

He gave a dollar to **me**.

1. Dave and (I, me) studied law together in school.
2. It is (I, me).
3. The cheetah is faster than (I, me).
4. She saved the last cookies for Stewart and (I, me).
5. For Kelly and (I, me), the dance was boring.

GROUP WORK

1. As a group, visit Ohio University's ESL Page at http://www.englishpage.com/verbpage/verbs1.htm and take the quiz on verb tense.
2. As a group, write a single sentence in each of the twelve tenses.
3. As a group, write two sentences starting with *here, there*, and *it*.

TEST (TRUE/FALSE)

1. Knowing two or more languages is an asset.
2. A digression is a sign of effective writing.
3. *I would like two beefs* is correct English.
4. *I will be swimming in the summer* is an example of the future progressive tense.
5. The past tense of *throw* is *threw*.
6. *I stopped to talk* and *I stopped talking* mean the same thing.

7. *If I was a millionaire, I would buy a mansion* is correct.

8. Effective writing avoids unnecessary tense shifts.

9. Generally speaking, writers should strive to write in passive voice.

10. *I can't get no satisfaction* is correct.

WRITING ASSIGNMENTS

1. Academic Assignment: Visit the Librarians' Index to the Internet at http://www.lii.org to research a significant person. Then, write a short essay in which you evaluate the strengths and weaknesses of that person. For assistance in common ESL problems, visit Ohio University's ESL Page at http://www.ohiou.edu/esl/english/grammar/index.html.

2. Journal Assignment: Explain everything that you have learned in this chapter: "Have ESL trouble spots been avoided?"

3. Creative Assignment: Visit the Aldrich Museum of Contemporary Art at http://www.aldrichart.org/, and find an image that you like. Describe that image in a paragraph or short essay. For tips on writing descriptions, return to Purdue University's Online Writing Lab at http://owl.english.purdue.edu/handouts/general/gl_describe.html.

Have words been spelled correctly?

"A professional writer is an amateur who didn't quit."

— Richard Bach

LEARNING OBJECTIVES

1. Learn why spelling words correctly is both difficult and important.
2. Learn four common spelling rules.
   - I Before E Rule
   - Silent E Rule
   - Y Rule
   - Doubling Rule
3. Learn how to form plurals.
4. Learn how to form possessives.
5. Learn how to form contractions.
6. Learn the most commonly misspelled words.
7. Learn the most commonly confused words.
8. Learn how to avoid common incorrect word forms.
9. Learn when to spell out numbers.
10. Learn about American and British differences in spelling.
11. Learn how to use a computer to aid in spelling.
12. Learn the steps to improved spelling.

PRE-READING QUESTIONS

1. Do you find spelling words correctly easy or difficult? Why?
2. What are some words in English that are not spelled the way that they sound?
3. What is one good method of learning how to spell words correctly?
4. When you want to be specific about an amount in a sentence, do you use a number (732) or do you write the number out with letters (seven hundred and thirty-two)?
5. What are the strengths and weaknesses of using a computer to help you spell correctly?

Pre-Reading Activity

Circle the word that is spelled correctly in the following pairs.

1. judgement or judgment
2. a lot or alot
3. begining or beginning
4. awkward or akward
5. accross or across
6. definitely or definately
7. friend or freind
8. restrant or restaurant
9. Febrary or February
10. knowledge or knowlege

You will be able to find the answers in the table of commonly misspelled words in this chapter.

WHY IS SPELLING WORDS CORRECTLY BOTH DIFFICULT AND IMPORTANT?

Spelling in English is difficult because words are not always spelled the way that they sound (e.g., kneel). Furthermore, English has many homonyms, words that sound alike but have different spellings and meanings (e.g., there, their, they're), which confuse writers. To complicate spelling further, some words in English may be spelled correctly in more than one way (e.g., theater, theatre).

Although spelling is difficult, it is also important. Just try sending out a résumé with a few misspelled words. Try sending an application to a university with a few misspelled words. What will be your chances of being selected? Probably slim because misspelled words detract readers from the intended message and reduce the credibility of the author. In other words, the reader may consider the writer unskilled and ignorant, despite the fact that many poor spellers are quite intelligent.

Spelling words correctly comes easily to a few people; however, many people struggle with spelling. Fortunately, anyone who learns a few spelling rules and techniques can improve his or her spelling.

Before learning four basic rules of spelling, recall the definitions of vowels and consonants:

Vowels include the following: *a, e, i, o, u*, and sometimes *y*. The letter *y* functions as a vowel when it has the *ee* sound in words like *daisy* and the *i* sound in words like *shy*.

Consonants include the following: *b, c, d, f, g, h, j, k, l, m, n, p, q, r, s, t, v, w, x, z*, and sometimes *y*. The letter *y* functions as a consonant when it has the sound of the letter, such as in *yell* and *young*.

WHAT ARE FOUR COMMON SPELLING RULES?

I Before E Rule

The following rhyme may help you to remember this rule.

Use *i* before *e*
except after *c*
or when sounding like *a*,
as in neighbor and weigh.

I before E Rule

I before E	Except after C	Or when sounding like A
Believe	Ceiling	Eight
Chief	Deceive	Freight
Field	Receive	Sleigh
Pie		Neighbor
Piece		Weigh

Some exceptions include the following: either, foreign, height, leisure, neither, science, seize, society, their, weird.

Silent E Rule

If the final *e* in a word is not pronounced, drop the final *e* when adding endings that start with vowels, and keep the final e when adding endings that start with consonants.

Silent E Rule	
Drop the final e when adding endings that start with vowels.	Keep the final e when adding endings that start with consonants.
love + ed = loved	definite + ly = definitely
smoke + ing = smoking	care + ful = careful
fame + ous = famous	love + less = loveless
guide + ance = guidance	achieve + ment = achievement

Some exceptions include the following: argument, awful, changeable, judgment, noticeable, simply, truly.

Y Rule

When adding an ending to a word, change the final *y* to an *i* when a consonant comes before the final *y*. Do not change the *y* to an *i* when a vowel comes before the final *y*.

Y Rule	
Change the y to an i	**Do not change the y to an i**
happy + est = happiest	monkey + s = monkeys
lucky + ly = luckily	boy + ish = boyish
worry + es = worries	toy + ing = toying
crazy + ness = craziness	play + er = player

Some exceptions include the following: daily, dryer, laid, paid, said.

Warning: When adding -*ing* to a word ending in y, always keep the y (e.g., worrying, paying).

Doubling Rule

Double the final consonant of a word in the following conditions:

1. The word is one syllable or accented on the last syllable.
2. The ending being added starts with a vowel.
3. The last three letters of a word are a consonant, a vowel, and a consonant (CVC).

Doubling Rule	
stop + ing = stopping	submit + ed = submitted
refer + ed = referred	plan + er = planner
hot + est = hottest	admit + ance = admittance

Some exceptions include the following: words ending in s, w, x, and y (gas + es = gases, mow + ed = mowed, tax + ed = taxed, pay + able = payable)

Summary of Spelling Rules	
Rule	**Examples**
Use *i* before *e* except after *c* or when sounding like *a*, as in *neighbor* and *weigh*.	believe/ceiling/eight
If the final *e* in a word is not pronounced, drop the final *e* when adding endings that start with vowels.	love + ed = loved
When adding an ending to a word, change the final *y* to an *i* when a consonant comes before the final *y*.	happy + est = happiest
Double the final consonant of a word in the following conditions: The word is one syllable or accented on the last syllable. The ending being added starts with a vowel. The last three letters of a word are a consonant, a vowel, and a consonant (CVC).	stop + ing = stopping

PRACTICE 1

Spell each word correctly, and name the rule that dictates the spelling.

Example: bel____ ____ve = believe (I before E Rule)

Example: motive + ation = motivation (Silent E Rule)

1. fr ____ ____ ght = _____
2. lazy + ness = _____

3. judge + ment = _____
4. rec ___ ___ ve = _____
5. begin + ing = _____
6. p ___ ___ ce = _____
7. stay + ed = _____
8. box + ing = _____
9. hide + ing = _____
10. commit + ed = _____

A General Guideline for Prefixes and Suffixes

Remember that a prefix is something that is added to the beginning of a word, and a suffix is something that is added to the end of a word. In general, if a prefix ends with the same letter that starts a word, keep both letters: dis + service = disservice. Also, if a suffix starts with the same letter that ends a word, keep both letters: drunken + ness = drunkenness.

HOW DOES A WRITER FORM PLURALS?

Eight general rules govern the formation of plurals:

1. **Most words form their plurals by adding -s.**

Singular	Plural
Dog	Dogs
Camper	Campers
Building	Buildings

2. **Words ending in -s, -ss, -z, -x, -sh, or -ch usually form their plurals by adding -es.**

Singular	Plural
Kiss	Kisses
Mix	Mixes
Wish	Wishes

3. **As you learned in the Y Rule, change the final y to an i before adding -es when a consonant comes before the final y.**

Singular	Plural
Country	Countries
Lady	Ladies
Family	Families

Exception: proper names ending in *y* (May/Mays, Kelly/Kellys).

4. **In general, words ending in *-f* or *-fe* change the ending to *v* and add *-es*.**

Singular	Plural
Half	Halves
Life	Lives
Knife	Knives

Some exceptions include the following: roof/roofs, belief/beliefs.

5. **Add *-s* to words that end in a vowel and *o*. Add *-es* to words that end in a consonant and *o*.**

Singular ending in vowel and o	Plural ending in vowel and o
Video	Videos
Patio	Patios
Radio	Radios

Singular ending in consonant and o	Plural ending in consonant and o
Potato	Potatoes
Hero	Heroes
Tomato	Tomatoes

Some exceptions include the following: burrito/burritos, piano/pianos, solo/solos, soprano/sopranos, taco/tacos.

6. **Some words have irregular plurals (see Chapter 17 for more irregular plurals).**

Singular	Plural
Child	Children
Sheep	Sheep
Woman	Women

7. **Plural forms of abbreviations and numbers take the -*s* ending. (They used to take -'*s* ending.)**

Singular	Plural
CD	CDs
1990	1990s
VCR	VCRs

Some exceptions include the following: Use -'*s* to form the plural of letters used as letters and words used as words (straight *A's*, six *no's*).

8. **Form the plural of a term consisting of two or more words by adding -*s* or -*es* to the main word (whether or not the term is hyphenated).**

Singular	Plural
Attorney at law	Attorneys at law
Brother-in-law	Brothers-in-law
Passerby	Passersby

When in doubt about how to spell the plural of a word, consult a dictionary.

PRACTICE 2

Create the plural form of the following words, and give the rule number (#1–8) that dictates the spelling:

Example: mouse: mice (Rule #6)

1. printer:_____
2. leaf:_____
3. mosquito:_____
4. box:_____
5. man:_____
6. VCR:_____
7. county:_____
8. sister-in-law:_____
9. belief:_____
10. criterion:_____

HOW DOES A WRITER FORM POSSESSIVES?

To show ownership or possession, a writer may use words like *belongs to, owns, of*, etc.

> The car *belongs to* Kerry.
> Someone *owns* the ranch.
> The nose *of* the dog was cut.

Using an *-'s* on the end of the word (the owner or possessor), however, is an even easier way of showing what is being owned or possessed.

> That is Kerry's car. (Kerry owns the car.)

> This is someone's ranch. (Someone owns the ranch.)

> The dog's nose was cut. (The dog owns its nose.)

When adding *-'s* to a word, remember the following guidelines.

First, ask to whom or to what does something belong. Then, look for the following situations.

Forming Possessives

Situations	Examples
If the owner word (possessive) does not end in -s, add *-'s* to the word.	Jessica's bike is yellow. The children's hands waved goodbye.
*If the owner word (possessive) does end in *-s* and the word is singular, add *-'s* to the word.	I will follow my boss's (singular: one boss) policy.
If the owner word (possessive) does end in *-s* and the word is plural, just add *-'* to the word.	We painted the boys' (plural: two or more boys) room.
To show individual ownership, add *-'s* to each noun.	Jan's and Beverly's experience helped them to produce a play.
To show joint ownership, add *-'s* to the last noun only.	Jan and Beverly's play will be performed next week.
To show ownership in a compound noun, add *-'s* to the last element.	I borrowed my sister-in-law's car.

*Exception: If the owner word (possessive) does end in -s and the word is singular but adding *-'s* creates an awkward pronunciation, simply add an apostrophe.
Incorrect: Jesus's idea
Revised: Jesus' idea

Some words already show ownership, so do not us an apostrophe with them to show ownership: *his, her, hers, its, your, yours, our, ours, their, theirs, whose.* Don't confuse them with words like *it's, they're, you're,* and *who's*; these are contractions and will be discussed next.

The dog raised *its* paw.

Our garden has weeds.

Whose book is on the desk?

PRACTICE 3

Show possession in the following phrases by adding -'s or -' to the words that need it. Write on a separate piece of paper or on a computer.

Example: the magazine of Sheila = Sheila's magazine

1. the application of Carmen = _____
2. properties of the gas = _____
3. bumpers of the cars = _____
4. jobs (individual) of John and Jack = _____
5. efforts (joint) of Mike and Juan = _____
6. talent of my sisters-in-law = _____
7. artifact of the museum = _____
8. tires of the two bikes = _____
9. money of the brother-in-law = _____
10. homes (individual) of Carolyn and Barbara = _____

HOW DOES A WRITER FORM CONTRACTIONS?

A contraction is two words combined into one. When two words are combined, an apostrophe replaces the missing letter(s).

Jose does not want to wait any longer.

Jose doesn't want to wait any longer. (the apostrophe replaces the *o* in *not*)

Common Contractions

I am = I'm	we have = we've	where is = where's
I have = I've	we will, we shall = we'll	were not = weren't
I shall, I will = I'll	they are = they're	would not = wouldn't
I would = I'd	they have = they've	could not = couldn't
you are = you're	are not = aren't	should not = shouldn't

Have words been spelled correcrtly?

you have = you've	cannot = can't	would have = wou..
you will = you'll	do not = don't	could have = could've
she is, she has = she's	does not = doesn't	should have = should've
he is, he has = he's	have not = haven't	that is = that's
it is, it has = it's	let us = let's	there is = there's
we are = we're	who is, who has = who's	what is = what's

Note: Avoid using *ain't* (for *am not, is not, are not,* or *have not*) in formal communication.

An exception follows: *Will not* becomes *won't.*

PRACTICE 4

Write the following words as contractions.

Example: was + not = wasn't

1. I + had = _____
2. we + are = _____
3. there + is = _____
4. could + have = _____
5. does + not = _____
6. let + us = _____
7. it + is = _____
8. who + is = _____
9. will + not = _____
10. they + are = _____

WHAT ARE THE MOST COMMONLY MISSPELLED WORDS?

The following words are frequently used and misspelled. Study the words twenty at a time. Your instructor may test you on twenty words per week to help you master these 252 troublemakers.

Commonly Misspelled Words

A lot	Accidentally	Acquire	Adolescence
Absence	Accommodate	Across	All right
Achieve	Achievement	Actually	Already
Academic	Acknowledge	Address	Amateur

(continued)

Commonly Misspelled Words (*continued*)

	Committee	Exaggerate	Irresistible
	Competition	Excellent	Jewelry
	Competitive	Exercise	Judgment
20	Complete	Exhaust	Knowledge
.y	Conceivable 60	Existence	Laboratory
Ap. ogize	Conferred	Experience 100	Leisure 140
Apparently	Conqueror	Explanation	Length
Appearance	Conscientious	Extraordinary	Library
Appreciate	Consider	Extremely	License
Argument	Convenient	Familiar	Likely
Arrangement	Criticism	Fascinate	Literature
Ascend	Criticize	February	Loneliness
Athlete	Decision	Finally	Lying
Athletics	Definitely	Foreign	Maintenance
Attendance	Dependent	Friend	Management
Awful	Descendant	Government	Maneuver
Awkward	Describe	Grammar	Marriage
Basically	Develop	Grateful	Mathematics
Becoming	Development	Guarantee	Meant
Beginning	Dictionary	Guard	Medicine
Belief	Difference	Guidance	Mischievous
Believe	Disappear	Harass	Necessary
Benefit	Disappoint	Hawaii	Neither
Bureau 40	Disastrous	Height	Ninety
Burry	Discipline 80	Hoping	Ninth
Buried	Discussed	Humorous 120	Noticeable
Business	Disease	Hypocrisy	Nuclear 160
Calendar	Divide	Illegal	Occasionally
Career	Dollar	Immediately	Occur
Cemetery	Dying	Incidentally	Occurred
Certain	Eighth	Incredible	Occurrence
Changeable	Eligible	Independent	Opinion
Character	Eliminate	Indispensable	Opportunity
College	Embarrass	Inevitable	Parallel
Column	Embarrassed	Intelligence	Particular
Coming	Emphasize	Interest	Perform
Commitment	Environment	Interfere	Perseverance
Commit	Especially	Involved	Persuade
Committed	Etc.	Irrelevant	Physically

Phenomenon	Recognize	Similar	Tragedy
Picnicking	Recommend	Sincerely 220	Tried
Planned	Reference	Sophomore	Tries
Pleasant	Referred	Speech	Truly
Possible	Relieve	Straight	Unfortunately
Practical	Religious	Strictly	Unnecessary
Preference	Repetition	Studying	Until
Preferred 180	Restaurant 200	Succeed	Unusual 240
Prejudice	Rhythm	Secretary	Using
Preparation	Ridiculous	Seize	Usually
Prevalent	Roommate	Senior	Vacuum
Privilege	Sacrifice	Sense	Vague
Probably	Safety	Separate	Vegetable
Professor	Sandwich	Sergeant	Vengeance
Prove	Scene	Successful	Villain
Psychology	Schedule	Suggest	Wednesday
Pursue	Severely	Supposed	Weight
Quizzes	Shining	Surprise	Weird
Receipt	Siege	Thoroughly	Writing
Receive	Significant	Though	Written 252

WHAT ARE THE MOST COMMONLY CONFUSED WORDS?

Words that sound alike, but that have different spellings and meanings, are often difficult to spell. Remember that if you choose the wrong word in one of the sets from the list below, your spell-checker will not be able to help you. Study these words twenty at a time. Your instructor may test you on twenty words per week to help you master these confusing words. Become familiar enough with this list to spot these words in your writing as you proofread; then, double-check to see that you have used these words correctly. Put a check by the words that continue to give you trouble, and study them until you know them.

PRACTICE 5

Fill in the blanks in the chart below with the correct form of the correct word. The first two have been completed as an example.

Commonly Confused Words

1	accept	to receive	He likes all flavors of ice cream, **except** vanilla.
2	except	to exclude (but)	She did **accept** the gift with thanks.
3	advice	opinions, suggestions (noun)	The _____ helped me to get a job.
4	advise	to give suggestions (verb)	My lawyer _____ me to testify.
5	affect	to influence (verb)	The _____ of hard work is progress.
6	effect	a result (noun)	The song _____ my mood.
7	all ready	completely prepared	She felt calm for the test since she had _____ studied a lot.
8	already	previously or before	The players were _____ to start the game.
9	all together	as one	The class _____ exited.
10	altogether	entirely or completely	The student was _____ correct.
11	altar	raised platform where sacrifices are made to a God	She prayed at the _____ of the temple.
12	alter	change	His education did _____ his perspective.
13	are	a form of *be*	This is _____ home.
14	our	belonging to us	The children _____ excited.
15	bare	naked; empty	The _____ room provided no place to sit.
16	bear	carry; produce; tolerate; large carnivore	I cannot _____ the screaming any longer.
17	brake	a device for stopping; to stop	When she saw the red light, she hit the _____.
18	break	to shatter or to pause	We stopped working and took a _____.
19	breath	air inhaled	The paramedic helped the victim to _____.
20	breathe	to inhale and exhale	I saw her _____ in the cold morning.
21	buy	to purchase	They drove _____ the park.
22	by	close to; no later than; through	Tim needed to _____ some ice.
23	capital	uppercase letter; punishable by death; wealth; city of government of a state or nation	Names of people start with a _____ letter.
24	capitol	the building where congress meets in Washington, D.C.	The president addressed the nation from the _____.

25	choose	to select (present tense)	Now, she wants to _____ a dress carefully.
26	chose	selected (past tense)	Last week, she _____ a dress carefully.
27	cite	to refer to or quote	He lost his _____ to diabetes.
28	sight	perception by the eyes; view	He will _____ a passage from *Hamlet*.
29	site	location	We could not find the _____ on the World Wide Web.
30	clothes	items that people wear	I wash my _____ every Saturday.
31	cloths	pieces of fabric	They washed the car with _____.
32	complement	to complete something or bring to perfection	I like receiving _____ about my hair.
33	compliment	praise	The new table _____ the living room furniture.
34	conscience	inner sense of right and wrong	His _____ told him not to steal.
35	conscious	aware	The victim was not yet _____.
36	coarse	common or rough	I used _____ sand paper for the job.
37	course	direction or path; school subject; part of a meal; naturally (of course)	The student was not sure which _____ to take.
38	council	a group of people chosen to administrate	The psychologist's _____ helped a lot.
39	counsel	advice; to give advice	We elected each member of the student body _____.
40	decent	proper or respectable	The plane began its _____ to the airport.
41	descent	going down	He has _____ behavior in school.
42	desert	to abandon; a dry sandy place	The camel walked across the _____.
43	dessert	sweet part of a meal	I'll have strawberry shortcake for _____.
44	deceased	dead	The accident left four people _____.
45	disease	illness	She contracted the _____ one year ago.
46	die	to stop living	The boy wore a tie-_____ shirt.
47	dye	color or substance used to give color	The girl thinks that she will never _____.
48	do	perform	I _____ my best at work.
49	due	owed	Rent is _____ on the first day of each month.

(continued)

Commonly Confused Words (*continued*)

50	fair	attractive; just	The bus _____ was one dollar.
51	fare	money paid for transportation	We signed the contract because it was _____.
52	fine	very good; money paid as a penalty	The judge gave me one month to pay the _____ or go to jail.
53	find	to get by searching; something discovered	She could not _____ her purse.
54	formally	according to fixed customs	Have we been introduced _____?
55	formerly	in the past	_____, people called him "the rocket."
56	forth	forward	She stood _____ in line.
57	fourth	the one following the third	Let's kick the ball back and _____.
58	hear	to receive sound through the ear	Please put the equipment over _____.
59	here	in this location	The neighbors can _____ the music.
60	heard	past tense of hear	I just _____ a gunshot.
61	herd	a group of animals	A _____ of buffalo drank at the water hole.
62	hole	a cavity or pit	The kids dug a _____ in the sand.
63	whole	complete or entire	He read the _____ book.
64	its	possessive form of *it*	_____ going to be a beautiful day.
65	it's	contraction for *it is* or *it has*	The dog raised _____ paw.
66	knew	clear understanding (past tense)	She _____ the definitions before the test.
67	new	not old; recent	Manny rode his _____ bike.
68	know	to understand clearly (present tense)	The child had _____ manners.
69	no	the opposite of *yes*; negative	He _____ the answer to the question.
70	lead	to direct or guide (present tense); soft metal	The principal _____ the school.
71	led	directed or guided (past tense)	The ranger _____ the tour last week.
72	lightening	becoming lighter	As the sun rose, the room started _____.
73	lightning	a discharge of electricity in the sky	_____ struck a tree.
74	loose	not tight or firmly attached	The Yankees did _____ on Saturday.
75	lose	to not win; misplace	She wears a _____ bracelet.

76	meat	the flesh of animals used as food	I want to _____ the president.
77	meet	to come face to face with	We ate _____ for dinner.
78	mine	belonging to me	The car is _____.
79	mind	intellect; to object to; to pay attention to	He did not _____ waiting in line for the tickets.
80	of	from; belonging to	That is a statue made _____ gold.
81	off	away from; not on	The light is _____.
82	pair	two items creating a set	He found a _____ in his lunch.
83	pear	a fruit	She bought a _____ of shoes.
84	passed	went by or beyond (past tense)	They _____ the restaurant.
85	past	of a former time; time gone by	Grandma loves to talk about her _____.
86	patience	ability to wait	The doctor cared for all of her _____.
87	patients	people receiving care	The coach had _____ with his players.
88	peace	freedom from war; calm	Both countries enjoyed a decade of _____.
89	piece	a part of a whole	May I have a _____ of apple pie?
90	personal	done by oneself	This is a _____ phone call.
91	personnel	employees	We need to hire more _____.
92	plain	simple	We boarded the _____ for Hawaii.
93	plane	aircraft; level	She wore a _____ dress to the prom.
94	pore	to read, consider, or study carefully	He will _____ over his notes before taking the test.
95	pour	to cause to flow in a stream	She _____ milk on her cereal.
96	precede	to be before	We were asked to _____ to the next window.
97	proceed	to go on	Your birthday _____ my birthday.
98	presence	existence or attendance	The girl received many Christmas _____.
99	presents	gifts	The judge has required your _____.
100	principal	chief; amount of money borrowed	The boys were sent to the _____ for fighting in school.
101	principle	a rule or law; standard	He lives by one _____: treat others the way that you want to be treated.
102	quiet	silent	The plumber _____ his job.
103	quit	to stop or withdraw	The hall was _____.
104	quite	really; entirely	They were _____ pleased with their new car.

(continued)

Commonly Confused Words (*continued*)

105	rain	drops of water falling to the earth	He lived during the _____ of King Henry IV.
106	reign	rule	_____ fell in the evening.
107	rein	strap of leather attached to the ends of a bit in a horse's mouth	Pull the _____ in the direction that you want to go.
108	riding	sitting on or in and moving along	He is _____ an article.
109	writing	putting words or symbols on paper	She is _____ on a horse.
110	right	good or correct; opposite of left; something to which one has a just claim	Take a _____ at the corner.
111	write	to put words or symbols on paper	I need to _____ an essay by Friday.
112	scene	a place in which an event occurs	She has _____ much progress in her time.
113	seen	past participle of *see*	Two people were wounded in the first _____ of the play.
114	sense	to feel or understand	He can _____ danger coming.
115	scents	smells or odors	The _____ of the flowers filled the room.
116	cents	pennies	The girl had four _____ in her pocket.
117	stationary	not moving	The note was written on special _____.
118	stationery	paper to write on	The car was _____ at the light.
119	statue	a carved or modeled figure	We saw the _____ of George Washington.
120	stature	height	He is a man large in _____.
121	statute	law	They passed the _____ in November.
122	than	used in comparisons	They eat, and _____ they sleep.
123	then	next; at that time	Fred works harder _____ Jim.
124	their	possessive form of they	He left his fork over _____.
125	there	that place or location; used with forms of *to be*	Dodger stadium is _____ home field.
126	they're	contraction for *they are*	_____ here now.
127	though	however; despite	He loves the flute _____ he hates the bass.
128	thought	idea; the act of thinking (past tense of *think*)	She _____ about where to take a vacation.
129	threw	tossed (past tense of throw)	The seagull flew _____ the cloud.
130	through	in one side and out the other side of	He _____ the ball to me.

131	to	in the direction of; used with infinitives	Dogs love running _____.
132	too	very; also	He has _____ motorcycles.
133	two	the number following one	The squirrel ran _____ the tree.
134	use	to bring into action	I will _____ a saw to cut the wood.
135	used	brought into action (past tense)	Yesterday, I _____ a brush to clean the sink.
136	waist	the part of the body between the ribs and the hips	She wore a red belt around her _____.
137	waste	destroy; fail to use properly	The Olympic athlete did not _____ her practice time.
138	weak	lacking in strength	Their vacation lasted one _____.
139	week	seven days	Her broken arm was _____.
140	wear	to have on the body (clothing)	She wants to _____ her red dress.
141	where	in or at what place	_____ are your shoes?
142	weather	the condition of the atmosphere	We enjoyed mild _____ last summer.
143	whether	if it be the case that	Time passes _____ we like it or not.
144	were	past tense of *are*	_____ in the home stretch.
145	we're	contraction for *we are*	The winners _____ happy.
146	whose	possessive form of *who*	_____ car is this?
147	who's	contraction for *who is* or *who has*	_____ coming with me to the beach?
148	your	possessive form of *you*	_____ very talented.
149	you're	contraction for *you are*	I found _____ ring.

HOW DOES A WRITER AVOID COMMON INCORRECT WORD FORMS?

Sometimes writers will use one or two words incorrectly. Study these incorrect uses of words until you can avoid them.

Common Incorrect Word Forms

Being that	Can't hardly	Could of	Irregardless	Whole nuther
	Couldn't hardly	Must of		
		Should of		
		Would of		

being that

Being that is incorrect. Instead, use *because* or *since*.

Incorrect: We will go camping being that summer is here.
Revised: We will go camping because summer is here.

can't hardly and couldn't hardly (see Double Negatives in Chapter 18)

Can't hardly and *couldn't hardly* are incorrect. Instead, *use can hardly* or *could hardly*.

Incorrect: She can't hardly keep her eyes open.
Revised: She can hardly keep her eyes open.
Incorrect: She couldn't hardly hear the radio.
Revised: She could hardly hear the radio.

could of, must of, should of, and would of

Could of, must of, should of, and *would of* are incorrect. Instead, use *could have, must have, should have,* and *would have*.

Incorrect: You could of gone with someone else.
Revised: You could have gone with someone else.

irregardless

Irregardless is incorrect. Instead, use *regardless*.

Incorrect: Irregardless of what the captain says, I will not participate in the event.
Revised: Regardless of what the captain says, I will not participate in the event.

whole nuther

Whole nuther is incorrect. Instead, use *another, whole new,* or *whole additional*.

Incorrect: She wants to stay and start a whole nuther game.
Revised: She wants to stay and start a whole new game.

WHEN DOES A WRITER SPELL OUT NUMBERS?

Use the following guidelines to help you in the use of numbers in your writing. These rules do not apply to technical or scientific writing.

1. In general, spell out numbers that can be written in one or two words. Use figures for numbers that require three or more words to spell out.

   Incorrect: The girl waited 4 years to get a dog.

   Revised: The girl waited four years to get a dog.

2. Always spell out numbers at the beginning of a sentence.

   Incorrect: 265 people signed up for the contest.

   Revised: Two hundred and sixty-five people signed up for the contest.

3. In general, use figures in the following situations:
   - Dates: September 29, 1998
   - Sections of books and plays: Chapter 7, page 34, act 3, scene 2
   - Addresses: 216 North Oak Street, Santa Barbara, CA 91230
   - Percents, decimals, and fractions: 10%, 1.25, ¼
   - Scores: Angels 3 Dodgers 5
   - Statistics (ratios and surveys): an average of 2 children per family
   - Exact amounts of money: $1, 247, 947
   - Identification numbers: 527-23-3456
   - Time of day: 7:30 a.m.

4. When several numbers are used in a sentence or paragraph, strive for consistency. Either use all words, or use all figures. In such cases, writers often choose to use all figures because they are easier to read.

   Incorrect: I saw three boys, 2 girls, five women, and 3 men standing near the entrance.

   Revised: I saw 3 boys, 2 girls, 5 women, and 3 men standing near the entrance.

5. When one number immediately follows another, use words for one number and figures for the other number.

   Incorrect: He caught three two-pound fish.

   Revised: He caught three 2-pound fish.

PRACTICE 6

Make corrections in word forms and use of numbers. Write on a separate piece of paper or on a computer.

Example: She went shopping for gifts being that the holidays are 10 days away.

   She went shopping for gifts because the holidays are ten days away.

1. The sun is melting the snow being that it's two-thirty P.M.
2. Little Corinne can't hardly read ten percent of the book.
3. We could of walked home on September fourth.
4. Irregardless of the cost, I will buy six keyboards, 3 phones, four copy machines, and 2 printers.
5. It's time to begin a whole nuther semester in 3 weeks.

SHOULD WRITERS BE AWARE OF DIFFERENCES IN AMERICAN AND BRITISH SPELLING?

Obviously, writers should be aware of differences in American and British spelling in English-speaking countries. These differences may be particularly challenging to students who are learning English as a second language. Of course, students should consistently apply the correct spelling according to the custom of the country in which they reside. Check a dictionary for words not listed below:

American	British
Airplane	Aeroplane
Analyze	Analyse
Canceled	Cancelled
Civilization	Civilisation
Check	Cheque
Color, humor	Colour, humour
Defense	Defence
Judgment	Judgement
License	Licence
Licorice	Liquorice
Mold	Mould
Realize	Realise
Skillful	Skilful
Theater, center	Theatre, centre
Tire	Tyre

HOW DOES A WRITER USE A COMPUTER TO AID IN SPELLING?

 In Chapter 12, you learned ways in which a computer can be helpful in the writing process, including how to use a spell-checker in a word processing program. Whenever using a spell-checker, remember the following ideas:

1. Run your spell-checker **after** you complete a draft. This will allow the computer to check all of the words that you have written. If you decide to add another paragraph to your essay after you run your spell-checker, then run it again when you are done writing. Of course, save your document before closing it.

2. A spell-checker cannot determine whether or not names are spelled correctly, so you will need to check the spelling of names in another source. If you use a name frequently, you may want to add it to your spell-checker's dictionary.

3. A spell-checker cannot tell if you have confused one correctly-spelled word for another. For example, if you write, "I would rather eat salad then hot dogs," it will not tell you that you should have used *than* instead of *then*.

4. Refer to a dictionary as needed to support your spell-checker. Because most spell-checkers do not define words, you may not know which word to choose when your spell-checker presents you with several alternative words. In these cases, consult your dictionary.

5. Always proofread your papers for spelling errors after you run your spell-checker, realizing that your spell-checker will not catch every error. Whenever you suspect that a word might not be spelled correctly, consult the list of commonly misspelled words and commonly confused words in this chapter, or look the word up in your dictionary.

HOW DOES A WRITER IMPROVE SPELLING?

In summary, several steps can be taken to improve one's ability to spell words correctly.

1. Study, memorize, and review the basic spelling rules.
2. Study, memorize, and review the most commonly misspelled words.
3. Study, memorize, and review the most commonly confused words.
4. Keep your own spelling list of words that you have misspelled.
5. Run your spell-checker after you have finished writing a draft; then, save the changes.
6. Proofread all of your writing after you run your spell-checker. Read from end to beginning, stopping to consider each word that could be misspelled or incorrectly used.
7. Use a dictionary as needed to correctly spell words that you have typed or handwritten.
8. Use either the American spelling or the British spelling of words, but not both.

GROUP WORK

1. As a group, visit Capital Community College and take their spelling quiz at http://webster.commnet.edu/cgi-shl/quiz.pl/spelling_quiz1.htm.

2. As a group, use the following five words correctly in original sentences: accept, already, lightening, precede, their. Consult the table in this chapter for definitions.

3. The following poem passed several spell-checkers. In a small group, see if you can find and correct the errors that the spell-checkers missed. Rewrite the poem correctly on a separate piece of paper or on a computer.

> Eye halve a spelling check her,
> It came with my pea see.
> It clearly marques four my revue
> Miss steaks eye kin knot sea.
> I strike a key and type a word
> And weight four it two say
> Weather eye am wrong oar write.
> It shows me strait aweigh.
> Whenever a mist ache is maid,
> It nose bee fore two long,
> And eye can put the error rite.
> Its rare lea ever wrong.
> I've run this poem threw it.
> I'm shore your please to no.
> Its letter perfect in it's weigh.
> My checker tolled me sew.

TEST (TRUE/FALSE)

1. Spelling English words correctly is easy for most people.
2. The letters *a, e, i, o, u,* and sometimes *y* are all consonants.
3. *Receive* is spelled correctly in this sentence.
4. Is the following word spelled correctly? definite + ly = definitely
5. *Dryer* is an exception to the "y rule."
6. Double the final consonant of *stop* when adding a suffix like *-ing*.
7. The plural of *knife* is *knifes*.
8. Is the following indication for possession correct? The teacher graded the thirty students' papers.
9. In a contraction, an apostrophe represents one or more missing letters.
10. A good spell-checker will catch all spelling errors all the time.

WRITING ASSIGNMENTS

1. Academic Assignment: Visit Michigan's Social Issues and Social Services Site at http://mel.lib.mi.us/social/SOC-index.html to research a social problem. Then, propose a solution to a social problem. Visit the University of Toledo's Writing Center at http://writingcenter.utoledo.edu/documents/comconf.txt for additional assistance with commonly misspelled words.

2. Journal Assignment: Explain everything that you have learned in this chapter97:"Have words been spelled correctly?"

3. Creative Assignment: Visit the American Museum of Photography at http://www.photographymuseum.com/, and find an image that you like. Describe that image in a paragraph or short essay. For tips on writing descriptions, return to Purdue University's Online Writing Lab at http://owl.english.purdue.edu/handouts/general/gl_describe.html.

Have capital letters been used as needed?

*"I write in order to attain that feeling of tension relieved
and function achieved which a cow enjoys on giving milk."*

— Mencken

LEARNING OBJECTIVES

1. Learn the four main rules of capitalization.
   - Capitalize the first word in a sentence.
   - Capitalize the first word in a direct quotation.
   - Capitalize names of specific people, places, and things.
   - Capitalize openings and closings of letters.
2. Learn to use computers to help with capitalization.

PRE-READING QUESTIONS

1. Are capital-letter errors more or less serious than grammar errors like run-ons and fragments? Why?
2. Why are some words capitalized while others are not?
3. How many categories (like names of people) can you think of that require a capital letter?

4. How many errors in capitalization do you see in the following sentence? Jerry and i sailed down the Columbia river in a boat full of Naturalists from the College.

5. Can a computer help you to find capital-letter errors? How effective are computers in finding these mistakes?

The word *capital* comes from the Latin word *caput*, which means *head*. Capital letters are used at the head of each new sentence as a means of indicating that a new unit of words has started, such as in the first word of each sentence in this paragraph. Capital letters are also used at the head of certain words as a means of indicating respect or significance, such as in specific names like Albert Einstein, Texas, and Norway. In this chapter, you will learn about these and additional situations that call for capital letters.

WHAT ARE THE FOUR MAIN RULES OF CAPITALIZATION?

The four main rules of capitalization are as follows.

1. **Capitalize the first word in a sentence**.

    Workers mine for copper in Zaire. They also mine for gold.

    Workers and *they* are capitalized because they are the first words in sentences.
    Do not capitalize the first word after a colon.

    Incorrect: Juan researched various aspects of Korean culture: Housing, clothing, art, diet, etc.

    Revised: Juan researched various aspects of Korean culture: housing, clothing, art, diet, etc.

    Exception: When a complete sentence follows a colon, a capital letter is optional.

    Juan researched various aspects of Korean culture: He (or he) studied housing, clothing, art, diet, etc.

2. **Capitalize the first word in a direct quotation**.

    He said, "Will you arrive at 7:30 or 8:00?"

    Do not capitalize the first word following an interruption in a quote:

    "Will you arrive," he said, "at 7:30 or 8:00?"

    Notice that *will* is capitalized in both examples because it is the head of a direct quote; however, *at* is not the head of a direct quote in either sentence. In the second sentence *at* is simply the first word in the second half of an interrupted quote, so it should not be capitalized.

3. **Capitalize names of specific people, places, and things**.

Names of People

Cindy Moore and Tony Ramirez outlined the report.

Titles and Abbreviations of Titles of People

Capitalize titles and abbreviations of titles with specific names of people.

Titles Before Names	Titles After Names
Mr. Edward March	Anita Wilde, Ph.D.
Mrs. Sylvia Jeffries	William Grate, Jr.
Dr. Elizabeth Jones	Gonzalo Hernandez, M.D.
Professor John Atkins	Patricia Wylie, D.D.S
District Attorney Kennedy	Rachel Dumain, M.A.

Do not capitalize titles without specific names of people.

Incorrect: My Doctor told me to exercise more and eat less junk food.
Revised: My doctor told me to exercise more and eat less junk food.

Names that Show Family Relationships

Capitalize names that show family relationships.

I hope that Grandma is coming over for dinner.
Will Dad and Uncle Mike come to watch the play?

Do not capitalize names that show family relationships when they are preceded by a possessive words such as *my, his, her, their, our,* or *-'s.*

My grandfather collects coins.
Her mom and grandparents gave her a birthday party.
Miguel's uncle lives just around the corner.

The Word *I*

Always capitalize the word *I*, even in contractions.

Yesterday, I talked to two of my old friends from high school.
On Monday, I'll take the driving test.

Names of Groups of People, Their Religions, and Their Languages

Capitalize nationalities, tribes, people, religions, deities, languages, and adjectives derived from them.

> Yesterday, a Canadian priest asked all Catholics to pray to God for world peace.
> Three Native Americans are studying Spanish in my class.
> Jerome is a descendant of the Cherokee, and he likes Japanese food.

Specific Places

Specific places like rivers, bridges, buildings, schools, and parks are capitalized when they accompany a specific name.

> Lake Ontario
> London Bridge
> Capitol
> Columbia University
> Central Park

Specific Areas

Specific areas like streets, cities, states, geographic locations, areas of the country, and areas of the world are capitalized.

> 2325 Oak Road
> Las Vegas
> Florida
> Rocky Mountains
> Midwest
> Near East

Do not capitalize directions (north, south, east, and west) or general locations.

> We drove south for one hour.
> She lives in northern Oregon.
> They live at the end of a beautiful road.

Do not capitalize for emphasis.

Incorrect: Magic Mountain is Really Fun!
Revised: Magic Mountain is really fun!

Specific Things

Calendar Items

The names of days of the week, months, and holidays are capitalized.

We will celebrate Christmas on the last Thursday of December.

Do not capitalize seasons: winter, spring, summer, fall.

We love to go camping early in the summer.

Commercial Items

The names of specific commercial items are capitalized.

For breakfast, the kids wanted Captain Crunch and Sprite.

Do not capitalize types of products.

For dinner, the kids wanted spaghetti and ice cream.

Titles of Works

Capitalize the major words in titles of literary and artistic works: books, magazines, articles, films, television shows, songs, cartoons, poems, stories, papers that you write. Capitalize the first and last words in a title and all other words except *a, an, the*, and unimportant words with fewer than five letters. Notice that short works also take quotation marks while long works are italicized or underlined (see *Quotation Marks* in Chapter 23).

Capitalized Words in Titles

Short Works	Long Works
"The Return of the Black Panther"	*Lord of the Flies*
"To an Athlete Dying Young"	*National Geographic*
"Hills like White Elephants"	*Los Angeles Times*
"The Most Dangerous Game"	*Romeo and Juliet*
"I'm Happy just to Dance with You"	*Who Wants to be a Millionaire?*
"Marley's Ghost"	*Jurassic Park*

Note: Traditionally, each line of poetry has been capitalized also, as in the first two lines of "Do not Go Gentle into that Good Night" by Dylan Thomas:

> Do not go gentle into that good night,
> Old age should burn and rave at close of day;

Sometimes, however, poets will not capitalized the first word of each line in order to obtain a certain effect, as in the last three lines of "High to Low" by Langston Hughes.

> well, you can see,
> we have our problems,
> too, with you.

When you quote lines of poetry, notice the capitalization patterns used by the author, and do not alter the poet's capitalization when you quote him or her.

Names of Organizations

Capitalize the names of organizations such as companies, associations, unions, clubs, religious and political groups, etc.

Albertson's
Aircraft Owners and Pilots Association
World Conservation Union
Boys & Girls Club
Republican Party

Abbreviations of names of organizations

FBI (Federal Bureau of Investigation)
EPA (Environmental Protection Agency)
ILO (International Labor Organization)
UNIDO (United Nations Industrial Development Organization)
UNESCO (United Nations Educational, Scientific, and Cultural Organization)
WHO (World Health Organization)

The first time that you use the name of an organization in your writing, write the entire name out with the abbreviation following the name in parentheses. When you refer to that organization again in your paper, simply use the abbreviation.

Some abbreviations are capitalized even though the words that they represent are not.

TV (television)
RBI (run batted in)

Specific School Courses

Capitalize specific school courses that are proper nouns or that are followed by a number.

Accounting I
Asian Studies 175
Business 1A
English
Psychology 100
Spanish

Do not capitalize general subject areas.

accounting
Asian studies
biology
computer science
economics
psychology

Historical Periods, Events, and Documents

Capitalize historical periods, events, and documents.

Bill of Rights
Great Depression
Roaring Twenties
Spanish Civil War
Super Bowl
World Festival of Animated Films
World War II

4. Capitalize openings and closings of letters.

Opening	Closing
Dear Gene,	With love,
Dear Madam:	Yours truly,
To Whom It May Concern:	Sincerely,

Notice that a comma is used after an informal opening of a letter while a colon is used after a formal opening of a letter. Also, notice that only the first word in the closing of a letter is capitalized.

CAN COMPUTERS HELP WITH CAPITALIZATION?

 Yes, computers can help with capitalization. They can tell you that sentences must begin with capital letters and that some words are always capitalized like *Ethiopia*. Some words like *aunt*, however, are capitalized only in certain contexts, and you will have to rely on yourself to know when to capitalize such words. Also, remember that a dictionary will be a helpful tool in determining when to capitalize words.

Summary of Capitalization

Remember to capitalize in the following situations:

1. The beginning of every new sentence.
2. The beginning of a direct quotation.
3. The names of specific people, places, and things.
4. The openings and closings of letters.

The following table provides many examples of names to capitalize and not to capitalize.

Capitals	No Capitals
Jerry Garcia	a singer
Dr. Mike Smith	the doctor
Uncle Albert	my uncle
I	me
Jehovah	a god
the Colorado River	a river
	(continued)

Capitals	No Capitals
Texas	a state
Monday	a day of the week
Hanukah	a holiday
Sprite	a drink
"America, the Beautiful"	a song
Vons	a supermarket
National Football League	professional football
NRA (National Riffle Association)	an organization
Anthropology 101	anthropology
the Vietnam War	a war

PRACTICE 1

Choose which words in the following sentences need capital letters. Write the capitalized words on the blank lines. The number of lines tells you how many words need to be capitalized.

Example: He said, "I will drive east to shaver lake on saturday."

<u>Shaver</u> <u>Lake</u> <u>Saturday</u>

1. She said, "please tell dr. Bernstein that grandmother is sick."

   _____ _____ _____

2. They drove from their city to santa barbara with their grandmother.

   _____ _____

3. We bought sprite and cookies at food for less on Monday.

   _____ _____ _____

4. My uncle and lisa's mom will visit us this winter after thanksgiving.

   _____ _____

5. We read "Anyone Lived in a pretty How Town" by E. E. cummings in english today.

   _____ _____ _____

6. During world war II, he worked for the fbi before studying computer science.

   _____ _____ _____

7. The letter began with "dear mom" and ended with "with love."

   _____ _____ _____

8. "please have mercy on me," he said. "I have children in montana," he continued, "who depend on me."

   _____ _____

9. She attends the university of los angeles in southern California.

   _____ _____ _____

10. This semester I'm taking the following classes: anthropology 1A, Business
    210, Computers 100, and psychology 1B.

    _____ _____

PRACTICE 2

Which words in the following corrupted dialogue from "Distance" in Fires
*by Raymond Carver need capital letters. Underline the ten words that need to
be capitalized as you rewrite the passage on a separate piece of paper or on a
computer.*

> "you're my wife," the boy said.
> "and we will always love each other?" the girl asked, enormously en-
> joying this conversation he could tell.
> "always," the boy said. "and we'll always be together. We're like the
> canada geese," he said, taking the first comparison that came to mind, for
> they were often on his mind in those days. "they only marry once. they
> choose a mate early in life, and they stay together always. if one of them
> dies or something, the other one will never remarry. it will live off by itself
> somewhere, or even continue to live with the flock, but it will stay single
> and alone amongst all the other geese."
> "that's sad," the girl said.

PRACTICE 3

*Choose which words in the following sentences need a lower case letter. Write the
words in lower case on the blank lines. The number of lines tells you how many
words need to be changed.*

Example: My Uncle teaches Psychology at a University.

  Uncle Psychology University

1. Grandma cooked a variety of food for the Holidays: Turkey, Stuffing Sweet Potatoes, Pie, etc.

_____ _____ _____

_____ _____ _____

2. He bought a Drink and a Hot Dog at Vons on the Weekend.

_____ _____ _____

_____

3. My Accountant has been working for a Tax Company since December.

_____ _____ _____

4. Last Summer, my Brother drove West to visit Disneyland.

_____ _____ _____

5. "Please pick me up in the Truck at Taco Bell," he said, "At 4:30."

_____ _____

GROUP WORK

1. As a group, visit Capital Community College and take their Capitalization Quiz at http://webster.commnet.edu/cgi-shl/par_numberless_quiz.pl/caps_quiz.htm.
2. As a group, generate five examples of proper nouns (capitalized) and five examples of common nouns (not capitalized).
3. As a group, find five words from this chapter whose capitalization depends upon the context of the sentence in which they are found. In other words, sometimes they are capitalized (*Uncle* George), and sometimes they are not capitalized (my *uncle*).

TEST (TRUE/FALSE)

1. Every new sentence begins with a capital letter.
2. The first word in a direct quotation is usually capitalized.
3. Names of specific people, places, and things (proper nouns) are capitalized.

4. The following sentence is capitalized correctly: My mom is always helping me.
5. The following sentence is capitalized correctly: Spring comes before summer.
6. The following sentence is capitalized correctly: I Love Labor Day.
7. Capitalize the first and last words in a title and all other words except *a, an, the,* and unimportant words with fewer than five letters.
8. The first lines of poems are usually capitalized.
9. Abbreviations are capitalized only when the words that they represent are capitalized.
10. The second word in the closing of a letter is always capitalized.

WRITING ASSIGNMENTS

1. Academic Assignment: Visit the International Partnership for Service Learning at http://www.ipsl.org to learn about service opportunities abroad. Then, write an essay in which you compare service learning in two different countries. For assistance with capitalization, visit NASA's Grammar, Punctuation, and Capitalization page at http://stipo.larc.nasa.gov/sp7084/sp7084ch4.html.

2. Journal Assignment: Explain everything that you have learned in this chapter: "Have capital letters been used as needed?"

3. Creative Assignment: Visit the Norton Simon Museum at http://www.nortonsimon.org, and find an image that you like. Describe that image in a paragraph or short essay. For tips on writing descriptions, return to Purdue University's Online Writing Lab at http://owl.english.purdue.edu/handouts/general/gl_describe.html.

Has parallel structure been used?

"The good writing of any age has always been the product of someone's neurosis. "

— William Styron

LEARNING OBJECTIVES

1. Learn what parallel structure is.
2. Learn why parallel structure is used.
3. Learn when parallel structure is used in the writing process.
4. Learn how to revise faulty parallelism.

PRE-READING QUESTIONS

1. What do two parallel lines look like?
2. What parallel items, besides lines, you have seen?
3. What is a possible benefit of two or more items being parallel?
4. What could parallel structure in writing involve?
5. Can a computer help you to create parallel structure in writing?

WHAT IS PARALLEL STRUCTURE?

To answer this question, first consider which of the following two sentences sounds better:

> Don't ask what your country can do to help you. Instead, think about what you can do for it.

> "Ask not what your country can do for you; ask what you can do for your country."
> — President John F. Kennedy

The second sentence sounds much better because it expresses its ideas in parallel or similar form.

Have you noticed that the tracks on a roller coaster ride are parallel? These tracks never separate, and they never meet. They run in the same direction, side by side, and they are equal in size. Because of their structure, they balance the car holding passengers, and the passengers can enjoy a wild and safe ride with sharp turns, sudden descents, and fast loops.

Parallel structure in writing involves repeating similar patterns of words, and this structure helps to avoid derailing the reader. For example, similar parts of speech should be connected: nouns with nouns, adjectives with adjectives, prepositional phrases with prepositional phrases, etc, as in the following example:

> Jan is tall, thin, and strong.

This simple sentence uses parallel construction because *tall, thin,* and *strong* are all adjectives (they describe a noun: Jan). Because three adjectives are used in a row, the sentence displays parallel structure.

Remember that this textbook is divided into three parts:

- Prewriting
- Writing
- Rewriting

These headings displays parallel structure because each word is a gerund (a verb form ending in *-ing*).

WHY IS PARALLEL STRUCTURE USED?

Parallel structure makes ideas easy to understand by expressing similar ideas in similar forms, creating order and balance, which enhances reader comprehension. Of course, if ideas are similar, and if those similar ideas are expressed in similar forms, then the reader can see the similarities in ideas quickly. As a result of understanding and employing parallel structure, one's writing becomes more effective.

In the table below, notice the rhythm and clarity of the sentences containing parallel structure compared to the sentences without it.

Nonparallel Construction	Parallel Construction
All human beings make mistakes, but to forgive is divine.	"To err is human, to forgive divine." —Alexander Pope
We are free. Our freedom has come. Thank God Almighty, we are finally free.	"Free at Last! Free at last! Thank God Almighty, we are free at last!" —Dr. Martin Luther King, Jr.
I came here; I liked what I saw, so we conquered the people.	"I came; I saw; I conquered." —Julius Caesar
Existing or not: that is my question.	"To be or not to be: that is the question." —William Shakespeare
Opinions change, but truth, on the other hand, does not change. If we cannot have both opinions and the truth, we should posses the older of the two.	"Opinion is a flitting thing, But truth, outlasts the Sun— If then we cannot own them both— Possess the oldest one—" —Emily Dickinson
There are times to weep, but then, again, there are times to laugh; times for mourning, and times to dance too.	"A time to weep, and a time to laugh; a time to mourn, and a time to dance;" —Ecclesiastes 3:4

Sometimes beginning writers discard parallel structure in an attempt to display variety and complexity in writing; however, as the examples above illustrate, many of the most-quoted writers have chosen to communicate through parallel structure.

PRACTICE 1

One item in each list is not parallel in form with the other items. Find the nonparallel item, put a line through it, and change it into a parallel item.

Example:

> loving
> ~~person that is friendly~~ Friendly
> caring

1. feeding
   producing
   to raise them

2. picking a counselor
   call for an appointment
   complete the forms

3. at the counter
   the line in the cafeteria
   on the table

4. is placing the order
   buys the merchandise
   takes the product

5. injured zebras
   infected giraffes
   elephants that are sick

WHEN IS PARALLEL STRUCTURE USED IN THE WRITING PROCESS, AND HOW IS FAULTY PARALLELISM REVISED?

Notice where this chapter on parallelism comes in this textbook, "Part Three: Rewriting." That is because in "Part Two: Writing" the writer focuses on finishing a complete draft of the work. In subsequent drafts in the process of rewriting, the writer focuses on polishing the work; this includes proofreading for faulty parallelism. In the process of checking for parallel structure, focus on four main areas.

1. Presenting a series of items in a list.

When you present two or more items, present them in parallel structure.

Incorrect: This semester we are studying poems, and reading plays, and some novels.
Revised: This semester we are studying poems, plays, and novels. (nouns)

Incorrect: She likes to *watch volleyball, basketball,* and *coach softball.*
Revised: She likes to *watch volleyball, play basketball,* and *coach softball.* (verb phrases)

Incorrect: *He took a shower, ate,* and *he drove to work.*
Revised: He took a shower, he ate breakfast, and he drove to work. (independent clauses)

PRACTICE 2

The following sentences have two items that are parallel and one that is not parallel. Change the non-parallel item to match the other items. Write on a separate piece of paper or on a computer.

Example:

> Pam is intelligent, funny, and has lots of enthusiasm.
>
> Pam is intelligent, funny, and enthusiastic.

1. The storm created rainy and windy conditions that were cold.
2. The ingredients included the following: cinnamon, sugar, and chopped up nuts.
3. The politician plans on running for election, campaigning throughout the state, and to win the office.
4. We learned how to train, groom, and showing a dog.
5. The facility provides services to people with physical or mental disabilities or anyone who is emotionally impaired.

   2. Comparing two items.

   Two items being compared should have parallel structure. In comparisons, writers often use *like, as,* or *than.*

   > Incorrect: *Driving Raul's car* is like *a rocket.*
   > Revised: *Driving Raul's car* is like *steering a rocket.* (verb phrases)
   > Incorrect: *Jack* is *as* fast as a *cheetah runs.*
   > Revised: *Jack* is *as* fast as a *cheetah.* (nouns)
   > Incorrect: *To work* is better than *procrastinating.*
   > Revised: *To work* is better than *to procrastinate.* (verbs in infinitive form)
   > Revised: *Working* is better than *procrastinating.* (verbs in gerund form)

   Notice that there is often more than one way to create parallel structure in a sentence.

PRACTICE 3

Revise the following comparisons to achieve parallel construction. Write on a separate piece of paper or on a computer.

Example:

> Paul's arm can throw a ball like a gun.
>
> Paul's arm can throw a ball like a gun can shoot a bullet.

1. To study is better than not studying.
2. Riding a horse is as fun as motorcycles.
3. To eat food is like filling the gas tank.
4. Clean air is as important as water that is clean.
5. Managing stress is like a clown who juggles three balls at once.

3. Offering paired ideas.

Certain paired words, called correlative conjunctions, join ideas, and the ideas that they join must be parallel.

Correlative Conjunctions

both . . . and (indicates addition)	neither . . . nor (indicates negative choice)	rather . . . than (indicates preference)
either . . . or (indicates choice)	not only . . . but also (indicates addition)	whether . . . or (indicates uncertainty)

When you use correlative conjunctions, remember to use both the first and the second part.

Incorrect: Danesha studies **both** *economics*
          and *speaking Spanish.*

Revised: Danesha studies **both** *economics*
          and *Spanish.* (nouns)

Incorrect: Adriana wants **either** *to play soccer*
          or *run.*

Revised: Adriana wants **either** *to play soccer*
          or *to run track.* (verb phrases)

Incorrect: Joseph seeks **neither** *fame*
          nor *to get a high salary.*

Revised: Joseph seeks **neither** *fame*
          nor *wealth.* (nouns)

Incorrect: Tandra earned a bachelor's degree **not only** *for herself*
          but also *she felt that she wanted to earn it for her family.*

Revised: Tandra earned a bachelor's degree **not only** *for herself*
          but also *for her family.* (prepositional phrases)

Incorrect: Josefina would **rather** *work*
                          than *to play*.

Revised: Josefina would **rather** *work*
                        than *play* (nouns).

Incorrect: Iesha couldn't decide **whether** *to earn her degree*
                              or *dropping out of school*.

Revised: Iesha couldn't decide **whether** *to earn her degree*
                            or *to drop out of school*. (verb phrases)

Correlative conjunctions must be placed as closely as possible to the words that are being compared.

Incorrect: Joseph **neither** seeks *fame*
                      nor *wealth*.

Revised: Joseph seeks **neither** *fame*

            nor *wealth*.

Remember to use a comma before a correlative conjunction that connects a second independent clause to a first independent clause.

Incorrect: **Either** *Adriana wants to play soccer*
                  or *she wants to run track*.

Revised: **Either** *Adriana wants to play soccer,*
                  or *she wants to run track*. (independent clauses)

PRACTICE 4

Revise the following sentences to achieve parallel construction by rewriting them on a separate piece of paper or on a computer. Underline the parts of the sentence that should be parallel.

Example:

> The meeting began with both the pledge of Allegiance and singing the national anthem.

> The meeting began with both <u>the pledge of Allegiance</u> and <u>the national anthem</u>.

1. Antonella learned both to play the piano and dancing.
2. Erin has to write a report on either a country or one of the U.S. presidents.

3. The stocks have neither risen nor fell.
4. Lorena created not only an organizational chart but also she drew up a production graph.
5. Buniel and Everett would rather ski than go down to the dock and fish.

4. Making a point effectively.

Great communicators have always used parallelism to make their points. Dr. Martin Luther King, Jr. eloquently expressed his hope for equality of all American citizens in his famous speech, "I Have a Dream," delivered at the Lincoln Memorial in Washington D.C. on August 28, 1963. Notice the parallel structure used in the last sentence of that address.

> And when this happens, when we allow freedom to ring, when we let it ring from every village and every hamlet, from every state and every city, we will be able to speed up that day when all of God's children, black men and white men, Jews and Gentiles, Protestants and Catholics, will be able to join hands and sing in the words of the old Negro spiritual, "Free at last, free at last. Thank God Almighty, we are free at last."

Notice that the sentence begins with parallel references to time, "When this happens . . . when we allow . . . when we let. . . ." The sentence goes on with parallel references to location, "Every village and every hamlet . . . every state and every city." The sentence continues with a parallel description of God's children, "Black men and white men, Jews and Gentiles, Protestants and Catholics." Then, King concludes with the parallel repetition of a phrase found in a Negro spiritual, "Free at last, free at last. Thank God Almighty, we are free at last." Although this speech was given many years ago, people will always be inspired by it, and the impact of it comes, in part, because of King's skillful use of parallel structure.

PRACTICE 5

Underline parallel structure in another section of King's speech, "I Have a Dream."

I have a dream that one day this nation will rise up and live out the true meaning of its creed: "We hold these truths to be self-evident: that all men are created equal."

I have a dream that one day on the red hills of Georgia the sons of former slaves and the sons of former slaveowners will be able to sit down together at a table of brotherhood.

I have a dream that one day even the state of Mississippi, a desert state, sweltering with the heat of injustice and oppression, will be transformed into an oasis of freedom and justice.

I have a dream that my four children will one day live in a nation where they will not be judged by the color of their skin but by the content of their character.

I have a dream today.

Summarizing Parallelism

Parallelism means expressing similar ideas in similar grammatical form to achieve a balanced structure in writing. Parallel structure is frequently found in the following areas:

1. Presenting a series of items in a list.

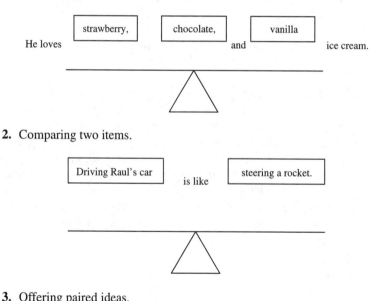

2. Comparing two items.

3. Offering paired ideas.

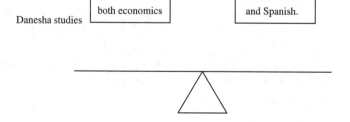

4. Making a point effectively.

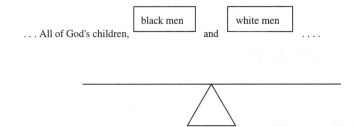

... All of God's children, [black men] and [white men] ....

GROUP WORK

1. Visit the Afro-American Almanac at http://www.toptags.com/aama/voices/ speeches/speech1.htm and read "I Have a Dream" by Dr. Martin Luther King, Jr. (or see page 399 for "I Have a Dream"). Describe five examples of parallel structure in this speech and explain why you chose each one by addressing how the parallel structure creates effective writing.

2. As a group, visit Capital Community College and take their Parallel Structure quiz at http://webster.commnet.edu/cgi-shl/quiz.pl/parallelism_quiz.htm.

3. Generate five examples of sentences with parallel structure. Make sure that your group includes one example of each type discussed in this chapter.

TEST (TRUE/FALSE)

1. Parallel lines never meet.
2. Parallel structure in writing means expressing similar ideas in similar grammatical forms.
3. In parallel structure, dissimilar parts of speech should be connected: adjectives with nouns, prepositional phrases with adverbs, etc.
4. Parallel structure makes writing easier to read and understand.
5. The following sentence is an example of parallel structure: Mary swam across the pool quickly and with ease.
6. Correcting faulty parallelism comes in the rewriting stage of the writing process.
7. Writers have only one option for correcting faulty parallelism.
8. With respect to correlative conjunctions, *Rather . . . than* is used to indicate addition.
9. Correlative conjunctions should be placed far away from the words that are being compared.

10. Understanding and employing parallel structure makes writing more effective.

WRITING ASSIGNMENTS

1. Academic Assignment: Visit Mississippi State University at http://www.
msstate.edu/dept/coop/interview/thank.html to learn how to write a
thank-you letter. Then, write a thank-you letter to a perspective employer,
or write a letter of appreciation to someone who has made a significant
contribution to your life in any way; this could be a friend, a family member,
a teacher, a coach, a leader, etc. Provide ample support through specific details about exactly what this person has done for you. Proofread your letter
for faulty parallelism. For assistance with parallel construction, visit Writers'
Workshop at the University of Illinois at Urbana-Champaign at http://
www.english.uiuc.edu/cws/wworkshop/tips/writtech.parallel.htm or the
Bellevue Community College Writing Lab at http://www.bcc.ctc.edu/
writinglab/Parallel.html.

2. Journal Assignment: Explain everything that you have learned in this chapter:"Has parallel structure been used?"

3. Creative Assignment: Visit the Morgan Library and view the Exhibitions at
http://www.morganlibrary.org/, and find an image that you like. Describe
that image in a paragraph or short essay. For tips on writing descriptions,
return to Purdue University's Online Writing Lab at http://owl.english.
purdue.edu/handouts/general/gl_describe.html.

Chapter 22

Has basic punctuation been used correctly?

"My attitude toward punctuation is that it ought to be as conventional as possible. The game of golf would lose a good deal if croquet mallets and billiard cues were allowed on the putting green. You ought to be able to show that you can do it a good deal better than anyone else with the regular tools before you have a license to bring in your own improvements."

— Ernest Hemingway

LEARNING OBJECTIVES

1. Learn what punctuation is and what it does for writing.
2. Learn what end marks are and how to use them.
3. Learn when to use commas.
4. Learn when not to use commas.

PRE-READING QUESTIONS

1. How do you define punctuation?
2. What problems could you expect in reading a paragraph with no punctuation?
3. Which of the following do you find to be the most difficult to use: the period, the question mark, the exclamation point, or the comma? Why?

4. When do you use a period, a question mark, and an exclamation point?

5. When do you use a comma?

WHAT IS PUNCTUATION AND WHAT DOES IT DO FOR WRITING?

First, read the following sentence:

> While we were driving a buffalo walked onto the road.

At first glance, the reader might think that the sentence is about people who are driving a buffalo. Notice how one punctuation mark clarifies the meaning of the sentence.

> While we were driving, a buffalo walked onto the road.

Now, consider the following opening paragraph of an essay:

> is there anyone in this world that can consider himself problem-free today many people especially young people are challenged by all sorts of problems in life the young people go through life like a person entering a martial arts tournament without taking any lessons first young people usually have problems like money love and family relationships to those people having problems the problems may seem impossible to solve but to an outsider with experience some solutions exist

This paragraph confuses readers because it lacks punctuation (and extra spaces and capital letters). Now, read the same paragraph below with punctuation (and extra spaces and capital letters).

> Is there anyone in this world that can consider himself problem-free? Today many people, especially young people, are challenged by all sorts of problems in life; young people go through life like a person entering a martial arts tournament without taking any lessons first. Young people usually have problems like money, love, and family relationships. To those people having problems, the problems may seem impossible to solve, but to an outsider with experience, some solutions exist.

> — Adapted from Toan Tran

The paragraph with punctuation is much easier to understand than the one without it because punctuation, the use of marks in sentences, clarifies meaning. These marks, based on standards established in Italy in the sixteenth century, work like road signs to indicate when to stop, start, or change direction. In speaking, one's tone of voice and pauses provide this same clarification. In writing, however, when the speaker is no longer present and the listener is interpreting writing, punctuation marks are indispensable in clarifying meaning.

WHAT ARE END MARKS AND HOW ARE THEY USED?

Recall that a sentence always begins with a capital letter and ends with some form of punctuation called an end mark: a period, a question mark, or an exclamation point.

Periods

When a sentence presents information, use a period as the end mark. This may include a statement, a request or mild command, or an indirect question.

One study noted a decline in hate crimes over a three-year period. (statement)
Please pass the salt and pepper. (request)
Kristy asked Laura when she obtained her job. (indirect question)

Notice that, in general, periods are also used after abbreviations.

Examples of Abbreviations

A.M. (ante meridian)	Etc. (et cetera)	Ms. (Miss or Mistress)
	Jr. (Junior)	P.M. (post meridian)
B.A. (bachelor of arts)	M.D. (doctor of medicine)	Sr. (Senior)
	Mr. (Mister)	St. (Saint or Street)
Dr. (Doctor)	Mrs. (Mistress)	

Exception: PC (personal computer), ASAP (as soon as possible), CA (California).

Dr. William H. Rollin performed the examination. (abbreviation)

Remember that if a sentence ends with an abbreviation, a second period is not used.

Our coach said that practice will start at 6:00 A.M. That is early.

Question Marks

When a sentence asks a direct question, use a question mark.

When will we have our final exam? (direct question)
Would you like some dessert now? (direct question)

Remember that an indirect question does not take a question mark. An indirect question explains to the reader what was asked in an earlier question.

Incorrect: Jane asked if I could go to the movies?
Revised: Jane asked if I could go to the movies.

Exclamation Points

When a sentence expresses strong emotions and commands, use an exclamation point. Sometimes, an exclamation point will follow a single word.

"Please help me!" he screamed. (strong emotions)
Ouch! (strong emotions)
Run for your life! (command)

Do not overuse the exclamation point in your writing, and never use more than one at a time.

Incorrect: Watch out for that rock!!!
Revised: Watch out for that rock!

Do not express mild emotions with an exclamation point.

Incorrect: Yes, the new printers are fast!
Revised: Yes, the new printers are fast.

PRACTICE 1

Insert periods, question marks, or exclamation points as needed.

Example: She asked me if I had any money

> She asked me if I had any money.

1. Streams feed the banana gardens of Kilimanjaro
2. How long have these ancient ruins been here
3. Shall we rise at 6:00 A.M.
4. Here comes the police. Run
5. Robert asked if Eric could attend the play
6. Dr Holmes performed the surgery
7. We have a fire in the boiler room
8. The British lost control of India with time
9. Venezuela rebelled against the domination of Spain
10. Please talk softly in the library

WHEN SHOULD A WRITER USE COMMAS?

Commas create more problems for writers than any other punctuation mark. Commas, like end marks, also serve as road signs. Imagine that some road signs were missing or incorrectly placed along the freeway. This would confuse drivers. Readers receive the same type of misinformation when writers place commas incorrectly. In general, commas are used to set off or separate elements of a sentence. Because beginning writers tend to misplace commas, remember not to use a comma unless the situation calls for one. The following rules will help readers to correctly identify those situations; these rules are important to learn since grammar checkers are not very helpful in placing commas correctly. Notice that correctly placed commas often create pauses in sentences.

1. Use a comma to set off introductory material such as words, phrases, or clauses. Use a comma to set off words.

   > *Suddenly,* a shadow appeared on the wall. (word)

   Use a comma to set off phrases. A phrase is a group of words that lacks a subject, a verb, or both.

   > *In the chill of the night,* she buttoned her parka. (prepositional phrase)

   Notice that a short prepositional phrase does not use a comma, unless one is required to clarify meaning.

At night she buttoned her parka. (short prepositional phrase)

At nine, thirty students began writing. (comma after short prepositional phrase clarifies meaning)

The comma is required, or the reader could conclude that students began writing at nine-thirty, not thirty students began writing at nine.

Use a comma to set off a dependent clause at the beginning of the sentence. A dependent clause is a group of words that contains a subject and a verb, but does not express a complete thought. See Chapter 15 for more information and practice with sentences of this type.

Dependent clauses often begin with words from the following table:

Words Often Found Starting Dependent Clauses

After	Before	Unless
Although	If	When (whenever)
As (as if)	Since	Whereas
Because	Until	While

If he saves enough money this year, he will buy a home. (dependent clause)

2. Use a comma to set off items in a series.
Do not use a comma before the first item or after the last item in a series. Do not use a comma between two items in a series. Finally, do not use a comma between three or more items in a series that are joined by *and*.

> Incorrect: Tam named the, composers, artists, and conductors, involved.
>
> Incorrect: Tam named the composers, and artists involved.
>
> Incorrect: Tam named the composers, and artists, and conductors involved.
>
> Revised: Tam named the composers and artists involved.
>
> Revised: Tam named the composers, artists, and conductors involved. (words)

You may notice in material that you read that some writers omit the comma before the last item in a series. Most experts agree, however, that including the final comma in a series makes the writing easier to understand than when it is omitted.

Use a Comma Between Coordinate Adjectives

When two or more adjectives each modify a noun separately, they are coordinate. You may test for coordinate adjectives by asking two questions:

- Can the adjectives be joined by *and*?
- Can the adjectives be placed in any order?

If the answer is yes, then they are coordinate (each adjective modifies the noun separately), and a comma is needed between each adjective.

Example: My mother is a *warm, intelligent, happy* person.

Test #1: My mother is a *warm* and *intelligent* and *happy* person. (This sounds okay.)

Test #2: My mother is a *happy, intelligent, warm* person. (This sounds okay.)

Since the answer to both questions is yes, the adjectives are coordinate, and commas are required to separate the adjectives.

Incorrect: My mother is a *warm intelligent happy* person. (Use commas to separate coordinate adjectives.)

Incorrect: My mother is a *warm, intelligent, happy*, person. (Do not use a comma to separate the last adjective and the noun or pronoun.)

Revised: My mother is a *warm, intelligent, happy* person.

If the answer to either of these questions is no, then the adjectives are cumulative, and commas are not needed. See Chapter 18 for a discussion of coordinate and cumulative adjectives.

Use a comma to set off three or more phrases in a series.

Jeremy trains for the competition by lifting weights in the morning, swimming in the afternoon, and running in the evening. (phrases)

Use a comma to set off three or more clauses in a series.

Amber raked the leaves, Keri mowed the lawn, and John swept the sidewalk. (clauses)

If Amber rakes the leaves, if Keri mows the law, and if John sweeps the sidewalk, the front yard will look good. (clauses)

Do not place only a comma between two independent clauses. Also, do not just place *and* between two independent clauses. Finally, do not place a comma after a coordinating conjunction. Instead, place a comma and a coordinating conjunction (*and, but, for, nor, or, so*, and *yet*) between two independent clauses. See Chapter 16 for a discussion of combining sentences in this way.

Incorrect: Amber raked the leaves, Keri mowed the lawn. (comma splice)

Incorrect: Amber raked the leaves and Keri mowed the lawn. (run-on)

Incorrect: Amber raked the leaves and, Keri mowed the lawn. (misplaced comma)

Revised: Amber raked the leaves, and Keri mowed the lawn.

3. Use a comma to set off contrasting elements. Contrasting elements are often introduced with words like *not, never*, and *unlike*.

Emily loves biology and chemistry, *not history*. (contrasting element)

Fish obtain oxygen from water, *unlike mammals*. (contrasting element)

4. Use a comma to set off information commonly found in letters such as openings and closings of letters, titles, numbers, dates, and addresses.

Openings and Closings of Letters

Dear Jack,	Yours truly,
Dear Mom,	Sincerely,

Note that a colon is used in openings of formal letters.

To Whom It May Concern:

Titles

When a title follows a person's name, set off the title with commas.

Mike Greenman, M.D., examined the x-ray and found a fracture.

Leslie Harris, Dean of Student Services, has proposed building a student center.

Numbers

When using numbers of four digits or more, place a comma after every three digits, starting at the right.

The campaign raised $43,000.

Do not place commas in telephone numbers, street numbers, zip codes, or years. See Chapter 19 for situations that require numbers to be spelled out.

Dates

Use commas to set off items in dates.

The committee met on Wednesday, December 3, 2002.

Note that a comma is not used between the day and the year when the day is given before the month. Also, a comma is not used when only the month and year are given.

The committee met on Wednesday, 3 December 2002.

The committee met in December 2002 to review the year.

Addresses

Set off parts of addresses with commas; however, do not separate the state and zip code with a comma.

We live at 316 Villanova Road, Costa Mesa, CA 91350.

They took a vacation to Waikiki, Hawaii, in 2001.

5. Use a comma to set off a direct quotation. Notice that the attribution (identification of speaker) may come at the beginning, middle, or end of the quotation. Notice also that commas and periods are usually placed inside quotation marks.

> John Dewey said, "We don't learn by experience. We learn by reflecting upon experience."
>
> "We don't learn," John Dewey said, "by experience. We learn by reflecting upon experience."
>
> "We don't learn by experience. We learn by reflecting upon experience," said John Dewey.

6. Use commas to set off non-essential words and transitional words.

Non-essential Words

Words that interrupt the flow of thought in a sentence and that are non-essential to the meaning of the sentence must have a comma before and after those words. On the other hand, if the interruption is essential to the meaning of the sentence, commas are not used. When reading a sentence out loud, you can usually hear where the commas should be placed.

> Essential: The mechanic *who has a mustache* fixed my car.
>
> Non-essential: Jerry Hubert, *who has a mustache*, fixed my car.

To understand why commas are needed in the second sentence and not the first, remove the interruption.

> Essential: The mechanic fixed my car.
>
> Non-essential: Jerry Hubert fixed my car.

In the first sentence, the reader does not know which mechanic fixed the car without the interruption, so it is essential to the meaning of the sentence because it identifies the mechanic. Interruptions that are essential are not set off with commas.

In the second sentence, the reader knows which mechanic fixed the car—Jerry Hubert—without the interruption, so the fact that Jerry wears a mustache is not essential to the meaning of the sentence. Interruptions that are not essential are set off with commas.

Transitional Words

Most transitional words or phrases interrupt the flow of a sentence and, therefore, must be set off with commas. As a general rule, if the transition appears at the beginning or end of a sentence, only one comma is needed. If it appears in the middle of a sentence, two commas are needed. Notice the location of the commas in the following sentences:

Each person in the family favors a different sport. *For example*, Jennifer prefers skiing.

Each person in the family favors a different sport. Jennifer, *for example,* prefers skiing.

Each person in the family favors a different sport. Jennifer prefers skiing, *for example*.

For more information about transitional words and punctuating them, see Chapter 10.

7. Use a comma to set off two independent clauses joined by a coordinating conjunction (*and, but, for, nor, or, so,* and *yet*). Remember that an independent clause contains a subject and a verb that combine to express one idea, which can stand alone.

> <u>Jade</u> <u>plays</u> the clarinet, and <u>Bridget</u> <u>sings</u> in a choir.

Because so many comma errors are made in combining independent clauses, be aware of the following four rules.

1. Do not set off two independent clauses with only a comma.
2. Do not only place *and* between two independent clauses.
3. Do not place a comma after a coordinating conjunction.
4. Do not place a comma and a coordinating conjunction between two elements that are not independent clauses.

> Incorrect: <u>Jade</u> <u>plays</u> the clarinet, <u>Bridget</u> <u>sings</u> in a choir. (comma splice)

> Incorrect: <u>Jade</u> <u>plays</u> the clarinet and <u>Bridget</u> <u>sings</u> in a choir. (run-on)

> Incorrect: <u>Jade</u> <u>plays</u> the clarinet and, <u>Bridget</u> <u>sings</u> in a choir. (misplaced comma)

> Incorrect: <u>Jade</u> <u>plays</u> the clarinet, and <u>practices</u> regularly. (misplaced comma)

Instead, place a comma and a coordinating conjunction between two independent clauses.

> Revised: <u>Jade</u> <u>plays</u> the clarinet, and <u>Bridget</u> <u>sings</u> in a choir.

See Chapter 16 for correcting run-on sentences.

Review of Commas

1. Use a comma to set off introductory material such as words, phrases, or clauses.
2. Use a comma to set off items in a series.
3. Use a comma to set off contrasting elements.

4. Use a comma to set off information commonly found in letters such as openings and closings of letters, titles, numbers, dates, and addresses.
5. Use a comma to set off a direct quotation.
6. Use commas to set off non-essential words and transitional words.
7. Use a comma to set off two independent clauses joined by a coordinating conjunction (*and, but, for, nor, or, so,* and *yet*).

PRACTICE 2

Insert commas as needed in the following sentences and put the rules (#1–7) used in parentheses at end of sentences. Write on a separate piece of paper or on a computer.

Example: Swimming across the pond a beaver carried a stick.

    Swimming across a pond, a beaver carried a stick. (#1)

1. Unless someone claims the wallet you may keep it.
2. The vegetables simmered on the stove and the casserole baked in the oven.
3. The blue wheelchair which has a rip in the seat cannot be used.
4. "This above all—to thine own self be true" wrote Shakespeare in *Hamlet*."
5. The Romeros donated $13000.
6. The scientists collect test and interpret information.
7. Tina is a kind witty and intelligent person.
8. Stay calm in an emergency never panic.
9. Josh who loves to chat eventually brought the food.
10. We downloaded the program yet it didn't work.

PRACTICE 3

Insert commas as needed in the following sentences and put the rules (#1–7) used in parentheses at end of sentences.

Example: Yes this is the place.

    Yes, this is the place. (#1)

1. Well who won the election?
2. Bats dolphins and whales use echolocation to pinpoint objects.
3. Identical twins share identical genes and the twins appear alike.
4. Melissa yelled "Stop that monkey!"

5. Stephen reads mostly news articles not fiction.
6. Professor Higgins who is walking towards us gives a lot of homework.
7. We attended the concert and it was great.
8. If we save enough money we can take a cruise to the Caribbean.
9. The food chain furthermore shows who eats whom.
10. Dear Renee

> Should we attend the party tonight? Let me know what you want to do.
>
> Your friend
>
> — Dave

WHEN SHOULD A WRITER NOT USE COMMAS?

1. Do not place a comma between a simple subject and verb.

Incorrect: The <u>box</u> of cookies on the table, <u>is</u> empty.

Revised: The <u>box</u> of cookies on the table <u>is</u> empty.

2. Do not place a comma before *that* unless *that* introduces a non-essential element.

Incorrect: Early in the semester the class felt, that *Hamlet* would not interest them.

Revised: Early in the semester the class felt that *Hamlet* would not interest them.

3. Do not place a comma between an independent clause and a dependent clause when the dependent clause is essential. See complex sentences in Chapter 16 for more information on independent clauses followed by dependent clauses.

Incorrect: <u>Jack</u> <u>will allow</u> his son to shoot a gun, if his <u>son</u> <u>takes</u> a safety course first.

Revised: Jack will allow his son to shoot a gun if his son takes a safety course first. (Essential elements require no commas.)

The *if* clause is essential to communicate the writer's intention. In other words, Jack is allowing his son to shoot only after his son completes a safety course.

4. Finally, only use the comma when it is called for in the situations described in this chapter. If you are in doubt about whether or not to use a comma and unable to check a handbook at the time, omit it.

PRACTICE 4

Remove commas as needed in the following sentences. Write on a separate piece of paper or on a computer.

Example: Of course, the trouble with being lazy is, that it doesn't pay off.

> Of course, the trouble with being lazy is that it doesn't pay off.

1. According to Carlos, personality traits, change little.
2. Adriana, Peter, and Joseph felt, that the game should continue.
3. By this time next year, Kyle will buy a car, if he has the money.
4. Kenny will take biology, psychology, chemistry, and, music.
5. She said, "What is it, that you want?"

BASIC PUNCTUATION SUMMARY

End Marks

Use a period with a statement, a request or mild command, or an indirect question.

> One study noted a decline in hate crimes over a three-year period.

Use a question mark with a direct question.

> When will we have our final exam?

Use an exclamation point to expresses strong emotions and commands.

> "Please help me!" he screamed.

Commas

Use a comma to set off introductory material such as words, phrases, or clauses.

> *In the chill of the night,* she buttoned her parka.

Use a comma to set off three or more items in a series.

> Tam named the *composers, artists,* and *conductors* involved.

Use a comma to set off contrasting elements.

> Emily loves biology and chemistry, *not history*.

Use a comma to set off information commonly found in letters such as openings and closings of letters, titles, numbers, dates, and addresses.

> The committee met on Wednesday, December 3, 2002.

Use a comma to set off a direct quotation.

> John Dewey said, "We don't learn by experience. We learn by reflecting upon experience."

Use commas to set off non-essential words and transitional words.

> Jerry Hubert, *who has a mustache*, fixed my car.

Use a comma to set off two independent clauses joined by a coordinating conjunction (*and, but, for, nor, or, so,* and *yet*).

> Jade <u>plays</u> the clarinet, and <u>Bridget</u> <u>sings</u> in a choir.

GROUP WORK

1. As a group, visit Capital Community College and take their Comma Quiz at http://webster.commnet.edu/grammar/quizzes/commas_fillin.htm.
2. Write three examples of direct questions and three examples of indirect questions.
3. Write three sentences with extra words that are essential elements, and write three sentences with extra words that are non-essential elements. Punctuate them correctly.

TEST (TRUE/FALSE)

1. Punctuation clarifies the meaning of a sentence.
2. End marks refer to periods, question marks, exclamation points, and commas.
3. Periods are used after indirect questions.

4. If a sentence ends with an abbreviated word, two periods are used.

5. When using exclamation points, three in a row is often too many, but one is often not enough.

6. A short introductory prepositional phrase must be set off with a comma.

7. Two items in a series joined by *and* require a comma.

8. Several coordinate adjectives modifying one noun are set off with commas.

9. In an address, place a comma between the state and zip code.

10. Most non-essential words are set off with commas.

WRITING ASSIGNMENTS

1. Academic Assignment: Visit Congress.org at http://www.congress.org/. Read about a national issue, become familiar with their tips on writing letters, and locate the name and address of a political leader. Then, formulate your opinion on a national issue in a letter to a senator, congressperson, or the President. Provide ample support through specific details. Proofread your letter for correct use of basic punctuation. For assistance with basic punctuation, visit the Weber State Writing Center at http://catsis.weber.edu/writingcenter/an_introduction_to_comma_usage.htm.

2. Journal Assignment: Explain everything that you have learned in this chapter: "Has basic punctuation been used correctly?"

3. Creative Assignment: Visit Philip's House of Stock Photography at http://www.photo.net/stock/. Select an image that you like and describe it in a paragraph or short essay. Proofread your essay for correct use of end punctuation. For tips on writing descriptions, return to Purdue University's Online Writing Lab at http://owl.english.purdue.edu/handouts/general/gl_describe.html.

Chapter 23

Has other punctuation been used correctly?

"In the writing process, the more a story cooks, the better."

— Doris Lessing

LEARNING OBJECTIVES

1. Learn how to use semicolons.
2. Learn how to use colons.
3. Learn how to use parentheses.
4. Learn how to use dashes.
5. Learn how to use quotation marks.
6. Learn how to use italics.
7. Learn how to use brackets.
8. Learn how to use ellipses.
9. Learn how to use apostrophes.
10. Learn how to use hyphens.
11. Learn how to use slashes.

PRE-READING QUESTIONS

1. Can you match the punctuation marks below with their names?

1. semicolon _____		a. " "
2. colon _____		b. [ ]
3. parentheses _____		c. ...
4. dash _____		d. /
5. quotation marks _____		e. '
6. italics _____		f. -
7. brackets _____		g. –
8. ellipses _____		h. :
9. apostrophe _____		i. ( )
10. hyphen _____		j. ;
11. slash _____		k. *word*

2. Which of these marks do you use frequently?
3. Which of these marks have you never used before?
4. How does using punctuation marks correctly affect written communication?
5. How does using punctuation marks incorrectly affect written communication?

HOW DOES A WRITER USE SEMICOLONS? ;

The semicolon is formed by placing a period above a comma; it signals more of a pause than a comma, but less of a pause than a period. Semicolons are used mainly in three situations.

1. Join two related independent clauses not joined by a coordinating conjunction (*and, but, for, nor, or, so, yet*) with a semicolon. This punctuation mark gives variety to writing.

    Incorrect: William Shakespeare wrote many plays; And his most famous play is *Hamlet.*

    Revised: William Shakespeare wrote many plays; his most famous play is *Hamlet.*

    Notice that both sentences are related: they are both about Shakespeare's plays. Also, notice that a coordinating conjunction is not used with the semicolon in the revised example above. Finally, notice that a capital letter does not follow a semicolon, as it does with a period.

    Be careful not to place an incomplete idea or fragment after a semicolon.

Incorrect: *Romeo and Juliet* tells a tragic love story; about two people from feuding families who fall in love.

Subject Verb

Revised: *Romeo and Juliet* tells a tragic love story; <u>it</u> <u>is</u> about two people from feuding families who fall in love.

2. Join two related independent clauses with a semicolon, a conjunctive adverb or transitional phrase, and a comma. Some useful conjunctive adverbs and transitional phrases include the following: *consequently, furthermore, however, in fact, indeed, moreover, nevertheless, then, therefore.* See Chapter 10 for additional transitional phrases and Chapter 16 for additional information about combining sentences using a semicolon.

Incorrect: Leah served as the president of the Key Club in high school; furthermore she participated on the debate team.

Revised: Leah served as the president of the Key Club in high school; furthermore, she participated on the debate team. (conjunctive adverb)

insert comma ➚

Again, both independent clauses are related; they are both about extra-curricular activities in high school. Notice also that a comma follows a conjunctive adverb.

3. Use a semicolon between items in a series containing internal punctuation.

Incorrect: On our vacation we visited Phoenix, Arizona, Las Vegas, Nevada, and Mammoth, California.

Revised: On our vacation we visited Phoenix, Arizona; Las Vegas, Nevada; and Mammoth, California.

Notice that the sentence refers to three vacation spots:

1. Phoenix, Arizona
2. Las Vegas, Nevada
3. Mammoth, California

Since each city and state must be separated by a comma, a semicolon—used in this case as a super comma—clarifies the separation of each of the three locations. Without the semicolon, the reader would have to figure out how many vacation spots were visited.

HOW DOES A WRITER USE COLONS? ⦂

The colon is formed by placing one period above another period. It is used after an independent clause to introduce something else by calling attention to words that follow it. The colon has four main uses. Notice that in the first three uses, the colon works like an equal sign.

1. Introduce a list, frequently with such words as *follows* or *following*. Use a lower case letter in the first word after the colon.

> A balanced diet might include the following: grain, fruit, vegetables, milk, and meat.

2. Introduce an explanation, which may explain, rename, or summarize. The explanation may be either an independent clause or a fragment, an incomplete idea. When a colon connects two independent clauses, either a capital letter or a lower case letter may begin the word after the colon.

> The athlete was skilled with a bow and arrow: he could hit a target the size of a quarter from one hundred feet. (colon introducing an independent clause)
>
> The athlete was skilled with a bow and arrow: He could hit a target the size of a quarter from one hundred feet. (colon introducing an independent clause with a capital letter)
>
> You will need two items to build the model: glue and sandpaper. (colon introducing a fragment)

3. Formally introduce a quotation with an independent clause. The colon frequently introduces a long quotation.

> Charles Dickens provides a clear example of parallel structure in the opening lines of *A Tale of Two Cities*: "It was the best of times, it was the worst of times, it was the age of wisdom, it was the age of foolishness, it was the epoch of belief, it was the epoch of incredulity, it was the season of Light, it was the season of Darkness, it was the spring of hope, it was the winter of despair, we had everything before us, we had nothing before us. . . ."

Use a comma, however, to introduce a quotation with *he said* or *she noted* (or a similar comment).

> She explained, "A security deposit will be required before you are able to move into the apartment."

4. Use in minor situations: after a salutation in a formal letter, between hours and minutes, in ratios, between titles and subtitles, between chapters and verses in scriptural references, and between city and publisher in bibliographic entries.

> Dear Professor Jackson:
>
> 3:30 P.M.
>
> The ratio of boys to girls was 3:1.
>
> *Savage Inequalities: Children in America's Schools.*
>
> Genesis 20:3
>
> New York: Prentice Hall, 2002

Colons are not usually used in the following situations.

1. Do not use a colon after a verb.

> Incorrect: The players were: Jill, Sarah, Kate, and Jessica.
>
> Revised: The players were Jill, Sarah, Kate, and Jessica.
>
> Revised: The players included the following: Jill, Sarah, Kate, and Jessica.

2. Do not use a colon between a preposition and its object.

> Incorrect: Weeds need to be pulled in: the front yard, in the back yard, and on the side yard.
>
> Revised: Weeds need to be pulled in the front yard, in the back yard, and on the side yard.

3. Do not use a colon after transitional phrases like *for example, for instance, including*, and *such as*, and *to illustrate*.

> Incorrect: For example: the tone of the first stanza is light-hearted.
>
> Revised: For example, the tone of the first stanza is light-hearted.

PRACTICE 1

Place semicolons (and sometimes commas) and colons where needed. Write on a separate piece of paper or on a computer.

Example: Kenny started a small business then he expanded it.

> Kenny started a small business; then, he expanded it.

1. The rancher brought the sheep to the barn he had to shear them.
2. Jose put the food in the pot Raymond stirred the pot.
3. The rattlesnake is venomous however the king snake is not venomous.
4. The committee met to examine natural resources land, rivers, lakes, and trees.
5. The committee met at 330 P.M.

HOW DOES A WRITER USE PARENTHESES?

Use parentheses like commas for extra material: supplemental information, numbers, afterthoughts, etc. Parentheses de-emphasize extra material. Parentheses are always used in pairs, so don't forget the second parenthesis.

> The Imperial Decree (March 3, 1861) freed Russian serfs in the same way that the Emancipation Proclamation (January 1, 1863) freed American slaves.
>
> After they caught their limit of fish (rainbow and brook trout), they hiked back to camp.

HOW DOES A WRITER USE DASHES?

A dash is formed by typing two hyphens on the computer or one solid line with no spaces before or after it. It creates a pause longer than a comma, but not as long as a period. Use the dash singly or in pairs. Dashes are less formal than parentheses. In general, dashes are used to set off words (an explanation, a clarification, new thought, a list) by drawing attention to them. Use them in the following ways:

1. Set off words for dramatic effect by emphasizing them.

> The paramedics carried the victim—screaming—into the ambulance.

2. Set off an abrupt change of thought.

> The museum featured paintings, photographs, sculptures—art you couldn't enjoy if you brought your children.

3. Set off a list.

> She volunteered to work one night per week at the shelter to help clients solve their problems—abuse, neglect, and addiction.

Use dashes sparingly, only when other punctuation marks are inadequate.

PRACTICE 2

Place parentheses and dashes where needed. Write on a separate piece of paper or on a computer.

Example: The collector examined the coins pre 1950 that we brought.

> The collector examined the coins (pre 1950) that we brought.

1. David bought a new computer IBM for his office.
2. The sheriff Wendell Roel arrested the suspect.
3. The climbing team suffered intensely dehydration and frostbite.
4. Alicia fell through the ice on the lake have you ever seen that happen to someone?
5. When the suspect was arrested, he stepped into the car smiling.

HOW DOES A WRITER USE QUOTATION MARKS? " "

Use quotation marks in the following four ways:

1. Quotation marks enclose a direct quote, the exact spoken or written words of someone.

She said, "Thank you for the wonderful gift."
Notice how the quotation was punctuated:

- Place a comma before the quote.
- Leave one space after the comma.
- Place quotation marks around the quote.
- Capitalize the first word of the quote.
- Place the period inside the second quotation mark.

Note: See the colon at the beginning of this chapter for a discussion of situations in which it may introduce a quote.
The quote may also be placed at the beginning of the sentence.

"Thank you for the wonderful gift," she said.

Finally, the quotation may be split.

"Thank you," she said, "for the wonderful gift."

Notice the punctuation in these situations.

- Split quotations require quotation marks around both parts of the quote.
- Commas surround the attribution (*she said*).
- The second part of the quote begins with a small letter, unless it is a separate sentence).

In dialogue, start a new paragraph for each new speaker.

"Thank you for the wonderful gift. I have been wanting a new phone since my old one broke down last month," said Trishia.

"You're welcome," said Nick.

Trishia said, "Shall we try it right now?"

"Sure," said Nick.

When punctuating direct quotations, keep the following rules in mind:

- Always place commas and periods **inside** quotation marks.

  He said, "Prospecting for gold had a major impact on the early economy."

- Always place semicolons and colons **outside** quotation marks.

  Aesha said, "The old house is vacant"; then she opened the door.

- Place question marks and exclamation points **inside** quotation marks if they are part of the quotation; place them **outside** the quotation marks if they are part of the entire sentence.

She asked, "May we retake the midterm?" (The quotation is a question, not the entire sentence.)

Will you say, "Please pass the potatoes"? (The entire sentence is a question, not the quotation.)

Never put quotation marks around an indirect quotation, someone's ideas not expressed in that person's exact words.

Incorrect: The bank teller said that "he would be right back."

Revised: The bank teller said that he would be right back. (indirect quotation)

Revised: The bank teller said, "I will be right back." (direct quotation)

ESL Note: Notice that in the example changing the indirect quotation to a direct quotation involves changing the pronoun *he* to *I* and changing the verb *would* to *will*.

Also, never put quotation marks around the title of your own short work, like an essay, unless you are referring to that work within another work.

2. Single quotation marks enclose a quotation or title within a quotation.

Our instructor continued, "Please read the last two lines of 'The Road Not Taken.' These lines say that taking the road less traveled 'has made all the difference.' What does that mean?"

3. Quotation marks enclose short publications. Long publications, on the other hand, require italics or underlining.

Identifying Literary and Artistic Works

Short Works Typically Require Quotation Marks	Long Works Typically Require Italics (or underlining)
The article "The Return of the Black Panther"	The book *Lord of the Flies*
The poem "To an Athlete Dying Young"	The magazine *National Geographic*
The short story "Hills like White Elephants"	The newspaper *Los Angeles Times*
The painting "Mona Lisa"	The play *Romeo and Juliet*
The song "I'm Happy just to Dance with You"	The television show *Who Wants to be a Millionaire?*
The chapter "Marley's Ghost"	
	The movie *Jurassic Park*
	The ship (including aircraft and trains) *Titanic*
	The *Statue of Liberty*

4. Quotation marks may be used to set off words used as words although this is usually indicated by italics or underlining.

The word "receive" is often misspelled.

The word *receive* is often misspelled.

Pick one method of setting off words, and be consistent in using that method throughout your paper.

When using quotation marks in any of the four ways mentioned above, remember that they are always used in pairs. Don't forget to include the second quotation mark, which is sometimes forgotten.

HOW DOES A WRITER USE ITALICS? | *Italics* |

Italics can be created by slanting words to the right when using a computer. The same effect is accomplished by underlining words when handwriting. Use italics in the following ways.

1. Set off long literary or artistic works (see table in quotation marks).

We read and discussed *The Heart of Darkness*.

2. Set off words used as words.

The word *principal* is often confused with the word *principle*.
The word principal is often confused with the word principle.

This is may be accomplished through quotation marks.

The word "principal" is often confused with the word "principle."

Pick one method of setting off words used as words, and be consistent in using that method throughout your paper.

3. Set off letters mentioned as letters and numbers mentioned as numbers (never set off these with quotation marks).

The letter *J* in John's signature was difficult to read.
The *6* on the speed limit sign had been replaced with a *7*.

HOW DOES A WRITER USE BRACKETS?

Use brackets to enclose words that you insert into a direct quotation.

Mrs. Jenkins told her employees, "If we reach our goal this year [sell more than one million dollars worth of inventory], everyone will get a raise in January."

The words of Mrs. Jenkins alone do not define the company's goal, so the information is added to the quote in brackets.

HOW DOES A WRITER USE ELLIPSES?

An ellipsis is three spaced periods, and it represents omitted words in a direct quotation.

> Dr. Long stated, "Neighborhoods with weekly waste collection programs that pick up recyclable waste . . . produce about 25 percent less waste than communities without such programs."

The original quote read as follows: "Neighborhoods with weekly waste collection programs that pick up recyclable waste *such as paper, plastic, and metal*, produce about 25 percent less waste than communities without such programs."

When you delete an entire sentence in a direct quotation, insert a period before the ellipsis dots.

> Patricia Ellis comments on the use of fluoride: "Applying substances with fluoride to the teeth make teeth more resistant to acids that cause dental decay. Adding fluoride ions to water also helps teeth to resist acids. . . . Fluoride ions in high concentrations, however, are toxic."

Note: Never use an ellipsis at the beginning of a quotation, and never use one at the end of a quotation unless you are deleting words from the last sentence quoted.

PRACTICE 3

Place quotation marks, italics (underline not using a computer), brackets, and ellipses where needed. Write on a separate piece of paper or on a computer.

Example: Please write me soon Christina asked.

> "Please write me soon," Christina asked.

1. Please pass me that magazine Armando asked.
2. Leda and the Swan is a poem in our text, An Introduction to Poetry.
3. Dr. Chan continued, "We must determine the effects of the disaster oil spill on marine life."
4. The football coach began swearing, "You idiots."
5. Please read the poem Oh Captain! My Captain! by Walt Whitman said Dr. Bingham.

HOW DOES A WRITER USE APOSTROPHES?

The apostrophe is used in the following ways.

1. Represent missing letters or numbers. When creating a contraction, place the apostrophe in the location of the missing letter(s). An apostrophe may also represent the first two numbers in a year.

   did + not = didn't

   1998 = '98

   Jose *didn't* want to move after *'98*.

Common Contractions

I am = I'm	we have = we've	where is = where's
I have = I've	we will, we shall = we'll	were not = weren't
I shall, I will = I'll	they are = they're	would not = wouldn't
I would = I'd	they have = they've	could not = couldn't
you are = you're	are not = aren't	should not = shouldn't
you have = you've	cannot = can't	would have = would've
you will = you'll	do not = don't	could have = could've
she is, she has = she's	does not = doesn't	should have = should've
he is, he has = he's	have not = haven't	that is = that's
it is, it has = it's	let us = let's	there is = there's
we are = we're	who is, who has = who's	what is = what's

Exception: *Will not* becomes *won't*, not *willn't*.

2. Show ownership or possession. Notice the situations below that show possession, and follow the examples in your writing.

Forming Possessives

Situations	Examples
If the owner word (possessive) does not end in -*s*, add -*'s* to the word.	Jessica's bike is yellow. The children's hands waved goodbye.
*If the owner word (possessive) does end in -*s* and the word is singular, add -*'s* to the word.	I will follow my boss's (singular: one boss) policy.
If the owner word (possessive) does end in -*s* and the word is plural, just add -*'* to the word.	We painted the boys' (plural: two or more boys) room. We'll meet you at the Johnsons' home. (plural: two or more Johnsons)
To show individual ownership, add -*'s* to each noun.	Jan's and Beverly's experience helped them to produce a play.

Situations	Examples
To show joint ownership, add -'s to the last noun only.	Jan and Beverly's play will be performed next week.
To show ownership in a compound noun, add -'s to the last element.	I borrowed my sister-in-law's car.

*Exception: If the owner word (possessive) does end in -s and the word is singular but adding -'s creates an awkward pronunciation, simply add an apostrophe. Incorrect: Jesus's idea Revised: Jesus' idea

Some words already show ownership, so do not us an apostrophe with them to show ownership: *his, her, hers, its, your, yours, our, ours, their, theirs, whose.* Don't confuse these words with contractions like *it's, they're, you're,* and *who's.*

Commonly Confused Words

its (possessive)	it's (it is)
their (possessive)	they're (they are)
your (possessive)	you're (you are)
whose (possessive)	who's (who is)

The dog raised *its* paw. (possessive)
It's going to be an nice day. (contraction)

The players brought *their* racquets. (possessive)
They're hoping to win the tournament. (contraction)

Your sweater is on the couch. (possessive)
You're a fast runner. (contraction)

She is a singer *whose* voice has not changed. (possessive)
Who's at the door? (contraction)

Incorrect: The lion bared it's teeth.
Revised: The lion bared its teeth. (possessive)

See Chapter 19 for a longer list of commonly confused words and use of the apostrophe.

Also, do not use an apostrophe to form the plural of a noun:

Incorrect: The vehicle's were lined up at the auto show.
Revised: The vehicles were lined up at the auto show.

3. Show plurals of abbreviations that end in periods, numbers mentioned as numbers, letters mentioned as letters, words mentioned as words.

The cashiers check customers' I.D.'s before selling alcohol.
She earned three *10*'s at the tournament.

He saw two *A*'s on his report card.

I don't want to hear any *if*'s, *and*'s, or *but*'s about it.

Notice that the *-s* is not italicized when it is used with an italicized number, letter, or word.

Also, plurals of abbreviations without periods and plurals of numbers mentioned as numbers may be written without apostrophes.

We own three VCRs.

She earned three *10*s at the tournament.

HOW DOES A WRITER USE HYPHENS?   -

The hyphen is one short mark used to connect or divide syllables or words in the following ways.

1. Combine words to form an adjective or noun. Many current words in English were used separately in the past, but have become joined through their use together. Words that are used together, then, may be found in one of three stages:

Separate	Hyphenated	Compound
fire engine	fire-eater (n)	firefighter
door prize	door-to-door (adj)	doorway
water polo	water-repellant (adj)	waterproof

Generally, only use the hyphen when the adjective comes before the noun.

He is a well-known player. (*well-known* comes before *player*)

The player is well known. (*well known* comes after *player*)

Consult a dictionary to see how words may be combined. If you do not see a word in a hyphenated or compound form in the dictionary, write it as separate words.

Also, notice that hyphens are suspended in a series:

The three fastest runners will win first-, second-, and third-place trophies.

2. Reduce confusion with double or triple letters:

pre-electric (easier to read than *preelectric*)

cross-stitch (easier to read than *crossstitch*)

Sometimes the hyphen helps the reader to differentiate between two different words.

re-collect (avoids the confusion with *recollect*)

re-creation (avoids the confusion with *recreation*)

The producer attempted a *re-creation* of the president's assassination in his film.

In the summer the kids swim at the community pool for *recreation*.

Check a dictionary to find the correct form of a word.

3. Combine words to create the written form of fractions and numbers between twenty-one and ninety-nine.

He ate *one-fourth* of the pie.

She will turn *twenty-eight* next month.

4. Set off certain prefixes like *all-, ex-* (former), *half-*, and *self-*, and the suffix *-elect*.

all-American

ex-husband

half-wit

self-employed

president-elect

Do not use a hyphen if one of the words ends in *-ly*.

Incorrect: We peered into the swiftly-moving stream.

Revised: We peered into the swiftly moving stream.

5. Express a range of pages.

In class we reviewed pages 235-248.

6. Divide words at the end of a line. Word processors allow writers to type continuously, so writers do not need to make decisions often about dividing words at the ends of lines with hyphens. When words do need to be divided in certain situations, however, remember the following guidelines:

• Divide words between syllables. (consult a dictionary for syllabification)

Incorrect: The doctors told me that I needed to schedule my *operati-on* in February.

Revised: The doctor told me that I needed to schedule my *opera-tion* in February.

• Do not divide one-syllable words.

Incorrect: The university gave him a grant to study the effects of urban *gr-owth* on native plants.

Revised: The university gave him a grant to study the effects of urban *growth* on native plants.

- Leave at least two letters at the end of a line and three letters at the beginning of a line.

    Incorrect: In her speech, she asked for board members to accept her a-
    pology.
    Revised: In her speech, she asked for board members to accept her apol-
    ogy.

- Only divide a hyphenated word at the hyphen.

    Incorrect: By working hard year after year, she became a self-em-
    ployed success.
    Revised: By working hard year after year, she became a self-
    employed success.

- Do not use a hyphen to divide a long e-mail or Internet address. Divide the address so that a punctuation mark begins the new line.

    For more information, please visit the site at http://www.whitehouse.gov
    /history/presidents/

In the above example, notice that a slash begins the second line.

HOW DOES A WRITER USE SLASHES? $\boxed{/}$

The slash or virgule is a diagonal line that has three main uses:

1. It separates lines of poetry in your text. In this context, use a space before and after
   the slash.

    In "Stopping by Woods on a Snowy Evening," Frost uses alliteration in the
    following lines: "He gives his harness bells a shake / To ask if there is some
    mistake."

2. It separates numbers that create fractions. In this context, do not use a space before
   or after the slash.

    ⅓ or ½

3. It separates paired words. In this context, do not use a space before or after the slash.

    She pointed out that opposites like *life/death, health/sickness*, and *happiness/
    misery* create choices for people.

When a paired word comes before and modifies a noun, use a hyphen instead of a
slash.

    We studied the life-death cycle of the black widow.

Do not use the slash frequently. Also, avoid *and/or, he/she*, and *his/her*.

PRACTICE 4

Place apostrophes, hyphens, and slashes where needed. Write on a separate piece of paper or on a computer.

Example: They couldnt earn enough money for a new car in 01.

They couldn't earn enough money for a new car in '01.

1. We wont be able to finish Lisas trench until Saturday.
2. The students hands shot up in response to the teachers question.
3. The store sells oil, water, and rubber based paints.
4. Tabitha is a self made millionaire.
5. The conflict between good bad, rich poor, powerful powerless appears throughout the work.

Other Punctuation Summary

Names and Marks	Main Uses	Examples
semicolon ;	Join independent clauses.	She is tall; he is short.
	Separate items in a series.	We visited Phoenix, Arizona; Las Vegas, Nevada; and Mammoth, California.
colon :	Introduce a list.	Our dog does the following: eats, sleeps, and barks.
	Introduce an explanation.	
	Introduce a quote.	He is lazy: he sleeps all day.
		She started again: "I believe . . ."
parentheses ( )	Insert extra material.	Her birthday (May 2) is close.
dash —	Set off for dramatic effect.	He fell—screaming.
	Set off a new thought.	I believe—no, I know—that we. . . .
	Set off a list.	She solves problems—abuse, neglect, and addiction.
quotation marks " "	Enclose a direct quote.	He said, "Thank you."
	Enclose titles of short works.	We read "A Black Wedding Song."
	Set off words used as words.	Don't confuse "affect" and "effect."
italics *this is italics* or <u>underlining</u>	Enclose titles of long works.	We read *A Christmas Carol.*
	Set off words used as words.	*They're* is a contraction.
	Set off letters and numbers used as letters and numbers.	She earned an *A* in math.
brackets [ ]	Insert words into a quote.	He said, "Thank you [for the bike]."
ellipses . . .	Omit words in a quote.	She said, "Remember this fun summer . . . and don't forget me."
apostrophe '	Represent missing letters.	We can't come to the party.
	Show ownership.	Is that Jasmine's book?
	Form some plurals.	He earned three *A*'s this semester.

(continued)

Other Punctuation Summary (*continued*)

Names and Marks	Main Uses	Examples
hyphen -	Combine words. Reduce confusion. Create numbers. Set off prefixes/suffixes. Express page numbers. Divide words ending a line.	We entered the high-rise building. We had to re-collect the payment. He is thirty-four now. She is self-employed. We covered 331-349 in our text. In school she wants to study psy- chology.
slash /	Separate lines of poetry. Create fractions. Separate paired words.	Langston Hughes wrote, "What happens to a dream deferred / does it dry up. . . ." Add ½ cup of sugar. We studied extremes like hot/cold and wet/dry.

PRACTICE 5

Place punctuation (all forms discussed in this chapter) where needed. Write on a separate piece of paper or on a computer.

Example: The bank loaned us the money now we can buy a home.

   The bank loaned us the money; now we can buy a home.

1. The recipe page 75 calls for 12 of a cup of chopped nuts.
2. In the lab, the computers monitors were all off.
3. Please read the poem called The Magi for homework, said the professor.
4. The well known writer was not well known before she won the Pulitzer.
5. Her pets included the following a dog, two cats, a bird, and four fish.
6. Shawn said, "Dont give that the camera to the children."
7. I remember part of the saying "Early to bed makes a man [person] healthy, wealthy, and wise."
8. Embarrass has two R's and two S's.
9. Last semester, we read Julius Caesar, the play by William Shakespeare we enjoyed it.
10. Sue sat in a chair by the casket for an hour crying.

GROUP WORK

1. As a group, visit Capital Community College and take their quiz on punctuation at http://webster.commnet.edu/grammar/quizzes/niu/niu12.htm.

2. As a group, pick any topic and write a paragraph together in which you use any five of the eleven marks discussed in this chapter.

3. As a group, write one separate sentence for each of the following eight words: *it's, its, they're, their, you're, your, who's,* and *whose.*

TEST (TRUE/FALSE)

1. A semicolon joins two related independent clauses.

2. A colon may not be used to join two related independent clauses.

3. Parentheses enclose extra material.

4. Dashes set off words by calling attention to them.

5. When punctuating direct quotations, commas and periods always go outside the quotation marks.

6. Italics may be used to set off words used as words.

7. Brackets enclose words that you insert into a direct quotation.

8. Ellipses may be used at the beginning, middle, or end of a quotation.

9. The following sentence indicates that two boys own one ball: "It was the boys' ball."

10. To create an adjective made up of two words, use either a hyphen or a slash (well-known woman or well/known woman).

WRITING ASSIGNMENTS

1. Academic Assignment: Visit Consumer Search at http://www.consumersearch.com and research at least five different brands of one type of product (cell phones, sport utility vehicles, etc.). Compare and contrast the products; then, rate them according to your own criteria. Provide ample support through specific details. Use at least five different types of punctuation described in this chapter. Proofread your essay for correct use of the punctuation. For assistance with punctuation, visit Capital Community College at http://webster.commnet.edu/grammar/marks/marks.htm.

2. Journal Assignment: Explain everything that you have learned in this chapter: "Has other punctuation been used correctly?"

3. Creative Assignment: Visit The Worldwide Art Gallery at http://www.theartgallery.com.au/. Select an image that you like and describe it in a paragraph or short essay. Proofread your essay for correct use of other punctuation. For tips on writing descriptions, return to Purdue University's Online Writing Lab at http://owl.english.purdue.edu/handouts/general/gl_describe.html.

REFERENCES

1. Anker, Susan. *Real Writing with Readings: Paragraphs and Essays for College, Work, and Everyday Life*. Boston: Bedford Books, 1998.
2. Bell, George E. *Writing Effective Sentences*. Boston: Allyn & Bacon, 1993.
3. Brandon, Lee. *At a Glance: Paragraphs*. Boston: Houghton Mifflin, 1999.
4. Brandon, Lee. *At a Glance: Sentences*. Boston: Houghton Mifflin, 1999.
5. Buchanan, Esther. *Just Plain English*. Fort Worth: Harcourt Brace, 1999.
6. Buscemi, Santi V., Albert H. Nicolai, and Richard Strugala. *The Basics: A Rhetoric and Handbook*. New York: McGraw-Hill, 1996.
7. Callahan, Steven. *Adrift: Seventy-Six Days Lost at Sea*. New York: Ballantine Books, 1986.
8. Carver, Raymon. *Fires: Essays, Pomes, Stories*. New York: Random House, 1989.
9. Choy, Penelope et al. *Basic Grammar and Usage*. Fort Worth: Harcourt Brace, 1998.
10. Clouse, Barbara Fine. *Jumpstart!: A Workbook for Writers*. New York: McGraw-Hill, 1996.
11. Coon, Dennis. *Introduction to Psychology: Exploration and Application, 3rd Ed.* St. Paul: West Publishing Company, 1983.
12. Dinesen, Isak. *Out of Africa*. New York: The Modern Library, 1937.
13. Emery, Donald W. et al. *English Fundamentals, Form A* (12th ed.). Boston: Allyn and Bacon, 2001.
14. Fawcett, Susan and Alvin Sandberg. *Grassroots with Readings: The Writer's Workbook* (7th ed.). Boston: Houghton Mifflin, 2002.
15. Frank, Anne. *The Diary of a Young Girl*. U.S.A.: Bantam, 1993.
16. "Frequently Asked Questions." *National Institute for Literacy*. 7 December 00 <http://novel.nifl.gov/nifl/faqs.html#literacy>.
17. Fung, Rosaline L. and Raymond F. Pike. *Patterns for Success: Taking the Mystery Out of the Paragraph*. Stockton: VisionKeeper, 1997.
18. Gibaldi, Joseph. *MLA Handbook for Writers of Research Papers* (4th ed.). New York: The Modern Language Association of America, 1995.
19. Glazier, Teresa Ferster and Paige Wilson. *The Least You Should Know about English: Writing Skills, Form B* (7th ed.). Fort Worth: Harcourt Brace, 1998.
20. Hacker, Diana. *The Bedford Handbook* (5th ed.). Boston: Bedford Books, 1998.
21. Hacker, Diana. *A Writer's Reference* (3rd ed.). Boston: St. Martin's Press, 1995.

22. Kelly, William J. and Deborah L. Lawton. *Discovery: An Introduction to Writing.* Boston: Allyn and Bacon, 1997.

23. Kelly, William J. and Deborah L. Lawton. *Odyssey: A Guide to Better Writing.* Boston: Allyn and Bacon, 1998.

24. Langan, John. *College Writing Skills with Readings* (4th ed.). New York: McGraw-Hill, 1997.

25. Langan, John. *Sentence Skills: A Workbook for Writers*, Form A (6th ed.). Boston: McGraw-Hill, 1998.

26. Langan, John. *Sentence Skills with Readings* (2nd ed.). Boston: McGraw-Hill, 2001.

27. Lee, Harper. *To Kill A Mockingbird.* New York: Warner Books, 1960.

28. Markline, Judy, Rose Hawkins and Bob Isaacson. *Thinking on Paper: A Reading-Writing Process Workbook* (4th ed.). Fort Worth: Harcourt Brace, 1999.

29. McKoski, Martin M. and Lynne C Hahn. *Developing Sentence Sense: A Sentence-Combining Worktext.* New York: HarperCollins College Publishers, 1994.

30. Mills, Helen. *Commanding Sentences* (3rd ed.). Salem: Sheffield Publishing Company, 1990.

31. Mills, Helen. *Commanding Sentences* (3rd ed.). *(Instrutor's Manual).* Salem: Sheffield Publishing Company, 1990.

32. Page, Jack. *Checkpoints: Developing College English Skills* (3rd ed.). New York: Longman, 1998.

33. Page, Jack. *Checkpoints with Readings: Developing College English Skills.* New York: Longman, 1997.

34. Peck, M. Scott. *The Road Less Traveled: A New Psychology of Love, Traditional Values, and Spiritual Growth.* New York: Simon & Schuster, 1978.

35. Rich, Susanna. *The Flexible Writer: A Basic Guide* (3rd ed.). Boston: Allyn and Bacon, 1998.

36. Robinson, William S. and Stephanie Tucker. *Texts and Contexts: A Contemporary Approach to College Writing* (3rd ed.). Belmont: Heinle & Heinle: 1997.

37. Rodriguez, Louis J. *Always Running: La Vida Loca: Gang Days in L.A.* New York: Simon & Schuster, 1993.

38. Roth, Audrey J. *The Elements of Basic Writing with Readings* (2nd ed.). Mass: Allyn & Bacon, 1996.

39. Salak, Ann M. *Improve Your Sentences.* New York: Glencoe/McGraw-Hill, 1995.

40. Salomone, William, and Stephen McDonald. *Inside Writing: A Writer's Workbook, Form A* (4th ed.). Belmont: Wadsworth Publishing, 1999.

41. Scarry, Sandra and John Scarry. *The Writer's Workplace with Readings* (3rd ed.). Fort Worth: Harcourt Brace, 1999.

42. Schachter, Norman, Alfred T. Clark, Jr., and Karen Schneiter. *Basic English Review: English the Easy Way* (7th ed.). Cincinnati: South-Western Educational Publishing, 1999.

43. Shepard, Alan and Deke Slayton. *Moon Shot: The Inside Story of America's Race to the Moon.* Atlanta: Turner Publishing, 1994.

44. Smart, Walter Kay. *English Review Grammar* (4th ed.). New Jersey: Prentice Hall, 1968.

45. Smilkstein, Rita. *Tools for Writing: Using the Natural Human Learning Process (Annotated Instructor's Edition)*. Fort Worth: Harcourt Brace, 1998.
46. Smilkstein, Rita. *Tools for Writing: Using the Natural Human Learning Process (Instructor's Manual)*. U.S.A.: Harcourt Brace, 1998.
47. Smith, R. Kent, John Langan, and Carole Mohr. *Basic English Brushup*. Marlton: Townsend Press, 1995.
48. Strong, William. *Writer's Toolbox: A Sentence-Combining Workshop*. New York: McGraw-Hill, 1996.
49. Strong, William. *Writing Incisively: Do-It-Yourself Prose Surgery*. New York: McGraw-Hill, 1991.
50. Strunk, William Jr. and E. B. White. *The Elements of Style* (3rd ed.). New York: Macmillian Publishing, 1979.
51. *Webster's New World College Dictionary* (4th ed.). Michael Agnes, ed. Ohio: IDG Books, 2000.
52. Winkler, Anthony C. *Writing Talk: Paragraphs and Short Essays with Readings*. New Jersey: Prentice Hall, 1997.
53. "Writing." *Britannica Online*. Encyclopaedia Britannica. 26 June 2000 <www.eb.com>.
54. Yarber, Mary Laine and Robert E. Yarber. *Reviewing Basic Grammar* (4th ed.). New York: Longman, 1996.

Appendix A

Readings for Writing

POEMS

Dreams
Langston Hughes

Hold fast to dreams
For if dreams die
Life is a broken-winged bird
That cannot fly.

Hold fast to dreams   5
For when dreams go
Life is a barren field
Frozen with snow.

DISCUSSION QUESTIONS

1. Why is this poem divided into two stanzas?
2. What two metaphors are being used in this poem?
3. What advice is this poem giving to its readers?

WRITING ASSIGNMENTS

1. Describe one of your most important dreams. What have you done to accomplish your dream? What still needs to be done to accomplish your
   dream?
2. What do dreams do for people? What are the advantages and disadvan-
   tages of having dreams? What does "hold fast to dreams" mean?

Dream Deferred
Langston Hughes

What happens to a dream deferred?

Does it dry up
like a raisin in the sun?

Or fester like a sore—
And then run?   5

Does it stink like rotten meat?
Or crust and sugar over—
like a syrupy sweet?

Maybe it just sags
like a heavy load.   10

Or does it explode?

DISCUSSION QUESTIONS

1. What is a "dream deferred"?
2. Why does this poem ask a series of questions?

WRITING ASSIGNMENTS

1. Describe an experience where you had a dream deferred. What were the consequences? To what can you compare your deferred dream?
2. Compare and contrast "Dreams Deferred" and "Dreams."

Fog
Carl Sandburg

The fog comes
on little cat feet.
It sits looking
over harbor and city
on silent haunches   5
and then moves on.

DISCUSSION QUESTIONS

1. How is fog like a cat?
2. Poets give life to things through personification. How does personification help the reader to understand fog?
3. What alliteration do you notice in "little cat feet"?

WRITING ASSIGNMENTS

1. Write a poem in which you give life to something through personification.
2. Write a short essay in which you propose a method for preserving an environmentally-delicate area.

To See a World in a Grain of Sand
William Blake

To see a world in a grain of sand
And a heaven in a wild flower,
Hold infinity in the palm of your hand
And eternity in an hour.

DISCUSSION QUESTIONS

1. How is the world like a grain of sand?
2. How does heaven resemble a wildflower?

WRITING ASSIGNMENTS

1. Metaphors are full of suggestions. Discuss the advantages of using metaphors in writing prose and poetry.
2. Write a short poem that is rich in metaphors.

Fish Story
Richard Armour

Count this among my heartfelt wishes:
To hear a fish tale told by fishes
And stand among the fish who doubt
The honor of a fellow trout,
And watch the bulging of their eyes   5
To hear the imitation flies
And worms with rather droopy looks
Stuck through with hateful, horrid hooks,
And fishermen they fled all day from
(As big as this) and got away from.   10

DISCUSSION QUESTIONS

1. What is the rhyme scheme of this poem?
2. Have you ever considered the tales that fish might tell? How difficult is generating new ideas or perspectives in a poem?

WRITING ASSIGNMENTS

1. Armour describes a common activity (fishing) from an uncommon perspective (the fish's point of view). Pick another common activity and describe it from an uncommon perspective in a short essay.
2. Write a short essay in which you compare and contrast one event (game, crime, job, etc.) from two opposing perspectives.

We Alone
Alice Walker

We alone can devalue gold
by not caring
if it falls or rises
in the marketplace.
Wherever there is gold   5
there is a chain, you know,
and if your chain
is gold
so much the worse
for you.   10

Feathers, shells
and sea-shaped stones
are all as rare.

This could be our revolution:
To love what is plentiful   15
as much as
what's scarce.

DISCUSSION QUESTIONS

1. Besides being "plentiful," what do "feathers, shells, and sea-shaped stones" have in common?
2. Explain the words, "Wherever there is gold there is a chain."
3. How does the title relate to the theme?

WRITING ASSIGNMENTS

1. In a short essay, analyze the three things that you love the most. Why are these things more important than other things? How are these things important in your life? How expensive are they?
2. Select one object of desire that comes with a chain or negative consequence. Examine the positive and negative consequences of pursuing that object of desire.

Alone
Maya Angelou

Lying, thinking
Last night
How to find my soul a home
Where water is not thirsty
And bread loaf is not stone   5
I came up with one thing
And I don't believe I'm wrong
That nobody,
But nobody
Can make it out here alone.   10

Alone, all alone
Nobody, but nobody
Can make it out here alone.

There are some millionaires
With money they can't use   15
Their wives run round like banshees
Their children sing the blues
They've got expensive doctors
To cure their hearts of stone.
But nobody   20
No nobody
Can make it out here alone

Alone, all alone
Nobody, but nobody
Can make it out here alone.   25

Now if you listen closely
I'll tell you what I know
Storm clouds are gathering
The wind is gonna blow
The race of man is suffering   30
And I can hear the moan,
Cause nobody,
But nobody
Can make it out here alone.

Alone, all alone   35
Nobody, but nobody
Can make it out here alone.

DISCUSSION QUESTIONS

1. How many stanzas does "Alone" contain? What is the purpose of the repetition of the three short stanzas?
2. According to this poem, why is "the race of man" suffering?

WRITING ASSIGNMENTS

1. Compare and contrast "We Alone" with "Alone."
2. If "nobody can make it out here alone," write an essay in which you propose a way for people to avoid that situation.

Elena
Pat Mora

My Spanish isn't enough.
I remember how I'd smile
listening to my little ones,
understanding every word they'd say,
their jokes, their songs, their plots.   5
    Vamos a pedirle dulces a mamá, Vamos.°
But that was in Mexico.
Now my children go to American high schools.
They speak English. At night they sit around
the kitchen table, laugh with one another.   10
I stand by the stove and feel dumb, alone.
I bought a book to learn English.
My husband frowned, drank more beer.
My oldest said, "*Mamá,* he doesn't want you
to be smarter than he is." I'm forty,   15
embarrassed at mispronouncing words,
embarrassed at the laughter of my children,
the grocer, the mailman. Sometimes I take
my English book and lock myself in the bathroom,
say the thick words softly,   20
for if I stop trying, I will be deaf
when my children need my help.

6. **Vamos . . . Vamos:** Let's go ask for sweets from mom. Come on.

DISCUSSION QUESTIONS

1. Who is speaking in the poem? What is her problem? Who wrote the poem? Could the speaker in the poem have written the poem? Why? Why not?
2. Have you or a family member ever struggled to learn a new language? What problems arose? How did you or that person handle the situation?

WRITING ASSIGNMENTS

1. What challenges exist for people who are assimilating into a new culture?
2. Write a short essay in which you propose methods for learning English as a second language and assimilating into a second culture.

Theme for English B
Langston Hughes

The instructor said,

    Go home and write
    a page tonight.

    And let that page come out of you—
    Then, it will be true.   5

I wonder if it's that simple?

I am twenty-two, colored, born in Winston-Salem.
I went to school there, then Durham, then here
to this college on the hill above Harlem.
I am the only colored student in my class.   10
The steps from the hill lead down to Harlem,
through a park, then I cross St. Nicholas,
Eighth Avenue, Seventh, and I come to the Y,
the Harlem Branch Y, where I take the elevator
up to my room, sit down, and write this page: 15

It's not easy to know what is true for you or me
at twenty-two, my age. But I guess I'm what
I feel and see and hear. Harlem, I hear you:
hear you, hear me—we two—you, me talk on this page.
(I hear New York, too.) Me—who?   20

Well, I like to eat, sleep, drink, and be in love.
I like to work, read, learn, and understand life.
I like a pipe for a Christmas present,
or records—Bessie, bop, or Bach.

I guess being colored doesn't make me not like   25
the same things other folks like who are other races.
So will my page be colored that I write?
Being me, it will not be white.
But it will be
a part of you, instructor.   30
You are white—
yet a part of me, as I am a part of you.
That's American.
Sometimes perhaps you don't want to be a part of me.

Nor do I often want to be a part of you.   35
But we are, that's true!
As I learn from you,
I guess you learn from me—
although you're older—and white—
and somewhat more free.   40

This is my page for English B.

DISCUSSION QUESTIONS

1. What does the speaker consider as he begins to respond to his writing assignment?
2. If you were an instructor receiving this poem in response to the assignment in lines 2 to 5, how would you grade and respond to it?

WRITING ASSIGNMENTS

1. The speaker asks, "So will my page be colored that I write?" How is everyone's writing colored by his or her perspective, culture, experience, etc.?
2. In a short essay, appraise "Theme for English B" as a response to the writing assignment at the beginning of the poem.

O Captain! My Captain!
Walt Whitman

O Captain! my Captain! our fearful trip is done,
The ship has weather'd every rack, the prize we sought is won,
The port is near, the bells I hear, the people all exulting,
While follow eyes the steady keel, the vessel grim and daring;
   But O heart! heart! heart!   5
     O the bleeding drops of red,
      Where on the deck my Captain lies,
       Fallen cold and dead.

O Captain! my Captain! rise up and hear the bells;
Rise up—for you the flag is flung—for you the bugle trills,   10
For you bouquets and ribbon'd wreaths—for you the shores a-crowding,
For you they call, the swaying mass, their eager faces turning;
     Here Captain! dear father!

> This arm beneath your head!
> It is some dream that on the deck,   15
>   You've fallen cold and dead.
>
> My Captain does not answer, his lips are pale and still,
> My father does not feel my arm, he has no pulse nor will,
> The ship is anchor'd safe and sound, its voyage closed and done,
> From fearful trip the victor ship comes in with object won;   20
> Exult O shores, and ring O bells!
>   But I with mournful tread,
>   Walk the deck my Captain lies,
>   Fallen cold and dead.

DISCUSSION QUESTIONS

1. To visualize this poem, sketch the image that this poem depicts; then, describe the details of your drawing.
2. What sensory details help to create a vivid image?

WRITING ASSIGNMENTS

1. This poem was written soon after the death of Abraham Lincoln. Write a short eulogy in which you pay tribute to someone who has died.
2. Write a letter of appreciation to a living person. Include specific details describing the words, traits, or actions of that person.

Sindhi Woman
Jon Stallworthy

> Barefoot through the bazaar,
> and with the same undulant grace
> as the cloth blown back from her face,
> she glides with a stone jar
> high on her head   5
> and not a ripple in her tread.
>
> Watching her cross erect
> stones, garbage, excrement, and crumbs

of glass in the Karachi slums,
I, with my stoop, reflect   10
they stand most straight
who learn to walk beneath a weight.

DISCUSSION QUESTIONS

1. Define any words that you do not know like *bazaar, undulant, excrement.*
2. The Sindhi are a predominantly Moslem people living in Sind, a province of Pakistan. Karachi is the capital of Sind. What do you learn about the setting of this poem from the description of the woman and the neighborhood?
3. What do the last two lines of the poem mean? Are they true? How?

WRITING ASSIGNMENTS

1. In a short essay, describe a hardship that produces positive results.
2. In the poem, the speaker juxtaposes the posture of him- or herself with the posture of the Sindi woman. Write a short essay in which you contrast an aspect of two people.

Welcome to Hiroshima
Mary Jo Salter

is what you first see, stepping off the train:
a billboard brought to you in living English
by Toshiba Electric. While a channel
silent in the TV of the brain

projects those flickering re-runs of a cloud   5
that brims its risen columnful like beer
and, spilling over, hangs its foamy head,
you feel a thirst for history: what year

it started to be safe to breathe the air,
and when to drink the blood and scum afloat   10
on the Ohta River. But no, the water's clear,
they pour it for your morning cup of tea

in one of the countless sunny coffee shops
whose plastic dioramas advertise
mutations of cuisine behind the glass: 15
a pancake sandwich; a pizza someone tops

with a maraschino cherry. Passing by
the Peace Park's floral hypocenter (where
how bravely, or with what mistaken cheer,
humanity erased its own erasure),   20

you enter the memorial museum
and through more glass are served, as on a dish
of blistered grass, three mannequins. Like gloves
a mother clips to coatsleeves, strings of flesh

hang from their fingertips; or as if tied   25
to recall a duty for us, *Reverence*
the dead whose mourners too shall soon be dead,
but all commemoration's swallowed up

in questions of bad taste, how re-created
horror mocks the grim original,
and thinking at last *They should have left it all*   30
you stop. This is the wristwatch of a child.

Jammed on the moment's impact, resolute
to communicate some message, although mute,

it gestures with its hands at eight-fifteen   35
and eight-fifteen and eight-fifteen again

while tables of statistics on the wall
update the news by calling on a roll
of tape, death gummed on death, and in the case
adjacent, an exhibit under glass   40

is glass itself: a shard the bomb slammed in
a woman's arm at eight-fifteen, but some
three decades on—as if to make it plain
hope's only as renewable as pain,

and as if all the unsung   45
debasements of the past may one day come
rising to the surface once again—
worked its filthy way out like a tongue.

DISCUSSION QUESTIONS

1. Evaluate the comparison of the cloud-blast from the dropping of the atomic bomb on Hiroshima and beer in a mug spilling over.
2. What is the theme of "Welcome to Hiroshima"?

WRITING ASSIGNMENTS

1. This poem contains several symbols like a child's broken wristwatch. Select one symbol, and analyze it. Why has the author included it in the poem? What does the symbol connote to you?
2. Should the atomic bomb be used in war? Defend your position with specific support.

Do Not Go Gentle Into That Good Night
Dylan Thomas

Do not go gentle into that good night,
Old age should burn and rave at close of day;
Rage, rage against the dying of the light.

Though wise men at their end know dark is right,
Because their words had forked no lightning they   5
Do not go gentle into that good night.

Good men, the last wave by, crying how bright
Their frail deeds might have danced in a green bay,
Rage, rage against the dying of the light.

Wild men who caught and sang the sun in flight,   10
And learn, too late, they grieved it on its way,
Do not go gentle into that good night.

Grave men, near death, who see with blinding sight
Blind eyes could blaze like meteors and be gay,
Rage, rage against the dying of the light.   15

And you, my father, there on the sad height,
Curse, bless, me now with your fierce tears, I pray,
Do not go gentle into that good night.
Rage, rage against the dying of the light.

DISCUSSION QUESTIONS

1. Whom does the speaker address? What is the speaker's advice?
2. This poem is a villanelle, a fixed form created by early French poets. What is its structure and rhyme scheme?

WRITING ASSIGNMENTS

1. How does one reconcile death? What perspective can be acquired to accomplish this?
2. The speaker of the poem says, "Do Not Go Gentle into that Good Night." Specifically, how can we live our lives in accordance with these words.

Stopping by Woods on a Snowy Evening
Robert Frost

Whose woods these are I think I know.
His house is in the village though;
He will not see me stopping here
To watch his woods fill up with snow.

My little horse must think it queer
To stop without a farmhouse near   5
Between the woods and frozen lake
The darkest evening of the year.

He gives his harness bells a shake
To ask if there is some mistake.   10
The only other sound's the sweep
Of easy wind and downy flake.

The woods are lovely, dark and deep,
But I have promises to keep,
And miles to go before I sleep,   15
And miles to go before I sleep.

DISCUSSION QUESTIONS

1. Sketch the scene described in this poem. What colors are used? What might these colors symbolize?

2. What is the rhyme scheme of the four stanzas in this poem?

3. Interpret the last stanza. What does the speaker mean in these four lines?

WRITING ASSIGNMENTS

1. Describe a favorite place, a place where you reflect upon life. Write using sensory details that communicate how we experience life: see, touch, smell, feel, and taste.

2. The speaker of the poem says, "I have promises to keep." What promises to yourself or others do you have to keep?

The Road Not Taken
Robert Frost

Two roads diverged in a yellow wood,
And sorry I could not travel both
And be one traveler, long I stood
And looked down one as far as I could
To where it bent in the undergrowth;   5

Then took the other, as just as fair,
And having perhaps the better claim,
Because it was grassy and wanted wear;
Though as for that the passing there
Had worn them really about the same,   10

And both that morning equally lay
In leaves no step had trodden black.
Oh, I kept the first for another day!
Yet knowing how way leads on to way,
I doubted if I should ever come back.   15

I shall be telling this with a sigh
Somewhere ages and ages hence:
Two roads diverged in a wood, and I—
I took the one less traveled by,
And that has made all the difference.   20

DISCUSSION QUESTIONS

1. What could a fork in the road symbolize?
2. What is meant by, "I doubted if I should ever come back"?
3. Explain the last three lines.

WRITING ASSIGNMENTS

1. Are some decisions irreversible? Provide specific evidence to support your claim.
2. Explain a time in your life when you did not follow the crowd. How did that decision pay off?

Your Children Are Not Your Children
Khalil Bibran

Your children are not your children.
They are the sons and daughters of Life's longing for itself.
They come through you but not from you,
And though they are with you yet they belong not to you.

You may give them your love but not your thought,   5
For they have their own thoughts.
You may house their bodies but not their souls,
For their souls dwell in the house of tomorrow, which you cannot visit,
    not even in your dreams.
You may strive to be like them, but seek not to make them like you.
For life goes not backward nor tarries with yesterday.   10

You are the bows from which your children as living arrows are sent forth.
The archer sees the mark upon the path of the infinite, and He bends you
    with His might that His arrows may go swift and far.
Let your bending in the archer's hand be for gladness;
For even as He loves the arrow that flies, so He loves also the bow that is stable.

DISCUSSION QUESTIONS

1. Do you agree with the title of this poem? How is the statement true? How is the statement not true?

2. Who are the arrows, the bows, and the archer?

3. How will a reader's belief or disbelief in God affect the way that this poem is received?

WRITING ASSIGNMENTS

1. What are the rights and responsibilities of a parent?
2. What are the rights and responsibilities of a child?

Sonnet 130
William Shakespeare

My mistress' eyes are nothing like the sun;
Coral is far more red than her lips' red;
If snow be white, why then her breasts are dun;
If hairs be wires, black wires grow on her head.
I have seen roses damasked, red and white,
But no such roses see I in her cheeks;
And in some perfumes is there more delight
Than in the breath that from my mistress reeks.
I live to hear her speak; yet well I know
That music hath a far more pleasing sound:
I grant I never saw a goddess go;
My mistress, when she walks, treads on the ground.
    And yet, by heaven, I think my love as rare
    As any she belied with false compare.

DISCUSSION QUESTIONS

1. What is ironic about this poem? Would a mistress receive this poem favorably? Why? Why not?
2. Explain the meaning of the following words: *dun, roses damasked, belied.*

WRITING ASSIGNMENT

1. In a poem, pay tribute to someone whom you love.
2. In a short essay, compare and contrast the strengths and weaknesses of a family member or close friend.

I Wandered Lonely as a Cloud
William Wordsworth

I wandered lonely as a cloud
   That floats on high o'er vales° and hills,   2. **vales:** valleys
When all at once I saw a crowd,
   A host, of golden daffodils,
Beside the lake, beneath the trees,   5
Fluttering and dancing in the breeze.

Continuous as the stars that shine
   And twinkle on the Milky Way,
They stretched in never-ending line
   Along the margin of a bay:°   10   10. **margin of a bay:** edge of
Ten thousand saw I at a glance,   water
Tossing their heads in sprightly dance.

The waves beside them danced; but they
   Outdid the sparkling waves in glee;
A poet could not but be gay,   15
   In such a jocund° company;   16. **jocund:** merry
I gazed – and gazed – but little thought
What wealth the show to me had brought:

For oft, when on my couch I lie
   In vacant or in pensive mood,   20
They flash upon that inward eye
   Which is the bliss of solitude;
And then my heart with pleasure fills,
And dances with the daffodils.

DISCUSSION QUESTIONS

1. What is the speaker's mood at the beginning of the poem? What causes the speaker's mood to change?
2. What is the "inward eye" described in line 21? How does it work?
3. What is the rhyme scheme of this poem? What similes and personification do you notice?

WRITING ASSIGNMENTS

1. Describe a favorite place in nature. Use specific sensory details. How does this place influence your mood?
2. Compose a short essay in which you explain what your "inward eye" sees and how those images affect your mood.

The Lightning is a Yellow Fork
Emily Dickinson

The Lightning is a yellow Fork
From Tables in the sky
By inadvertent fingers dropt
The awful Cutlery

Of mansions never quite disclosed   5
And never quite concealed
The Apparatus of the Dark
To ignorance revealed.

DISCUSSION QUESTIONS

1. The speaker says that "Lightning is a yellow Fork." Who dropped the fork? Can you know with certainty? The mansion is a symbol of what?
2. How effective is the symbolism in this poem? Does lightning work as a symbol of a spiritual force? How so?

WRITING ASSIGNMENTS

1. Select one symbol to represent you. Describe that symbol in detail, and explain how it represents you.
2. Pose one significant question to which you do not yet have an answer. Then in a short essay, explain how the answer could be obtained and why seeking an answer to this question is important.

The Eagle and the Mole
Elinor Wylie

Avoid the reeking herd,
Shun the polluted flock,
Live like that stoic bird,
The eagle of the rock.

The huddled warmth of crowds   5
Begets and fosters hate;
He keeps, above the clouds,
His cliff inviolate.

When flocks are folded warm,
And herds to shelter run,   10
He sails above the storm,
He stares into the sun.

If in the eagle's track
Your sinews cannot leap,
Avoid the lathered pack,   15
Turn from the steaming sheep.

If you would keep your soul
From spotted sight or sound,
Live like the velvet mole;
Go burrow underground.   20

And there hold intercourse
With roots of trees and stones,
With rivers at their source,
And disembodied bones.

DISCUSSION QUESTIONS

1. How are the eagle and the mole similar and different?
2. What are the pros and cons of not following the crowd, of foraging one's own path?

WRITING ASSIGNMENTS

1. Pick an animal that represents you. Describe the animal, and explain how its physical and behavioral characteristics are similar to yours.
2. Compare "The Eagle and the Mole" by Elinor Wylie to "The Road Not Taken" by Robert Frost.

Metaphors
Sylvia Plath

> I'm a riddle in nine syllables,
> An elephant, a ponderous house,
> A melon strolling on two tendrils.
> O red fruit, ivory, fine timbers!
> This loaf's big with its yeasty rising.   5
> Money's new-minted in this fat purse.
> I'm a means, a stage, a cow in calf.
> I've eaten a bag of green apples,
> Boarded the train there's no getting off.

DISCUSSION QUESTIONS

1. What do all of the metaphors in the poem reveal about the speaker?
2. How many syllables are in each line? How many lines are in the poem? How does this number relate to the speaker's condition?
3. What is the speaker's tone in the last line?

WRITING QUESTIONS

1. Pick three characteristics or traits that are essential for good parents to have. Prioritize them, and defend your claim.
2. In the last line of Plath's poem, the speaker says, "Boarded the train there's no getting off." Write a short essay in which you respond to that statement. Do you agree with it? Why? Why not? Under what conditions, if any, should passengers be able to get off that train?

The Day Is Done
Henry Wadsworth Longfellow

The day is done, and the darkness
   Falls from the wings of night,
As a feather is wafted downward
   From an eagle in his flight.

I see the lights of the village   5
   Gleam through the rain and the mist,
And a feeling of sadness comes o'er me.
   That my soul cannot resist:

A feeling of sadness and longing,
   That is not akin to pain,   10
And resembles sorrow only
   As the mist resembles the rain.

Come, read to me some poem,
   Some simple and heartfelt lay,°   14. **lay:** a ballad or story poem.
That shall soothe this restless feeling,   15
   And banish the thoughts of day.

Not from the grand old masters,
   Not from the bards sublime,°   18. **bards sublime:** poets who
Whose distant footsteps echo   wrote lofty, exalted poems.
   Through the corridors of time.   20

For, like strains of martial music,
   Their mighty thoughts suggest
Life's endless toil and endeavor;
   And tonight I long for rest.

Read from some humbler poet,   25
   Whose songs gushed from his heart,
As showers from the clouds of summer,
   Or tears from the eyelids start;

Who, through long days of labor,
   And nights devoid of ease,   30
Still heard in his soul the music
   Of wonderful melodies.

Such songs have power to quiet
   The restless pulse of care,
And come like the benediction°   35   35. **benediction:** state of blessed-
   That follows after prayer.   ness or grace.

Then read from the treasured volume
   The poem of thy choice,
And lend to the rhyme of the poet
   The beauty of thy voice.   40

And the night shall be filled with music,
   And the cares, that infest the day,
Shall fold their tents, like the Arabs,
   And as silently steal away.

DISCUSSION QUESTIONS

1. Longfellow makes many comparisons in this poem. Which similes appearing striking to you? In each simile, what two things are being compared? Why is each simile particularly effective here?
2. What is the speaker seeking? How does the speaker hope to obtain what is being sought?

WRITING ASSIGNMENTS

1. What are "the cares, that infest the day"? At school and work, what are your greatest challenges? What bothers or annoys you the most?
2. In the evening or on the weekend, how do you unwind from "the cares, that infest the day"? What specific hobbies, habits, and routines do you engage in to relax and recover? What impact do these activities have on your mental and physical health?

SHORT READINGS

Let's Get Specific

Beth Johnson

PREVIEW

What makes writing good? Good writing uses specific details to show instead of tell something. This may be accomplished by writing to the five senses, describing how things appear, smell, feel, taste, and sound. Beth Johnson, a journalist and teacher, discusses and demonstrates the use of specific details in her article.

BUILDING VOCABULARY

1. instinctive: natural
2. prospective: expected, future
3. vividly: clearly, in mental images
4. glaze: become glassy
5. blandly: dully and tastelessly
6. intuitively: immediately understood
7. parody: mocking imitation
8. anecdote: story
9. sustain: support

Imagine that you've offered to fix up your sister with a blind date. "You'll like him," you tell her. "He's really nice." Would that assurance be enough to satisfy her? Would she contentedly wait for Saturday night, happily anticipating meeting this "nice" young man? Not likely! She would probably bombard you with questions: "But what's he like? Is he tall or short? Funny? Serious? Smart? Kind? Shy? Does he work? How do you know him?"

Such questions reveal the instinctive[1] hunger we all feel for specific detail. Being told that her prospective[2] date is "nice" does very little to help your sister picture him. She needs concrete details to help her vividly[3] imagine this stranger.

The same principle applies to writing. Whether you are preparing a research paper, a letter to a friend, or an article for the local newspaper, your writing will be strengthened by the use of detailed, concrete language. Specific

5

10

language energizes and informs readers. General language, by contrast, makes their eyes glaze[4] over.

The following examples should prove the point.   15

Dear Sir or Madam:

Please consider my application for a job with your company. I am a college gradu-ate with experience in business. Part-time jobs that I have held during the school year and my work over summer vacations make me well-qualified for employ-ment. My former employers have always considered me a good, reliable worker. Thank you for considering my application.

Sincerely,

Bob Cole

Dear Sir or Madam:

I would like to be considered for an entry-level position in your purchasing de-partment. I graduated in June from Bayside College with a 3.5 GPA and a bache-lor's degree in business administration. While at Bayside, I held a part-time job in the college's business office, where I eventually had responsibility for coordinat-ing food purchasing for the school cafeteria. By encouraging competitive bidding among food suppliers, I was able to save the school approximately $2,500 in the school year 1998–1999. During the last three summers (1997–1999), I worked at Bayside Textiles, where I was promoted from a job in the mailroom to the position of assistant purchasing agent, a position that taught me a good deal about con-trolling costs. Given my background, I'm confident I could make a real contribu-tion to your company. I will telephone you next Tuesday morning to ask if we might arrange an interview.

Sincerely,

Julia Moore

Which of the preceding letters do you think makes a more convincing case for these job seekers? If you're like most people, you would choose the second. Although both letters are polite and grammatically acceptable, the first one suffers badly in comparison with the second for one important reason. It is *general* and *abstract,* while the second is *specific* and *concrete.*   20

Let's look at the letters again. The differing styles of the two are evident in the first sentence. Bob is looking for "a job with your company." He doesn't specify what kind of job—it's for the employer to figure out if Bob wants to work as a groundskeeper, on an assembly line, or as a salesperson. By contrast, Julia is immediately specific about the kind of job she is seeking—"an entry-   25
level position in your purchasing department." Bob tells only that he is "a col-

lege graduate." But Julia tells where she went to college, what her grade point average was, and exactly what she studied.

The contrast continues as the two writers talk about their work experi- 30
ence. Again, Bob talks in vague, general terms. He gives no concrete evidence to show how the general descriptions "well-qualified" and "good, reliable worker" apply to him. But Julia backs up her claims. She tells specifically what positions she's held (buyer for cafeteria, assistant purchasing clerk for textile company), gives solid evidence that she performed her jobs well (saved the school $2,500, was promoted from mailroom), and explains what skills she has acquired 35
(knows about controlling costs). Julia continues to be clear and concrete as she closes the letter. By saying, "I will telephone you next Tuesday morning," she leaves the reader with a helpful, specific piece of information. Chances are, her prospective employer will be glad to take her call. The chances are equally good that Bob will never hear from the company. His letter was so blandly[5] 40
general that the employer will hardly remember receiving it.

> "Vague, general language is the written equivalent of baby food. It is adequate; it can sustain life. But it isn't very interesting."

Julia's letter demonstrates the power of specific detail—a power that we all appreciate intuitively.[6] Indeed, although we may not always be aware of it, our opinions and decisions are frequently swayed by concrete language. On a restaurant menu, are you more tempted by a "green salad" or "a colorful salad 45
bowl filled with romaine and spinach leaves, red garden-fresh tomatoes, and crisp green pepper rings"? Would being told that a movie is "good" persuade you to see it as much as hearing that it is "a hilarious parody[7] of a rock docu-mentary featuring a fictional heavy-metal band"? Does knowing that a class-mate has "personal problems" help you understand her as well as hearing that 50
"her parents are divorcing, her brother was just arrested for selling drugs, and she is scheduled for surgery to correct a back problem"?

When we read, all of us want—even crave*—this kind of specificity. Con-crete language grabs our attention and allows us to witness the writer's world almost firsthand. Abstract language, on the other hand, forces us to try to fill in 55
the blanks left by the writer's lack of specific imagery. Usually we tire of the ef-fort. Our attention wanders. We begin to wonder what's for lunch and whether it's going to rain, as our eyes scan the page, searching for some concrete detail to focus on.

Once you understand the power of concrete details, you will gain consid- 60
erable power as a writer. You will describe events so vividly that readers will feel they experienced them directly. You will sprinkle your essays with nuggets of detail that, like the salt on a pretzel, add interest and texture.

Consider the following examples and decide for yourself which came from a writer who has mastered the art of the specific detail.

Living at Home

Unlike many college students, I have chosen to live at home with my parents. Naturally, the arrangement has both good and bad points. The most difficult part is that, even though I am an adult, my parents sometimes still think of me as a child. Our worst disagreements occur when they expect me to report to them as though I were still twelve years old. Another drawback to living with my parents is that I don't feel free to have friends over to "my place." It's not that my parents don't welcome my friends in their home, but I can't tell my friends to drop in anytime as I would if I lived alone.

But in other ways, living at home works out well. The most obvious plus is that I am saving a lot of money. I pay room and board, but that doesn't compare to what renting an apartment would cost. There are less measurable advantages as well. Although we do sometimes fall into our old parent-child roles, my parents and I are getting to know each other in new ways. Generally, we relate as adults, and I think we're all gaining a lot of respect for one another.

The Pros and Cons of Living at Home

Most college students live in a dormitory or apartment. They spend their hours surrounded by their own stereos, blaring Pearl Jam or Arrested Development; their own furnishings, be they leaking beanbag chairs or Salvation Army sofas; and their own choice of foods, from tofu-bean sprout casseroles to a basic diet of Cheetos. My life is different. I occupy the same room that has been mine since babyhood. My school pictures, from gaptoothed first-grader to cocky senior, adorn the walls. The music drifting through my door from the living room ranges from Lawrence Welk to . . . Lawrence Welk. The food runs heavily to Mid-American Traditional: meatloaf, mashed potatoes, frozen peas.

Yes, I live with my parents. And the arrangement is not always ideal. Although I am twenty-four years old, my parents sometimes slip into a time warp and mentally cut my age in half. "Where are you going, Lisa? Who will you be with?" my mother will occasionally ask. I'll answer patiently, "I'm going to have pizza with some people from my psych class." "But where?" she continues. "I'm not sure," I'll say, my voice rising just a hair. If the questioning continues, it will often lead to a blowup. "You don't need to know where I'm going, OK?" I'll say shrilly. "You don't have to yell at me," she'll answer in a hurt voice.

Living at home also makes it harder to entertain. I find myself envying classmates who can tell their friends, "Drop in anytime." If a friend of mine "drops in" unexpectedly, it throws everyone into a tizzy. Mom runs for the dustcloth while Dad ducks into the bedroom, embarrassed to be seen in his comfortable, ratty bathrobe.

On the other hand, I don't regret my decision to live at home for a few years. Naturally, I am saving money. The room and board I pay my parents wouldn't rent the tiniest, most roach-infested apartment in the city. And despite our occasional lapses, my parents and I generally enjoy each other's company. They are getting to know me as an adult, and I am learning to see them as people, not just my parents. I realized how true this was when I saw them getting dressed up to go out recently. Dad was putting on a tie, and Mom one of her best dresses. I opened my mouth to ask where they were going when it occurred to me that maybe they didn't care to be checked up on any more than I did. Swallowing my curiosity, I simply waved good-bye and said, "Have a good time!"

Both passages could have been written by the same person. Both make the same basic points. But the second passage is far more interesting because it backs up the writer's points with concrete details. While the first passage merely *tells* that the writer's parents sometimes treat her like a child, the second passage follows this point up with an anecdote[8] that *shows* exactly what she means. Likewise with the point about inviting friends over: the first passage only states that there is a problem, but the second one describes in concrete terms what happens if a friend does drop in unexpectedly. The first writer simply says that her room and board costs wouldn't pay for an apartment, but the second is specific about just how inadequate the money would be. And while the first passage uses abstract language to say that the writer and her parents are "getting to know each other in new ways," the second shows what that means by describing a specific incident.

Every kind of writing can be improved by the addition of concrete detail. Let's look at one final example: the love letter.

Dear April,

I can't wait any longer to tell you how I feel. I am crazy about you. You are the most wonderful woman I've ever met. Every time I'm near you I'm overcome with feelings of love. I would do anything in the world for you and am hoping you feel the same way about me.

Love,

Paul

Paul has written a sincere note, but it lacks a certain something. That something is specific detail. Although the letter expresses a lot of positive feelings, it could have been written by practically any love-struck man about any woman. For this letter to be really special to April, it should be unmistakably about her and Paul. And that requires concrete details.

Here is what Paul might write instead.

Dear April,

Do you remember last Saturday, as we ate lunch in the park, when I spilled my soda in the grass? You quickly picked up a twig and made a tiny dam to keep the liquid from flooding a busy anthill. You probably didn't think I noticed, but I did. It was at that moment that I realized how totally I am in love with you and your passion for life. Before that I only thought you were the most beautiful woman in the world, with your eyes like sparkling pools of emerald water and your chestnut hair glinting in the sun. But now I recognize what it means when I hear your husky laugh and I feel a tight aching in my chest. It means I could stand on top of the Empire State Building and shout to the world, "I love April Snyder." Should I do it? I'll be waiting for your reply.

Paul

There's no guarantee that April is going to return Paul's feelings, but she certainly has a better idea now just what it is about her that Paul finds so lovable, as well as what kind of guy Paul is. Concrete details have made this letter far more compelling.   90

Vague, general language is the written equivalent of baby food. It is adequate; it can sustain[9] life. But it isn't very interesting. For writing to have satisfying crunch, sizzle, and color, it must be generously supplied with specifics. Whether the piece is a job application, a student essay, or a love letter, it is concrete details that make it interesting, persuasive, and memorable.   95

DISCUSSION QUESTIONS

1. Johnson demonstrates specific details in the article by providing three pairs of examples: two job letters, two short writings about living at home, and two love letters. Compare the sets of letters. Which pair convinces you the most to use specific details? Why?
2. By examining the three vague examples and the three specific examples, which type of writing involves more effort and time by the author? How does this effort pay off for the reader?
3. Analyze the pair of love letters. Which specific details are the most effective? To which of the five senses do these details appeal?

WRITING ASSIGNMENTS

1. Compose an application letter for a job.
2. Assess the pros and cons of a step that you may take in the future: buying a car, focusing on a specific field or career, starting a family, etc.

3. Choose the three people whom you love the most. Write a letter to one of them expressing your love; this could be a romantic letter to a boyfriend, girlfriend, husband, wife, etc., or it could be a letter of appreciation to a parent, brother, sister, friend, etc.

Papa, the Teacher

Leo Buscaglia

PREVIEW

Leo Buscaglia's parents immigrated to the United States from Italy. Dirt poor and with only a fifth-grade education, Leo's father inspired his children to love learning through a family tradition.

BUILDING VOCABULARY

1. rural: of the country as opposed to the city
2. fathom: understand
3. protestations: objections
4. insular: isolated like an island
5. credo: a statement of belief
6. complacency: satisfaction or smugness
7. stagnation: a state of being foul from lack of movement
8. paternal: fatherly
9. pungent aromas: sharp, bitter odors
10. animated: lively
11. Piedmontese dialect: the language spoken in north-western Italy
12. *Cosi sia*: Italian for "so be it"
13. *E allora*: Italian for "oh, well"
14. Felice: The author's real first name (Felice Leonardo Buscaglia)
15. reverential: showing reverence or respect

Papa had natural wisdom. He wasn't educated in the formal sense. When he was growing up at the turn of the century in a very small village in rural[1] northern Italy, education was for the rich. Papa was the son of a dirt-poor farmer. He used to tell us that he never remembered a single day of his life when he wasn't working. The concept of doing nothing was never a part of his life. In fact, he couldn't fathom[2] it. How could one do nothing?

5

He was taken from school when he was in the fifth grade, over the protestations[3] of his teacher and the village priest, both of whom saw him as a young person with great potential for formal learning. Papa went to work in a factory in a nearby village, the very same village where, years later, he met Mama.

10

For Papa, the world became his school. He was interested in everything. He read all the books, magazines, and newspapers he could lay his hands on. He loved to gather with people and listen to the town elders and learn about "the world beyond" this tiny, insular[4] region that was home to generations of Buscaglias before him. Papa's great respect for learning and his sense of wonder about the outside world were carried across the sea with him and later passed on to his family. He was determined that none of his children would be denied an education if he could help it.

15

Papa believed that the greatest sin of which we were capable was to go to bed at night as ignorant as we had been when we awakened that day. The credo[5] was repeated so often that none of us could fail to be affected by it. "There is so much to learn," he'd remind us. "Though we're born stupid, only the stupid remain that way." To ensure that none of his children ever fell into the trap of complacency,[6] he insisted that we learn at least one new thing each day. He felt that there could be no fact too insignificant, that each bit of learning made us more of a person and insured us against boredom and stagnation.[7]

20

25

So Papa devised a ritual. Since dinnertime was family time and everyone came to dinner unless they were dying of malaria, it seemed the perfect forum for sharing what new things we had learned that day. Of course, as children we thought this was perfectly crazy. There was no doubt, when we compared such paternal[8] concerns with other children's fathers, Papa was weird.

30

It would never have occurred to us to deny Papa a request. So when my brother and sisters and I congregated in the bathroom to clean up for dinner, the inevitable question was, "What did *you* learn today?" If the answer was "Nothing," we didn't dare sit at the table without first finding a fact in our much-used encyclopedia. "The population of Nepal is . . . ," etc.

35

Now, thoroughly clean and armed with our fact for the day, we were ready for dinner. I can still see the table piled high with mountains of food. So large were the mounds of pasta that as a boy I was often unable to see my sister sitting across from me. (The pungent[9] aromas were such that, over a half century later, even in memory they cause me to salivate.)

40

Dinner was a noisy time of clattering dishes and endless activity. It was also a time to review the activities of the day. Our animated[10] conversations were always conducted in Piedmontese dialect[11] since Mama didn't speak English. The events we recounted, no matter how insignificant, were never taken lightly. Mama and Papa always listened carefully and were ready with some comment, often profound and analytical, always right to the point.

"That was the smart thing to do." "*Stupido*, how could you be so dumb?" "*Cosi sia*,[12] you deserved it." "*E allora*,[13] no one is perfect." "*Testa dura* ('hard-head'), you should have known better. Didn't we teach you anything?" "Oh, that's nice." One dialogue ended and immediately another began. Silent moments were rare at our table.

Then came the grand finale to every meal, the moment we dreaded most—the time to share the day's new learning. The mental imprint of those sessions still runs before me like a familiar film clip, vital and vivid.

Papa, at the head of the table, would push his chair back slightly, a gesture that signified the end of the eating and suggested that there would be a new activity. He would pour a small glass of red wine, light up a thin, potent Italian cigar, inhale deeply, exhale, then take stock of his family.

For some reason this always had a slightly unsettling effect on us as we stared back at Papa, waiting for him to say something. Every so often he would explain why he did this. He told us that if he didn't take time to look at us, we would soon be grown and he would have missed us. So he'd stare at us, one after the other.

Finally, his attention would settle upon one of us. "*Felice*,"[14] he would say to me, "tell me what you learned today."

"I learned that the population of Nepal is . . ."

Silence.

It always amazed me, and reinforced my belief that Papa was a little crazy, that nothing I ever said was considered too trivial for him. First, he'd think about what was said as if the salvation of the world depended upon it.

"The population of Nepal. Hmmm. Well."

He would then look down the table at Mama, who would be ritualistically fixing her favorite fruit in a bit of leftover wine. "Mama, did you know that?"

Mama's responses were always astonishing and seemed to lighten the otherwise reverential[15] atmosphere. "Nepal," she'd say. "Nepal? Not only don't I know the population of Nepal, I don't know where in God's world it is!" Of course, this was only playing into Papa's hands.

"*Felice*," he'd say. "Get the atlas so we can show Mama where Nepal is." And the search began. The whole family went on a search for Nepal. This same experience was repeated until each family member had a turn. No dinner at our house ever ended without our having been enlightened by at least a half dozen such facts.

As children, we thought very little about these educational wonders and even less about how we were being enriched. We couldn't have cared less. We   85
were too impatient to have dinner end so we could join our less-educated friends in a riproaring game of kick the can.

In retrospect, after years of studying how people learn, I realize what a dynamic educational technique Papa was offering us, reinforcing the value of continual learning. Without being aware of it, our family was growing together,   90
sharing experiences, and participating in one another's education. Papa was, without knowing it, giving us an education in the most real sense.

By looking at us, listening to us, hearing us, respecting our opinions, affirming our value, giving us a sense of dignity, he was unquestionably our most influential teacher.   95

DISCUSSION QUESTIONS

1. Analyze dinner conversation in your home as you grew up? What topics were discussed? Did someone guide the discussions through questions? If so, who did this?
2. Compare your attitude with your parents' attitude toward education? How educated are you? How educated are your parents?
3. What distinguishes your most influential teacher from all others? How did he or she influence and inspire you?

WRITING ASSIGNMENTS

1. Compose a letter of appreciation to your most influential teacher.
2. Examine in detail one positive family tradition.
3. Imagine that you are about to start a family. Select one value to teach to your children and create a family tradition that will instill the value.

Mrs. Flowers

Maya Angelou

PREVIEW

Maya Angelou (born Marguerite Johnson) is well known for her poetry and her autobiographical work *I Know Why the Caged Bird Sings*. In this book, Angelou tells of being raped at the age of eight and how she stopped speaking as a result of that experience. In "Mrs. Flowers," Angelou describes her experiences with the woman who helped her to recover and resume communication.

BUILDING VOCABULARY

1. aristocrat: a nobleperson or member of the upper class
2. taut: tight and tense
3. voile: a thin, sheer fabric
4. benign: kind and gentle, harmless
5. infuse: to fill

For nearly a year, I sopped around the house, the Store, the school and the church, like an old biscuit, dirty and inedible. Then I met, or rather got to know, the lady who threw me my first life line.

Mrs. Bertha Flowers was the aristocrat[1] of Black Stamps. She had the grace of control to appear warm in the coldest weather, and on the Arkansas summer days it seemed she had a private breeze which swirled around, cooling her. She was thin without the taut[2] look of wiry people, and her printed voile[3] dresses and flowered hats were as right for her as denim overalls for a farmer. She was our side's answer to the richest white woman in town.

Her skin was a rich black that would have peeled like a plum if snagged, but then no one would have thought of getting close enough to Mrs. Flowers to ruffle her dress, let alone snag her skin. She didn't encourage familiarity. She wore gloves too.

I don't think I ever saw Mrs. Flowers laugh, but she smiled often. A slow widening of her thin black lips to show even, small white teeth, then the slow effortless closing. When she chose to smile on me, I always wanted to thank her. The action was so graceful and inclusively benign.[4]

She was one of the few gentlewomen I have ever known, and has remained throughout my life the measure of what a human being can be. . . .

One summer afternoon, sweet-milk fresh in my memory, she stopped at the Store to buy provisions. Another Negro woman of her health and age would have been expected to carry the paper sacks home in one hand but Momma said, "Sister Flowers, I'll send Bailey up to your house with these things." 20

She smiled that slow dragging smile, "Thank you, Mrs. Henderson. I'd prefer Marguerite though." My name was beautiful when she said it. "I've been meaning to talk to her, anyway." They gave each other age-group looks. 25

Momma said, "Well, that's all right then. Sister, go and change your dress. You going to Sister Flower's." . . .

There was a little path beside the rocky road, and Mrs. Flowers walked in front swinging her arms and picking her way over the stones. 30

She said, without turning her head, to me, "I hear you're doing very good school work, Marguerite, but that it's all written. The teachers report that they have trouble getting you to talk in class." We passed the triangular farm on our left and the path widened to allow us to walk together. I hung back in the separate unasked and unanswerable questions. 35

"Come and walk along with me, Marguerite." I couldn't have refused even if I wanted to. She pronounced my name so nicely. Or more correctly, she spoke each word with such clarity that I was certain a foreigner who didn't understand English could have understood her.

"Now no one is going to make you talk—possibly no one can. But bear in mind, language is man's way of communicating with his fellow man and it is language alone which separates him from the lower animals." That was a totally new idea to me, and I would need time to think about it. 40

"Your grandmother says you read a lot. Every chance you get. That's good, but not good enough. Words mean more than what is set down on paper. It takes the human voice to infuse[5] them with the shades of deeper meaning." 45

I memorized the part about the human voice infusing words. It seemed so valid and poetic.

She said she was going to give me some books and that I not only must read them. I must read them aloud. She suggested that I try to make a sentence sound in as many different ways as possible. 50

"I'll accept no excuse if you return a book to me that has been badly handled." My imagination boggled at the punishment I would deserve if in fact I did abuse a book of Mrs. Flowers's. Death would be too kind and brief. 55

The odors in the house surprised me. Somehow I had never connected Mrs. Flowers with food or eating or any other common experience of common people. There must have been an outhouse, too, but my mind never recorded it.

The sweet scent of vanilla had met us as she opened the door.   60

"I made tea cookies this morning. You see, I had planned to invite you for cookies and lemonade so we could have this little chat. The lemonade is in the icebox."

It followed that Mrs. Flowers would have ice on an ordinary day, when most families in our town bought ice late on Saturdays only a few times during   65 the summer to be used in the wooden ice-cream freezers.

She took the bags from me and disappeared through the kitchen door. I looked around the room that I had never in my wildest fantasies imagined I would see. Browned photographs leered or threatened from the walls and the white, freshly done curtains pushed against themselves and against the wind. I   70 wanted to gobble up the room entire and take it to Bailey, who would help me analyze and enjoy it.

"Have a seat, Marguerite. Over there by the table." She carried a platter covered with a tea towel. Although she warned that she hadn't tried her hand at baking sweets for some time, I was certain that like everything else about her   75 the cookies would be perfect.

They were flat round wafers, slightly browned on the edges and butter-yellow in the center. With the cold lemonade they were sufficient for child-hood's lifelong diet. Remembering my manners, I took nice little lady-like bites off the edges. She said she had made them expressly for me and that   80 she had a few in the kitchen that I could take home to my brother. So I jammed one whole cake in my mouth and the rough crumbs scratched the insides of my jaws, and if I hadn't had to swallow, it would have been a dream come true.

As I ate she began the first of what we later called "my lessons in living."   85 She said that I must always be intolerant of ignorance but understanding of il-literacy. That some people, unable to go to school, were more educated and even more intelligent than college professors. She encouraged me to listen carefully to what country people called mother wit. That in those homely say-ings was couched the collective wisdom of generations.   90

When I finished the cookies she brushed off the table and brought a thick, small book from the bookcase. I had read A Tale of Two Cities and found it up to my standards as a romantic novel. She opened the first page and I heard poetry for the first time in my life.

"It was the best of times and the worst of times . . ." Her voice slid in and   95 curved down through and over the words. She was nearly singing. I wanted to look at the pages. Were they the same that I had read? Or were there notes,

music, lined on the pages, as in a hymn book? Her sounds began cascading
gently. I knew from listening to a thousand preachers that she was nearing the
end of her reading, and I hadn't really heard, heard to understand, a single   100
word.

"How do you like that?"

It occurred to me that she expected a response. The sweet vanilla flavor
was still on my tongue and her reading was a wonder in my ears. I had to speak.

I said, "Yes ma'am." It was the least I could do, but it was the most also.   105

"There's one more thing. Take this book of poems and memorize one for
me. Next time you pay me a visit, I want you to recite."

I have tried often to search behind the sophistication of years for the en-
chantment I so easily found in those gifts. The essence escapes but its aura remains. To be allowed, no, invited, into the private lives of strangers, and to share   110
their joys and fears, was a chance to exchange the Southern bitter wormwood
for . . . a hot cup of tea and milk with Oliver Twist.

I was liked, and what a difference it made. I was respected not as Mrs. Henderson's grandchild or Bailey's sister but for just being Marguerite Johnson.

Childhood's logic never asks to be proved (all conclusions are absolute). I   115
didn't question why Mrs. Flowers had singled me out for attention, nor did it
occur to me that Momma might have asked her to give me a little talking to. All
I cared about was that she had made tea cookies for *me* and read to *me* from
her favorite book. It was enough to prove that she liked me.

DISCUSSION QUESTIONS

1. What impressed Maya about Mrs. Flowers? What impresses you about Mrs.
   Flowers?

2. Examine the ways in which Maya writes using specific, concrete language
   that appeals to the five senses. Find examples of her descriptions of how
   things appear, smell, feel, taste, and sound.

3. Maya writes, "My imagination boggled at the punishment I would deserve
   if in fact I did abuse a book of Mrs. Flower's. Death would be too kind and
   brief." Why does Maya say, "Death would be too kind and brief"? What does
   this sentence tell you about their relationship? How does their relationship
   relate to her recovery?

WRITING ASSIGNMENTS

1. Use language to throw a "life line" to a disturbed family member or friend by composing a letter to a person in distress.
2. Mrs. Flowers states, "Be intolerant of ignorance but understanding of illiteracy." In a short paper, respond to this quote by differentiating between ignorance and illiteracy.
3. Mrs. Flowers explains, "But bear in mind, language is man's way of communicating with his fellow man and it is language alone which separates him from the lower animals." Examine the accuracy of this statement. Compare and contrast people and animals with respect to language. Do any animals communicate? What are the consequences of communicating through language?

Four Directions

Amy Tan

PREVIEW

Amy Tan, a Chinese-American novelist, writes about her gift for playing chess at the age of ten and how her vision of her opponents changed when she reached adolescence.

BUILDING VOCABULARY

1. irrevocable: unalterable
2. sponsors: people or companies who provide financial support
3. benevolent associations: charities
4. hovered over: watched carefully
5. erected: built
6. groping: searching about blindly
7. intersection: the line where two surfaces meet
8. prodigy: a child of unusual talent

I was ten years old. Even though I was young, I knew my ability to play chess was a gift. It was effortless, so easy. I could see things on the chessboard that other people could not. I could create barriers to protect myself that were invisible to my opponents. And this gift gave me supreme confidence. I knew at exactly what point their faces would fall when my seemingly simple and childlike strategy would reveal itself as a devastating and irrevocable[1] course. I loved to win.

    And my mother loved to show me off, like one of my many trophies she polished. She used to discuss my games as if she had devised the strategies.

    "I told my daughter, Use your horses to run over the enemy," she informed one shopkeeper. "She won very quickly this way." And of course, she had said this before the game—that and a hundred other useless things that had nothing to do with my winning.

    To our family friends who visited she would confide, "You don't have to be so smart to win chess. It is just tricks. You blow from the North, South, East, and West. The other person becomes confused. They don't know which way to run."

    I hated the way she tried to take all the credit. And one day I told her so, shouting at her on Stockton Street, in the middle of a crowd of people. I told her she didn't know anything, so she shouldn't show off. She should shut up. Words to that effect.

    That evening and the next day she wouldn't speak to me. She would say stiff words to my father and brothers, as if I had become invisible and she was talking about a rotten fish she had thrown away but which had left behind its bad smell.

    I knew this strategy, the sneaky way to get someone to pounce back in anger and fall into a trap. So I ignored her. I refused to speak and waited for her to come to me.

    After many days had gone by in silence, I sat in my room, staring at the sixty-four squares of my chessboard, trying to think of another way. And that's when I decided to quit playing chess.

    Of course I didn't mean to quit forever. At most, just for a few days. And I made a show of it. Instead of practicing in my room every night, as I always did, I marched into the living room and sat down in front of the television with my brothers, who stared at me, an unwelcome intruder. I used my brothers to further my plan; I cracked my knuckles to annoy them.

    "Ma!" they shouted. "Make her stop. Make her go away."

    But my mother did not say anything.

    Still I was not worried. But I could see I would have to make a stronger move. I decided to sacrifice a tournament that was coming up in one week. I would refuse to play in it. And my mother would certainly have to speak to me about this. Because the sponsors[2] and the benevolent associations[3] would start calling her, asking, shouting, pleading to make me play again.

And then the tournament came and went. And she did not come to me, crying, "Why are you not playing chess?" But I was crying inside, because I learned that a boy whom I had easily defeated on two other occasions had won.

I realized my mother knew more tricks than I had thought. But now I was tired of her game. I wanted to start practicing for the next tournament. So I decided to pretend to let her win. I would be the one to speak first.

"I am ready to play chess again," I announced to her. I had imagined she would smile and then ask me what special thing I wanted to eat.

But instead, she gathered her face into a frown and stared into my eyes, as if she could force some kind of truth out of me.

"Why do you tell me this?" she finally said in sharp tones. "You think it is so easy. One day quit, next day play. Everything for you is this way. So smart, so easy, so fast."

"I said I'll play," I whined.

"No!" she shouted, and I almost jumped out of my scalp. "It is not so easy anymore."

I was quivering, stunned by what she said, in not knowing what she meant. And then I went back to my room. I stared at my chessboard, its sixty-four squares, to figure out how to undo this terrible mess. And after staring like this for many hours, I actually believed that I had made the white squares black and the black squares white, and everything would be all right.

And sure enough, I won her back. That night I developed a high fever, and she sat next to my bed, scolding me for going to school without my sweater. In the morning she was there as well, feeding me rice porridge flavored with chicken broth she had strained herself. She said she was feeding me this because I had the chicken pox and one chicken knew how to fight another. And in the afternoon, she sat in a chair in my room, knitting me a pink sweater while telling me about a sweater that Auntie Suyuan had knit for her daughter June, and how it was most unattractive and of the worst yarn. I was so happy that she had become her usual self.

But after I got well, I discovered that, really, my mother had changed. She no longer hovered over[4] me as I practiced different chess games. She did not polish my trophies every day. She did not cut out the small newspaper item that mentioned my name. It was as if she had erected[5] an invisible wall and I was secretly groping[6] each day to see how high and how wide it was.

At my next tournament, while I had done well overall, in the end the points were not enough. I lost. And what was worse, my mother said nothing. She seemed to walk around with this satisfied look, as if it had happened because she had devised this strategy.

I was horrified. I spent many hours every day going over in my mind what I had lost. I knew it was not just the last tournament. I examined every move, every piece, every square. And I could no longer see the secret weapons of each piece, the magic within the intersection[7] of each square. I could see only my mistakes, my weaknesses. It was as though I had lost my magic armor. And everybody could see this, where it was easy to attack me.   85

Over the next few weeks and later months and years, I continued to play, but never with that same feeling of supreme confidence. I fought hard, with fear and desperation. When I won, I was grateful, relieved. And when I lost, I was filled with growing dread, and then terror that I was no longer a prodigy,[8] that I had lost the gift and had turned into someone quite ordinary.   90

When I lost twice to the boy whom I had defeated so easily a few years before, I stopped playing chess altogether. And nobody protested. I was fourteen.   95

DISCUSSION QUESTIONS

1. What causes the conflict between Amy and her mother? Is Amy justified in her position? Why? Why not?
2. When Amy decides to start playing chess again after quitting, her mother says, "No! It is not so easy anymore." This statement reveals that Amy's mother sees something that Amy misses. What is it?
3. Amy states, "And I could no longer see the secret weapons of each piece, the magic within the intersection of each square." Analyze how and why Amy lost her gift.

WRITING ASSIGNMENTS

1. Compose a letter to your parents or children in which you give advice by drawing on lessons available in "Four Directions."
2. Compose an essay in which you describe an experience when you learned a valuable lesson from a family conflict.
3. Examine the pros and cons of Amy's experience? During the last four years of playing chess, what did she lose, and what did she gain?

Cipher[1] in the Snow
A True Story

Jean Mizer

PREVIEW

Jean Mizer taught English at Blaine County School in Hailey, Idaho. In "Cipher in the Snow," she describes the unforgettable lesson she learned about her responsibility to her students. Jean Mizer received the Teacher of the Year Award for Idaho in 1964.

BUILDING VOCABULARY

1. cipher: the symbol indicating zero (0), a person or thing of no value
2. ailing: being in poor health
3. obituary: a notice of someone's death with a brief biography
4. resilience: the ability to bounce back
5. savage: pitiless, cruel
6. peaked: thin or weak from illness
7. veiled: concealed, hidden
8. alien: foreign, strange

It started with tragedy on a biting cold February morning. I was driving behind the Milford Corners bus as I did most snowy mornings on my way to school. The bus veered and stopped short at the hotel, which it had no business doing, and I was annoyed as I had to come to an unexpected stop. The boy lurched out of the bus, reeled, stumbled, and collapsed on the snow bank at the curb. The bus driver and I reached him at the same moment. The boy's thin, hollow face was white even against the snow.   5

"He's dead," the driver whispered.

It didn't register for a minute. I glanced quickly at the scared young faces staring down at us from the school bus. "A doctor! Quick! I'll phone from the hotel . . ."   10

"No use, I tell you, he's dead." The driver looked down at the boy's still form. "He never even said he felt bad," he muttered. "Just tapped me on the shoulder and said, real quiet, 'I'm sorry. I have to get off at the hotel.' That's all. Polite and apologizing like."   15

At school the giggling, shuffling morning noise quieted as news went down the halls. I passed a huddle of girls. "Who was it? Who dropped dead on the way to school?" I heard one of them half-whisper.

"Don't know his name. Some kid from Milford Corners," was the reply.

It was like that in the faculty room and the principal's office. "I'd appreciate   20
your going out to tell the parents," the principal told me. "They haven't a phone,
and anyway, somebody from the school should go there in person. I'll cover
your classes."

"Why me?" I asked. "Wouldn't it be better if you did it?"

"I didn't know the boy," the principal admitted levelly. "And in last year's   25
sophomore personalities column I noted that you were listed as his favorite
teacher."

I drove through the snow and cold down the bad canyon road to the
Evans' place and thought about the boy, Cliff Evans. His favorite teacher! I
thought. He hasn't spoken two words to me in two years! I could see him in my   30
mind's eye all right, sitting back there in the last seat in my afternoon literature
class. He came in the room by himself and left by himself. "Cliff Evans," I muttered to myself, "a boy who never talked." I thought a minute. "A boy who never
smiled. I never saw him smile once."

The big ranch kitchen was clean and warm. I blurted out my news some-   35
how. Mrs. Evans reached blindly toward a chair. "He never said anything about
bein' ailing[2]."

His stepfather snorted. "He ain't said nothin' about anything since I moved
in here."

Mrs. Evans pushed a pan to the back of the stove and began to untie her   40
apron. "Now hold on," her husband snapped. "I got to have breakfast before I go
to town. Nothin' we can do now, anyway. If Cliff hadn't been so dumb, he'd have
told us he didn't feel good."

After school I sat in the office and stared blankly at the records spread out
before me. I was to read the file and write the obituary[3] for the school paper. The   45
almost bare sheets mocked the effort. Cliff Evans, white, never legally adopted
by stepfather, five young half-brothers and sisters. These meager strands of information and the list of "D" grades were all the records had to offer.

Cliff Evans had silently come in the school door in the mornings and gone
out the school door in the evenings, and that was all. He had never belonged to   50
a club. He had never played on a team. He had never held an office. As far as I
could tell, he had never done one happy, noisy kid thing. He had never been
anybody at all.

How do you go about making a boy into a zero? The grade-school records
showed me. The first and second grade teachers' annotations read, "Sweet, shy   55
child," "timid but eager." Then the third grade note had opened the attack.
Some teacher had written in a good, firm hand, "Cliff won't talk. Uncooperative.
Slow learner." The other academic sheep and followed with "dull," "slow-witted,"
"low I.Q." They became correct. The boy's I.Q score in the ninth grade was listed

at 83. But his I.Q. in the third grade had been 106. The score didn't go under 100   60
until the seventh grade. Even the shy, timid, sweet children have resilience[4]. It
takes time to break them.

I stomped to the typewriter and wrote a savage[5] report pointing out what
education had done to Cliff Evans. I slapped a copy on the principal's desk and
another in the sad, dog-eared file. I banged the typewriter and slammed the file   65
and crashed the door shut, but I didn't feel much better. A little boy kept walking after me, a little boy with a peaked[6], pale face; a skinny body in faded jeans;
and big eyes that had looked and searched for a long time and then had become veiled[7].

I could guess how many times he had been chosen last to play sides in a   70
game, how many whispered child conversations had excluded him, how many
times he hadn't been asked. I could see and hear the faces that said over and
over, "You're nothing, Cliff Evans."

A child is a believing creature. Cliff undoubtedly believed them. Suddenly
it seemed clear to me: When finally there was nothing left at all for Cliff Evans,   75
he collapsed on a snow bank and went away. The doctor might list "heart failure" as the cause of death, but that wouldn't change my mind.

We couldn't find ten students in the school who had known Cliff well
enough to attend the funeral as his friends. So the student body officers and a
committee from the junior class went as a group to the church, being politely   80
sad. I attended the services with them, and sat through it with a lump of cold
lead in my chest and a big resolve growing through me.

I've never forgotten Cliff Evans nor that resolve. He has been my challenge year after year, class after class. I look for veiled eyes or bodies
scrounged into a seat in an alien[8] world. "Look, kids," I say silently. "I may not do   85
anything else for you this year, but not one of you is going to come out of here
as a nobody. I'll work or fight to the bitter end doing battle with society and
the school board, but I won't have one of you coming out of there thinking
himself a zero."

Most of the time—not always, but most of the time—I've succeeded.   90

DISCUSSION QUESTIONS

1. Cliff Evans' I.Q. was 106 in third grade but dropped to 83 in ninth grade.
   What contributed to the twenty-three point drop in I.Q.?
2. Jean Mizer says, "Not one of you is going to come out of here as a nobody."
   Create and prioritize a short list of practical suggestions for accomplishing
   this task.

3. Have you ever felt like a cipher in a particular situation? What made you feel that way? How did you find a resolution to the problem?

WRITING ASSIGNMENTS

1. Do you know a cipher? If so, what evidence exists to support your claim? Construct a plan for helping the cipher.
2. Who is responsible for Cliff Evans' death? Compose an essay in which you criticize those who contributed to the death of Cliff Evans.
3. Jean Mizer states, "A child is a believing creature." Write an essay in which you propose the types of positive experiences in the family and at school that a child must have while growing up to be healthy, happy, and productive.

Thank You, M'am

Langston Hughes

PREVIEW

In his early years, Langston Hughes lived a life of poverty with his mother after his parents separated. Later, Langston Hughes became a versatile author, writing fiction, drama, poetry, etc., and promoting African-American culture. He became one of the central figures of the Harlem Renaissance, a movement of African-American art and literature in the Harlem district of New York City during the 1920s.

BUILDING VOCABULARY: APPRECIATING BLACK ENGLISH AND STANDARD ENGLISH

1. "You a lie!": You're a liar!
2. "Ain't you got nobody home …?: Don't you have anybody at home …?
3. "I would not take you nowhere": I wouldn't take you anywhere
4. "Maybe you ain't been to your supper": Maybe you haven't had your supper
5. "You could of asked me": You could have asked me
6. "I were young once": I was young once
7. "I got to": I have to

She was a large woman with a large purse that had everything in it but a hammer and nails. It had a long strap, and she carried it slung across her shoulder. It was about eleven o'clock at night, dark, and she was walking alone, when a boy ran up behind her and tried to snatch her purse. The strap broke with the sudden single tug the boy gave it from behind. But the boy's weight and the weight of the purse combined caused him to lose his balance. Instead of taking off full blast as he had hoped, the boy fell on his back on the sidewalk and his legs flew up. The large woman simply turned around and kicked him right square in his blue-jeaned sitter. Then she reached down, picked the boy up by his shirt front, and shook him until his teeth rattled.

After that the woman said, "Pick up my pocketbook, boy, and give it here."

She still held him tightly. But she bent down enough to permit him to stoop and pick up her purse. Then she said, "Now ain't you ashamed of yourself?"

Firmly gripped by his shirt front, the boy said, "Yes'm."

The woman said, "What did you want to do it for?"

The boy said, "I didn't aim to."

She said, "You a lie!"[1]

By that time two or three people passed, stopped, turned to look, and some stood watching.

"If I turn you loose, will you run?" asked the woman.

"Yes'm," said the boy.

"Then I won't turn you loose," said the woman. She did not release him.

"Lady, I'm sorry," whispered the boy.

"Um-hum! Your face is dirty. I got a great mind to wash your face for you. Ain't you got nobody home[2] to tell you to wash your face?"

"No'm," said the boy.

"Then it will get washed this evening," said the large woman, starting up the street, dragging the frightened boy behind her.

He looked as if he were fourteen or fifteen, frail and willow-wild, in tennis shoes and blue jeans.

The woman said, "You ought to be my son. I would teach you right from wrong. Least I can do right now is to wash your face. Are you hungry?"

"No'm," said the being-dragged boy. "I just want you to turn me loose."

"Was I bothering *you* when I turned that corner?" asked the woman.

"No'm."

"But you put yourself in contact with *me*," said the woman. "If you think that that contact is not going to last awhile, you got another thought coming. When I get through with you, sir, you are going to remember Mrs. Luella Bates Washington Jones."

Sweat popped out on the boy's face and he began to struggle. Mrs. Jones stopped, jerked him around in front of her, put a half nelson about his neck, and continued to drag him up the street. When she got to her door, she dragged the boy inside, down a hall, and into a large kitchenette-furnished room at the rear of the house. She switched on the light and left the door open. The boy could hear other roomers laughing and talking in the large house. Some of their doors were open, too, so he knew he and the woman were not alone. The woman still had him by the neck in the middle of her room.   45

She said, "What is your name?"

"Roger," answered the boy.   50

"Then, Roger, you go to that sink and wash your face," said the woman, whereupon she turned him loose—at last. Roger looked at the door—looked at the woman—looked at the door—*and went to the sink.*

"Let the water run until it gets warm," she said. "Here's a clean towel."

"You gonna take me to jail?" asked the boy, bending over the sink.   55

"Not with that face, I would not take you nowhere[3]," said the woman. "Here I am trying to get home to cook me a bite to eat and you snatch my pocketbook! Maybe you ain't been to your supper[4] either, late as it be. Have you?"

"There's nobody home at my house," said the boy.

"Then we'll eat," said the woman. "I believe you're hungry—or been hungry—to try to snatch my pocketbook!"   60

"I want a pair of blue suede shoes," said the boy.

"Well, you didn't have to snatch *my* pocketbook to get some suede shoes," said Mrs. Luella Bates Washington Jones. "You could of asked me[5]."

"M'am?"   65

The water dripping from his face, the boy looked at her. There was a long pause. A very long pause. After he had dried his face, and not knowing what else to do, dried it again, the boy turned around, wondering what next. The door was open. He could make a dash for it down the hall. He could run, run, run, *run!*   70

The woman was sitting on the daybed. After a while she said, "I were young once[6] and I wanted things I could not get."

There was another long pause. The boy's mouth opened. Then he frowned, not knowing he frowned.

The woman said, "Um-hum! You thought I was going to say *but*, didn't   75
you? You thought I was going to say, *but I didn't snatch people's pocketbooks.*
Well, I wasn't going to say that." Pause. Silence. "I have done things, too, which I would not tell you, son—neither tell God, if He didn't already know. Everybody's got something in common. So you set down while I fix us something to eat. You might run that comb through your hair so you will look presentable."   80

In another corner of the room behind a screen was a gas plate and an ice-box. Mrs. Jones got up and went behind the screen. The woman did not watch the boy to see if he was going to run now, nor did she watch her purse, which she left behind her on the daybed. But the boy took care to sit on the far side of the room, away from the purse, where he thought she could easily see him out   85 of the corner of her eye if she wanted to. He did not trust the woman *not* to trust him. And he did not want to be mistrusted now.

"Do you need somebody to go to the store," asked the boy, "maybe to get some milk or something?"

"Don't believe I do," said the woman, "unless you just want sweet milk   90 yourself. I was going to make cocoa out of this canned milk I got here."

"That will be fine," said the boy.

She heated some lima beans and ham she had in the icebox, made the cocoa, and set the table. The woman did not ask the boy anything about where he lived, or his folks, or anything else that would embarrass him. Instead, as they   95 ate, she told him about her job in a hotel beauty shop that stayed open late, what the work was like, and how all kinds of women came in and out, blonds, redheads, and Spanish. Then she cut him a half of her ten-cent cake.

"Eat some more, son," she said.

When they were finished eating, she got up and said, "Now here, take this   100 ten dollars and buy yourself some blue suede shoes. And next time, do not make the mistake of latching onto *my* pocketbook *nor nobody else's*—because shoes got by devilish ways will burn your feet. I got to[7] get my rest now. But from here on in, son, I hope you will behave yourself."

She led him down the hall to the front door and opened it. "Good night!   105 Behave yourself, boy!" she said, looking out into the street as he went down the steps.

The boy wanted to say something other than, "Thank you, M'am," to Mrs. Luella Bates Washington Jones, but although his lips moved, he couldn't even say that as he turned at the foot of the barren stoop and looked up at the large   110 woman in the door. Then she shut the door.

DISCUSSION QUESTIONS

1. Mrs. Luella Bates Washington Jones says to Roger, "Ain't you got nobody home to tell you to wash your face?" What does she learn about Roger from his answer? How does his answer influence the way that she treats him?

2. Langston Hughes writes, "He [Roger] did not trust the woman [Mrs. Jones] *not* to trust him." Why is it so important that she trust him at this point in their relationship?

3. As Roger was about to leave, he couldn't even say, "Thank you, M'am." Why was he speechless?

WRITING ASSIGNMENTS

1. Have you ever been caught stealing or breaking a law? Compare and contrast your experience with Roger's experience.
2. Analyze the way that Mrs. Luella Bates Washington Jones treats Roger. What approach does she take? Why does she take this approach? Is she effective? Cite examples to support your point.
3. Langston Hughes writes, "Roger looked at the door—looked at the woman—looked at the door—and went to the sink." This is an example of showing, not telling, which is a trait of a good writer. Compose a short paper in which you examine three examples in this work of Langston Hughes showing something instead of telling it.

The Gift

Courtland Milloy

PREVIEW

This article first appeared in *The Washington Post*, December 23, 1992, and it describes one person's generosity in giving a life-saving gift.

BUILDING VOCABULARY

1. platonic: nonromantic
2. kidney dialysis machine: a machine that filters waste from blood for people with impaired kidney function
3. chronic fatigue: long-term exhaustion
4. hypertension: abnormally high blood pressure
5. ineligible: not qualified
6. coerced: forced
7. quelled: quieted
8. skeptics: people who doubt or question

When Jermaine Washington entered the barbershop, heads turned and clippers fell silent. Customers waved and nodded, out of sheer respect. With his hands in the pockets of his knee-length, black leather coat, Washington acknowledged them with a faint smile and quietly took a seat.

"You know who that is?" barber Anthony Clyburn asked in a tone reserved for the most awesome neighborhood characters, such as ball players and ex-cons.

A year and a half ago, Washington did something that still amazes those who know him. He became a kidney donor, giving a vital organ to a woman he described as "just a friend."

"They had a platonic[1] relationship," said Clyburn, who works at Jake's Barber Shop in Northeast Washington. "I could see maybe giving one to my mother; but just a girl I know? I don't think so."

Washington, who is 25, met Michelle Stevens six years ago when they worked for the D.C. Department of Employment Services. They used to have lunch together in the department cafeteria and chitchat on the telephone during their breaks.

"It was nothing serious, romance-wise," said Stevens, who is 23. "He was somebody I could talk to. I had been on the kidney donor waiting list for 12 months and I had lost all hope. One day, I just called to cry on his shoulder."

Stevens told Washington how depressing it was to spend three days a week, three hours a day, on a kidney dialysis machine.[2] She said she suffered from chronic fatigue[3] and blackouts and was losing her balance and her sight. He could already see that she had lost her smile.

"I saw my friend dying before my eyes," Washington recalled. "What was I supposed to do? Sit back and watch her die?"

Stevens's mother was found to be suffering from hypertension[4] and was ineligible[5] to donate a kidney. Her 14-year-old sister offered to become a donor, but doctors concluded that she was too young.

Stevens's two brothers, 25 and 31, would most likely have made ideal donors because of their relatively young ages and status as family members. But both of them said no.

So did Stevens's boyfriend, who gave her two diamond rings with his apology.

"I understood," Stevens said. "They said they loved me very much, but they were just too afraid."

Joyce Washington, Jermaine's mother, was not exactly in favor of the idea, either. But after being convinced that her son was not being coerced,[6] she supported his decision.

The transplant operation took four hours. It occurred in April 1991, and began with a painful X-ray procedure in which doctors inserted a metal rod into Washington's kidney and shot it with red dye. An incision nearly 20 inches long was made from his groin to the back of his shoulder. After the surgery he remained hospitalized for five days.   45

Today, both Stevens and Washington are fully recovered. Stevens, a graduate of Eastern High School, is studying medicine at the National Educational Center. Washington still works for D.C. Employment Services as a job counselor.

"I jog and work out with weights," Washington said. "Boxing and football are out, but I never played those anyway."   50

A spokesman for Washington Hospital Center said the Washington-to-Stevens gift was the hospital's first "friend-to-friend" transplant. Usually, it's wife to husband, or parent to child. But there is a shortage of even those kinds of transplants. Today, more than 300 patients are in need of kidneys in the Washington area.   55

"A woman came up to me in a movie line not long ago and hugged me," Washington said. "She thanked me for doing what I did because no one had come forth when her daughter needed a kidney, and the child died."

About twice a month, Stevens and Washington get together for what they call a gratitude lunch. Since the operation, she has broken up with her   60
boyfriend. Seven months ago, Washington got a girlfriend. Despite occasional pressure by friends, a romantic relationship is not what they want.

"We are thankful for the beautiful relationship that we have," Stevens said. "We don't want to mess up a good thing."

To this day, people wonder why Washington did it. To some of the men   65
gathered at Jake's Barber Shop not long ago, Washington's heroics were cause for questions about his sanity. Surely he could not have been in his right mind, they said.

One customer asked Washington where he had found the courage to give away a kidney. His answer quelled[7] most skeptics[8] and inspired even more awe.   70

'I prayed for it," Washington replied. "I asked God for guidance and that's what I got."

DISCUSSION QUESTIONS

1. Distinguish what heroic deeds have in common.
2. Under what conditions would you be willing to do what Jermaine Washington did? Do you give blood or make other sacrifices to help others?

3. According to Washington, where did he find the courage to make this sacrifice? How has his life changed as a result of his decision to donate a kidney?

WRITING ASSIGNMENTS

1. Have you ever met a real hero or been one yourself? Compose a short essay in which you describe someone's generosity and analyze why these actions could be considered heroic.
2. Michelle Stevens' boyfriend "gave her two diamond rings with his apology." Evaluate his position in refusing to be an organ donor. Provide ample support for your position.
3. Jermaine Washington said, "A woman came up to me in a movie line not long ago and hugged me. . . . She thanked me for doing what I did because no one had come forth when her daughter needed a kidney, and the child died." Whose needs are unmet in society today? Examine the reasons that these needs are not being met, and propose solutions to these problems.

I Have a Dream

Martin Luther King, Jr.

PREVIEW

King, a spiritual leader of the civil rights movement, advocated non-violent resistance to promote social change and equality. He delivered this speech on the steps at the Lincoln Memorial in Washington, D.C., on August 28, 1963. In December, 1964, he received the Nobel Peace Prize. Four years later, on April 4, 1968, at the age of thirty-nine he was assassinated.

BUILDING VOCABULARY

1. fivescore: five sets of twenty (one hundred)
2. Emancipation Proclamation: a document by President Lincoln freeing slaves, effective January 1st, 1963
3. decree: an official decision
4. manacles: handcuffs
5. segregation: the policy of requiring racial groups to use separate facilities.

6. languished: became weak
7. exile: banished or put away
8. heir: a person who inherits something
9. unalienable: not able to be transferred to someone else
10. defaulted: failed to do something
11. gradualism: seeking social changes gradually
12. democracy: government where the people hold power and rule (often through elections)
13. tranquility: calmness
14. revolt: rebellion
15. inextricably: cannot be separated
16. battlement: fortification
17. biracial: consisting of two races
18. tribulation: intense misery from oppression or sorrow
19. redemptive: serving to rescue
20. creed: a statement of belief
21. exalted: elevated
22. jangling: arguing
23. discords: disagreements
24. hamlet: small village

I am happy to join with you today in what will go down in history as the greatest demonstration for freedom in the history of our nation.

Fivescore[1] years ago, a great American, in whose symbolic shadow we stand today, signed the Emancipation Proclamation[2]. This momentous decree[3] came as a great beacon light of hope to millions of Negro slaves who had been   5
seared in the flames of withering injustice. It came as a joyous daybreak to end the long night of their captivity.

But one hundred years later, the Negro still is not free; one hundred years later, the life of the Negro is still sadly crippled by the manacles[4] of segregation[5] and the chains of discrimination; one hundred years later, the Negro lives on a   10
lonely island of poverty in the midst of a vast ocean of material prosperity; one hundred years later, the Negro is still languished[6] in the corners of American society and finds himself in exile[7] in his own land.

So we've come here today to dramatize a shameful condition. In a sense we've come to our nation's capital to cash a check. When the architects of our   15
republic wrote the magnificent words of our Constitution and the Declaration

of Independence, they were signing a promissory note to which every American was to fall heir[8]. This note was the promise that all men, yes, black men as
well as white men, would be guaranteed the unalienable[9] rights of life, liberty,
and the pursuit of happiness.   20

It is obvious today that America has defaulted[10] on this promissory note
in so far as her citizens of color are concerned. Instead of honoring this sacred
obligation, America has given the Negro people a bad check; a check which has
come back marked "insufficient funds." We refuse to believe that there are insufficient funds in the great vaults of opportunity of this nation.   25

And so we've come to this hallowed spot to remind America of the fierce
urgency of now. This is no time to engage in the luxury of cooling off or to take
the tranquilizing drug of gradualism[11]. Now is the time to make real the promises
of democracy[12]; now is the time to rise from the dark and desolate valley of
segregation to the sunlit path of racial justice; now is the time to lift our nation   30
from the quicksands of racial injustice to the solid rock of brotherhood; now is
the time to make justice a reality for all God's children. It would be fatal for the
nation to overlook the urgency of the movement. This sweltering summer of
the Negro's legitimate discontent will not pass until there is an invigorating au-
tumn of freedom and equality.   35

Nineteen sixty-three is not and end, but a beginning. And those who hope
that the Negro needed to blow off steam and will now be content, will have a
rude awakening if the nation returns to business as usual.

There will be neither rest nor tranquility[13] in America until the Negro is
granted his citizenship rights. The whirlwinds of revolt[14] will continue to shake   40
the foundations of our nation until the bright day of justice emerges.

But there is something that I must say to my people who stand on the
warm threshold which leads into the palace of justice. In the process of gaining
our rightful place we must not be guilty of wrongful deeds.

Let us not seek to satisfy our thirst for freedom by drinking from the cup   45
of bitterness and hatred. We must forever conduct our struggle on the high
plane of dignity and discipline. We must not allow our creative protest to de-
generate into physical violence. Again and again we must rise to the majestic
heights of meeting physical force with soul force.

The marvelous new militancy which has engulfed the Negro community   50
must not lead us to distrust of all white people, for many of our white brothers,
as evidenced by their presence here today, have come to realize that their destiny is tied up with our destiny and they have come to realize that their freedom is inextricably[15] bound to our freedom. This offense we share mounted to
storm the battlements[16] of injustice must be carried forth by a biracial[17] army.   55
We cannot walk alone.

And as we walk, we must make the pledge that we shall always march ahead. We cannot turn back. There are those who are asking the devotees of civil rights,"When will you be satisfied?: We can never be satisfied as long as the Negro is the victim of the unspeakable horrors of police brutality.   60

We can never be satisfied as long as our bodies, heavy with fatigue of travel, cannot gain lodging in the motels of the highways and the hotels of the cities. We cannot be satisfied as long as the Negro's basic mobility is from a smaller ghetto to a larger one.

We can never be satisfied as long as our children are stripped of their self-   65
hood and robbed of their dignity by signs stating "for whites only." We cannot be satisfied as long as a Negro in Mississippi cannot vote and a Negro in New York believes he has nothing for which to vote. No, we are not satisfied, and we will not be satisfied until justice rolls down like waters and righteousness like a mighty stream.   70

I am not unmindful that some of you have come here out of excessive trials and tribulation[18]. Some of you have come fresh from narrow jail cells. Some of you have come from areas where your quest for freedom left you battered by the storms of persecution and staggered by the winds of police brutality. You have been the veterans of creative suffering. Continue to work with   75
the faith that unearned suffering is redemptive[19].

Go back to Mississippi; go back to Alabama; go back to Louisiana; go back to the slums and ghettos of the northern cities, knowing that somehow this situation can, and will be changed. Let us not wallow in the valley of despair.

So I say to you, my friends, that even though we must face the difficulties   80
of today and tomorrow, I still have a dream. It is a dream deeply rooted in the American dream that one day this nation will rise up and live out the true meaning of its creed[20] — we hold these truths to be self-evident, that all men are created equal.

I have a dream that one day on the red hills of Georgia, sons of former   85
slaves and sons of former slave-owners will be able to sit down together at the table of brotherhood.

I have a dream that one day, even the state of Mississippi, a state sweltering with the heat of injustice, sweltering with the heat of oppression, will be transformed into an oasis of freedom and justice.   90

I have a dream my four little children will one day live in a nation where they will not be judged by the color of their skin but by the content of their character. I have a dream today!

I have a dream that one day every valley shall be exalted[21], every hill and mountain shall be made low, the rough places shall be made plain, and the   95
crooked places shall be made straight and the glory of the Lord will be revealed and all flesh shall see it together.

This is our hope. This is the faith that I go back to the South with.

With this faith we will be able to hear out of the mountain of despair a stone of hope. With this faith we will be able to transform the jangling[22] discords[23] of our nation into a beautiful symphony of brotherhood.

With this faith we will be able to work together, to pray together, to go to jail together, knowing that we will be free one day. This will be the day when all of God's children will be able to sing with new meaning — "my country 'tis of thee; sweet land of liberty; of thee I sing; land where my fathers died, land of the pilgrim's pride; from every mountain side, let freedom ring" — and if America is to be a great nation, this must become true.

Let freedom ring from the mighty mountains of New York.

Let freedom ring from the heightening Alleghenies of Pennsylvania.

Let freedom ring from the snow-capped Rockies of Colorado.

Let freedom ring from the curvaceous slopes of California.

But not only that.

Let freedom ring from the Stone Mountain of Georgia.

Let freedom ring from Lookout Mountain of Tennessee.

Let freedom ring from every hill and molehill of Mississippi, from every mountainside, let freedom ring.

And when we allow freedom to ring, when we let it ring from every village and hamlet[24], from every state and city, we will be able to speed up that day when all of God's children—black men and white men, Jews and Gentiles, Catholics and Protestants—will be able to join hands and to sing in the words of the old Negro spiritual, "Free at last, free at last; thank God Almighty, we are free at last."

DISCUSSION QUESTIONS

1. King explains, "America has given the Negro people a bad check; a check which has come back marked 'insufficient funds.'" Explain and evaluate the comparison between the experience of the Negro people in America and a bad check. How is this comparison effective or not effective in his speech?

2. King argues, "Again and Again we must rise to the majestic heights of meeting physical force with soul force." What does this mean? Assess the effectiveness of this advice?

3. King states, "I have a dream my four little children will one day live in a nation where they will not be judged by the color of their skin but by the content of their character." Compare and contrast the social condition in America at the time of King's remarks with the social condition in America today. Specifically, in what ways and to what degree has King's dream come to pass? How has it not come to pass yet?

WRITING ASSIGNMENTS

1. King claims that "unearned suffering is redemptive." Evaluate that statement. Provide ample support for your position.
2. King refers to the Declaration of Independence, which states, "We hold these truths to be self-evident, that all men are created equal." Examine the ways in which this statement is accurate and not accurate.
3. Compose a short essay in which you propose your dream for improving society.

RECOMMENDED BOOKS

Nonfiction

1. *I Know Why the Caged Bird Sings* by Maya Angelou. Angelou, a black poet and writer, tells her life story of growing up poor in the rural South, a moving account of life in the midst of death.
2. *Adrift: Seventy-Six Days Lost* at Sea by Steven Callahan. As Callahan sets sail from the Canary Islands to the Caribbean, his sloop sinks, and he finds himself adrift in a five-and-a-half-foot inflatable raft with only three pounds of food and eight pints of water. Callahan drifts eighteen hundred miles during seventy six days struggling with storms, sharks, and starvation.
3. *The Girl with the White Flag* by Tomiko Higa. Separated from her family during World War II at the age of seven, Higa struggles to survive on the battlefields of Okinawa, Japan while searching for her family in both a tragic and inspiring adventure.
4. *The Story of My Life* by Helen Keller. A wild child, Helen Keller begins life with the frustration and isolation of being both blind and deaf, but she triumphs through the journey of her education.
5. *I Rigoberta Menchu: An Indian Woman in Guatemala* by Rigoberta Menchu. Menchu chronicles her childhood and daily life, including the brutality and struggle faced by many in contemporary Latin American Indian communities. Because of

her tireless effort to promote justice, she was awarded the Nobel Peace Prize in 1992.

6. *Never Cry Wolf* by Farley Mowat. The Wildlife Services of Canada assigns naturalist Farley Mowat to study the bloodthirsty wolves that are slaughtering the artic caribou, but he finds that wolves are intelligent, skillful, devoted protectors of their young, and that the only savage and ruthless killers in the arctic are bounty hunters and government exterminators.

7. *March to Freedom: A Memoir of the Holocaust* by Edith Singer. The reader learns of Singer's unforgettable experiences and heroic acts of sabotage during her one year stay in Auschwitz and Taucha, two Nazi concentration camps, at the age of sixteen.

Fiction

1. *Lord of the Flies* by William Golding. As a result of an airplane crash, a group of boys find themselves stranded on a deserted island. The boys' struggle to maintain civilization in the face of instincts to hunt and kill serves as a parable for our time.

2. *To Kill a Mockingbird* by Harper Lee. A classic about growing up, Jem and Scout explore the mystery of Boo Radley while Atticus, father of Jem and Scout, defends a black man charged with raping a white girl. This book won the Pulitzer Prize in 1961.

3. *A Day No Pigs Would Die* by Robert Newton Peck. A boy receives a pet pig as a reward for a heroic act. After years of friendship with the pig, the boy's family faces hard times and starvation, and the boy learns about the sacrifices required to support a family.

4. *The Grass Dancer* by Susan Power. The Grass Dancer tells stories that authentically portray Native American culture and people, weaving ancient Indian practices with the realities of today.

5. *Holes* by Louis Sachar. Stanley Yelnats is sent to Camp Green Lake, a juvenile detention facility, for stealing a pair of shoes. To build character, the boys are ordered to dig holes, five feet deep and five feet wide, everyday. Soon Stanley realizes that the warden is not interested in building character, but in finding treasures. Stanley sets out to uncover the truth.

6. *The Kitchen God's Wife* by Amy Tan. Winnie Louie, an immigrant Chinese woman, explains her former painful life in China to her American-born daughter, Pearl. Family secrets, myths, traditions, and sensibilities shine through.

Additional Writing Topics

Each Chapter in this book concludes with writing activities, and Appendix A (Readings for Writing) also has writing prompts. In addition, you may wish to write about some of the topics below. For each writing topic, provide ample support through specific details. Be sure to follow all of the steps of the writing process within prewriting, writing, and rewriting.

1. Define *love* or *friendship*.
2. Find an incredible image, and obtain a copy of it. Then, describe it, and staple the image to the back of the short essay.
3. Describe the process of learning a new skill: skiing, skating, sailing, etc.
4. Tell about your first experience with something: a first airplane ride, a first visit to another country, a first kiss, etc.
5. Summarize a favorite book or movie.
6. Argue for or against a controversial issue like capital punishment, abortion, gay marriages, etc.
7. Explain the causes and effects of an action that placed you or someone else in the hospital.
8. What do you view as the most significant problem in society today? What is the solution to this problem?
9. Compare and contrast your public image with your private self.

10. If your doctor told you that you had six months to live, how would you spend your time?

11. Should American students be required to learn a second language? Why?

12. Write about a change that has occurred in your life.

13. Robert Frost said, "We come to college to get over our little mindedness." Discuss this idea in relation to your own experiences.

14. Which of the four seasons of the year appeals to you the most? Why?

15. What is the best advice you ever received? Explain.

16. According to Vince Lombardi, "Winning is not the most important thing; it's the only thing." Explain why you agree or disagree with this view.

17. What do you do to cope with stress?

18. Praise or criticize a person.

19. Illustrate a common mistake that teachers make. Explain the consequences of the mistake.

20. Create a new law. Why is it needed? Provide the consequence for breaking the law.

21. Write an essay in which you explain your plans for what you want to accomplish in the next ten years.

22. Consider five fast-food restaurants. Select several criteria by which to compare and contrast them (price, location, etc.). Then, rate the restaurants from best to worst based on your criteria.

23. Visit The Academy of American Poets at http://www.poets.org/poems/search.cfm. Browse poems by title, first line, or author's last name. Select a poem, and analyze it. In other words, examine and explain its parts (content and form) so as to discover their nature, function, and relationship.

24. Select an ineffective or offensive television advertisement, and criticize it. Consult the University of Washington at http://carmen.artsci.washington.edu/propaganda/contents.htm for an introduction to the seven devices of propaganda commonly used in advertising.

25. Research a group that is the target of intolerance (ethnicity, nationality, religion, etc.). Explain the extent of the problem, and propose a plan that provides solutions to the problem. Consult Teaching Tolerance at http://www.tolerance.org/maps/human_rights/index.html for a list of websites of human rights groups that identify current targets of intolerance and provide suggestions for promoting tolerance.

Basic Punctuation

Names and Marks	Main Uses	Examples
period .	Conclude a statement, a request or mild command, or an indirect question.	She is tall. Please defend me. Stand up. She asked me for some money.
question mark ?	Conclude a question.	When will we have our final exam?
exclamation point !	Conclude a statement that expresses strong emotions and commands.	"Please help me!" he screamed.
comma ,	1. Set off introductory material such as words, phrases, or clauses.	*In the chill of the night*, she buttoned her parka.
	2. Set off three or more items in a series.	Tam named the *composers, artists,* and *conductors* involved.
	3. Set off contrasting elements.	Emily loves biology and chemistry, *not history*.
	4. Set off information commonly found in letters such as openings and closings of letters, titles, numbers, dates, and addresses.	The committee met on Wednesday, December 3, 2002.

Names and Marks	Main Uses	Examples
	5. Set off a direct quotation.	John Dewey said, "We don't learn by experience. We learn by reflecting upon experience."
	6. Set off non-essential words and transitional words.	Jerry Hubert, *who has a mustache*, fixed my car.
	7. Set off two independent clauses joined by a coordinating conjunction (*and, but, for, nor, or, so,* and *yet*).	Jade plays the clarinet, and Bridget sings in a choir.

Other Punctuation Summary

Names and Marks	Main Uses	Examples
semicolon ;	Join independent clauses.	She is tall; he is short.
	Separate items in a series.	We visited Phoenix, Arizona; Las Vegas, Nevada; and Mammoth, California.
colon :	Introduce a list.	Our dog does the following: eats, sleeps, and barks.
	Introduce an explanation.	
	Introduce a quote.	He is lazy: he sleeps all day.
		She started again: "I believe . . ."
parentheses ( )	Insert extra material.	Her birthday (May 2) is close.
dash —	Set off for dramatic effect.	He fell—screaming.
	Set off a new thought.	I believe—no, I know—that we. . . .
	Set off a list.	She solves problems—abuse, neglect, and addiction.
quotation marks " "	Enclose a direct quote.	He said, "Thank you."
	Enclose titles of short works.	We read "A Black Wedding Song."
	Set off words used as words.	Don't confuse "affect" and "effect."
italics *this is italics* or <u>underlining</u>	Enclose titles of long works.	We read *A Christmas Carol*.
	Set off words used as words.	*They're* is a contraction.
	Set off letters and numbers used as letters and numbers.	She earned an *A* in math.

Names and Marks	Main Uses	Examples
brackets [ ]	Insert words into a quote.	He said, "Thank you [for the bike]."
ellipses . . .	Omit words in a quote.	She said, "Remember this fun summer . . . and don't forget me."
apostrophe '	Represent missing letters.	We can't come to the party.
	Show ownership.	Is that Jasmine's book?
	Form some plurals.	He earned three *A*'s this semester.
hyphen -	Combine words.	We entered the high-rise building.
	Reduce confusion.	We had to re-collect the payment.
	Create numbers.	He is thirty-four now.
	Set off prefixes/suffixes	She is self-employed.
	Express page numbers.	We covered 331–349 in our text.
	Divide words ending a line.	In school she wants to study psy-chology.
slash /	Separate lines of poetry.	Langston Hughes wrote, "What happens to a dream deferred / does it dry up. . . ."
	Create fractions.	Add 1/2 cup of sugar.
	Separate paired words.	We studied extremes like hot/cold and wet/dry.

Parts of Speech

Words can serve in different functions in sentences. This section reviews the eight parts of speech: nouns, pronouns, verbs, adjectives, adverbs, prepositions, conjunctions, and interjections.

1. *Nouns*

    A noun names a person, place, or thing. Common nouns are not capitalized while proper nouns are capitalized because they name something specific.

	Common	Proper
Person	woman	Joyce Johnson
Place	city	Newport Beach
Thing	car	Volkswagen

    Joyce Johnson drove her *car* to *Newport Beach*.

    See Chapters 14, 17, 18, 20, 21 for further explanation.

2. *Pronouns*

    A pronoun usually takes the place of a noun, so it allows us to avoid repetition. We have several types of pronouns in English.

Pronoun Type	Pronouns	Function and Example
Personal Pronouns	Singular: I, me, you, she, her, he, him, it Plural: we, us, you, they, them	Refer to specific person or things: When Mary wrote the letter, *she* was tired. See Chapters 10, 15, 18, 22 for further.
Possessive Pronouns	Singular: my, mine, your, yours, her, hers, his, its Plural: our, ours, your, yours, their, theirs	Indicate ownership: The Mustang is *mine*. See Chapter 18 for further explanation.
Intensive and Reflexive Pronouns	Singular: myself, yourself, himself, herself, itself Plural: ourselves, yourselves, themselves	Intensive pronouns add emphasize: The criminal *himself* apologized. Reflexive pronouns identify the receiver of an action as the same as the doer of the action: Jeffery can feed *himself*.
Relative Pronouns	who, whom, whose, which, that	Refer to someone or something already mentioned: The car *that* won the race is fast. See Chapters 15, 16, and 17 for further explanation.
Interrogative Pronouns	who, whom, whose, which, what	Introduce questions: *What* time is it?
Demonstrative Pronouns	this, that, these, those	Identify nouns: *This* towel is colorful.
Indefinite Pronouns	all, another, any, anybody, anyone, anything, both, each, either, everybody, everyone, everything, few, many, neither, nobody, none, no one, nothing, one, several, some, somebody, someone, something	Identify nonspecific persons or things: *One* (functioning as a noun) of the players will win. *All* (functioning as an adjective) players will win. See Chapters 14 and 17 for further explanation.
Reciprocal Pronouns	each other, one another	Express shared actions or feelings: We helped *eachother* up the trail.

3. *Verbs*

Verbs express something about the subject of a sentence, and two main types of verbs exist: action verbs and linking verbs.

Most verbs show action: The quail *ran* across the street.

Some verbs are linking verbs: Jessica *is* happy.

Linking verbs do not show action; instead, they describe or name the subject or show a state of existence. Linking verbs are usually forms of *be: be, am, is, are, was, were, being, been, will be, has been.* Other words like *act, appear, become, feel, get, grow, look, make, prove, remain, seem, smell, sound,* and *taste* are also linking verbs when they serve the same function.

See Chapters 17 and 18 for further explanation of verbs.

4. *Adjectives*

Adjectives describe nouns. They usually appear before a noun or after a linking verb.

Martha planted *red* flowers. (*Red* describes *flowers.*)

The flowers are *beautiful.* (*Beautiful* describes *flowers.*)

See Chapters 14 and 18 for further explanation.

5. *Adverbs*

Adverbs add details to sentences by describing verbs, adjectives, or other adverbs. Many adverbs end in *-ly.* Some adverbs do not end in-*ly: always, never, often, very, well.*

The student quickly drove home. (*Quickly* describes *drove.*)

She plays the flute well. (*Well* describes *plays.*)

See Chapter 14 for further explanation.

6. *Prepositions*

Prepositions connect nouns or pronouns to other words in sentences.

The bird *on* the fence is *black.* (*On* connects *bird* to *fence.*)

Common prepositions follow:

	Common Prepositions			
About	Behind	During	Of	Till (Until)
Above	Below	Except	Off	To
Across	Beneath	For	On	Toward
After	Beside	From	Onto	Under
Against	Besides	In	Out	Unfit
Among	Between	Inside	Outside	Up
Around	Beyond	Into	Over	Upon
At	By	Like	Through	With
Before	Down	Near	Throughout	Without

See Chapters 15, 17, and 18 for further explanation.

7. *Conjunctions*

Conjunctions connect words, phrases, or clauses, and they indicate the relationship between items.

Conjunction Type	Conjunctions	Function and Example
Coordinating Conjunction	*and, but, for, nor, or, so,* and *yet*	Connect equal elements: She wrote a paper on crime *and* punishment (connects two nouns). She wrote the paper, and the teacher graded it (connects two independent clauses). See Chapters 16 and 22 for further explanation.
Correlative Conjunctions	*either . . . or, neither . . . nor, not only . . . but also, whether . . . or,* and *both . . . and.*	Connect equal elements: *Either* you *or* I should attend the meeting. See Chapter 21 for further explanation.
Subordinating Conjunctions	after, although, as, because, before, if, since, unless, until, when, whereas, while	Introduce a subordinate clause, a group of words that cannot stand alone: *When* class ends, I will meet you for lunch. See Chapter 16 for further explanation.
Conjunctive Adverbs	consequently, furthermore, however, indeed, in fact, moreover, nevertheless, then, therefore	Join independent clauses with a semicolon: We needed gas; *however,* the gas station was closed. See Chapters 16 and 23 for further explanation.

8. *Interjections*

Interjections express emotions (*oh, wow, hey, ouch*). They may stand alone, and they usually do not appear in formal writing.

"*Hey!*" screamed the man. "That's my wallet."

Notice that a word may function as more than one part of speech.

They *slide* down the hill. (verb)

They bought a *slide* for the yard. (noun)

Block Business Letter Format

August 21, 20XX

Jack Parry
Ace Building Supply
1501 State Street
Santa Rosa, CA 91442

Dear Mr. Parry:

XXXXXXXXXXXXXXXXXXXXXXXXXXXXXXXXXXXXXXXXXXXXXXXXXXXXXXXX
XXXXXXXXXXXXXXXXXXXXXXXXXXXXXXXXX

XXXXXXXXXXXXXXXXXXXXXXXXXXXXXXXXXXXXXXXXXXXXXXXXXXXXXXXX
XXXXXXXXXXXXXXXXXXXXXXXXXXXXXXXXXXXXXXXXXXXXXXXXX

XXXXXXXXXXXXXXXXXXXXXXXXXXXXXXXXXXXXXXXXXXXXXXXXXXXXXXXX
XXXXXXXXXXXXXXXXXXXXXXXXXXXXXXXXXXXXXXXXXXXXXXXXXXXXXXXX
XX

Sincerely,

Signature

Ana Harmon

Answer Key to Exercises

CHAPTER 1 ANSWERS

Practice 1

1. An individual's ability to read, write, speak in English, compute and solve problems at levels of proficiency necessary to function on the job, in the family of the individual and in society.
2. functions that had previously been performed by oral language, such as indenturing of servants, deeding of property, displaying evidence at trials, recording the lives of saints, etc.
3. loose and unruly and lacking in social authority.
4. 89-94 million Americans.
5. First, writing preserves ideas more accurately than oral communication. Second, writing often carries a greater significance than oral communication. Third, democracy depends upon literacy. Fourth, writing often leads to truth, organization, and individualism. Fifth, literacy enhances opportunities and understanding.
6. teaching.
7. answers will vary.

CHAPTER 2 ANSWERS

Practice

1. The paper that you hand to your professor is the **product** of your writing. The steps that you go through to create that paper is the **process** of your writing.
2. The three stages of the writing process are prewriting, writing, and rewriting.
3. First, why are you writing this? Second, for whom am you writing this? Third, what will you write about that will be meaningful to you and your audience? Fourth, what attitude will you take towards your writing?
4. A cluster can be used to generate ideas.
5. An outline can be used to organize ideas.
6. A writer should not be concerned with writing error-free sentences on the first draft. Explanations will vary.
7. A friend, a tutor, and a teacher can read a paper and give feedback about it.
8. Global revisions are made first.
9. First, make a point. Second, support the point. Third, organize the ideas. Fourth, present the ideas in error-free sentences.
10. The first three traits of effective writing are addressed in the prewriting stage of the writing process. First, make a point. Second, support the point. Third, organize the ideas.

CHAPTER 3 ANSWERS

Practice

1. First, people are intelligent and can learn to write well. Second, people love to learn. Third, learning to write well is a life-long process, not a semester-long process.
2. A positive attitude toward writing makes writing enjoyable and productive.
3. The writing process will require endurance. Success will come by working hard long after the initial excitement of an idea passes.
4. Some writing tools include a pencil, paper, a quiet place, a disk, and a computer.
5. Following directions carefully will save you a lot of time and fundamentally influence the decision for a writing subject.
6. Authors write to entertain, to inform, or to persuade.
7. First, feeling strongly about a topic will sustain a writer through the writing process. Second, topics of significance to the writer tend to interest the reader. Third, writers usually know something about subjects that are significant to them.
8. Answers will vary but may include the following. First, is the audience interested in the subject? Second, how much does the audience know about the subject? Third,

what does the audience need to know about the subject? Fourth, does the audience already have an opinion or attitude about the subject?

  9. *Tone* refers to the attitude that an author has toward his or her writing and audience.

 10. Using an appropriate tone can contribute to effective writing by increasing the likelihood that an audience will consider and agree with a writer's point.

CHAPTER 4 ANSWERS

Practices 1–5

Answers will vary.

CHAPTER 5 ANSWERS

Practice 1

1.	3	people,	2	women,	1	literate women
2.	2	baseball,	3	sports,	1	pitching
3.	2	universities,	3	education,	1	classes
4.	1	key boards,	2	computer hardware,	3	computers
5.	1	city buses,	3	transportation,	2	public transportation

Practices 2–4 (Answers will vary)

Practice 5

1. Everyone should have the right not to be exposed to secondhand smoke.
2. Women should be free to have as many babies as they want, boys or girls.
3. Los Angeles city should put together a safe drag strip for legalized street racing because this would cut down on collision injuries.

CHAPTER 6 ANSWERS

Practice 1

1. Provide reasons for your argument.
2. Describe the steps in the process.
3. Provide the meaning or definition.
4. Analyze the causes and effects.
5. Explain the problems and the solutions.
6. Compare and contrast.
7. Explain the types or kinds in a classification.
8. Summarize through narration.
9. Illustrate through narration.
10. Explain by giving details.

Practice 2

1. upholstery, engine, headliner.
2. snout, skin color, roar.
3. rocks, pebbles, dead leaves and sticks.
4. 1966, Mexican Americans, Dolores Huerta.
5. coniferous forest, ponderosa pine, Douglas fir.

Practice 3–4

Answers will vary.

Practice 5

1. Tuition may only cost a hundred dollars.
2. Books, parking fees, health fees, and other fees are very reasonable.
3. The student housing costs are eliminated.
1. Applying and being accepted into a community college is much easier than at a university.
2. At a community college, an undecided student can take additional time to decide what major he or she will take.
3. The student can take classes in different fields to see which field he or she would like best.

1. There are more community colleges than universities in a state.
2. In fact, community colleges are usually within a few miles of home whereas universities can be much farther away.
3. Being located close to home makes the community college easier for students to attend, which helps cut the student's driving time and transportation costs.

CHAPTER 7 ANSWERS

Practice 1–5

Answers will vary.

CHAPTER 8 ANSWERS

Practice 1

1. 3   walk into the water
    2   wax the surfboard
    4   paddle out to the waves
    1   put on the wetsuit
    5   catch the wave and stand up
2. 2   narrow a topic
    3   generate a tentative thesis statement
    4   create an outline
    1   brainstorm some topics
    5   write a rough draft
3. 2   take your valentine to your favorite restaurant
    4   take a moonlit walk on the beach
    3   give your valentine a card and a gift
    5   kiss your valentine
    1   call your valentine and set up a date
4. 1   heard noise outside tent
    3   saw bear eating cookies out of icebox
    5   banged pans together and made noise
    4   talked about what to do
    2   unzipped tent door

5. 5   save the document
   1   locate the image that you want inserted
   4   adjust the size of the image to fit the document
   2   copy the image
   3   paste the image into the document

Practice 2–5

Answers will vary.

CHAPTER 9 ANSWERS

Practice 1

1. The second paragraph follows its outline.
2. . . . but they do not recognize that they make many mistakes themselves.

Practices 2–3

Answers will vary.

Practice 4

The most incredible thing happened to **Andy** today while **he** was bowling. Before **he** went up to bowl, this pretty girl came up to **him** and gave **him** her phone number. She told **him** to call her if **he** wanted to do something, but **he** could not move or believe what the woman was doing. She wanted to go on a date with **him**. **He is** not the manly man that women like. **He** was so surprised; then, she gave **him** a hug and left. The next day **he** called her and took her out to dinner. She is the most amazing girl **he has** ever met. She is very smart; in fact, she is brilliant, and her looks are wonderful. **He is** in a tough situation now because **he** already **has** a girlfriend.

CHAPTER 10 ANSWERS

Practice 1

1. for example
2. similarly

3. at the same time
4. for instance
5. however

Practice 2

1. process, process
2. doing, do
3. willing to take responsibility, willing to assume responsibility
4. will you, will you
5. be honest, be direct

Practice 3

1. they (Jesse and Stephen)
2. it (snake)
3. they (sticks)
4. it (snake)
5. they (Jesse and Stephen), it (snake)

Practice 4

Answers will vary

Practice 5

1. furthermore or moreover
2. furthermore or moreover
3. however
4. consequently or therefore
5. consequently or therefore

CHAPTER 11 ANSWERS

Practice 1

1. describe
2. summarize

    3. discuss the effects of
    4. compare and contrast
    5. evaluate

Practice 2

    1. h
    2. l
    3. p
    4. e
    5. d
    6. m
    7. o
    8. a
    9. j
    10. i
    11. n
    12. b
    13. f
    14. k
    15. g
    16. c

Practice 3

Answers will vary.

Practice 4

    1. c
    2. i
    3. c
    4. i
    5. c

Practice 5

1. It ran
2. the
3. is
4. presented. Finally,
5. classical

CHAPTER 12 ANSWERS

Practice 1–4

Answers will vary.

CHAPTER 13 ANSWERS

Practice 1

1. wine glass
2. two faces

Practice 2

1. young woman
2. old woman

Practice 3

1. phone
2. radio
3. vacation
4. tinfoil
5. rocks

Practice 4

1. Let the paper sit overnight.
2. This will help you to *see* more than if you read it quickly and silently.

3. Sentence-level editing builds upon global revision.

4. Use circles, lines, and arrows to move blocks of text around.

5. This will allow you to revisit deleted ideas.

6. It reflects the extra effort and discipline that creates success.

7. This will allow you to engage in sentence-level editing by considering each sentence out of context.

8. All in all, proofread your paper 10 times.

9. Combine sentences to produce the sentence variety that is typical of mature, college-level writing.

10. Ask peers, tutors, and your instructor to read your paper to give you additional feedback.

Group Work

1. ~~My mom also taught me how to cook. Exercise also relieves stress~~.

2. Dancing is way of expressing for me, and I love to dance. I always liked dancing when I was young; I was taught by my mother. (1) I used to just jump around when **I** was a young dancer. (2) Then, my mother **taught** me to dance with my sisters. (3) Although I **was** embarrassed to dance, I got used to it and danced with my mother and sisters. (4) As I grew older, I got less embarrassed about dancing in front of other people**. Now** I can't stop dancing. For me dancing is a great stress reliever. (5) **It** takes all my problems away. Dancing is a way to express yourself.

CHAPTER 14 ANSWERS

Practice 1–2

Answers will vary.

Practice 3 (answers may vary)

1. Education should be available to <u>everyone</u>.

2. The <u>firefighter</u> parked the truck at the park.

3. Average <u>citizens</u> will cast <u>their votes</u> against raising taxes.

4. Give the <u>customers</u> <u>their</u> change quickly.

5. When <u>swimmers</u> ask <u>their</u> <u>coaches</u> for advice, <u>they</u> usually get it.

6. <u>One's</u> attitude will determine <u>one's</u> future.

7. When <u>all workers</u> carry <u>their</u> weight, the work will end quickly.

8. Each speaker explained <u>his or her</u> views.

9. The job will take twenty <u>work-hours</u>.
10. <u>People</u> should express <u>their</u> opinions.

Practice 4 (answers may vary)

1. Playing sports may help someone to lose weight by burning calories.
2. Plant your garden in March.
3. Psychologists have studied how people behave.
4. Two birds migrate annually to forage in Canada.
5. People discussed employment issues at the conference in San Diego.
6. Communication enhances relationships between dogs and owners.
7. Snowboards are popular because they are fun today.
8. Now domestic violence has increased because of poverty.
9. About two thousand sea turtles were drowned because fishing nets trapped them.
10. Because of the length of the course, many skiers now are struggling to finish.

Practice 5

1. the
2. to
3. an
4. a
5. of

CHAPTER 15 ANSWERS

Practice 1

1. <u>Mark</u> <u>skated</u> across the rink.
2. The <u>microphone</u> <u>rested</u> on the table.
3. Poisonous <u>plants</u> <u>lined</u> the path.
4. <u>Circles</u> and <u>squares</u> <u>were</u> on the cover of the book.
5. <u>I</u> <u>visited</u> a chiropractor and a physician.
6. <u>Plants</u> and <u>animals</u> of all types <u>live</u> in the forest.
7. <u>He</u> <u>washed</u>, <u>ironed</u>, and <u>pressed</u> his clothes.
8. Indian <u>artifacts</u> and Indian <u>games</u> <u>are</u> at the museum.
9. <u>Jason</u>, <u>Patricia</u>, and <u>Claudia</u> <u>found</u>, <u>caught</u>, and <u>labeled</u> the insects.
10. The <u>girl</u> <u>appears</u> happy and <u>seems</u> intelligent.

Practice 2

1. The stars ~~in the sky~~ are bright ~~at night in the desert~~.
2. The heart pumps blood ~~throughout the body~~.
3. The crew performs routine maintenance ~~on the craft at the airport~~.
4. ~~In the spring~~ track events are held ~~at the stadium near the gym~~.
5. ~~In France~~ nuclear power plants produce much energy.
6. Vinyl and rubber are used extensively ~~in the automotive industry~~.
7. Hiking ~~in the mountains~~ fifteen miles each day conditions the legs.
8. Training, salary, and working conditions will be discussed ~~during the conference~~.
9. The restroom ~~for the fitness center~~ is ~~on the first floor of the gym~~.
10. The snow fell ~~throughout each day~~ ~~from the beginning of the week until the end of the week~~.

Practice 3 (answers may very)

1. We painted the birdhouse white. The color keeps the birds cool in the summer.
2. The servant bowed. He was showing reverence for the king.
3. They ate nutritious foods during breakfast, lunch, and dinner.
4. Walking through the park, a couple saw a flock of doves.
5. Squawking the entire time, the seagulls surrounded the fish.
6. The family raised enough money to take a vacation to Hawaii.
7. To lose weight, he ran three miles per day.
8. The laborers work hard every day, except for Larry.
9. She hates eating vegetable, especially broccoli.
10. He reads everything he can find, such as books, magazines, newspapers, etc.

Practice 4 (answers may vary)

1. The man who is standing behind the counter gave me a brochure.
2. Our minister, who wore a black robe, welcomed us.
3. The first advertisement, which interrupted our show, was distasteful.
4. The books that were on the second shelf fell onto us.
5. My only flashlight, which I have had for ten years, stopped working.

Practice 5

1. Because she drives quickly, she gets a ticket every month or two.
2. The parents paid the babysitter when they came home.

3. While attending school, he works at a restaurant.
4. The pioneers walked long distances since cars were not available.
5. The crowd went crazy after Joe hit a grand slam.

CHAPTER 16 ANSWERS

Practice 1

1. The <u>portrait</u> <u>hung</u> on the wall. <u>It</u> <u>had</u> a mahogany frame.
2. <u>She</u> <u>wanted</u> to know about job prospects. <u>She</u> <u>researched</u> her career.
3. <u>He</u> <u>studied</u> world religions. <u>Each one</u> <u>taught</u> him something new.
4. The <u>gear</u> <u>broke</u> after two miles. The <u>car</u> <u>was</u> twenty-five years old.
5. The <u>car</u> <u>could</u> not <u>be salvaged</u>. <u>They</u> <u>hauled</u> it to the junkyard.
6. <u>Writing</u> a history <u>may be</u> difficult. <u>It</u> <u>will require</u> research and time.
7. <u>She</u> <u>borrowed</u> ten thousand dollars to buy a car. Her <u>payments</u> <u>continued</u> for ten years.
8. Gas <u>prices</u> <u>have</u> risen. <u>They</u> <u>doubled</u> this month.
9. <u>Ants</u> <u>multiply</u> in the spring. <u>They</u> <u>may</u> even <u>come</u> into your home.
10. The tree <u>orchard</u> <u>is</u> old. <u>Most</u> of the trees no longer <u>bear</u> fruit.

Practice 2

1. She threw out all of her clothes**, but** some of them were in good shape.
2. They fired me**, so** I protested in a letter to the manager
3. The crime instilled rage in the victim**, for** he lost his entire savings.
4. She will take algebra**, or** she will take history.
5. He has high grades**, yet** he did not get into Harvard.

Practice 3

1. Dianna is an optimist**;** she believes that everything will work out.
2. They watch movies in the evening**;** the movies are free.
3. Family night is a ritual**;** they go out for ice cream.
4. She plays the piano and the violin**;** she wants to play the guitar.
5. The gas stove exploded**;** flames burned my hands.

Practice 4

1. She passed her final exam**; in fact,** she earned an *A* in the class.
2. They reduced their expenses**; moreover,** they raised their income.

3. The crew tracked the tiger; **however,** they never found it.
4. The laboratory report produced nothing; **furthermore,** investigators found no other evidence.
5. A candidate won; **therefore,** the election is over.

Practice 5 (answers may vary)

1. The police examined the fingerprints **after** they arrived.
2. They put the tools in the bin **when** they finished the work.
3. She stayed home from the concert **because** she had no money.
4. The horses crossed the river **although** it was deep.
5. Carrots are orange **whereas** strawberries are red.

Practice 6 (answers may vary)

1. **If** she wins the election, she will stay in office for four years.
2. **After** he went to school, he worked part time.
3. **When** they were trained, they worked on a locomotive.
4. **Until** Dania took over, Stacy led the discussion
5. **Since** prices have risen, houses are not affordable.

CHAPTER 17 ANSWERS

Practice 1

1. The man ~~in the red suit on the table~~ is a clown.
2. The stones ~~in the stream~~ appear black.
3. The cabinet ~~above the counter~~ has a broken door.
4. ~~For your information,~~ communication ~~throughout the world~~ does improve each year.
5. Ants ~~on the rim of the glass~~ scare the guests ~~at the party~~.

Practice 2

1. The detention facility ~~that is on the edge of town~~ needs refurbishing.
2. The fireplace, ~~which rests on a ledge~~, provides warmth in the winter.
3. The region ~~that was examined~~ appears suitable for building.
4. The woman ~~who is on the edge of the cliff~~ has a good view of the horizon.
5. For the passengers, the ride, ~~which is supposed to be short~~, seems to take hours.

Practice 3

1. The students who <u>are</u> in the class discussed the final exam. (plural)
2. The truck that <u>has</u> big tires will win the race. (singular)
3. The games, which <u>begin</u> in the afternoon, are for everyone. (plural)
4. In the evening, the sun, which <u>looks</u> red, sets around 6:30 p.m. (singular)
5. The white yacht, which <u>is</u> more than one hundred feet long, left before dawn. (singular)

Practice 4

1. A résumé and an application <u>are</u> required. (plural)
2. Her husband and lover <u>remains</u> faithful. (singular)
3. A mountain lion or a cougar <u>has</u> appeared on the trail. (singular)
4. Cookies or brownies <u>were</u> served for dessert. (plural)
5. Neither the employees nor the manager <u>knows</u> the cause of the malfunction. (singular)

Practice 5

1. Three **geese** walked across the road.
2. The army **fights** to win the conflict.
3. Everyone **supports** his or her leader.
4. Both of the dogs **attack** at once.
5. Most of the milk **is** gone.

Practice 6

1. How old **is** Susana?
2. Here **sit** my children.
3. The total number of students **is** twenty-five.
4. "Fog" **uses** personification.
5. *Receive* and *embarrass* **are** often misspelled.

CHAPTER 18 ANSWERS

Practice 1

1. She took <u>a train</u> home last week.
2. <u>The tires</u> on the car were new.

2. <u>Jogging</u> burns calories.
3. <u>Happiness</u> comes from within.
4. She moved to <u>the Rocky Mountains.</u>

Practice 2

1. They **grow** vegetables each summer (simple present tense).
2. The light **changed** in the evening (simple past tense).
3. Your physician **will prescribe** drugs (simple future tense).
4. The governor **has balanced** the budget (perfect present tense).
5. The students **had seen** the movie (perfect past tense).
6. The worker **will have dug** a pit (perfect future tense).
7. The lawyer **is asking** questions (present progressive).
8. The two fish **were swimming** in the stream (past progressive).
9. The business **will be prospering** in the community next year (future progressive).
10. Linda **has been studying** marine biology for two years (present perfect progressive).
11. The Chef **had been baking** the cake when the fire started (past perfect progressive).
12. By next January, the director **will have been producing** a movie for three months (future perfect progressive).

Practice 3

1. The dog **lay** on the grass last night.
2. Chris has **lain** on his bed.
3. Hector and Carlos **sat** in the front of the room.
4. Kerri **rises** at 5:00 a.m. for work.
5. The stars have **shone** all night.

Practice 4

1. I suggest **practicing** for thirty minutes daily.
2. I plan **to attend** the party.
3. Miguel advised me **to take** three classes.
4. The instructor let me **know** that I passed.
5. The couple agreed **to go** on a vacation.

Practice 5

1. The hotel **costs** two hundred dollars per night.
2. The counselor **understands** the problem.
3. Pam and Greg **know** the truth.
4. They **prefer** to dance.
5. The jars **contained** peaches.

Practice 6

1. The pedigree chart will **track** her ancestors.
2. Wax could **melt** in the sun.
3. Pollution should **be** reduced.
4. The sun shall **set** in two hours.
5. I will **meet** you at the park.

Practice 7

1. If I **were** preparing for the Olympics, I would train all the time.
2. If he **were** programming the computers, we would not have problems now.
3. They wish that I **were** punctual.
4. The officer insists that the driver not **move**.
5. The judge asks that he **tell** the truth.

Practice 8

1. The myth of romantic love **tells** us that for every young man in the world there **is** a young woman who **is** "meant for him," and vice versa.
2. Moreover, the myth **implies** that there **is** only one man meant for a woman and only one women for a man, and this **is** predetermined "in the stars."
3. When we **meet** the person for whom we are intended, recognition **comes** through the fact that we **fall** in love.
4. Since the match **is** perfect, we will then be able to satisfy all of each other's needs forever and ever, and **live** happily forever after in perfect union and harmony.
5. If we **do** not satisfy each other's needs, then we misread the stars, and we **live** unhappily, or get a divorce.

Practice 9

1. The wind blew the dessert sand.
2. The river polished the rocks.
3. Miguel read the magazine.
4. The crew prepared and launched the rockets.
5. Phillip waxed the snowboard.

Practice 10

1. The trees are beautiful this time of year.
2. The anchor that is on the left side is heavy.
3. Ice skating is good exercise.
4. The clown who is juggling is talented.
5. My essay, which discusses voter turnout, earned an *A*.

Practice 11 (answers may very)

1. Here is the information that you requested.
2. Here are road hazard signs.
3. There were seven people in attendance.
4. There are my keys.
5. Here comes the bride.

Practice 12

1. It is pleasant to walk on the beach.
2. It is 3:00 p.m.
3. It appears windy this afternoon.
4. It was a rainy day.
5. It seems like a ghost.

Practice 13 (answers may vary)

1. I own a **beautiful new red bike.**
2. We own an **oval brown wood desk.**
3. She is a **friendly, cheerful woman.**
4. He has a **big old book.**
5. He is an **outgoing, positive man.**

Practice 14

1. We saw a **depressing** movie.
2. That meal was **satisfying**.
3. Here comes an **exhausted** runner .
4. Brem is **annoyed** by procrastinators.
5. The book was **fascinating**.

Practice 15 (answers may vary)

1. The guide never left **any** one behind.
2. None of the nurses have **anything** to say.
3. Patty can't find **a** pen.
4. Jim-bob **can't** read a lick.
5. Little Tim **barely** walks.

Practice 16

1. **Can** auto accidents cause spinal injuries?
2. **Does** a chipmunk **dart** around quickly?
3. **Did** the Magna Carta guaranteed rights?
4. **Do** deciduous trees lose their leaves in the fall?
5. **Are** centipedes and spiders different?

Practice 17

1. I will see you at my house **at** 5:00 p.m.
2. Shall I type the essay **on** my computer?
3. Please call me **in** an hour.
4. The statue stands **by** the parking lot.
5. We wrote letters **on** Tuesday.

Practice 18

1. Dave and **I** studied law together in school.
2. It is **I**.
3. The cheetah is faster than **I**.

4. She saved the last cookies for Stewart and **me**.

5. For Kelly and **me**, the dance was boring.

CHAPTER 19 ANSWERS

Practice 1

1. fr __ __ ght = freight (I Before E Rule)
2. lazy + ness = laziness (Y Rule)
3. judge + ment = judgment (Silent E Rule)
4. rec __ __ ve = receive (I Before E Rule)
5. begin + ing = beginning (Doubling Rule)
6. p __ __ ce = piece (I Before E Rule)
7. stay + ed = stayed (Y Rule)
8. box + ing = boxing (exception to Doubling Rule)
9. hide + ing = hiding (Silent E Rule)
10. commit + ed = committed (Doubling Rule)

Practice 2

1. printers (Rule #1)
2. leaves (Rule #4)
3. mosquitoes (Rule #5)
4. boxes (Rule #2)
5. men (Rule #6)
6. VCRs (Rule #7)
7. counties (Rule #3)
8. sisters-in-law (Rule #8)
9. beliefs (exception to Rule #4)
10. criteria (Rule #6)

Practice 3

1. Carmen's application
2. gas's properties
3. cars' bumbers
4. John's and Jack's jobs

5. Mike and Juan's efforts
6. sisters-in-law's talent
7. museum's artifact
8. two bikes' tires
9. brother-in-law's money
10. Carolyn's and Barbara's homes

Practice 4

1. I'd
2. we're
3. there's
4. could've
5. doesn't
6. let's
7. it's
8. who's
9. won't
10. they're

Practice 5

1 He likes all flavors of ice cream, *except* vanilla.
2 She did *accept* the gift with thanks.
3 The *advice* helped me to get a job.
4 My lawyer *advises* me to testify.
5 The *effect* of hard work is progress.
6 The song *affects* my mood.
7 She felt calm for the test since she had *already* studied a lot.
8 The players were *all ready* to start the game.
9 The class exited *all together*.
10 The student was *altogether* correct.
11 She prayed at the *altar* of the temple.
12 His education did *alter* his perspective.
13 This is *our* home.
14 The children *are* excited.
15 The *bare* room provided no place to sit.
16 I cannot *bear* the screaming any longer.

17 When she saw the red light, she hit the *brakes*.

18 We stopped working and took a *break*.

19 The paramedic helped the victim to *breathe*.

20 I saw her *breath* in the cold morning.

21 They drove *by* the park.

22 Tim needed to *buy* some ice.

23 Names of people start with a *capital* letter.

24 The president addressed the nation from the *Capitol*.

25 Now, she wants to *choose* a dress carefully.

26 Last week, she *chose* a dress carefully.

27 He lost his *sight* to diabetes.

28 He will *cite* a passage from *Hamlet*.

29 We could not find the *site* on the World Wide Web.

30 I wash my *clothes* every Saturday.

31 They washed the car with *cloths*.

32 I like receiving *compliments* about my hair.

33 The new table *complements* the living room furniture.

34 His *conscience* told him not to steal.

35 The victim was not yet *conscious*.

36 I used *coarse* sand paper for the job.

37 The student was not sure which *course* to take.

38 The psychologist's *counsel* helped a lot.

39 We elected each member of the student body *council*.

40 The plane began its *descent* to the airport.

41 He has *decent* behavior in school.

42 The camel walked across the *desert*.

43 I'll have strawberry shortcake for *dessert*.

44 The accident left four people *deceased*.

45 She contracted the *disease* one year ago.

46 The boy wore a tie-*dye* shirt.

47 The girl thinks that she will never *die*.

48 I *do* my best at work.

49 Rent is *due* on the first day of each month.

50 The bus *fare* was one dollar.

51 We signed the contract because it was *fair*.

52 The judge gave me one month to pay the *fine* or go to jail.

53 She could not *find* her purse.

54 Have we been introduced *formally*?

55 *Formerly*, people called him "the rocket."

56 She stood *fourth* in line.

57 Let's kick the ball back and *forth*.

58 Please put the equipment over *here*.

59 The neighbors can *hear* the music.

60 I just *heard* a gunshot.

61 A *herd* of buffalo drank at the water hole.

62 The kids dug a *hole* in the sand.

63 He read the *whole* book.

64 *It's* going to be a beautiful day.

65 The dog raised *its* paw.

66 She *knew* the definitions before the test.

67 Manny rode his *new* bike.

68 The child had *no* manners.

69 He *knows* the answer to the question.

70 The principal *leads* the school.

71 The ranger *led* the tour last week.

72 As the sun rose, the room started *lightening*.

73 *Lightning* struck a tree.

74 The Yankees did *lose* on Saturday.

75 She wears a *loose* bracelet.

76 I want to *meet* the president.

77 We ate *meat* for dinner.

78 The car is *mine*.

79 He did not *mind* waiting in line for the tickets.

80 That is a statue made *of* gold.

81 The light is *off*.

82 He found a *pear* in his lunch.

83 She bought a *pair* of shoes.

84 They *passed* the restaurant.

85 Grandma loves to talk about her *past*.

86 The doctor cared for all of her *patients*.

87 The coach had *patience* with his players.

88 Both countries enjoyed a decade of *peace*.

89 May I have a *piece* of apple pie?

90 This is a *personal* phone call.

91 We need to hire more *personnel*.

92 We boarded the *plane* for Hawaii.

93 She wore a *plain* dress to the prom.

94 He will *pore* over his notes before taking the test.

95 She *pours* milk on her cereal.

96 We were asked to *proceed* to the next window.

97 Your birthday *precedes* my birthday.

98 The girl received many Christmas *presents*.

99 The judge has required your *presence*.

100 The boys were sent to the *principal* for fighting in school.

101 He lives by one *principle*: treat others the way that you want to be treated.

102 The plumber *quit* his job.

103 The hall was *quiet*.

104 They were *quite* pleased with their new car.

105 He lived during the *reign* of King Henry IV.

106 *Rain* fell in the evening.

107 Pull the *reins* in the direction that you want to go.

108 He is *writing* an article.

109 She is *riding* on a horse.

110 Take a *right* at the corner.

111 I need to *write* an essay by Friday.

112 She has *seen* much progress in her time.

113 Two people were wounded in the first *scene* of the play.

114 He can *sense* danger coming.

115 The *scents* of the flowers filled the room.

116 The girl had four *cents* in her pocket.

117 The note was written on special *stationery*.

118 The car was *stationary* at the light.

119 We saw the *statue* of George Washington.

120 He is a man large in *stature*.

121 They passed the *statute* in November.

122 They eat, and *then* they sleep.

123 Fred works harder *than* Jim.

124 He left his fork over *there*.

125 Dodger stadium is *their* home field.

126 *They're* here now.

127 He loves the flute *though* he hates the bass.

128 She *thought* about where to take a vacation.

129 The seagull flew *through* the cloud.

130 He *threw* the ball to me.

131 Dogs love running *too*.

132 He has *two* motorcycles.

133 The squirrel ran *to* the tree.

134 I will *use* a saw to cut the wood.

135 Yesterday, I *used* a brush to clean the sink.

136 She wore a red belt around her *waist*.

137 The Olympic athlete did not *waste* her practice time.

138 Their vacation lasted one *week*.

139 Her broken arm was *weak*.

140 She wants to *wear* her red dress.

141 *Where* are your shoes?

142 We enjoyed mild *weather* last summer.

143 Time passes *whether* we like it or not.

144 *We're* in the home stretch.

145 The winners *were* happy.

146 *Whose* car is this?

147 *Who's* coming with me to the beach?

148 *You're* very talented.

149 I found *your* ring.

Practice 6

1. The sun is melting the snow since it's 2:30 p.m.
2. Little Corinne can hardly read 10% of the book.
3. We could have walked home on September 4th.
4. Regardless of the cost, I will buy 6 keyboards, 3 phones, 4 copy machines, and 2 printers.
5. It's time to begin a whole new semester in three weeks.

CHAPTER 20 ANSWERS

Practice 1

1. She said, "**Please** tell **Dr.** Berstein that **Grandmother** is sick."
2. They drove from their city to **Santa Barbara** with their grandmother.
3. We bought **Sprite** and cookies at **Food** for **Less** on Monday.
4. My uncle and **Lisa's** mom will visit us this winter after **Thanksgiving**.

5. We read "Anyone Lived in a **Pretty** How Town" by E. E. **Cummings** in **English** today.

6. During **World War** II, he worked for the **FBI** before studying computer science.

7. The letter began with "**Dear Mom**" and ended with "**With** love."

8. "**Please** have mercy on me," he said. "I have children in **Montana**," he continued, "who depend on me."

9. She attends the **University** of **Los Angeles** in southern California.

10. This semester I'm taking the following classes: **Anthropology** 1A, Business 210, Computers 100, and **Psychology** 1B.

Practice 2

1. "**You're** my wife," the boy said.

2. "**And** we will always love each other?" the girl asked, enormously enjoying this conversation he could tell.

3. "**Always**," the boy said.

4. "**And** we'll always be together.

5. We're like the **Canada** geese," he said, taking the first comparison that came to mind, for they were often on his mind in those days.

6. "**They** only marry once.

7. **They** choose a mate early in life, and they stay together always.

8. **If** one of them dies or something, the other one will never remarry.

9. **It** will live off by itself somewhere, or even continue to live with the flock, but it will stay single and alone amongst all the other geese."

10. "**That's** sad, the girl said.

Practice 3

1. Grandma cooked a variety of food for the **holidays**: **turkey**, **stuffing**, **sweet pota-toes**, **pie**, etc.

2. He bought a **drink** and a **hot dog** at Vons on the **weekend**.

3. My **accountant** has been working for a **tax company** since December.

4. Last **summer**, my **brother** drove **west** to visit Disneyland.

5. "Please pick me up in the **truck** at Taco Bell," he said, "**at** 4:30."

CHAPTER 21 ANSWERS

Practice 1

1. feeding
   producing
   raising
2. **pick** a counselor
   call for an appointment
   complete the forms
3. at the counter
   in the cafeteria
   on the table
4. **places** the order
   buys the merchandise
   takes the product
5. injured zebras
   infected giraffes
   sick elephants

Practice 2 (answers may vary)

1. The storm created rainy, windy, and **cold** conditions.
2. The ingredients included the following: cinnamon, sugar, and **nuts**.
3. The politician plans on running for election, campaigning throughout the state, and **winning** the office.
4. We learned how to train, groom, and **show** a dog.
5. The facility provides services to people with physical, mental, or **emotional disabilities**.

Practice 3

1. To study is better than not **to study.**
2. Ridding a horse is as fun as **riding a motorcycle.**
3. **Eating** food is like filling the gas tank.
4. Clean air is as important as **clean water**.
5. Managing stress is like **juggling** three balls at once.

Practice 4 (answers may vary)

1. Antonella learned both <u>to play the piano</u> and <u>to dance</u>.
2. Erin has to write a report on either <u>a country</u> or <u>a U.S. president</u>.
3. The stocks have neither <u>risen</u> nor <u>fallen</u>.
4. Lorena created not only <u>an organizational chart</u> but also <u>a production graph</u>.
5. Buniel and Everett would rather <u>ski</u> than <u>fish</u>.

Practice 5 (answers may vary)

<u>I have a dream that one day</u> this nation will <u>rise up</u> and <u>live out</u> the true meaning of its creed: "We hold these truths to be self-evident: that all men are created equal."

<u>I have a dream that one day</u> on the red hills of Georgia the <u>sons of former slaves</u> and the <u>sons of former slaveowners</u> will be able to sit down together at a table of brotherhood.

<u>I have a dream that one day</u> even the state of Mississippi, a desert state, sweltering with the heat of <u>injustice</u> and <u>oppression</u>, will be transformed into an oasis of <u>freedom</u> and <u>justice</u>.

<u>I have a dream</u> that my four children will <u>one day</u> live in a nation where they will not be judged by the <u>color of their skin</u> but by the <u>content of their character</u>.

I have a dream today.

CHAPTER 22 ANSWERS

Practice 1

1. Streams feed the banana gardens of Kilimanjaro.
2. How long have these ancient ruins been here?
3. Shall we rise at 6:00 a.m.?
4. Here comes the police. Run!
5. Robert asked if Eric could attend the play.
6. Dr. Holmes performed the surgery.
7. We have a fire in the boiler room!
8. The British lost control of India with time.
9. Venezuela rebelled against the domination of Spain.
10. Please talk softly in the library.

Practice 2

1. Unless someone claims the wallet, you may keep it.   (#1)
2. The vegetables simmered on the stove, and the casserole baked in the oven.   (#7)

3. The blue wheelchair, which has a rip in the seat, cannot be used.   (#6)

4. "This above all—to thine own self be true," wrote Shakespeare in *Hamlet*."   (#5)

5. The Romero's donated $13000.   (#4)

6. The scientists collect, test, and interpret information.   (#2)

7. Tina is a kind, witty, and intelligent person.   (#2)

8. Stay calm in an emergency, never panic.   (#3)

9. Josh, who loves to chat, eventually brought the food.   (#6)

10. We downloaded the program, yet it didn't work.   (#7)

Practice 3

1. Well, who won the election?   (#1)

2. Bats, dolphins, and whales use echolocation to pinpoint objects.   (#2)

3. Identical twins share identical genes, and the twins appear alike.   (#7)

4. Melissa yelled, "Stop that monkey!"   (#5)

5. Stephen reads mostly news articles, not fiction.   (#3)

6. Professor Higgins, who is walking towards us, gives a lot of homework.   (#6)

7. We attended the concert, and it was great.   (#7)

8. If we save enough money, we can take a cruise to the Caribbean.   (#1)

9. The food chain, furthermore, shows who eats whom.   (#6)

10. Dear Renee,

    Should we attend the party tonight? Let me know what you want to do.

       Your friend,

       — Dave   (#4)

Practice 4

1. According to Carlos, personality traits change little.

2. Adriana, Peter, and Joseph felt that the game should continue.

3. By this time next year, Kyle will buy a car if he has the money

4. Kenny will take biology, psychology, chemistry, and music.

5. She said, "What is it that you want?"

CHAPTER 23 ANSWERS

Practice 1

1. The rancher brought the sheep to the barn; he had to shear them.

2. Jose put the food in the pot; Raymond stirred the pot.

3. The rattlesnake is venomous; however, the king snake is not venomous.

4. The committee met to examine natural resources: land, rivers, lakes, and trees.

5. The committee met at 3:30 p.m.

Practice 2

1. David bought a new computer (IBM) for his office.

2. The sheriff (Wendell Roel) arrested the suspect.

3. The climbing team suffered intensely (dehydration and frostbite).

4. Alicia fell through the ice on the lake—have you ever seen that happen to someone?

5. When the suspect was arrested, he stepped into the car—smiling.

Practice 3

1. "Please pass me that magazine," Armando asked.

2. "Leda and the Swan" is a poem in our text, *An Introduction to Poetry*.

3. Dr. Chan continued, "We must determine the effects of the disaster [oil spill] on marine life."

4. The football coach began swearing, "You . . . idiots."

5. "Please read the poem 'Oh Captain! My Captain!' by Walt Whitman," said Dr. Bingham.

Practice 4

1. We won't be able to finish Lisa's trench until Saturday.

2. The students' hands shot up in response to the teacher's question.

3. The store sells oil-, water-, and rubber-based paints.

4. Tabitha is a self-made millionaire.

5. The conflict between good/bad, rich/poor, powerful/powerless appears throughout the work.

Practice 5 (some answers may vary)

1. The recipe (page 75) calls for 1/2 of a cup of chopped nuts.

2. In the lab, the computers' monitors were all off.

3. "Please read the poem called 'The Magi' for homework," said the professor.

4. The well-known writer was not well known before she won the Pulitzer.

5. Her pets included the following: a dog, two cats, a bird, and four fish.

6. Shawn said, "Don't give that [the camera] to the children."

7. I remember part of the saying: "Early to bed . . . makes a man [person] healthy, wealthy, and wise."

8. *Embarrass* has two *R*'s and two *S*'s.

9. Last semester, we read *Julius Caesar*, the play by William Shakespeare; we enjoyed it.

10. Sue sat in a chair by the casket for an hour—crying.

About the Companion Website

Companion Website: *http://www.prenhall.com/kempler*

1. How to Use This Textbook
2. Sample Syllabus
3. Editing Exercises
4. Sentence-Combining Practices
5. Support for Each Chapter
   a. Objectives
   b. Self-Grading Quizzes
   c. Chapter-Test Answers
   d. Group Assignments
   e. Web Destinations
   f. Writing Assignments That Develop Critical Thinking Skills

Index

abstract words, 63
adjectives, 249, 412
   coordinate adjectives, 250
   cumulative adjectives, 250
   order, 249
   participles used as adjectives, 252
   punctuating, 250
adverbs, 412
"Alone," Maya Angelou, 350
Angelou, Maya, "Alone", 350
Angelou, Maya, "Mrs. Flowers",
   379
Armour, Richard, "Fish Story", 348
articles, 221
attitude, 26
audience, 29

Babran, Khalil, "Your Children Are Not Your
   Own", 361
bilingual, 220
Blake, William, "To See the World in a Grain
   of Sand", 348
body, 87
Buscaglia, Leo, "Papa, the Teacher", 375
business letter format, 414

capital letters, 287
   first word in a direct quotation, 287
   first word in a sentence, 287
   names of specific people, places, and
     things, 287
   openings and closings of letters, 293
   proper nouns, 292
"Cipher in the Snow: A True Story," Jean
   Mizer, 387
collective nouns, 212
comma splice, 189
commitment, 27
complex sentence, 193
compound sentence, 190
computer challenges, 147
computers, 113
computers, 143
   prewriting, 144
   rewriting, 145
   writing, 145
conclusion, 88
concrete details, 63

conjunctions, 413
   conjunctive adverbs, 413
   coordinating conjunctions, 413
   correlative conjunctions, 303, 413
   subordinating conjunctions, 413
conjunctive adverb, 192
contractions, 270
coordinate adjectives, 314
coordinating conjunction, 190
count nouns, 222

dangling modifier, 178
Dickinson, Emily, "The Lightning
   is a Yellow Fork", 364
directions, 28
"Do Not Go Gentle Into That Good Night,"
   Dylan Thomas, 358
double negatives, 253
"Dreams Deferred," Langston Hughes, 346
"Dreams," Langston Hughes, 345

editing, 154
effective writing, 20
"Elena," Pat Mora, 352
essay exam key words, 134
essay exams, 132 (*see also* succeeding on
   essay exams, 133)

faulty parallelism, 301
fiction, 402
first draft, 108 (*see also* first draft checklist,
   113)
first person, 112
"Fish Story," Richard Armour, 348
"Fog," Carl Sandburg, 247
"Four Directions," Amy Tan, 383
fragment, 176
Frost, Robert, "Stopping by Woods on a
   Snowy Evening", 359
Frost, Robert, "The Road Not Taken", 360
fused sentence, 189

here and *ther,e* 214, 247
Hughes, Langston, "Dreams Deferred", 346
Hughes, Langston, "Dreams", 345
Hughes, Langston, "Thank You, M'am", 390
Hughes, Langston, "Theme for English B",
   353

"I Have a Dream," Martin Luther King, Jr., 397
independent clauses, 173
interjections, 413
introduction, 87
it, 248
"I Wandered Lonely as a Cloud," William
          Wordsworth, 363

Johnson, Beth, "Let's Get Specific", 369

"Let's Get Specific," Beth Johnson, 369
literacy, 2
Luther King, Jr., Martin, "I Have a Dream", 397

"Metaphors," Sylvia Plath, 366
Milloy, Courtland, "The Gift", 294
Mizer, Jean, "Cipher in the Snow:
          A True Story", 387
Mora, Pat, "Elena", 352
"Mrs. Flowers," Maya Angelou, 379

narrowing a topic, 45
    circle diagram, 47
    clustering, 45
    flow chart, 46
noncount nouns, 222
non-essential elements, 121, 181, 317 (*see
          also* non-restrictive relative clauses,
          181)
nonfiction, 402
nouns, 410

"O Captain! My Captain!" Walt Whitman, 354
order for presenting ideas, 91
    importance method, 96
    space method, 94
    time method, 92
outline, 86 (*see also* guidelines for creating an
          outline, 99)

"Papa, the Teacher," Leo Buscaglia, 375
parallel structure, 299
parts of speech, 410
plagiarism, 82
Plath, Sylvia, "Metaphors", 366
plurals, 266
possessives, 269
prepositional phrases, 175
prepositions, 256, 412
prewriting techniques, 35
    brainstorming (listing), 36
    branching, 37
    clustering (webbing, mapping), 37

free writing, 37
idea mapping, 36
the internet, 35
journal writing 39
questioning (interviewing), 40
sketching, 35
prewriting, 9, 144
process, 9
product, 9
pronouns, 123, 410
    demonstrative pronouns, 411
    indefinite pronouns, 166, 212, 411
    intensive and reflexive pronouns, 411
    interrogative pronouns, 411
    object pronouns, 257
    personal pronouns, 411
    possessive pronouns, 257, 411
    reciprocal pronouns, 411
    relative pronouns, 180, 411
    subject pronouns, 257
proofreading, 138
proper nouns, 226
punctuation, 310
    apostrophes, 334, 409
    brackets, 332, 409
    colons, 326, 408
    commas, 313, 406
    dashes, 329, 408
    ellipses, 333, 409
    exclamation points, 312, 406
    hyphens, 336, 409
    italics, 332, 408
    question marks, 312, 406
    quotation marks, 329, 408
    parentheses, 328, 408
    periods, 311, 406
    semicolons, 325, 408
    slashes, 338, 409
purpose, 28

questions, 214
questions, 255

relative clause, 180, 207
repeating subjects, 247
restrictive clause, 181
revision, 152 (*see also* revision checklist, 154)
rewriting, 13, 145
rough draft, 108
run-on sentence, 188

Sandburg, Carl, "Fog", 247
second person, 112

sentences, 173
Shakespeare, William, "Sonnet 130", 362
show something, 63
significance, 28
"Sindhi Woman," Jon Stallworthy, 355
Slater, Mary Jo, "Welcome to Hiroshima", 356
"Sonnet 130," William Shakespeare, 362
sources of information, 72
    books, 73
    the Internet, 72
    journals, magazines, and newspapers, 73
    other people, 72
    reference materials, 72
    yourself, 72
specific details, 63
spelling, 262
    American and British differences in
        spelling, 282
    commonly confused words, 273
    commonly misspelled words, 271
    consonants, 263
    doubling rule, 265
    i before e rule, 263
    numbers, 281
    prefixes, 266
    silent e rule, 264
    suffixes, 266
    vowels, 263
    y rule, 264
Stallworthy, Jon, "Sindhi Woman", 355
"Stopping by Woods on a Snowy Evening,"
    Robert Frost, 359
subject, 173
subject-verb agreement, 202
subordinate clause, 182
subordinating conjunction, 193
summarizing, 74
summary and reaction, 78
support, 60

Tan, Amy, "Four Directions" 383
tell something, 63
"Thank You, M'am," Langston Hughes, 390
"The Day Is Done," Henry Wadsworth
    Longfellow, 367
"The Eagle and the Mole," Elinor Wylie, 365
"The Gift," Courtland Milloy, 294
"The Lightning is a Yellow Fork," Emily
    Dickinson, 364
"Theme for English B," Langston Hughes,
    353
"The Road Not Taken," Robert Frost, 360
thesis statement, 47

third person, 112
Thomas, Dylan, "Do Not Go Gentle Into That
    Good Night", 358
tone, 30
tools, 27
topic sentence, 47
"To See the World in a Grain of Sand,"
    William Blake, 348
transition, 117
transitional words and phrases, 119, 317

vague words, 63
verbs, 173, 227
    active verbs, 173, 227, 411
    gerunds, 239
    infinitives, 239
    irregular verbs, 231
        past participle, 232
        past tense, 232
        troublesome irregular verbs, 236
    linking verbs, 173, 227, 411
    modals, 242
    passive and active voice, 246
    perfect progressive tenses, 230
    perfect tenses, 228
    progressive tenses, 229
    progressives, 241
    simple tenses, 228
    subjunctive mood, 243
    tense shifts, 245

Wadsworth Longfellow, Henry, "The Day Is
    Done", 367
Walker, Alice, "We Alone", 349
"We Alone," Alice Walker, 349
"Welcome to Hiroshima," Mary Jo Salter, 356
Whitman, Walt, "O Captain! My Captain!",
    354
word choice, 162
    clichés, 164
    omitted words, 170
    sexist language, 165 (*see also* sexist terms,
        166)
    slang, 163
    wordiness, 167
Wordsworth, William, "I Wandered Lonely as
    a Cloud", 363
writing topics, 404
writing, 11, 145
Wylie, Elinor, "The Eagle and the Mole", 365

"Your Children Are Not Your Own," Khalil
    Babran, 361